IN SICKNESS AND IN HEALTH

Social dimensions of medical care

IN SICKNESS AND IN HEALTH

Social dimensions of medical care

RALPH HINGSON, Sc.D.

Associate Professor, Department of Socio-Medical Sciences and
Community Medicine and Department of Pediatrics,
Boston University School of Medicine, Boston, Massachusetts

NORMAN A. SCOTCH, Ph.D.

Director, School of Public Health; Professor and Chairman,
Department of Socio-Medical Sciences and Community Medicine;
Associate Dean, Boston University School of Medicine,
Boston University Medical Center, Boston, Massachusetts

JAMES SORENSON, Ph.D.

Associate Professor, Department of Socio-Medical Sciences and
Community Medicine; Chief, Social and Behavioral Sciences Section,
Boston University School of Public Health,
Boston University School of Medicine, Boston, Massachusetts

JUDITH P. SWAZEY, Ph.D.

Executive Director, Medicine in the Public Interest;
Professor, Department of Socio-Medical Sciences and
Community Medicine, Boston University School of Medicine,
Boston, Massachusetts

Illustrated

The C. V. Mosby Company

ST. LOUIS • TORONTO • LONDON   1981

MOSBY

1906 **75** 1981
YEARS

A TRADITION OF PUBLISHING EXCELLENCE

The C. V. Mosby Company
11830 Westline Industrial Drive, St. Louis, Missouri 63141

Library of Congress Cataloging in Publication Data

Main entry under title:

In sickness and in health.

    Bibliography: p.
    Includes index.
    1.   Social medicine.   I.   Hingson, Ralph,
1948-   [DNLM: 1.   Sociology, Medical. WA 31 I35]
RA418.I48   362.1′042   80-28794
ISBN 0-8016-4411-9

GW/D/D 9 8 7 6 5 4 3 2 1   02/A/229

To

Ephraim Friedman

and

John Sandson

Enlightened medical school deans whose broad
vision and sensitivity to the human dimensions of health care
provided us the opportunity and the support
to introduce medical students to the Socio-Medical Sciences

and to

Sol Levine

The perfect role model, a medical sociologist
whose profound teaching and research have made a difference

Contents

Illness is the night-side of life,
a more onerous citizenship. Everyone who
is born holds dual citizenship, in the kingdom
of the well and in the kingdom of the sick.
Although we all prefer to use only the good passport,
sooner or later each of us is obliged,
at least for a spell, to identify ourselves
as citizens of that other place.

Susan Sontag, *Illness as Metaphor*, 1978

Introduction

Most professional schools are so substantively oriented toward teaching the highly specialized technical knowledge requisite for their field of work that the broader interpersonal and social dimensions of professionalism tend to be neglected. The aim of the "revolution" in medical education, catalyzed by the Flexner report in 1910, was scientific excellence, and in pursuit of that goal American medical schools focused their curricula on basic and clinical sciences. As the years passed, Abraham Flexner himself became concerned about the way that medical education, under the aegis of his name, had placed what he considered too much emphasis on the purely scientific aspects of disease.

Flexner doubtless would approve of the fact that the crowded curricula of medical schools, as well as other schools for medical care professionals, in recent years gradually have begun to incorporate some exposure to knowledge and skills not previously thought to be of any great importance to the work of their graduates. These include interpersonal skills needed for a provider's work with patients, families, and other providers; knowledge of the psychologic and sociologic aspects of illness; awareness of the complex ethical, legal, and policy issues surrounding medicine; and an understanding of the complex organizations involved in the provision of medical care.

Courses aimed at providing at least portions of such knowledge, skills, and perspectives have been developed in numerous schools involved in training medical professionals. This book has evolved from one such course that we began teaching to medical students in 1975, when the Boston University School of Medicine inaugurated a new Department of Socio-Medical Sciences. Since then, we also have developed courses for public health students as well as undergraduate students.

As reflected by the diverse student groups whom we teach, we believe that the materials covered in this book are germane to the work of all those who are or will be involved in the provision of medical care. Although our intended audience is thus a broad one, we refer most frequently in the pages that follow to physicians and various aspects of their work with patients. Our focus on the physician in part reflects the fact that medical students were our first and still are one of our principal audiences and in part that much of the medical sociology literature that we draw on deals with physicians and their patients. In keeping with our focus on physicians and patients, we also have chosen to use the phrase *medical care* rather than *health care* in most instances, for we feel that *medical care* more accurately reflects what most providers and patients are involved in than does the more commonly used phrase *health care.*

Throughout the book we attempt to indicate that vast changes have occurred in the substance and format of medical care and that even more powerful and profound changes can be anticipated in both the short and long run. Our focus, however, is on examining, from a social science perspective, what we see as central and generic issues for providers and recipients of medical care rather than on the nature of and reasons for these changes or the particular mechanisms devised to deal with contemporary problems, such as the cost of medical care.

To the extent that any single book can affect the training and work of professionals, our hope is that this book will help to increase the effectiveness of those engaged in medicine by providing them with new knowledge and insights about the social dimensions of their work. Numerous problems are raised and discussed in the chapters ahead, with few solutions proposed. However discouraging it may be to read about critical problems in the provision of medical care, their existence should not be avoided or ignored. At a minimum, recognition of problems may well be the first step toward their eventual solution, particularly for those who will become change agents in their profession.

• • •

In our teaching, and in this text, our orientation toward health, illness, and medicine is that of medical sociology. Within its brief history as an academic discipline, medical sociology has studied medicine from two major perspectives, described by Strauss[1] in 1957 as *sociology of medicine* and *sociology in medicine*. Although the distinctions between these two approaches often are blurred in practice, they are of some use in orienting people to the work and objectives of medical sociologists. By *sociology of medicine*, Strauss referred to a detached, academic, and sociologic analysis of medicine, health professions, and institutions as part of a community or society. From a sociology of medicine perspective, medicine and its practice are viewed as sets of data that help us understand society and social change. The components of medicine, the roles it plays in society, and its similarities and dissimilarities to other institutions and professions are the focuses of attention.

By *sociology in medicine*, Strauss referred to an approach that is directed more toward actively using sociologic knowledge and skills to help providers better understand and deal with problematic aspects of their work. Sociology in medicine deals with subjects such as how social and economic forces influence the day-to-day practice of medical professionals; how social characteristics of providers and patients affect the relationships between them; how care seeking is influenced by people's knowledge, beliefs, values, backgrounds, and other variables; and how patients respond to diagnoses and treatments.

Although this book will include both types of analyses, its major perspective is that of sociology *in* medicine. We hope to help the reader explore facets of medical practice through the eyes of sociologists and understand the social forces that have contributed to some of the problems we cite, which may be key in their remediation. Parts I and II of the book have been organized to take the reader through a roughly temporal process that begins with health and its maintenance and ends, from the perspective of those who become patients, with recovery and rehabilitation from illness, or with death. Part III, in turn, draws on the perspective of sociology *of* medicine to explore selected aspects of what we refer to as the *medical domain,* including the training of physicians, the institutional contexts in which they practice, the nature of physicians as professionals, and, finally, the societal context of medicine in the United States.

To briefly describe the sequence and content of the chapters that follow, the four chapters of Part I focus on various aspects of maintaining health, seeking care, and becoming a patient. *Chapter 1* presents an overview of *social issues in medicine,* touching briefly on many topics dealt with more fully in later chapters. In this chapter, we try to give readers, particularly those who may have had little or no exposure to clinical medicine, a sense of some of the dimensions of their work that are not usually covered in their academic training. *Chapter 2* examines a number of *social factors in the prevention of disease.* Despite improvements in morbidity and mortality rates, there are many reasons for arguing that much can be done by medical and other social agencies to prevent disease, improve health, and increase life expectancy. After reviewing these arguments, Chapter 2 looks at the strengths and weaknesses of various disease prevention strategies that are being or could be employed. These include health education efforts by schools, mass media, and providers; clinical interventions to alter what are judged to be unhealthy behaviors; and legislative and regulatory efforts to promote health and reduce disease.

Chapter 3 examines the variables and processes involved in people deciding (1) whether or not they are ill, and (2) if so, whether they should seek assistance from a physician or an alternative source of care. Those who do decide to seek medical attention and gain access to a physician (or nurse) then enter a caregiving system that is shaped in many complex ways by the views of both medical professionals and society about the role of medicine in relation to health and illness. *Chapter 4* explores a number of social questions now being addressed and debated within and without medicine about what should constitute the boundaries, contents, and responsibilities of medical care. Our discussion of these issues is framed in terms of ambulatory care, which is the point of entrance into the medical system for most persons and constitutes the largest part of clinical practice.

Part II focuses on some major aspects of caring for and being a patient. *Chapter* 5 takes up a core aspect of medical care—the nature of the interactions that occur between providers and patients. Concentrating on the *doctor-patient relationship,* we present theories and data on the factors that help to shape the roles of physicians and patients, the ways that physicians and patients can interact, and the importance of the interactions or relationships as a determinant of the outcome of medical care. *Chapter 6* then analyzes a particularly important facet of the physician-patient relationship and of the success or failure of a treatment regimen—*compliance*. We examine the types of variables that have been shown to affect compliance, including characteristics of providers, patients, and treatment regimens, and suggest ways that providers can increase the likelihood that patients will follow their instructions and advice.

In the temporal sequence of becoming ill and seeking and receiving medical care, physician and patient interactions and the applications of medical knowledge and techniques can have several outcomes. For patients with an acute illness or trauma, there can be a cure or repair that returns them to health and, for the time being, lets them exit from the medical care system. Another increasingly large segment of the patient population have chronic illnesses that can only be managed palliatively or traumas, such as spinal cord injuries, that are irreparable. These patients and their caregivers are engaged in a long-term encounter, involving recovery and rehabilitation, but no cure. *Chapter 7* examines a number of social factors that play important roles in facilitating or inhibiting *recovery and rehabilitation:* particular types of patient and provider characteristics and attitudes, the patient's family context, the role of various social agencies, societal attitudes toward the handicapped, and the types of financial and other resources provided by our society.

For other patients the outcome of illness is death, and *Chapter 8* discusses various aspects of the *dying* process from the perspectives of both patients and providers. Also considered are why there has been such an upsurge of interest in and attention to death and dying in recent years and what this tells us about both lay and professional attitudes toward death and medical efforts to avert its occurrence.

Chapters 2 through 8, in sum, present in a roughly temporal order the sociologic aspects of patient care that we see as of direct clinical relevance to physicians and other medical providers. Our frame of reference, as we have pointed out, is sociology in medicine, in which we seek to identify social factors and issues in health, illness, and medical care that affect both providers and patients. Some of these factors and issues are new and others are timeless, but all of them can be anticipated to appear and reappear in the foreseeable future of medical practice.

In Part III, we turn our attention to some of the topics traditionally addressed by sociology of medicine that we feel are also crucial to a provider's understanding of medicine as a social science. *Chapter 9* looks at the nature of *medical education*, considering, from a historic and sociologic perspective, why undergraduate and graduate medical education has the form and content it has today, what sort of changes it may be undergoing, and what the process of becoming a physician entails, both substantively and experientially. During their training and subsequent practice, physicians and other providers work in a variety of medical care settings. *Chapter 10*, dealing with the institutional context of medicine, examines features of *hospitals and ambulatory care settings* and how these features shape the work of providers and the care of patients. *Chapter 11* turns to the *professional context of medicine*. Here we explore the ways that the characteristics and values of professionals affect the training and work of physicians, their interactions with each other and with other providers and patients, and the nature of the social controls that the medical profession uses to govern itself. Finally, *Chapter 12* reflects on *medicine as a social institution* in the United States. Why, from various quarters, do we hear the refrain "this is a 'time of crisis' for medicine"? What concerns are being voiced by providers, patients, and assorted groups of critics about the shape and substance of medical care? Are we in an era in which the "social contract" between medicine and American society is being renegotiated, and if so, what might be the elements of a new contract?

Immersion in the practice of medicine soon teaches the need to recognize, understand, and deal with the dimensions of medical care that have just been outlined. Over the years, we have watched numerous young physicians, nurses, and other providers move from the classroom to the world of practice and discover, often painfully, that they have only begun to learn what is involved in being a caregiver. We have also seen and heard how hundreds of our own students, who are at the beginning of their professional education, react to the materials dealt with in this text. Each year, some are angry or depressed about portions of what we say about the field of work they have chosen to enter. With time, we hope that those students and readers of this book, as do most whom we teach, will recognize that our aim is to help medical professionals better understand the complex world in which they will work and the difficult tasks they have chosen to perform. It is our belief that in doing so, we will expand the horizons and skills of providers to the benefit of their patients and in that measure to the benefit of society.

Reference

1. Strauss, R.: The nature and status of medical sociology, Am. Sociol. Rev. **22**:200, 1957.

Part I

HEALTH, ILLNESS, AND MEDICINE

Chapter 1

Social issues in medicine

"This is as difficult a time for medicine as it is one of achievement," wrote Glasser[18] in the preface to his autobiographic novel, *Ward 402.* "Despite all the successes a kind of leery feeling parallels the public applause, a suspicion that in making things better some things have been made worse, that in learning more too much has been forgotten."*

In this text, we deal with some of those aspects of learning to be an effective medical care provider that tend to have been forgotten in the teaching and practice of medicine as an applied science. Medical and other professional schools are reasonably effective in teaching students the technology of medicine and the basic knowledge of biologic, chemical, and physical sciences from which medicine is, in part, derived. But, in part because of how much of this information there is to be imparted and because of how central the advances of scientific medicine have been to the understanding and management of many diseases and disorders, the training of medical professionals has been a relatively unidimensional one. It has lost sight of a fact recognized clearly by one of the founders of medicine as an applied science, the nineteenth century German pathologist, Rudolph Virchow: *"Medicine is a social science."*[1]

Medicine, clearly, is not *only* a social science. But it is a body of knowledge and techniques, part science and part art, and a social institution that cannot be understood or practiced effectively if its social science dimensions are excluded. Although a largely ignored component of a student's formal education, clinical experience soon makes clear how important it is to recognize, understand, and attempt to deal with these dimensions of medical care.

"I finished medical school," Glasser continues in his preface, "much the same as any other medical student—eager, confident, sure that a year of internship would be all I needed to put the whole thing together."

I was wrong. My internship was not the end I expected it to be, but a wrenching beginning.

It had never occurred to me when I was in school that as a physician there would

---

*Reprinted from WARD 402 by Ronald J. Glasser, M.D. by permission of the publisher, George Braziller, Inc. Copyright 1973 by Ronald J. Glasser.

be anything I'd have to face which was not covered in my classes, anything my professors had not yet worked out, or at least would not have warned us about. Becoming an intern was like passing through a curtain into a world that had never been mentioned, a world I was quite unprepared for.

Ready for hearts and lungs and kidneys, I was confronted with a whole person. In the midst of all the familiar precision, of laboratory values and X-rays, suddenly there were human concerns: grief and heartache, personal problems, economics, distrust, fears, and even anger. So seemingly well turned out, with all of science to draw on, I found myself stumbling; all of us were, with only our own strengths and weaknesses to get us through.*†

What novice practitioners soon begin to realize, and must continuously confront throughout their careers, as Glasser suggests, is that there are many complicated aspects of being a provider or patient and functioning, in either capacity, within our system of delivering health and illness care. In this chapter, we will look at a few selected examples of the range of often unanticipated problems and issues that students meet as they move from the classroom to the clinic. These include, but are by no means limited to, problems in interacting with patients and other health care professionals, issues about the status and role of physicians, and changes in our society's views about the role of medicine in relation to health and illness. These are all facets of medicine as a social science. Although the social sciences have no magic solutions, they can offer an understanding of such problems and issues that can help the provider to deal with them better and, perhaps, contribute to improvements in the context and quality of medical care.

Interactions with patients

For the physician, nurse, or other provider, the essence of clinical medicine is caring for patients. Since the major focus of this book is on social dimensions of patient care, we will touch only briefly on a few aspects of interacting with patients that providers are apt to find particularly problematic, especially when beginning clinical training. The examples we have chosen to highlight are some facets of patient behavior and attributes and the difficulties of dealing with chronic diseases.

Patient behavior. Many patients simply do not behave in the idealized or stereotyped ways that new providers may anticipate. In the idealized view, fondly portrayed in television shows such as "Marcus Welby, MD," the patient recognizes a symptom and, without delay or procrastination, reaches the physician. The physician, after careful thought, diagnoses the illness and recommends a treatment plan, which the patient follows. The treatment works, the patient gets better, and is duly grateful to the physician.

---

*Reprinted from WARD 402 by Ronald J. Glasser, M.D. by permission of the publisher, George Braziller, Inc. Copyright 1973 by Ronald J. Glasser.
†A number of recent physician autobiographies and novels emphasize these themes. See, for example, references 7, 12, 23, 25, 35.

Reality, of course, is less simple; it tends to be more frustrating and less satisfying for both the patient and the physician. Physicians often are dismayed to find that most of the illnesses brought to them by patients cannot be cured; at best, some of the symptoms can be controlled. Moreover, many patients seek care for problems that require more interpersonal and psychologic skill than disease-focused medical knowledge.

Most frustrating of all, when the medical condition is serious and the knowledge and technology are available to truly help the patient, the physician often finds one or more of the following: (1) The patient has waited too long, and it is too late for medical care to make much of a difference. (2) The patient is so unsure of what is happening or so anxious or inarticulate that it is almost impossible to learn just what is happening. These same factors make it difficult for the patient to understand both the physician's questions and explanations regarding the illness and what must be done about it. (3) The patient does not follow the physician's advice. For example, he or she does not take medication in the right amount or at the right time, if it is taken at all; does not return for follow-up care; or does not alter the behaviors that led to the illness in the first place.

In terms of expectations about one's status as a physician, it also can be discomforting to find that patients do not always treat physicians with the expected deference to their expertise and obedience to their authority. Instead, patients do question their diagnosis and treatment, do not follow the sound advice they are given, are not properly grateful, and may not even pay their bill.

The physician's interactions with and responses to patients also can be affected, usually negatively, by patient attributes that are difficult for the physician to deal with. For example, the patient may not speak the same language as the physician, may be elderly or unattractive or both; or may have a condition as unpleasant for the physician as for the patient, such as a fecal impaction. The patient's relatives may interfere with physician-patient transactions. They may wish to override the patient's wishes; may openly disagree with each other and with the physician; or are nowhere to be found when their help could make the crucial difference between costly hospitalization and home care. The patient may be poor, may not be covered by health insurance, and, regardless of the physician's own fees, cannot possibly pay for medication, hospitalization, or nursing home care. In short, physicians often cannot do as much to help as they would hope, and the process of helping often is not as rewarding as they had anticipated.

Dealing with chronic diseases. A major contributor to the frequent mismatch between provider expectations and actual experiences derives from changes in the types of problems now brought to providers. There have been major shifts in morbidity and mortality and an increase in life expectancy over the last 50 years. At the turn of this century, for example, the average American male at birth could expect to live just over 40 years, while currently, he can anticipate living over 70 years.

Much of this increase in life expectancy is attributable to better nutrition, sanitation, and the general rise in the standard of living. Some of the increase also is due to medical advances, such as immunization and means to treat infectious diseases.

As life expectancy has increased, there has been a major shift in morbidity. The leading causes of illness and death now are the chronic diseases, rather than infectious and other acute diseases. Consequently, providers must be prepared to deal with an expanding population of elderly patients, who often suffer from several concurrent chronic illnesses.

Moreover, with few exceptions, the chronic diseases are not yet amenable to prevention or cure.[32] Thus, physician and patient alike must cope, over time, with disorders whose etiologies often are not well understood and whose symptoms can, at best, be palliated. Consider, for example, the problem of migraine. As one authority on pain and migraine headaches has acknowledged, after 46 years of specialization, he can *describe* many aspects of migraine, especially how and when they strike. But he and other experts still are uncertain as to *why* migraine headaches occur and are unable to provide treatments that offer much relief from these severely painful headaches that afflict many people year in and year out. His attitude toward this aspect of his practice is described by an interviewer:

> Patients who are not cured do not represent a failure to him. He has patients of 25 years' standing who still get headaches. But, he says, "you learn as a doctor to set your sights on something less than curing. You establish a relationship that is meaningful and useful."[26]

Patients, on the other hand, may take a less sanguine view of the limitations of knowledge and technology and the problems of uncertainty in the area of chronic illness. Didion[11] writes:

> . . . after a series of periodic visual disturbances, three electroencephalograms, two complete sets of skull and neck X-rays, one five-hour glucose tolerance test, two electromyelograms, a battery of chemical tests and consultations with two ophthalmologists, one internist and three neurologists, I was told that the disorder was not really in my eyes, but in my central nervous system. I might or might not experience symptoms of neural damage all my life. These symptoms, which might or might not appear, might or might not involve my eyes. They might or might not involve my arms or legs, they might or might not be disabling. Their effects might be lessened by cortisone injections, or they might not. It could not be predicted. The condition had a name, the kind of name usually associated with telethons, but the name meant nothing and the neurologist did not like to use it. The name was multiple sclerosis, but the name had no meaning. This was, the neurologist said, an exclusionary diagnosis, and meant nothing.
>
> I had, at this time, a sharp apprehension . . . of what it was like to open the door to the stranger and find that the stranger did indeed have the knife. In a few lines of dialogue in a neurologist's office . . . the improbable had become the probable, the norm: things which happened to other people could in fact happen to me. I could be struck by lightning, could dare to eat a peach and be poisoned by the cyanide in the stone. The startling fact was this: my body was offering a precise physiologic equivalent

to what had been going on in my mind. "Lead a simple life," the neurologist advised. "Not that it makes any difference that we know about."*

As the passage tells us so eloquently, both patients and caregivers often must come to terms with the fact that medicine, for all its achievements, cannot explain, prevent, or cure many human ills. In turn, people see medical care as offering them a variety of things and have many expectations about what should or may result from their interaction with a physician or other provider. It is a mistake, we believe, to equate *cure* with *success* in medical care, for physicians, nurses, and others provide a wide range of caregiving services, not the least of which is simple reassurance.

The role of the physician has changed as the types of conditions brought to the attention of medicine have changed and, even more important, it will continue to change significantly in the foreseeable future. With the exception of acute episodes of illness or trauma, which represent a small fraction of provider-patient encounters, the physician and other professional colleagues will play less of a technical role and more of a managerial and educational role. Physicians who define their roles narrowly as diagnosing and treating disease, with the implication that the many other dimensions of caregiving are not their responsibility, simply do not understand what patients and society expect of them. In treating chronic disease, for example, one incurs responsibilities to see that people understand what is known about the cause and prognosis of their disease and that they understand and are able to do those things that help and avoid those things that hurt their condition. Technologic medicine is only one part of a complex whole. Other integral parts of that whole include interpersonal skills, such as the ability to listen, communicate, and motivate patients. The development of these skills depends on understanding a patient's *behavior* and not just a patient's *symptoms*. Medical care today focuses heavily on controlling, palliating, and limiting the consequences of disease. However, the importance of interpersonal skills and services is often underestimated, by both the public and those within the medical professions.

Professional interactions and the status of physicians

Another important aspect of clinical practice that falls outside the applied science orientation of medical care education are the often complex social system interactions that occur between peers, such as physician-physician or nurse-nurse, and between different providers, such as physician-nurse. The nature of those interactions, as well as provider-patient interactions, in turn, are being affected by a related social phenomenon—the changing status of the physician.

---

*From Didion, J.: The white album, New York, 1979, Simon & Schuster.

The hospital as a social system

Interactions with colleagues. As new graduates of medical school enter residency training, they find that they must learn to function in the intricate social system of the hospital, with its various groups and hierarchies of trainees, staff physicians, attending physicians, nurses, and administrative personnel.[8,15,16] Almost all house officers can cite individuals in each such group who have been enormously helpful in their professional development and in helping them weather the acute and chronic stresses and strains of internship and residency.[22] Providers, both at the beginning of and throughout their careers, find others who will help them through crises, teach them new technical knowledge and skills, and show them better ways to approach clinical problems and deal with anxious patients and relatives.

Relationships with colleagues, however, also can be extraordinarily difficult, calling for as much "diagnostic and management" skill as does a complex disease entity. In residency training, for example, the competitiveness often experienced in the premedical and medical school years may persist, even to the extent that "doing better" and "being smarter" than one's fellow trainees may override the needs of patients. In addition to the vivid accounts of residency by physician-authors, sociologists such as Mumford[24] and Bosk[4] have examined aspects of training, such as the processes by which house officers must either "climb the pyramid" to obtain the limited number of senior and chief residencies at their institution or seek training elsewhere.

The informal and formal teaching methods of senior house officers, staff, and attending physicians also can be difficult to accept. Seniors may be brutally impatient when the intern makes the inevitable mistakes of a new initiate. The hard questioning of new physicians in front of peers and advanced colleagues may at times have a calculated tendency to humiliate the learner, with the hope of reducing the occurrence of errors in patient care. It may also have the unintended effects of producing anxiety about one's skill and judgment and raising the unpleasant possibility that one will never be able to learn it all.[4]

Trainees also learn that they must adapt their professional behavior to conform to the accepted norms of the service they are on and find that these standards usually are dictated by the seemingly all-powerful chief of service. A related aspect of this adaptation process involves dealing with the strong pressures for young physicians to ultimately defer to the clinical judgment of their superiors, no matter how brilliant, knowledgeable, and up to date in the clinical literature trainees may be. Arguments, debates, or appeals to superior tribunals are discouraged. In the clash between scientific and clinical knowledge it may seem that attending physicians believe they are always right, no matter what was just printed in last week's journal.

The pressures of time. Another difficult facet of becoming a physician, one that is most graphic during internship but recurs throughout practice, is the extreme pressures of time and the work load. House officers must meet grueling demands on their time, which undeniably interfere with some aspects of learning and patient care. One wonders how priorities, attitudes, and habits in patient care are shaped, both in short- and long-term ways, by the limits fatigue and time place on provider-patient interactions. To what extent do effective history taking, treatment, and building of rapport in provider-patient relationships suffer because house officers are too tired to be sympathetic with a patient's problems or too rushed to even explore what those problems might be? What long-term attitudes toward providing care are developed when the exhausted resident on call, awakened repeatedly during the night, wishes that Mr. X would "just die so I don't have to get up and go to the ward again?" What message is conveyed to new physicians about the nature of their superior's priorities when they are asked to render effective care under such constraints?[27]

Incompetency in colleagues. In discovering what is expected of them in their professional interactions, young physicians sooner or later will also encounter incompetence in a colleague and the dilemma of how to deal with it. We are not referring to those incompetencies caused by inexperience or limitations in the state of the art, which all physicians must confront. Rather, as virtually every experienced physician will acknowledge, we are referring to the problem of those practitioners who, because of negligence, substance abuse, or emotional difficulties, are incompetent enough to endanger their patients.[10,19] Detecting and dealing with this problem is or should be an unsettling personal and professional experience for a young physician. As they are socialized into the culture of medicine, physicians learn that it is rarely considered appropriate to "turn" on one's incompetent colleague. Rather, the physician is expected to accommodate to a colleague's inadequacies, trying to make sure in the process that the colleague's patients are not harmed. In the hospital setting, this practice of covering for an impaired physician is sometimes referred to as "grayzoning."[20] It is the type of problem and practice that produces a classic clash of professional values—duties to patients versus duties to colleagues—and throws into sharp focus issues of social control within the medical profession.[4,17]

Working with "the team." In addition to fellow physicians, other professionals within the social system of the hospital, and later in other practice settings, provide both educational and collaborative benefits and often unanticipated interpersonal problems. Experienced nurses have saved many an intern from medical catastrophe, and it is well understood on hospital units that there is no substitute for experience, regardless of the level of professional training. Yet at the same time, conflicts arise out of this dependency of the doctor on the nurse. The traditional hierarchy places the physician at the top and role expectations imply that the physician has superior medical knowledge and skills. Most young physicians eventually learn to work their way through this thorny maze of conflicting roles, expectations, obligations, and status with but a few scratches.

What complicates this situation more is the movement of nursing toward greater professional autonomy and more of a collaborative role with, rather than a subordinate role to, medicine. Moreover, young physicians often fail to appreciate the difficulty nurses have in interacting with doctors, traditionally their superiors, while actually being responsible to nursing supervisors. Considerable conflict may be generated for nurses from these two lines of authority.[2]

As medicine becomes more complex, clinically and socially, physicians also are finding that they often must lean more on other specialists, not only nurses, but social workers, health educators, medical technicians, occupational and physical therapists, and sometimes even lawyers. The emerging roles of professionals such as nurse practitioners and physician's assistants, as well as the reemergence of some old roles such as nurse midwives, also contribute to current unrest regarding these issues.[3] The relationship of these groups to one another is still in transition, and conflict is inevitable during any such rearrangement of status, duties, and rights.

The changing status of the physician

The physician's interaction with fellow physicians, nurses, and other colleagues and with patients and the public more generally is further complicated these days by changes in the status and image of the physician and of medicine as a profession. The perhaps mythical but nonetheless gleaming image of the selfless, dedicated, omniscient physician has been tarnished.[27] In an age when television comics satirize the presumed altruism of physicians by suggesting that people not get ill on weekends or Wednesday afternoons unless they happen to be on the golf course, we can state with confidence that we are witnessing a powerful change in the public image of physicians.

Many factors seem to be contributing to the changing status of the physician and of medicine as a profession. Some factors are related to medicine itself. These factors include, for example, public concern about the disappearance of generalists, the rise of subspecialists, and the geographic maldistribution of physicians; the perceived focus of medicine on organs and disease and concomitant loss of interest in patients as human beings; the development of practices and procedures that, some charge, are more beneficial to practitioners than to patients; and a deepening concern about the rising costs of medical care.

Other contributing factors that we have alluded to include increasing public awareness of the impaired physician and other social control problems within medicine, which, in part, entails recognition of the seemingly obvious fact that physicians, too, are imperfect human beings. The physician's traditional status, authority, and autonomy also are being altered by the growing affirmations of the patient's legal and ethical rights to be an informed, consenting participant in decisions about his or her care, rather than the passive recipient of the physician's benevolent paternalism.

The physician's status also is being altered by more widespread societal changes, for which medicine often serves as a lightning rod. These changes include challenges to the wisdom and authority of the expert or professional in our society and a mounting distrust in the leadership of both private and public institutions. For all these reasons, most of which are not well understood, the physician and the profession of medicine are in evolving roles that seem to signal the development of a new form of social contract between providers and the public in which the status and role of physicians may be substantially altered.[6,21,30]

The changing status of American physicians, however, needs to be kept in perspective, for it has almost always been very high in the twentieth century, compared both to the status of other professional groups and of physicians in other countries. Although it is true that physician status has dropped significantly, this has been true of *all* professions, and medicine has not dropped as much as most of the others, such as law and education. Moreover, the status of physicians may have been so extraordinarily high that it contributed to unrealistic expectations among the public. Although high status may have salutory effects in some aspects of professional practice, its side effects, such as the corresponding expectation of perfection and the ability to solve *all* medical problems, certainly have not been healthy or constructive for the profession or for the public. It is important that both groups have realistic expectations that will not be crushed so easily and create a deep-seated cynicism and distrust of the medical care world.

The social context of medical practice

Interactions between physicians, patients, and other providers, complex as they are when considered by themselves, do not occur in isolation. Instead, they take place in various settings, such as the hospital, health center, or physician's office. Each of these delivery settings can be viewed as a small social system in its own right, with structural and functional features that condition the processes of giving and receiving medical care. Additionally, when we think of medicine as one of many institutions in our society, we can begin to define at a more macro level the ways that various social, cultural, political, and economic forces shape the nature of medicine and health care.

Economic and regulatory forces. Many aspects of training and practice that seem, at first glance, to be professionally determined are conditioned by governmental decisions about how health care monies should be distributed and how practices should be regulated.[5,28,36] The specific requirements attached to provisions for the manpower training funds awarded to medical and nursing schools affect the numbers of students admitted for training and, together with federal research funds, the orientation of that training. Economic factors associated with clinical training and practice, over time, also are linked to changes in clinical programs, such as the increasing emphasis on primary care training, and to patterns of physician and nurse practice specialization, geographic distribution, and practice settings in which care is offered.

Economic and other societal factors also condition and constrain practice in many ways at more immediate provider-patient levels. For example, the neophyte clinician working in an emergency room, ward, or outpatient department soon learns that the medical condition of patients is by no means the only or sometimes even the major factor in deciding which persons should be treated and sent home and which should be hospitalized. Hospital administrators, for example, are deeply concerned about the hospital census, for which they are responsible and which determines much of a hospital's financial viability. When the census is high and beds are limited, house staff are told to decrease admissions; when the census is low, they are told to increase admissions. Requirements for professional review standards and third-party reimbursements exert further pressures on the length of hospital stays.

In nonemergency situations, a patient's ability to pay for services is considered, and some outpatient clinics actually direct patients to billing offices before services are rendered. In teaching hospitals, intern and resident colleagues also convey strong opinions regarding the appropriateness of admissions, the goal being to admit more medically interesting patients and to send home those with repetitive, uninteresting problems.

New professionals in nursing and social work as well as medicine also discover that patient placement for those needing long-term, chronic care involves problems of which they are rightly incredulous. Many nursing homes, for instance, will send critically ill patients to hospitals in emergency circumstances and will then fill their spaces so that the patients cannot return when ready for discharge. Patients with no money and no medical insurance coverage become particularly difficult to place in other homes. Likewise, other medical institutions set up barriers to block referrals of such patients to themselves. A maze of federal and local regulations, a swamp of payment schemes, and other factors have led some observers to the conclusions that nursing homes represent a national scandal, yet home health services or centers for independent living are only meagerly supported, if at all.

In cases such as these, the young clinician learns that when the medical condition of the patient conflicts with the training needs of the house staff, the fiscal needs of the administration, or the financial and regulatory binds on types of required care, the patient's needs may come second. What effect will such decision-making pressures have on this young physician's values? How do they compare with expectations brought from medical school to act in the patient's best interests? By accommodating to these unforeseen pressures, will the house officer's view of medical care and appropriate behavior undergo significant and lasting change?

Medicine's expanding scope. Beyond the specific economic and regulatory forces that condition medical care, we are in an era in which the scope of what society views as medicine's responsibilities is an expanding one. Providers increasingly must contend with the fact that they are asked to deal with social problems for which they have had little or no training. On one hand, powerful social influences can bend, damage, or destroy their best treatment and prevention efforts with patients. Grinding poverty, lack of education, social isolation, societal prejudice, indifference to the needs and capacities of some patients, environmental hazards, and occupational health risks all can bring certain types of illnesses and traumas to hospitals in a seemingly endless cycle or can impede the best efforts of providers to help patients recover from serious illnesses and return to meaningful lives. On the other hand, providers are asked to treat and cure social or psychologic problems such as drug and alcohol abuse, delinquency, gambling, and child and wife abuse as if they were medical diseases with a definitive etiology, natural history, and cure.[31]

The complex issue of whether or to what extent we are "overmedicalizing" many social problems (defining them as illness or disease and turning to medicine for their prevention, treatment, or cure) is one that disturbs many contemporary observers of American society.[14] One simplistic view is that the medical care industry is essentially imperialistic and seeks to extend the borders of its influence and offer pronouncements and treatments for a wide variety of social ills including hyperactive children, substance use, and marital disharmony. Another view asserts that in the vacuum of human services aimed at dealing with such problems, medicine has been invited, perhaps dragged in, to deal with problems no other institutions are willing or able to deal with.

Whether imperialistic or altruistic, medicine's involvement in such areas has been extraordinarily problematic. These social problems, though they contain threats to health, are not well understood in terms of traditional medical competencies in the areas of etiology, diagnosis, prognosis, and treatment. With very few exceptions, medicine has been unable to substantially alter, modify, or reduce such problems for society as a whole or even for particular individuals.

The net effect on medicine has been to include yet another huge category of problems in its domain for which it can do little and for which, once again, its performance is currently judged as inadequate. Our own view is that medical involvement is motivated less by imperialistic designs than by public solicitations. The mistake is the profession's ready acceptance of the redefinition of problems from social to medical and its failure to appreciate the limits of a traditional clinical approach when dealing with social problems.

The health consciousness of Americans. Another set of questions associated with the issues of medicine's expanding scope and the extent to which America has become an overmedicalized society has to do with whether we have become preoccupied, if not obsessed, with health. We do live in a society that devotes considerable attention and resources to health, illness, and medicine, and to some observers of the American scene, such as Dr. Lewis Thomas, this attention has been excessive.

"As a people," Thomas believes, "we have become obsessed with health. There is something fundamentally, radically unhealthy about this. We do not seem to be seeking more exuberance in living as much as staving off failure, putting off dying. We have lost confidence in the human body."[33] To Thomas, this "obsession" seems paradoxical in view of the reduced mortality, increased life expectancy, and reduction of acute infectious diseases that have occurred in the United States in the past 50 years.

Are Americans as concerned about health as we appear? Is the phrase "the worried well" or the title of the important book, *Doing Better and Feeling Worse*,[13] apt and accurate? If it is true that Americans are obsessed with health, why is this the case?

If we assessed American health consciousness first in terms of physician and hospital visits, we would see that these are high compared to the rest of the world and appear to be rising. Yet it would be a mistake to identify all these visits as patient-*initiated*. Many visits are, in fact, due to the direct recommendations of physicians or are in response to highly publicized and ubiquitous public service media messages. The health-medical care system must thus take some responsibility for motivating much of the public to seek care.

A second assessment is the highest per capita consumption of prescription drugs in the world, plus the consumption of a staggering amount of over-the-counter or patent medicines. Obviously, some of this usage also is physician-initiated, even though many physicians report that medication is requested by patients themselves. Much drug usage and the vast purchases of other products perceived as health-related also are stimulated by a media barrage of advertising. Thomas[31] has written:

> Watching television, you'd think we lived at bay, in total jeopardy, surrounded on all sides by human-seeking germs, shielded against infection and death only by a chemical technology that enables us to keep killing them off. We are instructed to spray disinfectants everywhere, into the air of our bedrooms and kitchens and with special energy into bathrooms, since it is our very own germs that seem the worst kind. We explode clouds of aerosol, mixed for good luck with deodorants, into our noses, mouths, underarms, privileged crannies—even into the intimate insides of our telephones. We apply potent antibiotics to minor scratches and seal them with plastic. Plastic is the new protector; we wrap the already plastic tumblers of hotels in more plastic, and seal the toilet seats like state secrets after irradiating them with ultraviolet light. We live in a world where the microbes are always trying to get at us, to tear us cell from cell, and we only stay alive and whole through diligence and fear . . .*

A third, softer assessment of a high level of concern is the sheer volume of attention that the American media pay to health issues. Virtually every major newspaper and magazine in the country has standard columns of information and advice about topics such as health, nutrition, drugs, and sex. Much of the hard

---

*From THE LIVES OF A CELL by Lewis Thomas. Copyright © 1971, 1972, 1973 by the Massachusetts Medical Society. Reprinted by permission of Viking Penguin Inc.

news in all daily newspapers also deals with local and national health-related issues such as health care costs, epidemics, malpractice suits, hospital closings, medical school admissions, transplants, lifesaving emergency treatment, and new develop ments in technology.

Comparably, television and radio programming includes an array of medical documentaries, regularly scheduled presentations, and medical news consultants who provide spot information and advice. Medical dramas, too, have long been winners in the ratings game, as have books on health and medicine in the fiction and nonfiction best-seller charts.

The public also receives a steady barrage of information, appeals, and warnings from the disease-oriented voluntary health organizations, such as the American Cancer Society, the American Heart Association, and the March of Dimes. These organizations seek both to raise funds for research and treatment and to alert people to the dangers of specific diseases and their impacts on individuals and the public. In a strange way, each organization has to compete with the others to maintain public concern and funding for "their" disease. Each thus tends to escalate and amplify the message of research and treatment needs. One, perhaps inadvertent, message transmitted by the clamor, begging, and warnings of the public service messages is a sense that one is truly vulnerable to numerous devastating diseases.

In part because people receive so many different types of health-illness-medicine messages from so many different sources, a peculiar juxtaposition of public ignorance about the most elementary aspects of health and illness combined with considerable sophistication about other aspects can be found, often in the same individual. For example, people gravely concerned about cancer-causing food additives may misunderstand the basics of nutrition, and those who swear by untested home remedies or faith healing may know the subtleties of arguments for and against certain operations or drug therapies. The range of lay knowledge and ignorance often is surprising to medical personnel, who initially tend to assume that their patients will be either uneducated or sophisticated about the problems for which they are seeking care. Given this mixture of the health knowledge of patients and the beliefs and potentially miscalculated impressions of providers, the recommendations of medical professionals are likely to get a mixed reception.

Americans tend to be an activist people, not merely passive recipients of information. Thus a sizable and growing proportion of the population is engaging in a variety of "health"-related behaviors. Some of these behaviors are thought to be beneficial and others are thought to be dubious by medical professionals. Endeavors such as jogging, marathoning, swimming, biking, backpacking, weight watching, stopping smoking, and health and natural food consumption are attempts by many to attain or retain their youth, vigor, and health.

However, for a sizable and perhaps major group of Americans, the presumed powerful concern with health does not seem to produce healthful behavior or reduce unhealthful behavior. Many Americans continue to smoke, overeat, drink excessively, and live sedentary lives. Many avoid medical checkups, delay seeking medical care in the presence of significant physical symptoms, and, when diagnosed and treated for a particular disorder, notoriously fail to comply with recommended regimens.

Medical or health care as a "right." A final aspect of the social context of medical practice that we will note, related both to the expanding scope of medicine's responsibilities and to concerns about health and illness, is the more and more widely shared value that all citizens have a *right* to medical or health care.[34] Though prior to World War II medical care was regarded like any other purchasable service, the notion of health care as a right has been supported publicly by Congress and the last five United States presidents. Legislation such as Medicare and Medicaid has been passed, and various national "health insurance" plans have been proposed to help ensure that such a "right" is not denied by lack of financial resources. Because concepts of "rights" are related to the prevalent values of the time, society, and culture in which they arise, such value changes tend to be slow. But the direction in the case of medical care appears unmistakably clear: American society, through its political institutions, is expected and intends to extend more care to more people.

Efforts to act on the belief that medical care is a right, in terms of providing services that are available, accessible, and affordable, appear to be on a collision course with powerful and escalating concerns about the costs of such care. The rapidity and steepness of the rise in those costs has alarmed large segments of the American public and government as well as the medical community. The leading chapter of the important Department of Health, Education, and Welfare Report to the President, *Health United States, 1978*, deals not with the status of our nation's health but with cost containment.[9] The conflict between extending services and, at the same time, cutting the labor and equipment intensive costs of those services is readily apparent, and, for the foreseeable future, will place both providers and patients between the proverbial rock and hard place, in terms of expectations about what types of services should be delivered at what costs.

Summary

In this first chapter, we have touched briefly on selected problems of which new providers often are not aware until they first encounter them in the clinical setting and with which they must continue to deal throughout their practice. These social science dimensions of medical care, and others that we will cover more fully in the chapters that follow, are ones that the crowded curricula of professional schools leave little room to address.

These topics are difficult and often bleak ones, both at the individual provider and patient level and with respect to the larger social context of medical care in the United States; we have not balanced our attention to them in this chapter by discussing the many positive aspects of learning to become and being a medical care professional.

It is currently fashionable for critics of American medicine to argue that a significant part of what they diagnose as being wrong with medical care is due to the characteristics of its major providers. One strand of this argument contends that physicians are motivated chiefly by a desire for status, power, and wealth. These motives are seen variously as (1) inherent in those who chose medicine as a career, (2) reflective of a faulty medical school selection process, or (3) the result of a training period that is so lengthy, costly, and dehumanizing that its survivors believe they are entitled to rewards that obscure their original more idealistic and altruistic motives. A second common criticism involves the personality of physicians. Often invoking comparisons with the idealized kindly old doctor of horse and buggy days, this refrain is that today's physicians, while technically competent, are no longer warm, friendly, and compassionate in their dealings with patients.

Like any comparable statements about the motivations and characteristics of a class of individuals, these two lines of criticism obviously are neither completely true nor completely false for physicians as a class. Moreover, we would argue that, personal idiosyncrasies apart, the vast majority of physicians and other medical care providers strongly desire to act as professionals in the best sense of that word. That is, they want to be *experts* at what they are doing, and they want to be *effective*. They want the respect of their patients and colleagues for doing their job well and would like to think that what they do is beneficial not only for individual patients, but for society as well.

Neither individual providers nor their professions as a whole, we believe, can attain satisfactory levels of expertise or effectiveness unless the social science dimensions of health and medical care become an integral part of training and practice. To that end, as we have indicated in this chapter, this book addresses some of the social factors in health, illness, and medical care that we feel are particularly important for providers to be aware of as they enter clinical training and practice.

References

1. Ackernecht, E.: Rudolph Virchow: doctor, statesman, scientist, Madison, 1953, University of Wisconsin Press.
2. Anderson, P.: Nurse: the true story of Mary Benjamin, R.N., New York, 1978, St. Martin's Press, Inc.
3. Bliss, A., and Cohen, E., editors: The new health professionals, Germantown, Md., 1977, Aspen Systems Corp.
4. Bosk, C.: Forgive and remember: managing medical failure, Chicago, 1979, University of Chicago Press.
5. Burger, E.: Protecting the nation's health: the problems of regulation, Lexington, Mass., 1976, Lexington Books.
6. Chapman, C.: Doctors and their autonomy: past events and future prospects, Science **200:** 851, 1978.
7. Cook, R.: The year of the intern, New York, 1972, Harcourt Brace Jovanovich, Inc.
8. Coser, R.: Life in the ward, East Lansing, 1966, Michigan State University Press.
9. Department of Health, Education, and Welfare: Health United States 1978, Washington, D.C., 1978, DHEW Publication No. (PHS) 78-1232.
10. Derbyshire, R.: Medical licensure and discipline in the United States, Baltimore, 1969, The Johns Hopkins University Press.
11. Didion, J.: The white album, New York, 1979, Simon & Schuster, Inc.

12. Doctor X: Intern, New York, 1965, Harper & Row, Publishers, Inc.
13. Doing better and feeling worse: health in the United States, Daedalus **106**:Winter, 1977.
14. Fox, R.: The medicalization and demedicalization of American society, Daedalus **106**: 9, 1977.
15. Freidson, E.: The hospital in modern society, New York, 1966, The Free Press.
16. Freidson, E.: Professional dominance: the social structure of medical care, New York, 1970, Atherton Press.
17. Freidson, E.: Doctoring together: a study of professional social control, New York, 1975, American Elsevier Publishers, Inc.
18. Glasser, R.: Ward 402, New York, 1974, Pocket Books.
19. Green, R., Carroll, G., and Buxton, W.: The care and management of the sick and incompetent physician, Springfield, Ill., 1978, Charles C Thomas, Publisher.
20. Holoweiko, M.: Grayzoning, Medical Economics, p. 187, Feb. 19, 1979.
21. Jonsen, A.: The rights of physicians: a philosophical essay, Washington, D.C., 1973, National Academy of Sciences–Institute of Medicine.
22. Lowenstein, L., and Shapiro, E., editors: Becoming a physician: development of values and attitudes in medicine, Cambridge, Mass., 1979, Ballinger Publishing Co.
23. MacNab, J.: The education of a doctor: my first year on the wards, New York, 1971, Simon & Schuster.
24. Mumford, E.: Interns—from students to physicians, Cambridge, Mass., 1957, Harvard University Press.
25. Shem, S.: The house of God, New York, 1978, Richard Marek Publishers.
26. Siegel, E.: The search for migraine cause, Boston Globe, Oct. 2, 1979.
27. Siegler, M., and Osmond, H.: Aesculapian authority, Hastings Cent. Stud. **1**:41, 1973.
28. Somers, A., and Somers, H., editors: Health and health care: policies in perspective, Germantown, Md., 1977, Aspen Systems Corp.
29. Straus, A., editor: Where medicine fails, New Jersey, 1970, Transaction Books.
30. Swazey, J.: Health, professionals, and the public: toward a new social contract? Philadelphia, 1979, Society for Health and Human Values.
31. Thomas, L.: Germs. In The lives of a cell, New York, 1975, Bantam Books, Inc.
32. Thomas, L.: On the science and technology of medicine, Daedalus **106**:35, 1977.
33. Thomas, L.: The health-care system. In The medusa and the snail, New York, 1979, The Viking Press.
34. Veatch, R., and Branson, R., editors: Ethics and health policy, Cambridge, Mass., 1976, Ballinger Publishing Co.
35. Viscott, D.: The making of a psychiatrist, New York, 1972, Arbor House Publishing Co., Inc.
36. Weeks, L., and Berman, H., editors: Economics in health care, Germantown, Md., 1977, Aspen Systems Corp.

Chapter 2

Social factors in the prevention of disease

Between 1970 and 1975 something startling happened in the United States: the average life expectancy in this country rose 2 years, largely because of a decline in the rates of death from coronary heart disease.[97]

This sudden increase in life expectancy followed 15 years of frustration and disappointment for those interested in disease prevention. Between the late 1800s and 1955, improved standards of living, better nutrition and housing, as well as medical and public health breakthroughs such as the implementation of sterile surgical techniques, modern sewage disposal, purification of public drinking water, pasteurization, mass immunization against numerous infectious diseases, and the advent of antibiotic therapy had all contributed to a spectacular increase in life expectancy at birth from around 50 years to 70 years.[19] Most of this increase was the result of infectious disease control. From 1900 to the 1950s, the contribution of infectious diseases as the primary reported cause of death in the United States declined from 40% to slightly over 5% of all deaths.[9]

Unfortunately, in the mid-1950s these gains slackened markedly. Despite an ever increasing fund of medical knowledge and rapidly increasing *per capita* expenditures on medical care, the ability of modern medicine to increase further life expectancy came into question.

Some argued that advances earlier in the century had primarily focused on childhood diseases. This produced a gradual shift in the age composition of the population with increasing proportions in the middle-aged and elderly groups. As a result, deaths from chronic degenerative diseases assumed greater importance. Between 1900 and 1963, the death rate for cardiovascular disease rose from 137 per 100,000 people to 375 per 100,000 people. Similarly, deaths from malignant neoplasms rose from 64 per 100,000 people to 151 per 100,000 people, making those two illnesses the leading causes of death.* In the early 1960s many physicians, researchers, and epidemiologists believed the United States had reached an upper limit in life expectancy until a new breakthrough could be achieved in the preven-

---

*Since then mortality for heart disease dropped to 337 per 100,000 people, while the rate for cancer rose to 175 per 100,000 people in 1976.

tion of the major chronic diseases.[9] Moreover, the prevention of most major chronic diseases appeared quite unlikely, mainly because these were degenerative diseases of old age. Perhaps the best that could be done would be to delay the onset of these diseases. But even then, delaying the onset of one disease by no means ensured that people would not succumb to other chronic diseases within a short period of time, anyway.

Nonetheless, others believed that the level of medical knowledge and technology should enable the United States to make marked advances in preventing or delaying the onset of a variety of diseases, which, in turn, would prolong life expectancy. They questioned why, with ostensibly the best-trained physicians in the world, the best medical facilities, physician population ratios as high as those of any country, and the greatest *per capita* expenditure on health, the average life expectancy at birth for both males and females in the United States was several years less than in European countries such as Norway, Sweden, and Denmark.[2] Infant mortality rates in the United States in 1963, in particular, were higher than those in many other developed nations.[106] In the United States, 25 of every 1,000 infants born died within the first year of life, compared, for example, to only 15 of every 1,000 infants in Sweden.*

In this chapter we will first explore the potential for disease prevention in the United States by reviewing various explanations for why the United States had not in the 1960s and still today has not achieved as high a life expectancy at birth as many European countries. Several explanations have been offered, ranging from scarcity of available medical services to the personal habits and life-styles of individuals to the chemical and physical environments to which we are exposed. Then we will review specific approaches that medical care providers can consider to promote more healthful behavior among the public and a more healthful environment: patient and public education, clinical behavior modification interventions, and legislative efforts to alter individual behavior and protect the public from common health hazards.

The potential for disease prevention in the United States
Disadvantaged populations

Many of those who sought to understand the different life expectancies of the United States and European countries in the 1960s were struck by the disparities in the morbidity and mortality of subpopulations within the United States. They pointed out that reducing these disparities would undoubtedly improve overall life expectancy.

In the United States it was well established that both morbidity and mortality were higher among racial minority groups and persons with lower socioeconomic

---

*These differences persist. In 1976 infant mortality had dropped to 15.2 in the United States, compared to 8.0 in Sweden.[107]

status. Although the inverse relation between morbidity and socioeconomic status may in part result from a status drift downward of persons with chronic or disabling illnesses, the drift hypothesis cannot account for socioeconomic differentials in mortality and racial differences in morbidity and mortality. For example, in the United States, infant mortality in the mid-1960s for nonwhites was over 40 per 1000 infants, almost twice the rates for whites. Between the ages of 35 and 45, mortality for nonwhite males was three times that of their white counterparts. Even if a nonwhite person lived to age 40, his projected life expectancy was four years less than that of a white person the same age.[1]

Access to medical care

Some attributed these disparities to inequities in medical care delivery. They believed that the United States system, or nonsystem, of health and medical care delivery was in such disarray that many groups in the population simply could not obtain the medical and health care they needed. The poor, elderly, and nonwhites all had markedly less access to medical care services.

In 1963 only 54% of persons living below the poverty level saw a physician, compared to 75% of the rest of the population.[42] Only 58% of pregnant women living below the poverty level obtained prenatal care during the first trimester, compared to 87% of the rest of the population.[94] These differences and the current situation will be further discussed in Chapter 3.

Others, however, doubt that lack of access to health and medical care is really the key to prevention. They note that, even when prevention programs such as screening or immunization have been made available, the poor, disadvantaged minority groups, and elderly have still been consistently less likely than the rest of the population to participate in these programs.[25] Moreover, differences in life expectancy observed in the 1960s persist today despite programs such as Medicare and Medicaid, which have reduced the disparities in medical care access.

Environmental factors

Another school of thought has focused on the environment to which socially disadvantaged groups are exposed. Those groups were and still are more likely to experience inadequate housing, pollution, violent crime, and occupational risk.

One of the most obvious and first recognized examples of these relationships is the connection between poverty, nutrition, and illness. Because of their need for extra nutrition for growth, infants are particularly vulnerable to failure to thrive and to specific disorders like pellagra because of inadequate caloric intake and protein and vitamin deficiencies. Inadequate nutritional intake can have a deleterious effect on physical growth and mental functioning, and protein deficiency can also leave the child more susceptible to infection.[80]

Occupational risks pose another example. It has been estimated that occupational risks alone account for 100,000 deaths in the United States. Such risks are disproportionately found in lower income occupations, such as mining, agriculture, and construction. Although the overall national death rate is 18 per 100,000 people, it is 100 per 100,000 workers in mining, 72 per 100,000 workers in construction, and 67 per 100,000 workers in agriculture. Not only are blue-collar workers and laborers exposed to immediate risks such as mine explosions, fires, and vehicular accidents, but they are also exposed to long-term risks from chemicals and pesticides. There are as many as 12,000 materials of known toxicity in commercial use, many of them carcinogens.[4]

Other major health risks that disproportionately produce ill health among the lower income groups in society are environmental pollution and poor sanitation. Persons with low incomes are much more likely than the rest of the population to live in the congested inner cities, where older houses with inadequate plumbing are more common and when faulty electrical systems pose fire risks. Peeling paint in houses built before the 1950s poses a lead poisoning hazard, which is particularly severe for young children who may eat peeling paint chips. Between 1973 and 1978, over 160,000 children screened for lead absorption nationwide were found to have excessive lead levels, and over 20,000 of the children required chelation therapy.[32]

The level of air pollution is also much higher in the inner cities, not only because of the higher amount of motor vehicle travel, but also because of the proximity to industrial manufacturing. It is difficult to obtain firm epidemiologic proof that chronic exposure to air pollution produces excess rates of lung and other forms of cancer because of the high levels of geographic mobility and the potential confounding effects of smoking and social class. But the higher incidence of cancer in industrialized, urbanized areas, particularly those in which the petrochemical industry is located, suggests that pollution may increase the risk of these illnesses. Moreover, the notable pollution crises of Donora, Pennsylvania, in 1948 and London in 1952 clearly indicate that general atmospheric pollution can pose an acute risk for young children and elderly persons with respiratory or cardiovascular illnesses.[6]

Individual behavior

Another focus of preventive health efforts has rested on the belief that individual changes in life-style and personal habits in every segment of society could produce the most substantial increase in life expectancy.[52] One basis for this conviction is data on the leading causes of death in the United States, which suggest that many deaths could be prevented or delayed if one could promote alterations in the living habits of the American people (Tables 1 and 2).[56]

Adults. Looking first at adults, it has been estimated that smoking contributes to approximately 300,000 deaths in this country each year, including 200,000 respiratory and cardiovascular deaths and 80,000 cancer deaths, over one fifth of all deaths

Table 1. Deaths and death rates for the 10 leading causes of death in 1976 and death rates for these same causes in 1900*†

Rank, 1976	Cause of death and category numbers of the Eighth Revision International Classification of Diseases, Adapted, 1965		Number of deaths, 1976	Rate per 100,000 population	
				1976	1900
	ALL CAUSES		1,909,440	889.6	1,719.1
1	Diseases of heart	390-398, 402, 404, 410-429	723,878	337.2	137.4
2	Malignant neoplasms, including neoplasms of lymphatic and hematopoietic tissues	140-209	377,312	175.8	64.0
3	Cerebrovascular diseases	430-438	188,623	87.9	106.9
4	Accidents	E800-E949	100,761	46.9	72.3
5	Influenza and pneumonia	470-474, 480-486	61,866	28.8	202.2
6	Diabetes mellitus	250	34,508	16.1	11.0
7	Cirrhosis of liver	571	31,453	14.7	12.5
8	Arteriosclerosis	440	29,366	13.7	–
9	Suicide	E950-E959	26,832	12.5	10.2
10	Certain causes of mortality in early infancy†	760, 769.2, 769.4-772, 774-778	24,809	11.6	62.6

*From Facts of life and death, U.S. Department of Health, Education, and Welfare Pub. No. (PHS) 79-1222, 1978.
†Relates to causes such as birth injuries, asphyxia, infections of newborn, ill-defined diseases, and immaturity.

from cancer.[31] At present, an estimated 45 million Americans smoke cigarettes. The hazards of smoking have been clear since the Surgeon General's report in the early 1960s,[100] and recent estimates reveal that 80% of smokers have considered stopping at one time or another and that some 1.5 million persons do manage to stop each year in the United States.[21] However, 39% of adult men and 29% of adult women continue to smoke cigarettes regularly.[93] Moreover, among teenage girls the proportion who smoke rose from 22% in 1964 to 27% in 1977.[101]

Another major contributor to heart disease, as well as stroke and renal disease, is hypertension. In the United States over 23 million people are estimated to be hypertensive, between 9% and 14% of all American adults.[38] Yet, even though diagnosis is easy and painless, and treatment can prevent many serious consequences,[103] less than one third of all persons with hypertension have been treated and have the disease under control. Although some progress is being made, between 30% and 40% of hypertensives are unaware that they have hypertension, and almost one third of those aware of their illness are receiving inadequate therapy.[105]

Still other preventable problems are those caused by excessive alcohol consumption or by the erratic behavior of persons who have been drinking. It has long been suspected that alcohol often plays a major contributing role in the nearly 30,000 annual deaths from cirrhosis of the liver.[89] Alcohol has also been considered a con-

Table 2. Major diseases susceptible to primary prevention in adults*

Disease	Number of deaths	Major risk factors	Deaths attributable to major risk factors (%)	Comment
Cancer				
Lung	83,880†	Heavy cigarette smoking	>80	Good prospective studies
Oral cavity	8,300†	Alcohol, tobacco	76	Both factors seem to be important
				Retrospective studies
Esophagus	6,600†	Alcohol, tobacco (USA)	>67	
Larynx	3,250†	Alcohol, tobacco	>67	
Penis	280‡	Poor hygiene, noncircumcision	>90	Retrospective, but convincing
Coronary heart disease	682,910‡	Hypertension, smoking, cholesterol	73§ (males)	Prospective, convincing studies
Chronic bronchitis and emphysema	28,350‡	Heavy smoking, air pollution	67	Good retrospective and prospective studies
Stroke	214,650‡	Hypertension	Not known, probably 50%	Reduction in blood pressure probably effective
Cirrhosis (liver)	33,630‡	Alcohol	Estimated 67%	Data changing constantly
Accidents	115,040‡			
Motor vehicle	55,690	Drunken driving, lack of seat belt use, excess speed	Estimated 50% driver and pedestrian deaths	Recent dispute over precise figures
Homicide	19,510†	Guns, alcohol	Not known; 67% killed by guns, alcohol implicated in 50%.	

*From Louria, D., et al.: Primary and secondary prevention among adults: an analysis with comments on screening and health education. Prev. Med. **5:**549-572, 1976.
†Estimated 1976.
‡1973 Vital Statistics data.
§For those with all three risk factors: diastolic > 90 mm/hg, cholesterol > 250 mg/%, any smoking.

tributor to approximately one half of motor vehicle fatalities (about 27,000 to 28,000 yearly).[99]

Each year, there are also 25,000 traffic fatalities in which alcohol has not been implicated, many because of excessive automobile speed or failure to wear seat belts. In addition, each year in the United States since 1961, over 20,000 persons have ended their lives by suicide.[71] Homicide in the United States has annually accounted for over 20,000 deaths since 1973.[96]

Infants and children. The leading causes of infant and childhood death suggest that parental behavior can directly influence the health of children (Tables 3 and 4).[108] During the first year of life most deaths result from congenital abnormalities and prematurity. Though not all of these are related to parental behavior, and no one knows exactly what proportion of these deaths ultimately can be prevented, a variety of *behavioral maternal risk factors during pregnancy* have been identified: poor maternal nutrition, smoking, use of some psychoactive drugs such as heroin, maternal alcoholism, pregnancy past age 38, and lack of prenatal care. Not all of these have been clearly linked to congenital or neurologic infant abnormality, but even those which have not, such as maternal smoking or heavy alcohol intake, have been found to be independently associated with prematurity and lower infant birth weight, which, in turn, may lower a child's chance of survival.[15,43]

From ages 1 to 14, accidents are by far the leading cause of death. The accident rate has dropped markedly during this century, but careful control of potentially dangerous household items, such as use of containers so that toxic products cannot be easily opened and ingested by children, and increased traffic safety could all reduce the death rates still further.

Effects on life expectancy. What impact would altering the types of life-styles

Table 3. Infant mortality by age and selected causes in the United States*†

	1977	1976	1972	1968
Age				
<1 yr	14.0	15.2	18.5	21.7
<28 days	9.8	10.9	13.6	15.9
28 days to 11 months	4.2	4.3	4.8	5.8
Cause of death				
Certain gastrointestinal diseases (004, 006-009, 561, 563)	0.2	0.2	0.2	0.3
Influenza and pneumonia (470-474, 480-486)	0.5	0.6	1.3	2.3
Congenital anomalies (740-759)	2.4	2.6	2.9	3.2
Birth injuries (764-768 [0-.3], 722)	0.4	0.6	0.6	0.7
Asphyxia of newborn, unspecified (776.9)	0.9	1.1	2.1	3.0
Immaturity, unqualified (777)	1.2	1.3	1.9	2.8
Other diseases of early infancy (remainder of 760-778)	4.5	4.9	5.8	5.7
All other causes (residual)	3.9	3.9	3.7	3.7

*From Wegman, M.: Annual summary of vital statistics 1977, Pediatrics **62:**947-954, 1978.
†Rates per 1000 infants.

Table 4. Deaths and death rates for the 10 leading causes of death, ages 1 to 4 and 5 to 14: 1976*

Rank	Age, cause of death, and category numbers of the Eighth Revision International Classification of Diseases, Adapted, 1965		Number	Rate per 100,000 population in specified group
1 to 4 years, both sexes				
	ALL CAUSES		8,606	69.9
1	Accidents	E800-E949	3,439	27.9
2	Congenital anomalies	740-759	1,114	9.0
3	Malignant neoplasms, including neoplasms of lymphatic and hematopoietic tissues	140-209	656	5.3
4	Influenza and pneumonia	470-474, 480-486	480	3.9
5	Homicide	E960-E978	306	2.5
6	Diseases of heart	390-398, 402, 404, 410-429	227	1.8
7	Meningitis	320	220	1.8
8	Cerebrovascular diseases	430-438	90	0.7
9	Meningococcal infections	036	90	0.7
10	Enteritis and other diarrheal diseases	008, 009	82	0.7
5 to 14 years, both sexes				
	ALL CAUSES		12,901	34.7
1	Accidents	E800-E949	6,308	17.0
2	Malignant neoplasms, including neoplasms of lymphatic and hematopoietic tissues	140-209	1,849	5.0
3	Congenital anomalies	740-759	745	2.0
4	Homicide	E960-E978	392	1.1
5	Influenza and pneumonia	470-474, 480-486	362	1.0
6	Diseases of heart	390-398, 402, 404, 410-429	332	0.9
7	Cerebrovascular diseases	430-438	206	0.6
8	Suicide	E950-E959	163	0.4
9	Benign neoplasms and neoplasms of unspecified nature	210-239	112	0.3
10	Anemias	280-285	98	0.3

*From Facts of life and death, U.S. Department of Health, Education, and Welfare DHEW Pub. No. (PHS) 79-1222, 1978.

and specific behaviors we have mentioned have on the life expectancy of the average American? No one knows for sure, and the question is a vigorously debated one. It is impossible to do experimental studies that require individuals or groups to live certain life-styles for research purposes. The best one can do is compare individuals who choose different habits. Though people who choose not to smoke or overeat may be healthier to begin with, it is unlikely that such habits alone account for the health status differences that have been reported.

There are some data that suggest that individual habits and life-styles have an important influence on morbidity and mortality. In his book *Who Shall Live?*

Fuchs[33] compared the inhabitants of Utah and Nevada. These are contiguous states with similar climate, income, education, urbanization, and health care services, but their residents have very different life-styles. Utah is heavily populated with abstemious followers of the Mormon religion, whereas the life-style of substantial segments of the population in Nevada revolves around the casino and entertainment centers of Las Vegas and Reno. For men ages 40 to 49, the death rate in Nevada is 54% higher than in Utah. For women ages 40 to 48, the death rate in Nevada is 69% higher than in Utah.

Even more striking evidence comes from a study by Breslow[10] and Belloc[7] on the life habits of an area probability sample of nearly 7000 people in Alameda County, California in 1965. A computer matching operation recorded all deaths from their sample over a 5½ year period. (Those who may have died outside the state were not included.) They found that practicing a number of health habits was markedly correlated with increased life expectancy. These habits included (1) eating three meals a day instead of snacking; (2) eating breakfast every day; (3) moderate exercise, for example, long walks, swimming, bicycling, and gardening three to five times a week; (4) sleeping 7 to 8 hours a night; (5) not smoking; (6) drinking only one or two drinks at a time; and (7) maintaining a moderate weight, neither drastically above nor below normal.

The life expectancy for men age 45 who practice zero to three of these habits was 21.6 years, or almost to age 67. Those practicing six to seven of these habits could, on average, be expected to live 33.1 years, or almost to age 78. Thus, a difference of 11 years was found among comparably aged men who practiced most of the habits listed above as compared to those practicing only a few. Among women the difference was 7 years. Moreover, marked differences in life expectancy were found regardless of the respondents' incomes or health status at the start of the study. A follow-up on the same sample has revealed that though somewhat diminished, differences between groups persist even when deaths were monitored over a 9½-year period.[99] Although evidence concerning some of these habits, for example, eating breakfast or sleeping 8 hours a night, has not been extensively corroborated, the findings with regard to smoking, drinking, and exercise are consistent with results from numerous other studies.

Government emphasis on prevention

A final explanation for the higher morbidity and mortality rates in the United States is that our society has not given disease prevention the attention it deserves. The United States in 1977 spent over $165 billion ($737 per person) on what is termed health care.[98] Yet less than 6% was spent on disease prevention, and most of this money was devoted to pollution control and abatement.[54]

According to one estimate, less than 0.5% of health care expenditure is devoted to health education activities.[70] For example, although the federal, state, and local governments collect about $6 billion in tobacco taxes annually, and the National Cancer Institute has a current annual budget of $900 million, less than $2 million is spent by the National Cancer Institute on educational programs related to prevention. This compares with over $400 million spent annually by the tobacco industry on cigarette advertising in magazines and newspapers. Moreover, even when money is earmarked for prevention, it is often neutralized by other government policies, such as the $97 million spent in 1977 by the government for direct and indirect support of the tobacco industry, including a $50 million grant to study better ways to grow and process the tobacco crop.

While the National Heart and Lung Institute allocated $175 million in research for heart and vascular diseases in 1975, the United States Department of Agriculture that year placed its highest seal of approval, "prime", on marbleized beef with high fat content.[70] Although there is considerable latitude for reimbursement of health education activities for Medicaid outpatients, any activities labeled "preventive" are not allowed for Medicaid and Medicare inpatients.[70]

Multiple causation of illness and death

The presence of many different explanations for the less favorable mortality experience of the United States, as compared to some other industrialized nations, reflects an important fact about disease prevention. Whether or not individuals will acquire a given illness or die from it is influenced by *many* different factors, including (1) the *biologic characteristics of individuals*, such as age, sex, nutritional status, resistance to infection, and genetic makeup; (2) the *biologic environment* to which individuals are exposed, such as the infectious agents in the environment, reservoirs of infection like other humans, animals, soil, and vectors that transmit disease like mosquitoes or flies; (3) the *social environment*, such as economic factors as well as nutritional habits, receptivity to behavior change, and social pressures that affect smoking or drinking; and (4) the *physical environment* to which people are exposed, such as heat, light, air, water, radiation, and chemicals.

This multiple interaction in disease acquisition has been called the *web of causation*.[60] Mausner and Bahn[61] have used a wheel diagram to depict the multiple factors that influence the acquisition of illness (Fig. 1). At the core of the wheel is man, the potential host of illness. Each person has a unique genetic makeup, which can influence the acquisition and course of illness. The relative contribution of the biologic, social, or physical environment obviously depends on the disease under consideration.

Though people interested in disease prevention are often able to isolate a specific agent that may cause a disease, such as tubercle bacillus or lead paint, more often than not all of these environments influence who will acquire an illness and die from it. For example, who will acquire tuberculosis is determined not only by exposure to the tubercle bacillus, but also by age, nutrition, and social class. Simi-

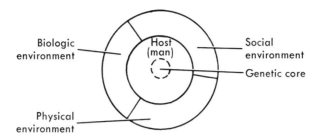

Fig. 1. Wheel model of man-environment interactions. (From Mausner, J., and Bahn, A.: Epidemiology: an introductory text, Philadelphia, 1974, W. B. Saunders Co.)

larly, exposure to lead poisoning depends on the age of the housing people live in, the condition of that housing, the ages of the children who live in the housing, and the degree of nutrition and parental supervision given to those children.

Other illnesses, particularly degenerative diseases that accompany aging, such as heart disease or stroke, do not have a single causative agent, but rather are influenced by each of the environments.

The multiplicity of factors that influence the acquisition and development of diseases and patterns of morbidity and mortality often means that prevention can be approached from many directions, only one of which is direct contact between patients and physicians or other health professionals in clinical settings. Not all morbidity and mortality results from disease, and even reductions in the death rate from specific diseases like tuberculosis can be approached by either antibiotic treatment of the disease, immunization, case finding and quarantine, alteration of personal habits like uncovered coughing or spitting in public places, or improved nutrition. Tuberculosis is like many diseases in that the spectrum of action to lower the death rate from the disease ranges from highly clinical interventions to patient education and prevention by altering the social environment. Though medical care providers often tend to focus their actions on one end of this continuum, early diagnosis and treatment and nonclinical interventions often can achieve similar goals.

Historically, the major strategies to prevent disease and other causes of morbidity and mortality have included health education of the public, patient education, specific clinical interventions to alter patient behaviors, professionally run voluntary disease prevention and detection programs, legal regulation designed to *prohibit* personal health-threatening behavior, legal inducements to discourage certain health-threatening behavior, legislation to promote environmental and occupational safety, and legislation to improve economic conditions and the general standard of living.

The multiplicity of approaches is at once a reason for optimism about the potential for prevention and a source of skepticism about the likelihood that prevention can be achieved. On one hand, the multiplicity of approaches might lead some to believe that we currently have so many ways to encourage preventive health behavior that even if one approach fails, another will be successful. On the other hand, the presence of so many strategies (1) indicates that many approaches are inadequate when pursued alone and (2) leaves the overall responsibility for disease prevention fragmented among a variety of professions and public agencies.

Moreover, the multiplicity of approaches forces clinicians and health care providers to question where their responsibilities lie. Should they systematically devote time during each patient visit to health education? Should they develop educational materials for their clinic population? Should they attempt clinical interventions to alter unhealthy behaviors? Do their responsibilities in prevention extend beyond their own patients to their community or region? Should they initiate or participate in detection or prevention programs? Should they try to play a role in the formation of community and national policy on health? In the next sections we will examine health education, clinical behavioral interventions, and legal regulation commonly employed in prevention.

Health education and the responsibility of providers

Should providers take time during patient visits to encourage more healthful life habits among patients? Many medical care providers do not believe that making recommendations to patients about appropriate health behaviors will modify what their patients do. It has been argued that evidence of successful health education efforts is, at best, modest.[41] One review of all empirical studies reported in 11 health education journals between 1975 and 1977 indicated that 40% had inadequate designs, 20% yielded insignificant results, 33% showed significant results but only minimal improvement, and only 7% demonstrated significant results with major improvements.[20]

These and other studies[63] have suggested that health education tends to focus on the individual's responsibility to change behavior and engage in a more healthy life-style, when social and economic interests promote and indeed thrive on people living stressful lives, with unhealthful habits like smoking, drinking, and consuming fatty foods offered as a relief from those stresses. Indeed, powerful industries inundate our culture with images of the suave smoker or the debonair drinker and pressure us to consume products that discourage exercise and careful diet.[63] Also, persons in the most economically disadvantaged segments of society may simply be unable to afford to follow some recommendations, for example, eating a diet that is low in fat but has adequate protein or removing lead paint from their homes.

It is naive for providers to believe that single recommendations at one or even several times with a patient will alter every patient's health beliefs and behaviors. But it is also naive to assume that patient behavior is intractable and therefore educating patients serves little purpose. Unquestionably, life-styles and habits

Table 5. Changes in per capita consumption in the United States between 1963 and 1973*†

Product	Change
All tobacco products	22.4% decline
Fluid milk and cream	19.2% decline
Butter	31.9% decline
Eggs	12.6% decline
Animal fats and oils	35.7% decline
Vegetable fats and oils	44.1% increase

*Reprinted from The New England Journal of Medicine, **297:**163-165, 1977.
†Figures for calculating percentage changes were obtained from U.S. Department of Agriculture.

in the United States are changing. Since the early 1960s, when the Surgeon General[100] reported on the hazards of smoking, and the American Heart Association began its campaign to alter the American diet by reducing the intake of saturated fat and cholesterol in an effort to lower the incidence of heart disease and stroke, a remarkable shift in public behavior has occurred. There has been a sizable shift in the *per capita* consumption of a variety of products thought to affect health (Table 5).[104]

According to the 1979 Surgeon General's report on smoking and health, *per capita* cigarette consumption in 1978 reached its lowest level in 30 years.[101] At the same time, Americans seem to have discovered exercise. A 1977 Gallup poll indicated that the proportion of adults who exercise had almost doubled since 1960 to close to 50% of the population.[87] Though the effects of clinical recommendations cannot be disentangled from those of school and media public health education programs as well as other social forces, one cannot dismiss the cumulative effect as trivial or inconsequential. A social climate has been created where smoking and certain dietary habits are perceived as less desirable, and activities such as exercise are more desirable than they once were.

Despite such overall changes in health behavior, many providers still fear that continual cautions to patients about their habits will make them less likely to come in for preventive checkups or illness care. There are also financial barriers to preventive health education by clinicians. Such activities are time-consuming and are not reimbursable under most medical care payment plans. Moreover, most physicians have little or no training in patient education, and many would prefer to spend their time using the diagnostic and therapeutic skills their training gave them.

The effectiveness of mass media

There is a tendency for medical care providers to feel that recommendations about life-style and personal habits should be left to mass media campaigns and school educators, communication sources that can reach large audiences. The argument for use of mass media, particularly television, has great appeal. More people watch television than make use of any other mode of mass communication. Ninety-six percent of American homes have one or more television sets, and in the average home, one set is on more than 6 hours a day.[70]

However, there is evidence that mass media messages exert a direct impact on human behavior only in very limited circumstances.[49] Rather than mass media being a powerful communication hypodermic needle injecting behavior-modifying information into our social system, its impact has been likened to an aerosol spray: "As you spray it on the surface, some of it hits the target; most of it drifts away, and little of it penetrates."[62] It has been argued that mass media communications have persuasive impact only where (1) the issues at hand are not important to the audience, (2) the communications reinforce initial predispositions of the audience, and (3) mediating factors, such as predisposition, social ties, and personal influence, do not contradict this message.[24]

Audiences targeted for mass media messages are not passive recipients waiting to absorb and be changed by messages. People selectively expose themselves to communications and selectively perceive, interpret, and retain what they hear.[22] People question what they hear and discuss it with others. Studies of political behavior have shown that the influence of messages is often transmitted in stages.[73] Although a population may hear of a new idea or innovation, they will look to opinion leaders in their social network before accepting new information or acting on it. Of course, opinion leaders do not always promote change in the direction mass media messages intend.

Beliefs, attitudes, and values

People bring their own *beliefs, attitudes,* and *values* to each communications situation. *Beliefs* are judgments people make about themselves and their environment (e.g., Florida is warmer than Massachusetts; cold weather causes illness). *Attitudes* are based on beliefs and are predispositions to action (e.g., "I'd rather live in Florida than Massachusetts, because I'll stay healthier"). *Values* are based on beliefs and attitudes. They are enduring beliefs about the worth of specific modes of conduct or end states of existence (e.g., Stealing is wrong; it is good to be healthy). Each individual holds many more beliefs than attitudes and many more attitudes than values. *Beliefs are easier to change than attitudes, which, in turn, are easier to change than values.*[75]

One reason mass media messages do not have much impact is that preserving health is not necessarily man's highest value. It competes with many other values, including wealth, love, power, security, beauty, knowledge, and social acceptance.

Over the last two decades numerous mass media campaigns have tried to alter people's beliefs, attitudes, and values about health in an effort to alter their behavior. Most studies have reported that people's knowledge is, indeed, increased and beliefs are changed by media campaigns.

However, although mass media have been effective in conveying information and increasing the salience of issues, they have not been as effective as interpersonal communication in molding attitudes or values and in influencing behavior.[49]

This is true for several reasons.[72,112] First, the credibility of mass media, especially television, is low. The association of mass media with the advertising industry raises suspicions about the accuracy of health information transmitted and the motives behind it. One content analysis of health-related messages broadcast on television suggests that as much as 70% may be misleading or false.[83] Second, interpersonal communication can be more persistent in the face of apathy. It is harder to turn away a person than to flick off a television or radio. Third, if an audience does not understand a message, it is easier to detect and correct in an interpersonal interaction. Fourth, it is more difficult for mass media messages to convey social approval if someone disagrees with the messages conveyed. Advertisements often have people in the background nodding their heads in approval of a person in the ad and accepting the ad's message, but this is a small substitute for actual personal approval.

Finally, and most importantly, as we will discuss in Chapter 6, each person has a set of beliefs about illness and treatment that influences behavior. Numerous studies of immunization programs and screening programs have shown that beliefs about *susceptibility* to illness, *severity* of illness, if acquired, in terms of health and life-style disruption, *effectiveness* of the procedure in diagnosis or prevention of the disease, and *barriers* or obstacles to engaging in preventive behaviors are related to whether people will engage in preventive behaviors.[76] People's health beliefs vary from disease to disease, person to person, or even in the same person over time. The major handicap of mass media compared to individual communication is that mass media cannot customize messages to the beliefs of specific individuals. Mass media messages to persuade people of the seriousness of a disorder in an effort to foster preventive behavior may not affect people who already believe a disease to be serious. (Some fear arousal studies suggest it may even be counterproductive because fears may be elevated to an immobilizing level.) Such people might be more influenced by messages about the effectiveness of preventive action. In interpersonal communication, specific beliefs can be identified before recommendations are offered.*

Another example can be seen in efforts to dissuade people from smoking. People derive different benefits from smoking. Some people smoke to relax, whereas others seek stimulation. Some smoke when they want to reduce loneliness, sad-

---

*If mass media are not as effective as interpersonal communication, it is reasonable to ask: Why do so many companies spend millions of dollars each year in mass media advertising? Probably the main reason is that the goal of advertising often differs from that of health educators trying to encourage changes in life-style. Advertisers are not only trying to foster entirely new behaviors or have people abandon old ones. Sometimes, rather than persuade people to use more bars of soap, they are more interested in having people shift from Brand X to their brand. Even shifts of only 2% to 3% of the buying public from one product to another can prompt dramatic shifts in the profits of a national company.

ness, or anxiety. Some enjoy manipulating the cigarette, package, and matches with their hands. Some feel the need to light up whenever they see someone else smoking. Some smoke as part of habit patterns, for example, after meals, with drinks, or with coffee. Some smoke because they feel more glamorous or sophisticated.[90] Mass media messages can hardly be expected to address each of these reasons for smoking, whereas individual communications could explore individual reasons or benefits from smoking and address these needs.[48]

Schools and health education

The limitations of mass media in health education prompt some clinicians to look to the school system as an alternative avenue for promoting healthful behaviors. Nearly 50 million children are currently enrolled in kindergarten through the twelfth grade, constituting a vast captive audience for interpersonal communication.

Despite the tremendous potential for health education in schools, most would agree that school health education attempts have been meager and inadequate. The following comments of the President's Committee on Health Education in the early 1970s reflect the situation.[95]

> Our findings are that school health education in most primary or secondary schools either is not provided at all or loses its proper emphasis because it is tacked onto another subject such as physical education or biology, assigned to teachers whose interests and qualifications lie elsewhere. . . . While large amounts of health information materials find their way into the schools because they are free or inexpensive, such materials are rarely evaluated in terms of real value to the children. . . . Antiquated laws, indifferent parents, unaggressive school boards, teachers poorly equipped to handle the subject, lack of leadership from the government or the public, lack of funds, lack of research, lack of evaluation—all of these hobble a comprehensive program that could provide the nation's 55 million schoolchildren with adequate health education of an interesting, permanent, and objective nature. . . . Evidence abounds that health education in schools is not effective even when it is attempted.

One reason for this problem is the small number of persons trained in health education. Though estimates vary, there are probably fewer than 20,000 health educators in the entire nation. This compares, for example, with 295,000 active practicing physicians and 815,000 active registered nurses.[70] Without a dramatic shift in present educational priorities and an enormous effort to train health educators for the school system, it is unlikely that school health education can conceivably reach its potential.

However, even if resources could be shifted to school health educators, numerous obstacles would have to be surmounted for such programs to be effective in promoting more healthful behaviors. The traditional thrust of most school health education programs has been to argue *against* behaviors that many students see as being "adult." School health education, like mass media communications, is not introduced into a social vacuum. Students will compare what they hear with their own experiences and the practices of their friends and families. In this context, urging students not to smoke or drink when their parents do can appear as just another message from the school system that they are still children, not adults.

Most school health education efforts also have been heavy on moralism and weak on content. Sessions on venereal diseases discourage sex, rather than inform students of means of prevention or the need for prompt treatment, if the diseases are acquired. Alcohol messages tend to have a prohibitionist ring, rather than helping students learn the ways and amounts in which alcohol can be consumed safely. Even more problematic, some school health education efforts have so elaborately exaggerated the dangers of certain substances, like marijuana, that the overall credibility of all their messages has been called into question. Indeed, exaggerated portrayal of hazards of certain behaviors may, in fact, only reinforce the motivation of students for whom risk taking is seen as a way of gaining the respect of their peers.[109]

Provider-patient interactions

In making these comments, we are not trying to suggest that mass media and school education programs are not potentially valuable aspects in preventive health. Indeed, their potential is much greater than it has yet been realized. However, both approaches to health education have limitations when contrasted to direct communication between patients and medical care providers. Because of its interpersonal nature, provider-patient contact offers greater interaction potential than the formal education system. In any given year, three fourths of the nation's population will have contact with a physician, and the average person has nearly five contacts per year.[102] During these contacts, not only physicians or nurses, but each medical care team member can potentially serve as a health educator.

Whether they realize it or not, providers also play an important role in health education by virtue of being opinion leaders who can legitimize or deflate the ideas their patients encounter in the media or from their friends and families. In any given year the public is apt to encounter a bewildering variety of facts, promises, and arguments about what is healthy or unhealthy. Sometimes even medical professionals seem at odds with each other, for example, over whether saccharin is carcinogenic, whether alcoholics can learn to drink in moderation, or whether jogging prevents heart disease.

In large measure, the credibility of medical care providers as opinion leaders who can influence patient behavior rests on their ability to interpret and explain such controversies to their patients. In recent years there has been a tendency to think that the only effective form of health education is that which produces immediate desired behavior change in the public. Although fostering certain behaviors is a desirable end, it should be only one aspect of health education. It is equally important to convey an accurate understanding of current knowledge on important health issues to patients so that decisions on their behavior will be informed decisions (even if they do not coincide exactly with what providers want).

Effective health education not only consists of skills in persuasion. It includes an ability to succinctly summarize differing points of view on controversial medical issues and weigh key evidence on both sides of issues with patients. It also involves being able to admit the limitations or gaps in our knowledge and admit that some prevention recommendations advanced by medical professionals are, at best, guesses based on limited knowledge.

Failure to present information and recommendations in this fashion weakens the credibility of medical professionals and health education and creates confusion in the public about what is clearly established, compared to what is suspected or feared.

The credibility of providers is particularly vulnerable if their recommendations appear to carry judgmental, moral overtones or appear to the public to be self-serving by inflating the importance of a problem in an effort to gain public attention and funding. Three examples illustrate these types of credibility problems. The first example involves education on the use of psychoactive drugs or alcohol. When discussing the dangers of these substances, health care providers should be particularly careful to separate their own political, social, and moral views from their instruction about the effects of such substances. Inflated prevalence estimates or depiction of potential risks as certainties on the basis of meager and often subjective evidence not only undermines public acceptance of many prevention efforts, but may actually hinder professional understanding of these problems. In an area so heavily permeated by moralism, it is particularly important for providers to have read firsthand the major scientific studies ascribing risks to these substances before conveying information to the public. Failure to understand the strengths and limitations of such studies may lead to inadvertent exaggeration of some dangers at the expense of their credibility on other dangers, which may be real and serious.

A second example is advocating or supporting diagnostic screening programs. Physicians and other medical care providers should critically weigh the benefits of such programs against their potential risks. The rationale behind screening programs differs from that of using advanced diagnostic techniques to detect possible illnesses in a patient who seeks a physician's care.[78] In the latter situation, the encounter is initiated by the patient, and the purpose is a comprehensive assessment of health, with no guarantee that the patient will benefit. Instead, clinicians are simply attempting to provide the best standard of care that is available. Screening, however, is different. Because the medical care professional is initiating the encounter, not the patient, there is an implicit promise that those who volunteer to be screened will benefit in that (1) the illness in question can be accurately diagnosed (the rate of false negatives and false positives is low); (2) the illness can be treated more effectively than if the patient waited until symptoms were present; (3) the treatment and follow-up facilities are accessible and affordable to anyone diagnosed positively; and (4) the disease in question is sufficiently severe and the benefits sufficiently great that being screened is worth the effort.

Though screening is often a useful tool in prevention, it may not be warranted for disorders where early diagnosis offers little therapeutic benefit. The prevention potential of screening is minimal in those instances where treatments are only marginally effective, such as lung cancer. When treatment is ineffective, patients only learn sooner that they have an incurable illness. Screening programs are also less desirable when the illness diagnosis confers social stigma that can be only partially dispelled by treatment, as in certain forms of mental illnesses or behavior disorders such as alcoholism. Any medical or health care professional should critically weigh these issues before publicly advocating screening.

A third example concerns promotion of mass immunization programs. The potential costs to the individual and society of any given immunization should be carefully weighed before large-scale programs are begun. If the need for a program is not overwhelming, then the public should be told this before programs are initiated. Risks and procedures for dealing with them should be carefully detailed in advance. Programs that fail to do this (e.g., the swine flu program) can erode the value placed by the public in other immunization efforts that are, in fact, needed.[12,27]

In sum, the health education approach focuses on individual decision making and behavior. It appeals to the reasonableness and rationality of the public and values libertarianism as a social good. The underlying assumptions are that (1) individuals should be permitted as much free choice as possible as long as no harm to others results from that choice, and (2) given correct information, most individuals will take action to protect their health.

The emphasis in recent years on behavior change has left the clinician in a difficult spot. Though interpersonal interactions are more effective in altering behavior than mass media or school education programs, providers still have only a mixed record in achieving long-term behavior changes in patients. Although fostering healthful behaviors is important, this certainly should not be the only goal of health education. The major goal of health education that providers can achieve is providing a complete, unbiased, accurate appraisal of our current state of knowledge, including not only what we know, but also admitting what we do not know and what we only suspect. The ability of providers and mass media or school education programs to alter individual behavior ultimately depends on the record of credibility established by earlier appeals and recommendations.

Medical interventions to alter hazardous behaviors

Some medical professionals have questioned whether people who fail to engage in minimal preventive health behaviors, particularly in the face of clinical recommendations, might be either physically or psychologically ill. If so, they argue, providers have an obligation to intervene clinically in an effort to prevent additional health and psychologic problems for the individual, especially when the person's behaviors are viewed as self-destructive in nature (e.g., drug abuse, gross overeating, suicide, alcohol abuse, and, more recently, even cigarette smoking).

Crudely simplified, there is a medical view which holds that these are behaviors over which people can lose personal control either as a result of physical addiction, psychologic dependence, or compulsion to self-destruction. Having lost behavioral control, these persons are sick and could benefit from medical intervention.

Once a person is classified as sick or ill, the armamentarium of the various medical professions can then be brought to bear on the individual behavior in an effort to prevent additional behavioral or physical impairment. This armamentarium includes (1) therapeutic listening, (2) psychoanalysis, (3) behavioral modification by conditioning, (4) hypnosis, (5) learning group therapies, (6) hospitalization or live-in facilities, (7) outpatient group therapies like Alcoholics Anonymous or Synanon, (8) a variety of drug treatments, for example, methadone or Antabuse, and (9) programs that either apply a variety of these treatments simultaneously or coordinate their staging.

Limitations

Medical treatment of behavioral problems has achieved some success in preventing some people from engaging in self-destructive acts and is more humane than legal punishment. But this approach, too, has limitations. Perhaps the most glaring problem is a definitional one: when can people be defined as ill, and when does a person's behavior reach the point that the person can be called, for example, suicidal, alcoholic, or a drug addict?

Defining what constitutes an illness, as we discuss in Chapter 4, is not an easy task, especially when the criteria used in making the diagnosis are behavioral and hence susceptible to social, cultural, and political influences. To begin with, it is not uniformly accepted by medical professionals that self-destructive behavior is indeed *sick* behavior. Although many believe that medical professionals have an obligation to intervene when someone is behaving in a self-destructive manner, others believe that people have the right to engage in any behavior, including self-destructive behavior, as long as it does not violate the rights of others.

Secondly, even if one accepts the view that providers should intervene to prevent self-destructive behavior, it is not always clear when, in fact, a particular behavior is self-destructive. Until recently, it has been commonly assumed that heavy consumption of alcohol is a self-destructive behavior. The World Health Organization, for example, defines alcoholism as a chronic behavior disorder manifested by repeated drinking of alcoholic beverages in excess of dietary and social use in a community and to an extent that interferes with the health, social, or economic functions of the drinker.[81]

Nevertheless, a number of persons have come to question whether the destructive consequences of drinking large amounts of alcohol have been exaggerated. They point out that many of the conclusions about the self-destructive or violent character of heavy alcohol consumption have been based on examination of highly unusual populations, often skid row drunks. Because persons in these populations of heavy drinkers often exhibit numerous physical and mental problems, it was widely assumed that alcohol consumption fostered such problems.

Critics of this view point out that examining the role of heavy drinking in such a manner overlooks (1) questions of cause and effect, (2) persons who have similar serious health and behavioral problems even though they do not drink, (3) persons who drink heavily but do not exhibit health or behavioral problems, and (4) persons who actually use alcohol to help themselves cope with personal problems that might otherwise overwhelm them. Although prolonged excessive alcohol consumption indisputably can have deleterious physical effects and may well cause some people to face additional problems at home and at work, one might hypothesize that were it not for their heavy alcohol consumption, some other people would engage in far more self-destructive or violent behavior than they now do. Some clinical researchers have cautioned that a portion of patients who restrict their alcohol intake as a result of therapeutic interventions may actually experience an increase in other psychologic problems.[35]

Conversely, some behaviors that may be highly self-destructive are not classified as sick and indeed are often not given much attention by the medical professions. For example, research on accidents, both automotive and others, suggests that certain types of people may be more prone to accidents. Yet how many physicians ever seek or explore or identify why some patients are accident-prone?

Similarly, Goode has pointed out that many legally prescribed drugs are far more dangerous than the medical profession admits. He argues, "It is ironic that physicians who lead the attacks in declaring all nonmedical drug use as harmful and pathologic are probably society's most avid consumers and peddlers of legal drugs."[37]

Alcoholism as an example

The current situation regarding alcoholism reflects the problems that are created by the disagreement over whether a particular behavior is an illness, and exactly what distinguishes normal behavior from pathologic behavior. Many different diagnostic criteria of alcoholism are evident in medical literature, ranging from definitions examining the amount that a person drinks to those examining the psychologic meaning of drinking to the person who drinks to the social or physical impact of drinking.[50,86]

The net effect of many different definitions is that a very wide range of human behavior is called alcoholism. Problems of a different nature, for example, being aggressive after drinking and drinking to alleviate stress, are lumped under the same rubric.[45] This has led to broad diagnostic criteria that include many people. Though some alcohol treatment professionals and agencies honestly believe that such wide-ranging definitions will facilitate early identification of alcoholism and easier treatment, such definitions suit the political purposes of treatment agencies by raising the presumed prevalence. This leaves the impression that more treatment services and research are needed.

At this point there is little or no evidence that alcohol problems follow a uniform trajectory[13,74] or that early identification and treatment will increase the likelihood that a person will be able to gain control over the problem.[65] Of course, if intervention is successful at an early stage, numerous health and personal problems may be avoided.

However, using wide-ranging diagnostic criteria to identify someone as an alcoholic brings so many different types of problems to treatment that no single form of treatment can hope to be effective for all the problems called "alcoholism." Although a wide variety of drugs and psychologic treatments have been tried, no single treatment appears to be clearly superior.[3,8,14,28] Even Alcoholics Anonymous (AA), the most widely used treatment, has never been scientifically demonstrated to be superior to others.[5,91] (AA will not allow its treatment and members to be scientifically researched.)

Of course, some people with severe drinking problems do benefit from an organized treatment program. At this point it does appear that for people willing to seek help, treatment is preferable to no treatment, but is not markedly better.[28,51] Only about one third of those who go through treatment are reported to gain total abstinence, and in total about one half to two thirds show some improvement, either a reduction in alcohol consumption or improvement in related social areas like marriage or work.[29] This is only somewhat higher than the reported rate of spontaneous remission for those who do not seek treatment.[13] Also, it is not clear that elaborate, expensive, lengthy treatment programs have a greater impact than short-term counseling.[26,68]

If medical care providers decide to recommend a treatment program, they should make some effort to match the patient with the type of program that seems to be most effective for people with the patient's characteristics. They then should follow the patient's progress in the program, because even patients carefully matched to a specific program may not do well and may need a referral to a different program.

Medical professionals also should recognize that the diagnosis of alcoholism carries considerable social stigma. Though the movement to label alcoholism a disease in part grew out of an attempt to reduce that stigma and to move social response to alcohol problems away from punitive, often inhumane, legal approaches, the image many people have of an alcoholic is a skid row derelict who has rejected responsible behavior and the work ethic of our society. A medical diagnosis of alcoholism can make it more difficult for people to obtain and maintain employment, and others may tend to interpret their behavior in light of their alcohol problem. Taking a sick day from work or having a drink at lunch would be viewed as signs of illness, probably not the way they would be viewed if someone else did the same. The label of alcoholism is particularly difficult for people to shed because of the widespread but unsubstantiated belief that once a person is an alcoholic, that person will always be an alcoholic.

In short, although the diagnosis of alcoholism may point the way to alcoholism treatment and help some people, diagnosing heavy drinkers who are not really alcoholics as alcoholics and encouraging them to be treated will probably not help and may hurt these individuals. The tendency of some professionals to do this has actually confused alcoholism research on etiology and retarded progress in alcoholism treatment.

Though we have chosen to detail the record of treatment for alcohol problems, its record of mixed success and failure and the risks of stigmatization are not unique. Drug treatment programs,[37,44,57] weight loss programs,[18] and smoking cessation programs[79,82,88] have achieved only modest levels of success, and the quality and quantity of research evaluating treatment effectiveness varies enormously.

All of these clinical efforts at prevention are expensive, require considerable professional time, and, most important, rely heavily on the sustained motivation of the person with the unhealthful habit or addiction. Consequently, although these approaches may help some people for whom legal and educational efforts alone are not sufficient, they can only be expected to reach a rather limited segment of individuals who cannot control their unhealthful behavior on their own and who want to be helped. Although such medical attempts to alter behavior provide secondary prevention against a variety of health problems, certain levels of self-destructive behavior must be present even before medical treatment is invoked. Furthermore, some clinical prevention programs may overestimate the ability of clinical interventions to reduce other health problems that are known to be associated with certain forms of self-destructive behavior, such as violent crime with drug addiction or traffic accidents with alcohol abuse. This latter example has recently been systematically studied.

In several parts of the United States, drivers arrested and convicted of driving while intoxicated are given the option of attending education sessions in lieu of the previously established penalties. At the impetus of the federal government, over $88 million was spent on such Alcohol Safety Action Programs (ASAP education and rehabilitation programs),[55] and between 1971 and 1976 more than 200,000 drivers were referred to these programs. The evidence regarding the effectiveness of this intervention is unclear. Apparently 12 of the 35 ASAP sites that have been studied had significant declines in nighttime fatal crashes, and there is the suggestion that blood alcohol content (BAC) surveys of drivers in some of these sites were lower.[55]

Although over 500 fatalities were apparently prevented, the evidence implies that the increased enforcement of laws and the deterrent impact of this enforcement were responsible for the decline in mortality, rather than the clinical rehabilitation component of the ASAP program. One study specifically concerned with evaluating the education and clinical rehabilitation component of the ASAP programs concluded that ". . . on the whole, ASAP education and treatment programs had at best a small specific deterrent effect and, at worst, a slightly negative effect."[67]

Finally, all these clinical therapeutic approaches place the burden of overcoming alcohol (or drug or smoking) problems on those who obviously are having the most difficulty changing their behavior. Although useful, the goals of such programs will be much more difficult to obtain if simultaneous efforts are not in place to discourage the promotion, production, and distribution of alcohol, drugs, or tobacco to begin with.

Legal efforts to promote health

Legal regulation and legislative incentives offer another approach to promoting more healthful behaviors. While clinically trained providers are often reluctant to assume patient education as a responsibility, they tend to be even more reluctant to attempt shaping of legislation and governmental policy and programs to promote public health. Often shaping of law and health care programs seems far removed from the task of actually caring for individual patients with visible illness and pain.

Learning how to develop such programs and legislation means venturing into areas that are seldom taught in medical or nursing schools—economics, political and social science, and law. It also requires learning about existing health-related laws. Exploring the labyrinthian structure of the Public Health Service, the Department of Health and Human Services (formerly the Department of Health, Education, and Welfare), the Department of Labor, the Food and Drug Administration, or the Environmental Protection Agency, let alone state and local health departments, is a task that seems both forbidding and uninteresting to many providers. Learning how to mold public opinion, develop constituencies, or lobby for legislative reform may not appeal to students struggling to learn the complexities of their preclinical and clinical curricula.

Yet there can be little question that these topics bear directly on the health of the nation and the types of patients and illnesses that clinical providers will encounter in their practices.

The government's responsibility for health protection has been divided among local, state, and federal sectors. Federal power derives from the United States Constitution, which does not specifically mention health but charges the federal government to promote the general welfare. The legal basis for state and local activities is the mandate to exercise police power to regulate internal affairs for the promotion of public health, safety, prosperity, and general welfare.[16]

The development of laws can be influenced at three levels: (1) in their formulation at the legislative level, (2) in their interpretation by the courts, and (3) in the drafting of regulations and programs that implement legislation. Medical care providers can have impact at each of these levels, but particularly as opinion leaders in the formulation of laws and as participants in their implementation and in the evaluation of their impact.

Legal efforts in disease prevention have been of two basic types. First, legislative efforts have attempted to influence individual behavior that might be harmful to the health of that individual. Second, laws have been passed to protect citizens from diseases or bodily damage that might be (1) inflicted on them by environmental hazards or (2) communicated to or inflicted on them by their fellow citizens. The former is illustrated by laws establishing water filtration systems and sewage, rodent, and insect controls. The latter has been approached by establishing agencies such as the United States Public Health Service and the Center for Disease Control as well as laws enforced by police and the courts.

Laws to promote individual health behavior

Although some of this legislation has reduced morbidity and mortality, such laws are more difficult to enact and enforce than laws protecting the public from external health hazards. The first and most obvious problem is that such legislation requires considerable political support before it can be enacted into law. This can be particularly difficult in a nation that places high value on individual liberty. If a behavior that is harmful to an individual's health is engaged in by substantial segments of the population, for example, not wearing automobile seat belts or smoking cigarettes, then it is extremely unlikely that legislation prohibiting its use can ever be passed.

Second, even if the legislation prohibiting or restricting certain unhealthful behaviors is passed and succeeds in reducing the problem it was targeted to reduce, widespread opposition may force its repeal or undermine its effect. This is especially true of laws where (1) most people do not perceive themselves to be directly jeopardized if they or someone else does not adhere to the law and (2) detection of violators is difficult. For example, though the prohibition of alcohol in the 1920s succeeded in reducing the death rate from liver cirrhosis, the opposition to it fostered development of bootlegging by organized crime and ultimately achieved its repeal.[40]

Similarly, the British Road Safety Act of 1967 initially had a dramatic impact on reducing traffic casualties and fatalities in that nation. The law permitted British police to test the blood alcohol level of drivers by use of roadside breath tests and carried a penalty of automatic suspension of a driver's license for one year if a driver was intoxicated. Though the law produced a 20% to 25% reduction in traffic fatalities during the first two years following its enactment, it was so unpopular that British police did not enforce it vigorously, and its deterrent impact diminished as the public learned that the risk of being caught under the law was minimal.[77]

Because opposition by a sizable minority can force repeal of many laws, behaviors that have been prohibited over long periods of time in this country have tended to be those engaged in by only a small minority of the population, particularly politically weak or even disenfranchised segments,[40] such as users of heroin,[45] motorcycle drivers who do not want to wear helmets, or teenage drinkers. Though the health of the groups affected by such laws may be improved, they still may feel that society has inequitably singled out their behavior for prohibition, thus undermining their support for all societal laws.

In some instances, such as illicit drug use, the laws and the uncontrolled nature of illegal marketplaces that they produce actually are more dangerous to the user than the drugs themselves. The most significant sources of heroin-related morbidity and mortality appear to be (1) accidental overdose, because in an unregulated marketplace users do not know the potency of the drugs they purchase, and (2) infection resulting from the use of unsterilized needles and syringes.[37]

Even laws that have merely *discouraged* the use of unhealthful substances through taxation have at times faltered because of illicit bootlegging that has emerged to circumvent such laws. Moreover, increasing taxes on alcohol or tobacco does not have a uniform effect across the population. Direct taxation falls most severely on the poor, whereas persons with higher incomes can afford the higher prices. This makes such laws particularly inequitable for those substances where health risk is posed only by excessive use and some benefit and pleasure is derived by moderate use, such as use of alcohol.

Third, the Bill of Rights ensures individual rights that even so well intentioned a pursuit as disease prevention cannot violate. The governmental power to request individuals to undergo a medical procedure such as immunization or screening for disease cannot be used to require individuals to protect themselves, but rather can be called on only to protect the general health and welfare of others or their children.[39] Consequently many argue that legal action usually should be taken against a behavior only if it poses direct harm to someone else; for example, they feel that action should be taken against a person whose drinking in public threatens others, but not against one who drinks alone in private.[69] Likewise, legal action should be considered to restrict smoking in public buildings, but not against persons who wish to smoke in their own homes.

Fourth, laws to promote preventive health behaviors or to discourage potentially self-destructive behaviors are often difficult to enforce because it is difficult to determine humane and reasonable yet effective punishments.

Immunization laws are examples of laws intended to promote a preventive action. Even though the immunization status of a population can affect infant and child mortality, recent surveys in the United States reveal that 5.8 million of 14 million preschool children in the United States are not adequately immunized. Moreover, the proportion of preschool children immunized against measles, rubella, diphtheria, pertussis, tetanus, and polio has dropped in recent years. The most striking drop is in polio immunization. In 1963 84.1% of preschool children were immunized against polio. By the mid-1970s, 60% were protected. Among the nonwhite poverty population, the percentage of preschool children immunized in this country falls below 50%.[92]

In response to this problem, 38 of the 50 states in the United States legally require children to obtain immunizations prior to entering public schools. Several states additionally require immunization of any preschool child before the child can be enrolled in day-care centers or attend nursery schools.[111] Yet these laws have proven difficult to enforce, in part because of the difficulties in identifying an appropriate punishment for those who refuse immunization. Some have argued that parents who refuse to allow their child to be immunized can be accused of willful neglect, but few persons would be willing to have the state assume legal custody of a child because a parent refuses immunization for the child. Other control measures have been to refuse a child admittance to a public school or cut off federal funding to neighborhood health centers or clinics that fail to achieve a certain percentage of completely immunized children in their patient population.

Though some studies suggest that such measures have increased immunization receptivity,[34,58,64] one has to question whether these punishments might not actually harm the very people they are trying to help. Indeed, it is difficult to identify a penalty that is not either too severe or so mild that it would not affect immunization receptivity.[46]

It is perhaps even more difficult to develop an appropriate punishment to deter people from engaging in clearly self-destructive behaviors. Suicide poses the most clear-cut example. How can punishment deter an individual bent on self-destruction? Punishment could be interpreted by such a person as (1) compatible with self-destruction, (2) irrelevant, or (3) simply another reason why one should engage in self-destructive behavior.[36]

For problems such as alcohol or drug abuse, it has been argued that criminal punishment and prosecution served only to ostracize the individual from (1) persons who discourage such behavior and (2) opportunities in life that would help the individual to be economically self-sufficient.

Spradley[84] in his book on skid row likens legal prosecution of alcohol abusers on disorderly conduct, vagrancy, and loitering charges to a "rite of passage." Legal conviction of persons on alcohol abuse charges and subsequent detention or incarceration stigmatizes and transforms the identities of these people without providing a way for them to control their drinking. Instead, the social margin of tolerance allowed by society for their idiosyncratic behavior may even be reduced.[59] The "once an alcoholic, always an alcoholic," or "once a junkie, always a junkie" philosophy of many people and organizations makes obtaining or maintaining employment or personal dignity in social relations especially difficult.[110] Legal prosecution and punishment can not only stigmatize individuals; it can also alienate people from the very mores and behaviors the laws are trying to instill.

In sum, although legal controls at times have been successful in altering individual behaviors that place people at a higher risk for injury and disease, they have important limitations in promoting individual health behaviors. These range from lack of acceptance and adherence in the population to difficulties in developing effective and equitable penalty structures.

Those hoping to employ legislation to promote individual health behaviors must address these issues if their efforts are to have any chance of success. They should recognize that it is difficult to enact and enforce laws prohibiting acts that have direct deleterious effects on only the person who engages in the behavior being prohibited. This is especially true when the presumed ill effects are not immediate, but may be delayed for years or even decades. Oftentimes groups attempting to prohibit or restrict such behaviors will invoke health reasons into their arguments when, in reality, they are far more concerned with limiting what they regard as antisocial or immoral behavior.[40,85] When health care providers become enmeshed in this situation, their motives may well be viewed with skepticism by those they are trying to change. Even the efforts of those whose sole concern is to promote or protect the health of the individual may be called into question. Whether the hoped-for health benefits of laws that are so difficult to enact or enforce are worth the mistrust they may engender is an issue that should be carefully weighed by medical care professionals.

Legislation to protect the public from common environmental hazards

During this century some of the most notable advances in disease prevention have emerged from legislation to protect the public from common health hazards such as inadequate or unsafe housing, unsafe drinking water, contaminated food, cosmetic additives, hazardous drugs, air pollution, and occupational hazards.[31,53,66] The major legislation that attempts to do this is discussed in the following paragraphs.

Water. State and local legislation and, more recently, federal laws have been passed to control water pollution and ensure safe drinking water. The most comprehensive legislation is the federal Water Pollution Control Acts of 1948 and 1956, which were amended in 1972 and 1973. These acts limit the discharge of toxic pollutants into surface and other waters. More recently the federal Safe Drinking Water Act of 1974 requires that every community water supply serving 25 or more people must meet at least the minimal standard of purity established by the federal government.

Food and drugs. In 1906 (the same year that Upton Sinclair published *The*

Jungle), the federal Food and Drug Act was passed in an effort to prevent bacterial contamination and poisonous adulterants from entering meat. Thirty years later, the federal Food, Drug, and Cosmetic Act of 1938 gave the Food and Drug Administration authority over food additives, cosmetics, and drugs. It prohibits marketing of food that contains a natural or added substance that may render it injurious to health. Toxic substances may be permitted within prescribed tolerance limits, but the manufacturer must prove that the additive is safe under the conditions of proposed use.

A particularly important amendment to that law, the 1958 Delaney Amendment, states that "no additive shall be claimed to be safe if it is found after tests which are appropriate for the evaluation of food additives to induce cancer in man or animal." Under the law, responsibility for demonstrating possible carcinogenic or other hazards of cosmetics rests with the Food and Drug Administration. Though manufacturers are not required to do toxicologic testing on their products, untested products must be so labeled when they are marketed. The Act requires that drugs be tested to show that they are safe for use under the conditions of use prescribed in their labeling, and the 1962 Kefauver-Harris amendments to the law require formal proof of effectiveness from their manufacturers and authorized banning on the grounds of imminent hazard.

Air. The Clean Air Act of 1970 gives the Environmental Protection Agency of the federal government authority to set ambient air quality standards for hazardous air pollutants. Section 112 authorizes regulation of hazardous air pollutants that pose risk of serious adverse effects such as cancer even at relatively low exposure levels.

The workplace. In addition to state and local regulations, several pieces of federal legislation have been passed in an attempt to make the workplace safe from accident risks and toxic or carcinogenic exposures. The Walsh Healey Public Contract Act of 1936 gave the government direct jurisdiction over the safety of working conditions in each state in industries that held government contracts above $10,000 for the manufacturing and furnishing of materials and equipment. The law was expanded in 1959 to protect workers from contaminants in the working atmosphere that might be hazardous to health. Also in 1959 the Longshoreman Act established safety standards for shipyard workers. The federal Metal and Nonmetal Mine Safety Act of 1966 gave the Secretary of the Interior authority to promulgate health and safety accidents standards in the mining industry. The federal Coal Mine Safety Act of 1969 established standards for the amount of respirable dust permissible in coal mine atmosphere, and the federal Mine Safety and Health Amendments Act of 1977 established a Mine Enforcement Safety Administration in the Department of Labor.

The most important recent legislation focusing on the workplace was the Occupational Safety and Health Act of 1970. This law requires the Secretary of Labor to promulgate mandatory standards for safety and health in all workplaces and to create an Occupational Safety and Health Review Commission for carrying out adjudication under the law. Appeals are taken to federal court. The Act is to be carried out with state agencies.

Though the Act permitted rights of entry and inspection of work sites without advance notice, this aspect of the law was modified by a Supreme Court decision in 1978 requiring inspectors to obtain search warrants before making surprise inspections.

Under the 1970 Act, the National Institute for Occupational Safety and Health (NIOSH) was started in the Department of Health, Education, and Welfare. Three of the responsibilities delegated to NIOSH are to develop criteria as a basis for the health and safety standards to be set by the Labor Department, to publish annual lists of known toxic substances, and to conduct epidemiologic surveys and health hazard evaluations for industries where major problems of occupational health and safety are suspected.

A final important piece of legislation is the 1976 Toxic Substances Act, which authorizes the Environmental Protection Agency of the federal government to require industrial firms to provide data on a chemical's structure, composition, and health or environmental effects before marketing a new chemical or using existing chemicals in new ways. The Environmental Protection Agency can seek a court order banning or restricting chemicals believed to be imminently hazardous and can take action against chemicals it considers to be unreasonable risks.

Issues in enforcement

Though each of these laws represents a major achievement for public health officials, most were difficult to pass, and many still believe that they are inadequate to protect the environment and workplace from the thousands of chemicals, pollutants, and industrial by-products now being produced.[4,31] The passage of each law was opposed by industrial or commercial interests afraid that the law would increase the costs of their products, making them less desirable and competitive on national and international markets. Small firms, in particular, with less capital and discretionary resources, have been concerned about the costs and amount of changes they would have to make to comply with such laws. Moreover, although the impact of improved sanitation earlier in this century was dramatic and obvious because those measures reduced communicable disease outbreaks, the more recent controls are aimed at preventing toxic or carcinogenic effects that may not become evident in people until years after exposure.

The laws leave a great deal of discretionary power in development of regulations and enforcement to the federal government. The relevant federal agencies make decisions about which substances are toxic or carcinogenic and which companies to investigate or prosecute. At present there is considerable controversy in this country among public health officials, medical professionals, and commercial and industrial interests about the nature of evidence that needs to be marshaled before action is warranted to prohibit the production of certain chemicals or pesticides or prohibit the discharge of industrial pollutants or by-products into the environment.

Although commercial and industrial interests tend to coalesce in their opposition to pollution controls or restrictions on chemicals, not all firms are uniformly opposed, nor are all health professionals in complete agreement about what is or what is not hazardous, mutagenic, or carcinogenic.[17,31]

The enormous inventiveness and diversity of American business brings vast numbers of new chemicals into the workplace and environment. According to one source, there are now some 13,000 different chemicals in common use,[31] and approximately 500 new chemicals are introduced into industry each year.[4] Many public health officials believe that unless great caution is exercised in permitting new chemicals in our food, consumer products, workplace, and environment, this nation could face an unprecedented increase in the incidence of cancer. The task of weighing evidence for and against use or restrictions of these substances in the environment is staggering. Health professionals and federal agencies often must make decisions based on assumptions and educated guesses rather than firmly established facts. Because of (1) the rapidity with which new products are developed, (2) the considerable lengths of time that may be required for a chemical or pollutant to produce a toxic or carcinogenic impact on humans, and (3) the considerable time, expense, and difficulty in undertaking longitudinal epidemiologic research in humans on these substances, the government has been forced to give considerable weight to animal studies. Most often, definitive epidemiologic studies in human populations simply do not exist.

Carcinogenicity

In the area of carcinogenicity the problem is further compounded because vast numbers of animals are needed to test the cancer-causing potential of certain chemicals that are released in only small doses in the environment or that may cause cancer in only a small fraction of the population. As an alternative, animal researchers have instead given small groups of animals much larger doses than humans are exposed to.

Use of animals in cancer research relies on a variety of assumptions.[30] The first assumption is that if a cancer occurs in an animal, it will also occur in humans. The suitability of animal testing has been challenged by industry, which claims that rodents are unusually sensitive to cancer. However, all chemicals known to cause cancer in man also do so in experimental animals (with the possible exception of arsenic compounds). Also although most substances, if given in sufficient doses, will cause toxic reactions in animals, only a small fraction produce cancer. Indeed, one difficulty in animal research is testing animals with sufficiently high doses to produce cancer in populations small enough to be controlled by the researcher, while not killing animals from toxic but not carcinogenic effects of the substance.[30]

Second, it is assumed that results from administration of large doses of a chemical to small groups of animals provide the same information as would be gleaned from administration of smaller doses to large groups of animals. The assumption is that a linear dose response extrapolation is possible. This latter assumption has also been questioned, and some have even argued that there may be certain thresholds of exposure that are necessary before an agent will produce cancerous effects in humans. At present this second assumption has been neither verified nor disproven, and how to interpret animal data is a source of contention.

The case of saccharin is perhaps the most widely known example of this controversy. On one hand, those opposed to banning the use of saccharin point to the seeming absurdity of basing decisions on studies that exposed rats in Canada to the amounts of saccharin that, if translated to human consumption, would require a person to drink 800 cans of diet soda daily. On the other hand, those fearful of saccharin's potential carcinogenic effects point out that because the threshold of risk is unknown and because several animal studies have shown carcinogenic effects, even if saccharin produced cancer in only a small fraction of the population in a nation of over 200 million people, thousands of people might be affected. Because of the time lag between exposure and development of cancer, perhaps as long as 20 years, epidemiologic research in humans that measured levels of saccharin exposure and compared those with high and low exposure would be nearly impossible to conduct with a high degree of follow-up and certainty of exposure levels over time. Moreover, by the time such research could be completed, millions of people might have been unnecessarily exposed to a potential risk, however small.

Implications for providers

The debate over saccharin and potentially carcinogenic substances in industry has direct relevance to providers. During their practice patients will ask about the effects of many substances. Clinicians will encounter people who work or live in places that expose them to substances whose level of toxicity or carcinogenicity has not been proven in humans, but has been suspected or established in animals. Although the risk to an individual patient may not be high in every instance, it would be an error for the clinician to dismiss the research to the patient without first providing some outline of the concerns it raises and the assumption behind it. Providers should realize that the decision about personal risk is not the same as the decision that public health officials make about large populations. Although a clinician can tell a patient that the personal risk is minimal, a small risk translated to an entire community, state, or national population may involve thousands of people.

Providers not only have the responsibility to provide information on risk to the patient, but must also decide whether their responsibility extends to the community at large. If they encounter a series of patients working for the same factory or on the same farm with a similar set of maladies or complaints, they must decide whether to raise their concerns to the laborers, the industry involved, the government, or the labor organizations that work in the plant. As Brodeur's[11] discussion of the events that precipitated the closing of a factory producing asbestos insulation in Texas indicates, different physicians exposed to the same data implicating an industrial health hazard among factory workers responded in a variety of ways. Some aggressively sought to inform the public or seek governmental assistance to clean up or regulate a hazardous work environment. Others, including physicians in no way involved with the industry concerned but who saw affected persons as private patients, were slow to act. Some doubted the health risks of asbestos, and some feared the economic repercussion that closing a factory, even temporarily, might have on the economic welfare of their community. This represents but one of many documented examples of inaction on the part of some medical providers in the face of occupational health hazards.[4,9] It is noteworthy because it points out that even in a situation where health risks have been repeatedly identified in separate epidemiologic surveys in humans, not just in laboratory animals, one cannot assume that all physicians will recognize and act on their responsibilities to individual patients.

Some physicians and other providers are actively informing patients and their families as well as labor and community organizations about the possible health risks that have been attributed to the products or pollutants in their workplace or local environment. And some even actively seek government resources to research or monitor possible hazards or alter industrial or agricultural production practices. But only a small proportion of providers become actively involved in developing legislation or evaluating its impact.

Part of the reason may be that though medical care providers are trained to diagnose and treat the illnesses caused by environmental hazards, few are trained to study the etiology of these problems, develop control programs, or evaluate the impact of legilsative or regulative measures. In addition, active attempts to formulate legislation require providers to move beyond their professional community in writing and public speaking. Building support for legislation or developing programs with any likelihood of implementation means that providers will have to deal with community agencies or groups that may or may not be interested in these issues. It means that they will have to translate what they know into terms understandable to all political factions that might support their work. In effect they must be willing to take the time and effort to popularize the knowledge they have and the reforms they seek. This is not a task with great economic, professional, or academic rewards. It also requires skills that not all medical care providers possess, and it demands taking time away from the care of individual patients. Moreover, it can be extremely frustrating because providers can expect at least some opposition, usually organized opposition, to virtually any proposal they put forth.

Nonetheless, physicians and other medical care providers, even if not in the forefront of such legislative endeavors, should provide information to their patients about risks to which they may be exposed. Also, they can be important opinion leaders in the legislative process. Their own expertise and that of the professional organizations to which they belong will be called on to evaluate and support or reject a variety of public health programs designed to protect the public from health hazards.

Because clear, definitive data about the risk of certain substances are often not available in studies of humans, the skill of medical and health professionals in interpreting the meaning of data and the need for legal restriction of some substances will be called on.

When decisions are made about the need for legal restriction on a potentially toxic or carcinogenic substance, a key issue that merits consideration is the extent to which exposure to the substance is voluntary. Certainly chemical impurities entering our air, our water, or our food create a situation where ingestion is not voluntary. Even in the case of food, where many additives serve useful functions as preservatives and where labeling of ingredients is required, it is not reasonable to expect that every purchaser will read and understand the contents of every package. In the workplace, exposures are completely involuntary if workers are not informed of hazards, but, even if informed, workers may be able to leave an unhealthful work environment only at the expense of salary, seniority, and job security.

In situations where exposure is involuntary, providers should be more willing to press the government to restrict exposure to suspected hazards identified in animal studies even before risk can be proven in human studies. In situations where exposure is voluntary, medical care providers and the government, at a minimum, have the responsibility to provide full information about the suspected hazard and pertinent data supporting as well as not supporting the risk.

Summary and conclusions

The past decade has brought renewed optimism to those interested in disease prevention. Overall life expectancy has increased as infant mortality and the rate of deaths from coronary heart disease and stroke have declined. Though many people continue to engage in unhealthful behaviors, the public is starting to reduce its consumption of cigarettes and fatty foods and has increasingly begun to exercise.

But the past decade has also been a time during which the rate of death from various forms of cancer has been rising. New chemicals, pesticides, and industrial by-products are being introduced at an increasingly rapid rate into our consumer products, our workplaces, our communities, and our homes. Researchers attempting to assess the safety of new products have not been able to keep pace with the variety of new materials industry has produced. At the same time the public has been told that so many substances cause cancer that some have become fatalistic about their ability to maintain a safe environment.

As the costs of medical care soar, an ever-growing number of medical care providers, researchers, and administrators are calling for more emphasis to be placed on disease prevention. Their argument, not a new one, but perhaps more relevant today in view of soaring medical costs, is that prevention can save lives and money. It is easier to prevent illness than to treat it, and preventing illness takes less time and costs less money. Though direct medical care costs may not be dramatically reduced by efforts to prolong life because those whose life spans are altered may still experience acute and chronic illnesses requiring medical care, such persons will be economically productive longer.[47]

An important theme running through the current discussion of disease prevention is the call for individuals to engage in life-style behaviors that will promote their own health.[52] Although no doubt shifts in individual behaviors can promote longer and healthier lives, disease prevention is not just a do-it-yourself activity. As we have discussed, external environmental forces beyond individual control also influence the acquisition of disease. Certain subgroups in society—the poor, elderly, and children—are particularly vulnerable to health risks beyond their control. Moreover, although individuals do bear some responsibility for their own health, that in no ways diminishes the obligation of medical care providers to engage in disease prevention activities with their patients and to exert their opinions in the development and evaluation of public health legislation and programs.[23,27]

Yet despite the importance of disease prevention, medical care providers have not been encouraged by our society to engage their patients in disease prevention activities. Providers are seldom reimbursed by the government or third-party payers for trying to promote health education with their patients or attempting to promote new laws and public health programs. Moreover, most providers receive little or no professional training in disease prevention, and, as any provider willing to venture into prevention activities quickly learns, disease prevention, either by patient education, clinical intervention, or legislative reform, is not an easy task. Disease prevention activities are time-consuming, and their successes are often not readily visible.

Nonetheless, medical care providers can play a strategic role in disease prevention, not only as educators and clinicians, but as opinion leaders, developers, and evaluators of prevention efforts. Those providers willing to move beyond the deterrents previously cited should recognize that not all activities aimed at prevention have an equal likelihood of success, and that some efforts can even be counterproductive.

As we have noted in this chapter, efforts that clinicians can invoke directly with their patients range from health education to specific clinical interventions to help those who have difficulty in avoiding certain substances on their own.

Use of education to persuade individuals not to engage in behaviors that harm their health is consistent with our society's libertarian values. Although this approach is time-consuming and does not always change behavior, it serves the important function of permitting patients to make informed choices about their personal behavior. In the long run, the ability of this approach to promote healthful behaviors depends on medical care providers accurately understanding and being able to present to patients why certain behaviors are undesirable, without exaggerating the certainty of dangers or appearing judgmental. Its success depends on patients' perceiving the intent of providers as a concern with their health, not a concern with their morals. Though mass media and school education reach wide audiences, their potential for altering behavior is not as direct as that of providers. Although it is unreasonable to expect that everyone will respond to their recommendations, medical care providers can foster prevention activities in some patients. The clinician's ability to foster healthful behavior through education has not been used to its fullest potential. Even on such an unequivocally dangerous but widespread behavior as smoking, only about one third of medical care providers routinely ask their patients if they smoke and recommend that they stop.[101]

At the other end of the spectrum some medical care providers attempt to promote more healthful behaviors in their patients through the use of clinical treatments, for example, to stop patients from drinking or taking drugs. These treatments are warranted for patients who have been unable on their own to stop the behaviors in question. Although treatment success rates have not been great because of the difficulty of the task they address, these efforts nonetheless have helped many persons. However, it is unlikely that systematic extension of these efforts as a means of disease prevention is feasible. They are extremely expensive, can be stigmatizing, and seem to work best only with the populations who actively seek them out. Also few clinicians are trained or motivated to attempt such interventions.

Perhaps one reason that many clinicians prefer not to make even minimal educational recommendations or treatment interventions is that they do not feel their efforts will be fruitful, given the vast social and economic resources that promote unhealthful behaviors or expose the public to health hazards.

To some extent such concerns are correct, particularly with respect to those in lower income groups. The poor are less able to live in conditions that are healthful or engage in life-styles that promote health. The poor in our nation predominantly live in either the more heavily polluted, crowded, deteriorating housing of our inner cities where crimes, fires, and accidents are more common or they live in remote rural areas, where human services, plumbing, and medical care are less available. Moreover, lack of income makes it difficult to purchase a healthful, balanced diet with sufficient vitamins and proteins that is low in fat and salt.

Because clinicians feel powerless to alter individual behaviors of their patients or environmental health hazards to which all of us are exposed, but which seem to fall most heavily on the poor, many have attempted to address these problems through legislation.

Some advocate legislative reforms that will require their patients to forego unhealthful personal habits, such as drinking or drug taking. Such prohibitionary legislation has its greatest chance of success only when the behavior adversely affects others besides the individual involved, such as excessive speeding or driving while intoxicated. Such legislation has the least chance of success when it attempts to prohibit behaviors that mainly affect only the individual involved, for example, laws prohibiting use of psychoactive substances such as heroin or alcohol. This is particularly true when violators are difficult to detect.

The one area where laws have been able to win widespread support has been in protecting the public from involuntary health risks, such as infectious disease, and exposure to chemical or biologic hazards in our food, water, and environment. Widespread support is especially possible when such hazards pose a threat to all segments of society, not just to disadvantaged groups.

At present a major concern is that as the number of chemicals being introduced in the environment increase at an ever-faster pace, the risk of toxic or cancer-causing effects is also increasing. Some researchers fear that this country may soon face an epidemic of environmentally produced cancer. Because cancer takes so long to develop after exposure, it is impossible to undertake studies in humans of the cancer risks or safety of each new chemical, pesticide, drug, or pollutant. Waiting for such data might expose thousands of people to cancer risks. Medical care providers have a responsibility to understand this dilemma and our need to evaluate cancer risks through animal research, despite its limitations. Workers exposed to potentially hazardous substances should be informed of their dangers by their medical care providers. Though it is unreasonable to expect all medical care providers to become active legislative reformers, they should be active in educating the public about risks to which they may be exposed, and they should act as opinion leaders who point out why a cautious approach is needed in deciding which new products and chemicals will be permitted in our consumer products, workplaces, food, and environment.

In sum there are numerous actions that medical care providers can take to promote disease prevention. Not all work equally well, and some require providers to move beyond their traditional interaction with patients. Although patient education and clinical interventions to produce more healthful individual behaviors no doubt can prevent many diseases, other health problems require legislative reform to ensure that our environment, goods, and homes are free of toxic agents and to raise the economic standard of living of the poor. Though medical care providers are seldom directly rewarded for engaging in disease prevention, they nonetheless can play a crucial role as educators, opinion leaders, and advocates of public health reform.

References

1. Allen, C.: The health of the disadvantaged, Public Health Rep. **89:**499-503, 1974.
2. Anderson, O.: Health care: can there be equity? New York, 1972, John Wiley & Sons, Inc.
3. Armour, D., and Polich, J. M.: Alcoholism and treatment, Santa Monica, Calif., 1976, Rand Corporation.
4. Ashford, N.: Crisis in the work place, Cambridge, 1977, Massachusetts Institute of Technology Press.
5. Baekeland, F.: Evaluation of treatment method in chronic alcoholism. In Kissin, B., and Begleiter, H., editors: The biology of alcoholism, New York, 1977, Plenum Publishing Corp.
6. Baetjer, A.: Atmospheric pollution. In Sartwell, P., editor: Preventive medicine and public health, New York, 1973, Appleton-Century-Crofts.
7. Belloc, N.: Relationships of health practices and mortality, Prev. Med. **2:**67-81, 1973.
8. Blum, E. M., and Blum, R.: Alcoholism: modern pyschological approaches to treatment, San Francisco, 1969, Jossey-Bass, Inc., Publishers.
9. Bogue, D.: Principles of demography, New York, 1969, John Wiley & Sons, Inc.
9a. Breslow, J. E.: Persistence of health habits and their relationship to mortality, Prev. Med. **9:**469-483, 1980.
10. Breslow, L., and Belloc, N.: Relationship of physical health status and health practices, Prev. Med. **1:**409-421, 1972.
11. Brodeur, P.: Expendable Americans, New York, 1974, The Viking Press.
12. Buttery, C., and Merchant, D.: Further thoughts in swime flu immunization, Am. J. Public Health **69:**820, 1979.
13. Cahalan, D.: Drinking practices and problems: research perspectives on remedial measures, Public Affairs Rep. **14:**1-6, 1973.
14. Chafetz, M., Blane, H., and Hill, M.: Frontiers of alcoholism, New York, 1970, New York Science House.
15. Chez, R. A., Haire, D., Quilligan, E. J., and Wingate, M. B.: High risk pregnancies: obstetrical and perinatal factors. In Brent, R., and Harris, M., editors: Prevention of embryonic, fetal, and perinatal disease, D.H.E.W. Publication no. 76-853, Bethesda, Md., 1976, National Institutes of Health.
16. Clark, D.: Governmental health programs and services. In Clark, D., and MacMahon, B., editors: Preventive medicine, Boston, 1967, Little, Brown & Co.
17. Claxton, L., and Barry, P.: Chemical mutagenesis: an emerging issue for public health, Am. J. Public Health **67:**1037-1043, 1977.
18. Coates, T., and Thorenson, C.: Treating obesity in children and adolescents: a review, Am. J. Public Health **68:**143-151, 1978.
19. Coe, R.: Sociology of medicine, New York, 1970, McGraw-Hill, Inc.
20. Cohen, C. I., and Cohen, E. J.: Health education: panacea, pernicious or pointless? N. Engl. J. Med. **299:**718-720, 1978.
21. Corwin, E.: Smoking: The challenge for change, Public Health Rev. **2:**93-103, 1973.
22. Cox, D.: Clues for advertising strategies. In Dexter, L., White, D. M., editors: People, society, and mass communication, New York, 1968, The Free Press.
23. Crawford, R.: You are dangerous to your health, Int. J. Health Serv. **7:**663-680, 1977.
24. DeFleur, M.: Theories of mass communication, New York, 1966, David McKay Co., Inc.
25. Douglas, C. W.: A social psychological view of health behavior for health research, Health Serv. Res. **6:**6-15, 1971.
26. Edwards, G., Orford, J., and Egert, S., et al.: Alcoholism: a controlled trial of treatment and advice, J. Stud. Alcohol. **38:**1004-1031, 1977.
27. Eisenberg, L.: The perils of prevention, N. Engl. J. Med. **297:**1230-1232, 1977.
28. Emrick, C. D.: A review of psychologically oriented treatment of alcoholism, Q. J. Stud. Alcohol. **35:**523-549, 1974.
29. Emrick, C. D.: A review of psychologically oriented treatment of alcoholism, J. Stud. Alcohol. **36:**88-108, 1975.
30. Epstein, S.: Environmental determinants of cancer, Cancer Res. **34:**2425-2435, 1974.
31. Epstein, S.: The politics of cancer, San Francisco, 1978, Sierra Club Books.
32. Fu, J. L.: Lead exposure among children: a reassessment, N. Engl. J. Med. **300:**731-733, 1979.
33. Fuchs, V.: Who shall live? Economics and social choice, New York, 1974, Basic Books, Inc., Publishers.
34. Gee, L., and Sowell, R. F.: A school immunization law is successful in Texas, Public Health Rep. **90:**21-24, 1975.

35. Gerard, D. L., Saenger, G., and Wilie, R.: The abstinent alcoholic, Arch. Gen. Psychiatry 6:83-95, 1962.

36. Gibbs, J.: Suicide. In Merton, R., and Nisbet, R., editors: Contemporary social problems, New York, 1971, Harcourt Brace Jovanovich, Inc.

37. Goode, E.: Drugs in American society, New York, 1972, Alfred A., Knopf, Inc.

38. Goodwin, N.: Hypertension: a perspective, J. Urban Health 2:11, 1973.

39. Grad, F. P.: Public health law manual: a handbook of legal aspects of public health administration and enforcement 5, Ann Arbor, Mich., 1965, The Ann Arbor Health Association, Inc.

40. Gusfield, J.: Symbolic crusade: status, politics, and the American temperance movement, Urbana, 1966, University of Illinois Press.

41. Haggerty, R.: Changing life styles to improve health, Prev. Med. 6:276, 1977.

42. Hardy, L. A., Anderson, R., and Anderson, O.: Social surveys and health policy, Public Health Rep. 92:512, 1977.

43. Hemminki, E., and Starfield, B.: Prevention of low birth weight and pre-term birth, Milbank Mem. Fund Q. 56:339-361, 1978.

44. Henry, G.: Treatment and rehabilitation of narcotic addiction. In Gibbins, R., Israel, Y., and Kalant, H., et al., editors: Research advances in alcohol and drug problems, New York, 1974, John Wiley & Sons.

45. Hingson, R., Scotch, N., and Matthews, D.: The use and abuse of psychoactive substances. In Reider, M. L., editor: Handbook of medical sociology, Englewood Cliffs, N.J., 1979, Prentice-Hall, Inc.

46. Holden, A. P.: Compulsory immunization statutes, J.A.M.A. 228:1059-1060, 1974.

47. Holtzman, N.: Prevention rhetoric or reality, Int. J. Health Serv. 9:25-39, 1979.

48. Horn, D.: Some factors in smoking and its cessation. In Borgetta, E., and Evan, R., editors: Smoking health and behavior, Chicago, 1968, Aldine Publishing.

49. Katz, E., and Lazarsfeld, P.: Personal influence, Glencoe, Ill., 1955, Free Press.

50. Keller, M.: Problems of epidemiology in alcohol problems, J. Stud. Alcohol. 36:1442-1451, 1975.

51. Kissin, B., Rosenblatt, S., and Mackover, S.: Prognostic factors in alcoholism, Psychiatric Research Reports 24:22-43, 1968.

52. Knowles, J.: The responsibility of the individual. In Knowles, J., editor: Doing better and feeling worse—health in the United States, New York, 1977, W. W. Norton & Co., Inc.

53. Kruse, C.: Sanitary control of food. In Sartwell, P., editor: Preventive medicine and public health, New York, 1973, Appleton-Century-Crofts.

54. Lee, P., and Franks, P.: Primary prevention and the executive branch of the federal government, Prevention 6:209-226, 1977.

55. Levy, P., Voas, R., Johnson, P., and Klein, T.: An evaluation of the Department of Transportation's alcohol safety action projects, J. Safety Research 10:162-176, 1978.

56. Louria, D. B., Kidwell, A. P., and Lavenhar, M. A., et al.: Primary and secondary prevention among adults: an analysis with comments on screening and health education, Prev. Med. 5:549-572, 1976.

57. Louria, D. B.: Some aspects of drug abuse, Public Health Rev. 6:61-93, 1977.

58. Lovejoy, G., Giandela, J., and Hicks, M.: Successful enforcement of an immunization law, Public Health Rep. 89:456-458, 1974.

59. MacAndrew, C., and Edgerton, R.: Drunken comportment, Chicago, 1973, Aldine Publishing Co.

60. MacMahon, B., and Pugh, T.: Epidemiologic methods, Boston, 1960, Little, Brown & Co.

61. Mausner, J.: Epidemiology: an introductory text, Philadelphia, 1974, W. B. Saunders Co.

62. Mendelson, H.: Mass communication and cancer control. In Cullen, J. W., Fox, B. H., and Ison, R. H., editors: Cancer: the behavioral dimensions, New York, 1976, Raven Press.

63. Miller, L.: Healthy, wealthy, and wise: an essay on doing better and feeling worse: health in the United States, Soc. Sci. Med. 2:429-433, 1978.

64. Minear, R., and Guyer, B.: Assessing immunization services at a neighborhood health center (1975), Pediatrics 63:416-419, 1979.

65. Moberg, D. P.: Treatment outcomes for earlier-phase alcoholics, Ann. N.Y. Acad. Sci. 273:543-551, 1976.

66. Moore, E.: General consideration of water supply. In Sartwell, P., editor: Preventive medicine and public health, New York, 1973, Appleton-Century-Crofts.

67. Nichols, J., and Weinstein, E.: The specific deterrent effect of ASAP education and re-

habilitation programs, J. Safety Research **10**: 177-187, 1978.
68. Pittman, D., and Tate, R.: A comparison of two treatment programs for alcoholics, Int. J. Soc. Psychiatry **18**:183-193, 1972.
69. *Powell* vs. *Texas* 392 U.S. 514 (1968), rehearing denied 393 U.S. 898 (1968).
70. Preventive medicine USA, health promotion and consumer health education: a task force report, sponsored by the John E. Fogarty International Center for Advanced Studies in the Health Sciences, National Institute of Health and the American College of Preventive Medicine, New York, 1976, Prodist.
71. Roberts, A. R.: Suicide and suicide prevention: an overview, Public Health Rep. **2**: 4, 1973.
72. Rogers, E.: Diffusion of innovations, Glencoe, Ill., 1962, Free Press.
73. Rogers, E., and Shomaker, F.: Communication of innovation, Glencoe, Ill., 1972, Free Press.
74. Rohan, W.: Criteria for diagnosis of alcoholism, J. Stud. Alcohol. **29**:211-218, 1978.
75. Rokeach, M. R.: Beliefs, attitudes, and values, San Francisco, 1968, Jossey-Bass, Inc., Publishers.
76. Rosenstock, I.: Why people use health services, Milbank Mem. Fund Q. **44**:94-127, 1966.
77. Ross, H. L.: Law, science, and accidents: the British Road Safety Act of 1967, J. Legal Studies **2**:1-78, 1973.
78. Sackett, D. L., and Holland, W. W.: Controversy in the detection of disease, Lancet **2**:356-359, 1975.
79. Schwartz, J. L.: A critical review and evaluation of smoking control methods, Public Health Rep. **84**:483-506, 1969.
80. Sebrell, W.: Malnutrition and nutrition in preventive medicine. In Sartwell, P., editor: Preventive medicine and public health, New York, 1973, Appleton-Century-Crofts.
81. Seely, J. R.: Notes and comments on the World Health Organization definition of alcoholism, Q. J. Stud. Alcohol. **20**:352-365, 1959.
82. Shewchuk, L. A.: Smoking cessation programs of the American Health Foundation, Prev. Med. **5**:454-474, 1976.
83. Smith, F. A., Trivax, G., and Zuechlke, D. A., et al.: Health information during a week of television, N. Engl. J. Med. **286**: 516-520, 1972.
84. Spradley, J.: You owe yourself a drunk, Boston, 1970, Little, Brown & Co.
85. Suchman, E.: Sociology and the field of public health, New York, 1963, Russell Sage Foundation.
86. Suchman, E.: The addictive disorders as socio-environmental health problems. In Freeman, H., Levine, S., and Reeder, L., editors: Handbook of medical sociology, Englewood Cliffs, N.J., 1972, Prentice-Hall, Inc.
87. Thomas, G.: Physical activity and health: epidemiological and clinical evidence and policy implications, Prev. Med. **8**:89-103, 1979.
88. Thompson, E. L.: Smoking education programs, Am. J. Public Health **68**:250-257, 1978.
89. Tokuhata, G. R.: Cirrhosis of the liver: an epidemiological review, Public Health Rev. **2**:36-41, 1973.
90. Tomkins, S. S.: Psychological model for smoking behavior, Am. J. Public Health **56**: 17-20, 1966.
91. Tournier, R. E.: Alcoholics Anonymous as treatment and as ideology, J. Stud. Alcohol. **40**:230-240, 1979.
92. U.S. Department of Health, Education, and Welfare: United States immunization survey, U.S. D.H.E.W. Publication, no. CDC 75-3221, Atlanta, 1975, Center for Disease Control.
93. U.S. Department of Health, Education, and Welfare, Center for Disease Control: Cigarette smoking in the United Sates, Morbidity and Mortality Report **25**:237-238, 1976.
94. U.S. Department of Health, Education, and Welfare, Health Resources Administration: Health of the disadvantaged: chartbook, U.S. D.H.E.W. Publication no. HRA 77-628, Washington, D.C., 1977, U.S. Government Printing Office.
95. U.S. Department of Health, Education, and Welfare Public Health Service: The report of the President's Committee on Health Education, Washington, D.C., 1973, U.S. Government Printing Office.
96. U.S. Department of Health, Education, and Welfare, National Center for Health Statistics: Vital statistics, final mortality statistics, Washington, D.C., 1975, U.S. Government Printing Office.
97. U.S. Department of Health, Education, and Welfare, National Center for Health Statis-

tics: Advance report final mortality statistics, Washington, D.C., 1975, U.S. Government Printing Office.

98. U.S. Department of Health, Education, and Welfare, National Center for Health Statistics: Highlights: health United States, U.S. D.H.E.W. Publication P.H.S. 78-1232-1, Washington, D.C., 1978, U.S. Government Printing Office.

99. U.S. Department of Health, Education, and Welfare, National Institute on Alcoholism and Alcohol Abuse: First special report to the U.S. Congress on alcohol & health, U.S. D.H.E.W. Publication no. HSM 9031, Washington, D.C., 1973, U.S. Government Printing Office.

100. U.S. Department of Health, Education, and Welfare: Surgeon General of the United States, Smoking and health, U.S. D.H.E.W., Public Health Service Publication 1103V, Washington, D.C., 1964, U.S. Government Printing Office.

101. U.S. Department of Health, Education, and Welfare: Smoking and health: a report of the Surgeon General, D.H.E.W. Publication no. PHS 79-50066, Washington, D.C., 1979, U.S. Government Printing Office.

102. Utilization rate remains stable, The Nation's Health (official monthly newspaper of the American Public Health Association) 3:2, 1978.

103. Veterans Administration cooperative study group on anti-hypertension agents, Effects of treatment on morbidity in hypertension I and II, J.A.M.A. **202**:116-121 and **213**:1143-1152, 1967.

104. Walker, W. J.: Changing United States lifestyle and declining vascular mortality: cause or coincidence? N. Engl. J. Med. **297**:163-165, 1977.

105. Ward, G.: Changing trends in hypertension, Public Health Rep. **93**:31-34, 1978.

106. Wegman, M.: Annual summary of vital statistics—1966, Pediatrics **40**:1035-1045, 1967.

107. Wegman, M.: Annual summary of vital statistics—1974, Pediatrics **56**:960-966, 1975.

108. Wegman, M.: Annual summary of vital statistics—1977, Pediatrics **62**:947-954, 1978.

109. Williams, A. F.: Personality and other characteristics associated with cigarette smoking among teenagers, J. Health Soc. Behav. **14**:374-380, 1973.

110. Wiseman, J.: Stations of the lost: treatment of skid row alcoholics, Englewood Cliffs, N.J., 1970, Prentice-Hall, Inc.

111. Witte, J.: Recent advances in public health immunization, Am. J. Public Health **64**:939-944, 1974.

112. Wornecke, R., Grahm, S., Mosler, W., Montgomery, E., and Schats, W.: Contact with health guides and use of health services among blacks in Buffalo, Public Health Rep. **90**:212-222, 1975.

Chapter 3

Decisions to seek care

Everyone who reads this chapter has probably, at least once, debated about whether or not to seek medical care. Suppose you had a headache that persisted for 2 days even though you had taken analgesics. Would you seek medical care? Would it be appropriate to seek care for fatigue and nausea, for a low-grade fever and sore throat, or for a sore back and stiff shoulders?

The control and management of illness often depends on the willingness of people to seek medical care when it is needed. But many providers complain that medical care often is not sought "appropriately."

On one hand, many people seek medical care for problems that some physicians consider an intrusion on the *proper bounds* of their *medical* practice, a topic we will look at in Chapter 4. Rather than being afflicted with a diagnosable organic illness, these patients' problems are more often psychologic, social, or behavioral in nature. A 1977 national study, for example, estimated that 14% of all patients present ill-defined symptoms having no diagnosable organic basis, and 6% of patients present some psychiatric or major social problem.[6] These patients are hard to help by conventional medical knowledge and techniques and also can make providers worry about whether they have missed diagnosing an important physical problem. Additionally, in a time of spiraling medical costs, many believe that such persons consume medical resources that could be devoted to patients who could benefit more immediately from medical care. For these and other reasons, including seeking care at odd hours or in emergency room settings, physicians often characterize such patients as malingerers, gomers, turkeys, crocks, or hypochondriacs.

On the other hand, other persons fail to seek needed medical care or do so only after waiting so long that treatment is rendered more difficult or ineffective. Some estimates suggest that about two thirds of illnesses have not been treated by a physician.[49] Moreover, failure to seek medical care and delay in seeking medical care are not confined to less serious diseases or disorders.[39,40,42,52] Hackett[30] has observed that one third of myocardial infarction patients delay at least 12 hours after the onset of chest pain before seeking medical care. He has also estimated that 10% to 20% of cancer patients *never* consult a physician.[31] In a study of over 500 cancer patients who did seek care, he reported that two thirds of the patients waited longer than 1 month after noticing signs or symptoms before seeing a physician. Such delay time, moreover, has not significantly diminished since the 1920s.[63]

Knowledge that some persons present complaints that many physicians consider nonmedical whereas many others fail or delay in seeking care even for problems like cancer and coronary heart disease raises serious issues for the medical professionals and society. When should people see a physician? Is there a clear common understanding among members of society about what symptoms or disorders ought to be brought to medical attention? If there is such a consensus, to what extent is it shared by providers, and how does this influence who seeks medical care? What other factors affect decisions to seek medical care?

In this chapter we will examine (1) what factors foster or inhibit people from seeking medical care, (2) what groups in our society are most likely to seek and not to seek needed medical care, (3) what measures are being taken on national and state levels to foster medical careseeking, and (4) what individual providers can do to encourage their patients to seek medical attention when it is needed.

Medical careseeking as a process

The seeking of medical care is not just the single act of contacting a physician or visiting a clinic or hospital that is recorded in health care utilization data.[76] Rather it is a process of events, decisions, and behavior that can occur in different persons or even in the same person over varying durations of time.[67] For analytic purposes careseeking can be divided into three separate stages: (1) *symptom perception* — the time between the emergence of some change in physical or psychologic state and the individual's recognition of that change as a medical symptom; (2) *decision making* — the time the individual takes after noticing a symptom to decide whether or not medical care is needed; and (3) *actual careseeking* — the time that elapses between the individual's decision to seek care and contact with a medical care provider.

Although these careseeking stages usually occur sequentially, behavior during the process is not uniform.[48] Numerous factors both promote and impede medical careseeking during each stage. For example, studies of myocardial infarction patients reveal that most of their delay occurs while they decide whether or not to seek professional care. One study, in fact, suggests that only about 10% of the time between symptom onset and physician contact was consumed by actual travel to a hospital.[55]

Symptom perception

A common complaint of many physicians is that people *deny* having symptoms that indicate a medical problem when in fact they are experiencing changes in their physical or psychologic status. Although many people do deny that certain signs are symptoms of illness, in many other cases denial is not a factor. There is simply a large degree of ambiguity among members of society about what constitutes a medical symptom.

Most people worry about whether a body change is indicative of a medical symptom if it is *painful, incapacitating,* or *unusual.* But different groups in society vary systematically in their perceptions of these changes. Thus, although earlier research and theory suggested that the threshold of *pain* is the same for all human beings regardless of social or cultural differences,[32] recent evidence reveals that perception of pain is systematically influenced by the unique history of the individual, the meaning given to the pain-producing situation, and present thoughts and fears for the future.[51]

An individual's ethnic and cultural background also affects the perception of and response to pain. Zborowski's[74] comparison of Irish, Italian, Jewish, and Old Yankee hospital patients indicates that Old Yankee and particularly Irish patients are less likely to acknowledge pain than Jewish or Italian patients. In general, although Italian patients most often expressed concerns about relief from pain, Irish patients tended to focus their concerns on what the pain indicated about the state of their health. Of the different groups he studied, Zborowski reported that Jewish persons were most likely to quickly consult physicians after the onset of symptoms whereas Irish and Old Yankee persons were more likely to delay in seeking care.

Not only the degree of pain, but also the extent to which pain *incapacitates* or interferes with one's *normal occupational and living functions* indicates illness to most Americans.[9] But just as pain is not uniformly perceived in society, so too incapacitation is not uniformly perceived. Back pain can incapacitate a farm laborer, but not a clerk. Hearing loss may be more serious to a truck driver than to an accountant.

A third factor that influences whether a body change is considered a medical symptom is how *unusual or unexpected* it is.[11] Many symptoms of chronic illnesses appear slowly and especially among older people may be considered an inevitable part of aging rather than a symptom of a treatable disorder. Oftentimes people learn to accommodate to such symptomatology in ways that permit normal functioning to continue.[13] Even acute body changes may not be considered symptoms if they occur with frequent regularity among a population. Zola[75] reports that diarrhea is so widespread among certain groups of Mexican Americans that it is not considered symptomatic of illness sufficient to require medical attention. Likewise fatigue is such a common occurrence among certain groups, such as students and physicians, that it often goes unnoticed when in fact it is the result of a medical disorder.

Decisions to seek care

Most of the delay in seeking medical care occurs as people debate whether or not to take symptoms to a provider. Just as people vary in their perceptions of symptoms, they also vary in their beliefs of what symptoms should be brought to medical

attention. Among both the general public and medical professionals there is a surprising lack of consensus about what symptoms should be brought to a physician's
attention.

*First of all it is often difficult to distinguish symptoms of very serious medical
disorders from symptoms of trivial consequence.* For example, nausea and fatigue
may represent nothing more than nausea and fatigue or they may in fact be symptomatic of a heart attack, an ulcer, hepatitis, or a variety of other disorders. Frequent headaches may indicate too much daily stress or they may signal sinusitis,
hypertension, glaucoma, or a brain tumor. Weight loss may reflect effective dieting
or bowel cancer. More often than not, when such symptoms occur they do not in
fact represent the more serious disorders we have mentioned.

Because a great deal of symptomatology can represent either minor and self-
limiting illnesses or serious illnesses, potential patients must make complex judgments about whether or not to seek medical care. These judgments involve comparing the *benefits, risks,* and *costs* of seeking medical care with benefits, risks,
and costs of alternative behaviors, such as waiting to see if the symptoms subside,
taking over-the-counter medications or home remedies, or contacting an alternative
type of healer.

For each person and every symptom, the benefits, risks, costs, and alternatives
vary.

Benefits of seeking care

Although often difficult for inexperienced providers to accept, a patient's problem need not be physical or biologic in origin or manifestation or even alterable by
medical treatment for the patient to perceive a possible benefit in seeking medical
attention. The benefit a patient may be seeking *may not* involve the diagnostic or
treatment skills the provider has worked so hard to learn.

For most people *reassurance that one is not seriously ill is the most important
benefit in seeking care.* A national survey conducted for the American Cancer Society
asked respondents what they liked most about having a physical examination. Of
those responding 54% indicated that learning that they were all right or not sick
was what they liked most.[4]

Also, many people seek medical care to find social and psychologic assistance.[60]
People who are lonely or anxious often complain of illness when in fact they are
seeking reassurance and social support.[50] Some persons may describe and seek care
for physiologic disorders when in fact they are facing a social or family problem but
find that problem difficult to understand and articulate. Seeking care for organic
complaints appears to many people as less threatening or stigmatizing than contacting a social worker, psychiatrist, family counselor, or psychologist, assuming
that such resources are available in the first place.

Other patients may actually desire to be told they are sick. As we will discuss more fully in Chapter 5, illness is often used by people as a legitimate excuse for failing to meet goals, aspirations, and responsibilities.[18] Furthermore, medically diagnosed illness can prove useful in obtaining financial and other dispensations. Most physicians have probably encountered patients requesting written confirmation of a medical disability to collect financial assistance or avoid military or other duties.

Finally, if a person is ill, the compassion and understanding offered by the medical staff can be extremely important and rewarding even if treatment is not completely effective. Although physicians take greatest pride in their ability to cure disease, in many instances no cure is available. In those instances palliative treatment and offering sympathy and emotional support can be crucial to helping the patient cope with what has happened.

Risks of seeking care

Though seldom discussed by medical professionals, seeking medical care is not without a variety of risks. Rather than learning that they are well or that they have an easily treated condition, patients may learn that their conditions are incurable or even fatal. The woman with a lump in her breast may have her worst fears confirmed. The man with nausea and shortness of breath may in fact be having a heart attack.

Even if a disorder is not fatal, the only available therapies may be painful, unpleasant, or frightening. People seeking medical care may learn that their conditions require hospitalization, which even in the best of institutions can be an unpleasant experience. Patients must leave their usual surroundings, activities, and social relations. Hospitalization requires people to drastically change their usual levels of autonomy and authority. Once in hospitals patients are expected to forego their normal freedom and activities. Clothes and belongings are removed, and patients are required to dress in institutional garb. Time spent eating and sleeping is determined by institutional needs, not by those of the patients. Patients are expected to restrict their behavior and often must seek permission to engage in such simple activities as going to the toilet or showering. Lastly, once in the hospital patients must expose their bodies and their lives to a host of professionals, students, and technicians, many of whom have little or no personal interest in patients and their overall treatment care.

Not only may a person's disorder require hospitalization, it may also involve surgery. The thought that someone will cut into and excise part of one's body, especially when one has been made unconscious, is indeed scary. People also may worry about the disfiguring aspects of surgery. Women with breast lumps or people with oral or facial lesions may be particularly fearful of what surgery will do to their appearance. Most frightening of all, of course, is the possibility that once anesthetized one will not come out of surgery alive. The growing literature and discussion about "unnecessary" surgery and iatrogenic illness has undoubtedly increased many people's skepticism about the safety of hospital care.

Even patients who are not hospitalized are expected to expose their bodies and lives to the physician and in so doing run the risk that the physician will be critical of them or their behavior. Patients who may need immediate medical attention may delay in seeking it for fear of physician disapproval. Patients experiencing intense chest pain have been known to be so concerned about their appearance that they return home to change clothes or even take showers before seeking care. Patients who have not adhered to their physicians' recommendations to diet or stop smoking or drinking excessively may be reluctant to seek care for symptoms even when their disorders are in no way related to these behaviors. Even more threatening to some is the possibility that divulging personal or family problems will call their mental and emotional health into question.

Often patients who feel sick may learn that no physical cause for their behavior can be found. One evaluation of patient complaints, for example, revealed that physicians diagnosed problems for only about two thirds of the complaints they were given.[61] This situation is particularly difficult for both the provider and the patient. Such patients are often considered "problem patients" by physicians, who do not see any way to help them.[26] The physician's frustration in turn may leave the patient wondering if he or she is regarded as neurotic or frivolous.

Also, as was discussed in Chapter 2, the diagnosis of certain illnesses is obviously stigmatizing and may reveal or raise questions about aspects of people's behavior. It has long been known that people delay in seeking treatment for venereal disease.[54] Unwed pregnant adolescents are an example of those who may delay in seeking prenatal care because of moral stigma attached to their behavior.

Costs in seeking care

Regardless of diagnosis or treatment, there also are numerous costs involved in seeking medical care. First and most obvious is the *financial cost of care*. While emergency room and ambulatory visits can run from approximately $50 to $150 depending on the facility and the tests deemed necessary, an inpatient day in an intensive care unit can cost over $500.

Seeking medical care is also very *time-consuming*. Based on a national survey Sloan[64] reported in 1977 that the average time spent in traveling and waiting to see a provider varies depending on locale from 1 to 2 hours, and most of that time is spent in waiting rooms. Coupled with the time that patients spend actually seeing a physician, waiting for tests, and returning home, it becomes apparent that a medical visit most often means disrupting at least half a day's activities.

In considering the time and money spent in seeking medical care, it should be remembered that the need for good health competes with other motivations, such as desire for love, money, drugs, work, cigarettes, alcohol, sex, or salvation.[58] Medical professionals often perceive people's delay or failure to seek care as irrational in part because as providers selected, trained, and paid to be concerned about health and illness, they are likely to see maintaining health as paramount. Most people, however, are most concerned about other facets of life and could just as legitimately question the reasonableness of the many providers who so focus on their job of promoting health that they neglect their families and financial affairs and forsake the many pleasures of leisure time. Many people perceive the seeking of medical care as *incurring opportunity costs* by diverting the individual from pursuing other worthwhile goals.

Alternatives to medical care

Finally, there are a wide variety of available alternatives to medical care, many of which are less costly and time-consuming. *Self-medication* is the most often used substitute for a physician's care. Coe[17] reports that in the United States one third of the annual expenditure for pharmaceuticals is used in the purchase of nonprescription medicine for self-medication. Additionally, no one knows how much prescription medicine is saved by people and later used without professional consultation. Although much of this self-medication may be harmless, it may prolong hope that symptoms will go away until damage from a disorder reaches serious proportion. In a national survey nearly 3000 respondents were asked, "If you had a certain ailment and knew a medicine that would control it with continuous use, how long would you wait before asking a doctor about it?" The ailments mentioned included sore throat, cough, stomach acidity, headache, and skin rashes. Approximately 20% of those queried said they would wait 1 week and 10% 2 weeks before consulting a physician.[56]

Other alternatives to seeking conventional medical care include sources that range from *chiropractors to acupuncturists to faith healers and quacks.* In the early 1970s, for example, there were over 20,000 practicing chiropractors in the United States who saw over 3,000,000 patients annually.[10] Although use of their services is most common among lower income groups, more often than not such alternatives are sought only after more traditional medical care has been obtained but not found completely satisfactory.[71] The recent controversy over the dispensing of laetrile exemplifies the fears of many providers that such alternatives might lure treatable patients away from conventional medical care.

Of course, it is always possible that people seek out services other than traditional medicine for reasons beyond the hope that these services can provide cures that medicine cannot. It may be that these healers appear as more understanding, supportive, and receptive to some patients or that they offer less costly or painful treatments. Certainly the proliferation of numerous self-help groups to deal with certain medical disorders suggests that many people identify needs that they do not feel are adequately served by medical professionals.

Thus one can see that the decision to seek medical care involves considering a complex range of issues. Even if medical professionals were in complete agreement about exactly what should be brought to medical attention and when it should be reported, the sheer complexity of the decision to do so militates against widespread uniformity in what people decide.

But *physicians and other medical professionals are often not even in agreement among themselves about what should be brought to medical attention.* The most striking disagreements revolve around whether it is legitimate to bring personal, nonorganic complaints to a physician for help. Many physicians regard their time as a particularly precious commodity that should not be wasted on activities other than the diagnosis and treatment of identifiable organic diseases. They question whether medicine should respond to the range of human needs that previously were addressed mostly by families, churches, schools, and social services.

Others, however, feel that personal and behavioral issues are legitimate to bring to a physician because so many organic disorders have behavioral and psychological antecedents and consequences. White[73], for example, has estimated that one third to one half of disorders seen in medical practice have behavioral or psychologic concomitants. Moreover, many feel that even when no pharmacologic or surgical cure is possible, the sympathy, reassurance, and compassion that a medical professional can provide is a form of treatment in that it often reduces pain and alleviates anxiety.[25] Moreover, disorders that may benefit from psychiatric treatment may go unnoticed if personal issues are not discussed with patients.[27]

It is also not always clear to physicians which organic symptoms require treatment. For example, a study in Washington of over 250 acute myocardial infarction patients reported that three fourths of those patients contacted their physician or the ancillary staff before going to the hospital. Although 57% of those providers had the patient hospitalized in 15 minutes, 33% took more time to decide to hospitalize the patient than the patient took to contact them, ranging from 2 hours to 4 days.[1]

Acting on decisions to seek care

Even after a person has decided to seek medical care, it is still necessary to establish contact with a provider and travel to a hospital, clinic, or physician's office. That is not equally easy for all people to do. First, the distance people must travel to obtain medical care varies across the country. The small numbers of primary care providers in rural areas and inner-city neighborhoods has long been a concern. Although the active physician-population ratio nationwide is one physician per 650 people,[62] in many inner cities it is between one per 2000 and one per 10,000 people.[62] In a 1975 report the AMA identified 140 rural counties in 26 states with a combined population of over 500,000 people in which there was not a single physician.[2]

Second, travel is not equally convenient for all people. Those who must rely on public transportation, especially the elderly and disabled, may find traveling to a clinic, hospital, or physician's office a particularly arduous task.

Numerous factors have contributed to the lack of primary care physicians in inner-city and rural areas. For the most part physicians are free to practice wherever and in whatever branch of medicine they prefer. The shift away from primary care medicine has resulted in part from the dramatic increase in medical knowledge. Rather than assume the difficult responsibility of keeping up with many areas of medicine, many prefer to confine their practice to more circumscribed areas where they can more easily manage to keep abreast of new advances and have greater control over their time. Since the number of specialists has increased, the general practice physician has increasingly been regarded as nonexpert.

Specialization in turn affects geographic distribution because of the specialist's need for interrelations with other physicians for referrals. This need prompts specialists to locate in urban areas. Also, the risks involved in solo practice make rural and inner-city practice less desirable. Finally, like most Americans, physicians prefer to live and work in areas other than remote rural ones or the congested, run-down, and often dangerous inner cities.[27]

In summary, a review of the factors influencing the different stages of medical careseeking underlines, first, that people do not uniformly recognize certain medical symptoms. Second, the reasons for seeking care are more diverse than being diagnosed, treated, and cured of illness. Third, numerous risks and costs deter people from seeking care, and still others make care difficult to obtain even if it is desired.

Groups in society least likely to seek needed medical care

Failure to seek needed medical care and delay in seeking care are common among all groups in society. Predictably, however, they are most common among those groups that have the fewest resources to meet the varied costs of careseeking and the greatest likelihood of learning that they have acquired a serious, chronic, disabling, or perhaps even fatal illness.

Poverty and lack of education mark those groups in society least likely to seek and obtain medical care promptly when it is needed.[68] The elderly, blacks, and some other ethnic minority groups all have disproportionate numbers who are poor and less educated. Individuals in these groups are much more likely to be sick and to experience life-threatening illness than individuals in any other group in society.[57] Yet as recently as 1963 the number of physician visits and hospital admissions among these segments of our society was much less than any other group.[8] At that time the poor had less access to medical care but spent a higher proportion of their meager income for medical services.[21] Persons over 65 were at a particular disadvantage. Although they constituted only 9% of the population,[14] they accounted for 25% of the poor in the United States.[47] Most elderly lived in one- and two-person families.

The median income of such family units with a head of household over 65 was less than one half that of families with a head of household under 65. Yet the elderly were twice as likely to suffer from some form of chronic illness and spent over twice as much per capita on medical care.[43]

Medicare and Medicaid

For these reasons many hoped that the joint passage in 1965 of Medicare and Medicaid would diminish failure and delay in seeking medical care among the poor and elderly (p. 77). *Medicare* is a federal insurance program providing partial hospital and outpatient coverage to persons over age 65 and to those under 65 who receive social security because of disabilities that prevent them from working. *Medicaid* was passed in an attempt to give poor persons under 65 access to medical care. Although the legislation requires states to provide medical coverage to all persons receiving cash assistance under the federal Aid to Families of Dependent Children (AFDC), participating states have the option of including or excluding other needy children and their families, the elderly, the blind, and the disabled.[72]

Medicare and Medicaid have had a substantial impact on the use of health services by the poor. In the years since they were passed the disparity in use of physician services between the poor and other segments of society has been substantially reduced.[12,53] As can be seen in Table 6 the percentage of poor people seeing a physician during a given year has increased and almost reached the percentage of nonpoor who see a physician.

Although on the surface it would appear that the poor are almost as likely as others to seek medical care when it is needed, such a conclusion is premature. It must be remembered that the poor segments of society experience much more illness than do other groups. A closer look at the data also indicates that among the poor, children under 5 years of age and adults over age 65 are still less likely in any given year to see a physician than children and elderly who are not poor. These are the age groups that experience the most illness.[20] When adjustments are made for health status, it appears that the poor still use fewer physician and hospital services than the rest of the population.[21] Among the elderly and the general population, if one controls for health status, there is still a strong direct relation between income and use of physician services[22] (Tables 7 and 8). Similarly, if one considers symptoms that physicians feel should receive medical attention, lower-income persons are still less likely to seek needed care.[7]

Several factors contribute to this continued disparity. First, though Medicare and Medicaid have dramatically helped to reduce financial barriers to medical care-seeking among the poor, financial barriers have not been eliminated. Second, approximately one third of the people living under the poverty level (between 8 and 12 million people) are not covered by Medicaid. Davis[19] has compiled the following list of people not covered.

Medicare and Medicaid

Medicare

Payment mechanism Administered through the Federal Social Security Administration

Persons eligible

1. Persons over age 65 who contributed to social security
2. Persons over age 65 who did not contribute to social security but are willing to pay a $69 per month premium
3. Persons under age 65 who receive social security because of disabilities that prevent them from working

Cost to recipient $8.70 per month

Benefits

Ambulatory care

$60 deductible each year, 80% reimbursement on allowable charges
1. Physician costs exceeding the rate set are not covered.
2. Prescription drugs are not covered.

Hospital care

$160 deductible each year; no charge for the first 60 consecutive days' hospitalization; days 61 to 90 at $40 per day; after 90 consecutive days 60 lifetime reserve days at $80 per day
1. The coverage for days 1 to 90 can be applied repeatedly as long as the individual remains out of the hospital at least 60 consecutive days after each hospitalization.
2. The coverage after 90 consecutive days can be used only once.

Medicaid

Payment mechanism Federal funds under general guidelines are funneled to participating states, which have considerable discretion on how they are spent.

Persons eligible

1. Persons who qualify for public assistance
2. Persons whose medical expenses would produce indigence without assistance
3. All states are *required* to provide medical coverage to persons receiving cash assistance under Aid to Families of Dependent Children (AFDC).
4. Each state has the option of including other needy children and their families, the aged, the blind, and the disabled.

Cost to recipient None

Benefits Inpatient and outpatient hospital, nursing, and physician service (exact coverage varies from state to state)

Table 6. Percentage of respondents who saw a physician in 1963, 1970, and 1976 by poverty level and age group in the United States*†

Age	1963	1970	1976
1 to 15			
Nonpoor	76	71	76
Poor	48	46	68
16 to 44			
Nonpoor	68	69	77
Poor	55	59	70
45 to 64			
Nonpoor	67	69	77
Poor	62	68	76
65+			
Nonpoor	70	81	82
Poor	62	68	71
TOTAL			
Nonpoor	70	70	77
Poor	54	59	71

*From Hardy, L. A., Anderson, R., and Anderson, O.: Public Health Rep. **92:**512, 1977.
†Data based on National Health Survey data.

Table 7. Physician visits by family income, 1969*

	All persons	
Income level†	Unadjusted	Adjusted for health status
All family incomes	4.6	4.6
Under $5000	4.9	3.7
Public assistance	6.6	4.5
No public assistance	4.7	3.6
$5000 to $9999	4.2	4.6
$10,000 to $14,999	4.4	4.9
$15,000 and over	4.8	5.2

*© 1976 National Bureau of Economic Research, Inc. (Distributed by Neale Watson Academic Publications, Inc.)
†Excluding individuals reporting family income unknown; those under 17 for whom head of household's education was unknown; and those 17 and older for whom individual education was unknown.

Table 8. Average physician visits for the elderly by health status and family income, adjusted for other morbidity indicators*

Family income	Health status†		
	Perfect	Average	Poor
Under $5000			
No Aid‡	2.78	5.64	10.47
Aid	3.86	7.52	13.42
$5000 to $9999	3.14	6.60	11.70
$10,000 to $14,999	3.75	7.27	12.98
$15,000 and over	5.35	9.53	16.98

*© 1976 National Bureau of Economic Research, Inc. (Distributed by Neale Watson Academic Publications, Inc.)
†Perfect health status is defined as without any chronic conditions, limitation of activity, or restricted activity days. Average and poor health status are defined at the mean and twice the mean level of the three morbidity indicators used.
‡Aid indicates public assistance recipients.

1. Widows under age 65 or other non-elderly single persons.
2. Most two-parent families, which account for 70% of rural poor family members and almost half of poor family members in metropolitan areas.
3. Families with a father working at a marginal, low-paying job.
4. Families with an unemployed father in the 26 states that do not extend welfare payments to this group, and families with an unemployed father receiving unemployment compensation in other states.
5. Medically needy families in the 21 states that do not voluntarily provide Medicaid coverage.
6. Women pregnant with their first child in the 27 states that do not provide welfare aid or eligibility for the "unborn child."
7. Children of non-AFDC poor families in the 36 states that do not take advantage of the optional Medicaid category called "all needy children under 21."*

Several million persons just above the poverty level also have no health insurance coverage.

Even though almost all persons over 65 are covered by Medicare, it does have deductibles and limits to the number of hospital bed days it will cover. Though the deductibles and limits were intended to reduce seeking of unnecessary care and unnecessarily protracted hospital stays, their utility in accomplishing those goals is questionable.[27] Furthermore, the deductibles and limits pose the heaviest burden on the poor and still leave most people with unpredictably expensive medical care. Few medical professionals, much less elderly persons, take the time to read or memorize the 51-page document that outlines eligibility and coverage under the Medicare program.[69] Similarly, it is doubtful that many indigent persons keep abreast of what conditions, services, and medications are covered for them by Medicaid. As a result even when the poor and elderly do qualify for medical coverage, they are still less likely to seek needed medical care.[70]

Other deterrents

Apart from financial barriers the poor have less education and awareness of what physical changes or bodily signs constitute medical illness. In his landmark study *The Health of Regionville*, Koos[41] found that persons in the lower socioeconomic classes are much less likely to believe that a variety of bodily changes are symptoms indicating the need for medical care. More recent data gathered by the American Cancer Society[4] reveal that lower social class individuals still are less likely to recognize the potential dangers posed by a number of bodily changes (Table 9).

Additionally, numerous studies have shown that poor persons are much more skeptical about the ability of medicine to cure illness.[38] This may result in part from their tendency to delay so long in seeking care that treatment becomes more difficult. Average length of hospital stay is much longer among the poor. But they are

---

*From Davis, K.: Achievements and problems of Medicaid, Public Health Rep. **91**:309-316, 1976.

Table 9. Symptoms mentioned as a sign of cancer according to respondent income national random sample survey conducted for the American Cancer Society*†

Symptoms	Under $6000/year (%)	$6000 to $9999/year (%)	$10,000 and over/year (%)
A lump or thickening in the breast or elsewhere	82	89	93
A sore that does not heal	73	79	84
Unusual bleeding and discharge	71	78	86
A change in a mole or wart	67	77	87
A change in bowel or bladder habits lasting 2 or more weeks	48	54	66
A persistent cough	45	54	62
Continuing hoarseness	31	46	59
Difficulty in swallowing	36	44	53
Persistent indigestion	24	32	41
Number of respondents	713	798	450

*From the American Cancer Society, A study of motivational, attitudinal, and environmental deterrents to the taking of physical examinations that include cancer tests, New York, 1966, Lieberman Research, Inc.
†NOTE: Based on the statement: "Here is a list of symptoms. Look through the list and tell me the letters of symptoms you think might be the first signs of cancer."

also more distrustful of physicians.[4] This distrust may stem in part from the differences in background and status of the physician and the patient. It may also derive from impressions about how poor people have been treated by medical care providers. The municipal and charity hospitals that have provided care to the indigent, for example, do not offer as pleasant surroundings or the personal attention that other hospitals offer. Until the passage of Medicare and Medicaid admission of non-paying patients to private teaching hospitals depended heavily on the value of their particular disorder for teaching and research.[23,37] Even after the passage of Medicare and Medicaid differences have persisted in the types of medical services poor people are able to obtain. Poor people are the least likely to have a personal physician and more often rely on the emergency room and public clinic care. For example, one study of over 4000 families with children revealed that only 15% of parents on welfare had a physician who usually looked after their children, compared to 85% of those with an income of over $10,000 per year.[3]

It is difficult to make across-the-board statements about the quality of care offered by clinics as opposed to private physicians; obviously the quality of service rendered varies from physician to physician and service to service. Many clinics, emergency rooms, and hospital outpatient departments are organized to provide only episodic treatment for specific ailments, and the development of a personal relationship between a physician and a patient is very difficult.[59] Poor people with little education understandably feel more vulnerable in approaching a bureaucratic setting offering medical services than more educated, wealthier people do in approaching a private physician they have known for years.[45]

Even those low-income persons who have a regular source of care may experience more difficulty traveling to receive that care and slower service when they arrive.[36] According to 1970 National Health Survey data, persons below the poverty line were three times more likely than the rest of the population to need 30 minutes or more to reach their source of care, and once in the clinic or office they were twice as likely to wait an hour or more before being seen and examined by their provider.[68]

Distrust and skepticism of medicine can also result from continuing reports of discrimination in service delivery. For example, recent studies have documented that minority and poor patients are more likely to undergo elective surgery,[44] which some consider to be unnecessary, and in at least some institutions are much more likely to be operated on by staff in training than by board-certified surgeons.[24]

Other problems arise from the fact that minority ethnic groups and recent immigrants are disproportionately represented among the poor. Members of such groups often carry unique beliefs about the causes of disease and how best to treat them, which at times conflict with modern medicine.[33,65,66] They may also experience language difficulties that limit their interaction with medical professionals. Even though language barriers are commonplace and predictable in many areas, few hospitals and medical schools require students and staff to have proficiency in one or more of the languages of the different peoples they will serve.

Additionally, a sizable number of low-income individuals are illegal immigrants to the United States. Though their economic circumstances would often qualify them for medical care coverage were they United States citizens, such persons are reluctant to seek medical care unless they can pay out of pocket for services because they fear being identified by immigration authorities and deported.

Conclusions: what can be done?

Our look at seeking medical care as a behavior process has demonstrated that factors that promote inappropriate or delayed careseeking arise at all stages of the process of seeking medical care. First, there is considerable *ambiguity about what is a medical symptom.* This ambiguity, although in part the result of social forces, permits social influences not directly related to a potential medical disorder to have considerable influence over decisions about whether or not one should seek care.

The decision to seek medical care is laden with *risks*, especially for the poor and the elderly who have the greatest likelihood of learning that they have a serious, untreatable, or even fatal disorder. Moreover, the *costs* of seeking medical care are not equitably distributed. Although the perception of what medical care costs is clear (it is expensive), understanding of how much of that cost is covered by medical insurance such as Medicare or Medicaid is murky. Deductibles, limits to coverage, and fluctuating regulations all contribute to delay in seeking care. Medical care also demands a great deal of *trust* from patients. Medicine pokes and prods and invades both the physical and the behavioral privacy of people's lives. To the extent that a specific provider or institution appears insensitive or impersonal, people will be hesitant to seek care, especially those with the least resources.

Finally, for many who desire care there are *direct barriers* to obtaining it. As we have mentioned the ratio of primary care practitioners to the population is very low in inner-city and some rural areas. And for some, especially the elderly and disabled, travel to and from medical care can be difficult and time-consuming.

Efforts to foster more appropriate seeking of health care need to focus on social and psychologic factors during all three stages in the careseeking process: symptom perception, decision making, and decision actualization. But what can realistically be done at each of these stages?

To begin, recognition of symptoms and deciding that certain symptoms should be brought to medical attention is the initial necessary step that if not taken makes all others superfluous. *Strategies to alert the population to crucial signs of illness need to be further explored.*

Many such efforts are under way with cumulative effects that have been quite beneficial. At the beginning of this chapter we reported the finding that people delay in seeking professional medical care as long as they did 50 years ago. What we did not mention is that people are noticing their symptoms sooner today than they did even 25 years ago. For example, from 1970 to 1976 the percentage of women who do breast self-examinations doubled from 14% to 35%.[29] In a review article on breast cancer management Cady[15] cited 10 different studies that reported that patients are presenting breast cancer symptoms earlier in the disease process. For example, at the New England Deaconess Hospital, where data on breast cancer characteristics have been kept for 40 years, statistically significant trends toward presentation of small primary cancers and fewer axillary metastases have been recorded, especially in the last 20 years. These trends have coincided with introduction by the American Cancer Society of public education efforts to encourage prompt careseeking and breast self-examination.[16]

Another illustration comes from data at the same institution on malignant melanoma.[16] Comparing records before and after 1949 reveals that both diameter and depth of invasion are less for patients who sought care after the introduction of American Cancer Society education. This in part has contributed to better survival rates for melanoma patients. In the absence of changes in the disease pathology over time or drastic changes in patient characteristics, neither of which appear likely in this case, one can suggest that public education has caused people to note symptoms and seek care sooner. Whether or not they delay less or more after noting symptoms may not have changed, but it is apparent that people are noticing and reporting danger signs sooner than before public education endeavors began.

Providers should make special efforts to inform patients about the symptomatology of disorders that would most benefit from prompt treatment. For example, delay in seeking care for heart attack symptoms greatly reduces survival chances. Patients with known cardiovascular disease and patients with high risk factors for heart disease should be informed about what symptoms might signal a heart attack and how to respond in the event they experience such symptoms. Although some might argue that such educational campaigns could trigger a rash of unnecessary careseeking, we are unaware of such an effect from any public health education program.

One might also ask if similar education efforts should be undertaken to discourage inappropriate medical careseeking. The answer, we believe, is "no." Although almost all providers would agree that symptoms indicating disorders like skin cancer or heart disease require professoinal medical attention, *disagreement* is widespread about what should *not* be brought to medical attention. What a surgeon feels is inappropriate may well differ from what a pediatrician or a psychiatrist feels is inappropriate, and consensus may be limited with each of these fields. Agreement would prove difficult to reach on who should not seek care. Probably agreement could only be reached about situations that constitute a minute fraction of patients seeking medical care.

Moreover, early detection of warning signals for problems like cancer, heart disease, or mental illness requires people to make subtle judgments about unclear symptoms. Consequently, if seeking medical care when it is deemed inappropriate by certain physicians is discouraged, some persons may, in confusion, be discouraged from seeking medical care when it is appropriate. The price of early detection for the health care system may well be patients who present without medical pathology.[34] When physicians disagree about what lies in the province of medical care, some persons seeking medical assistance for nonmedical problems are inevitable. Attention must therefore concentrate on persuading people to seek care for disorders that all or most physicians agree require medical attention, not on discouraging the seeking of care for disorders that physicians may disagree about.

We recognize the frustration that some patients with no definable illness can bring to physicians if they repeatedly seek care. However, the fact that no organic pathology may be diagnosable does not mean that physicians and other providers cannot offer desired help to these people, either by facilitating referral to others who can offer assistance or by a willingness to listen to patient concerns. There is some evidence suggesting that when services are offered to such patients, the subsequent number of visits will be fewer than the number made by patients not offered such services.[28]

Efforts also are needed to foster decisions to seek medical care once symptoms are noticed. First, educational research is needed. If one looks at medical and public health research on how to persuade people to behave in ways that will improve their health, one finds that most of this research has focused first on preventive health behavior and second on compliance behavior. Almost no research exists on how to persuade people to seek care once they know they have a medical symptom. Whether the findings about fear arousal, fear allaying, or other emotional appeals or providing information about how to most easily obtain care that have been reported in preventive health behavior studies can be generalized to the case where people know they have a medical symptom is not clear. Also, because family and friends can be important sources of advice about whether or not to seek care,[35,36,46] we need to test efforts aimed at persuading people to encourage careseeking among friends and relatives who may have noticed signs of illness.

Even before such studies are conducted, physicians and other providers can take steps to create medical care environments that appear more inviting. Though professional medical ethics prohibit competitive advertising of services, providers should try to learn why all new patients chose their services rather than other services. Asking new patients about how they chose their provider may offer insight into the problems they have perceived with previous providers and clinics. Patients also should be periodically queried about how easy or difficult they perceive obtaining services to be and what barriers to seeking care they encounter. When patients seek care for symptoms that might indicate serious illness, the appropriateness of their behavior should be confirmed for them even when no illness is diagnosed. If patients are made to feel welcome and appreciated, some of the risks incurred in seeking care may appear less frightening.

On a national level increased efforts are urgently needed to increase the accessibility of service. Much delay and failure to consider certain symptoms as appropriate for medical attention may really be attributable to lack of access.

The experience of Medicare and Medicaid illustrates that programs to reimburse medical expenses can have a marked effect in reducing financial barriers to care. A national health insurance program covering all persons could overcome many inequities and insufficiencies of the present system. These include the mosaic of deductibles present in Medicare that accomplish little, deter prompt careseeking, and should be abandoned. Likewise the limits placed on hospital duration should be reviewed and exceptions considered.

Although many people legitimately worry about the economic costs of a national health insurance program, these should be weighed against the costs of continuing the present situation, in particular poor health, disability, additional hospital costs, lost work, and loss in tax revenues that result from delay or failure to seek needed medical care. Also, the high administrative costs of our current complex and often unpredictable billing and reimbursement arrangements should be considered.

Though we support the concept of national health insurance, we believe that efforts on the reimbursement side must be coupled with strategies to discourage and detect abuse of the system, such as performing unneeded tests and procedures.

While Medicare and Medicaid undoubtedly have helped to reduce financial barriers to care for some, they also have contributed to the spiral in medical costs that makes care even more difficult to obtain for those not covered. A national health insurance program must be accompanied by an increase in the accessibility of providers.

Numerous strategies to accomplish this goal have been attempted in recent years, including the following:

1. Efforts to train more physicians
2. Efforts to train a higher proportion of physicians in the primary care-family care practice areas
3. Medical education loan programs that assume education costs if students will practice in underserved areas on completion of their training
4. Development of new health practitioners
5. Funding and establishment of neighborhood health centers in underserved urban areas
6. Promotion of health maintenance organizations
7. National health service corps
8. Children and youth projects focused on specific target populations in need

The relative impact of these various programs on access has been carefully documented elsewhere.[43] It is apparent that changes in medical education alone, either in the numbers or types of physicians or other practitioners being trained, will not produce the needed redistribution of providers unless programs are simultaneously undertaken to develop desirable practice organizations in underserved areas. To the extent that the factors that have discouraged physicians and other providers from practicing in inner city and rural areas can be addressed, the desirability of such organizations can be increased. Special attention should be devoted to reducing the professional isolation of those working in such areas, increasing the professional prestige and the amount of control such individuals have over their work, and providing ample support and referral resources for such individuals. As Fein[27] has argued, planning and development of such practice organizations around a community enrollment principle increases the likelihood that responsibility for the service needs, as well as the overall health status of the community served, can be identified.

But even if the direct impediments imposed by income and the distribution of providers are eliminated the legacy of past difficulties may obscure the symptom perception and otherwise impede the decision making of certain groups to seek medical care. Ingrained reluctance to seek care will not evaporate for all persons overnight. Lower-income persons may still remain more skeptical of medical services for reasons other than inability to pay or difficulty in getting to care. What patients encounter when they do seek care is crucial in this regard. As we shall describe in subsequent chapters, the conduct of all providers toward these patients is central both to how patients perceive the quality of their care and how they respond to care. Costs of seeking medical care are not only monetary, and so long as patients encounter other costs in seeking care delay will continue.

If early detection of disease symptoms facilitates patient treatment, then prompt careseeking must be promoted even if that requires extra effort on the part of medical professionals. Otherwise, a cycle of continued skepticism, delay, and difficulty in treatment will limit the ability of modern medicine to detect, treat, and control disease.

References

1. Alconzo, A.: The impact of physician consultation on care seeking during acute episodes of coronary heart disease, Med. Care **15**:34-50, 1977.
2. Allen, C.: The health of the disadvantaged, Public Health Rep. **89**:499-503, 1974.
3. Alpert, J. J., Kosa, J., Haggerty, R. J., et al.: The types of families that use an emergency clinic, Med. Care **7**:55-61, 1969.
4. American Cancer Society: Americans look at cancer and the check-up, New York, 1966, Lieberman Research, Inc.
5. Andersen, R., Smedby, B., and Anderson, O.: Medical care use in Sweden and the United States, Chicago Center for Health Administration Studies Research Series 27, Chicago, 1970, University of Chicago Press.
6. Andersen, R., Francis, A., Leon, J., and Dougherty, V.: Psychological related illness and health services utilization, Med. Care **15**:59-73, 1977.
7. Andersen, R.: Health status indices and access to medical care, Am. J. Public Health **68**:458-463, 1978.
8. Anderson, O., Anderson, R.: Patterns of use of health services. In Freeman, H., Levine, S., and Reeder, L., editors: Handbook of medical sociology, Englewood Cliffs, N.J., 1972, Prentice-Hall, Inc.
9. Apple, D.: How laymen define illness, J. Health Human Behav. **1**:219-225, 1960.
10. Ballantine, H. T.: Will delivery of health care be improved by the use of chiropractic services? N. Engl. J. Med. **288**:237-242, 1972.
11. Banks, F. R., and Keller, M.: Symptom experience and health action, Med. Care **9**:498-502, 1971.
12. Bice, T., et al.: Economic class and use of physician services, Med. Care **11**:287-296, 1973.
13. Blackwell, B.: The literature of delay in seeking medical care for chronic illness, Health Educ. Monogr. **16**:3-33, 1963.
14. Bogue, D.: Principles of demography, New York, 1969, John Wiley & Sons, Inc.
15. Cady, B.: Modern management of breast cancer, Arch. Surg. **104**:270-275, 1972.
16. Cady, B.: Skin cancers: "what's new?", discussion at the Fifth Annual Medical Symposium of the American Cancer Society, Metropolitan Boston Unit, Dec. 2, 1973.
17. Coe, R.: Sociology of medicine, New York, 1970, McGraw-Hill, Inc.
18. Cole, S., and Lejeune, R.: Illness and the legitimation of failure, Amer. Sociol. Rev. **37**:347-356, 1972.
19. Davis, K.: Achievements and problems of Medicaid, Public Health Rep. **91**:309-316, 1976.
20. Davis, K., and Reynolds, R.: The impact of Medicare and Medicaid on access to medical care. In Rosette, R., editor: The role of insurance in the health sector, New York, 1976, National Bureau of Economic Research.
21. Donabedian, A.: Benefits in medical care programs, Cambridge, Mass., 1976, Harvard University Press.
22. Donabedian, A.: Effects of Medicare and Medicaid on access to and quality of medical care, Public Health Rep. **91**:322-331, 1976.
23. Duff, R., and Hollingshead, A.: Sickness and society, New York, 1968, Harper & Row, Publishers, Inc.
24. Egbert, L., and Rothman, I.: Relation between the race and economic status of patients and who performs their surgery, N. Engl. J. Med. **247**:90-91, 1977.
25. Eisenberg, L.: The search for health care. In Knowles, J., editor: Doing better and feeling worse: health in the United States, New York, 1977, W. W. Norton & Co., Inc.
26. Fabrega, H. J., Moore, R. J., and Strawn, J. R.: Low income medical problem patients:

some medical and behavioral features, J. Health Soc. Behav. **10:**334-343, 1969.

27. Fein, R.: On achieving access and equity in health care. In McKinlay, J., editor: Economic aspects of health care, New York, 1973, Prodist Milbank Fund.

28. Follette, W., and Cummings, N.: Psychiatric services and medical utilization in a prepaid health plan setting, Med. Care **5:**25-35, 1967.

29. Gallup Poll: Summary: a survey concerning cigarette smoking health checkups, cancer detection tests, conducted for the American Cancer Society, Princeton, N.J., 1977, Gallup Organization.

30. Hackett, T., and Cassem, N. H.: Factors contributing to delay in responding to the signs and symptoms of acute myocardial infarction, Am. J. Cardiol. **24:**651-658, 1969.

31. Hackett, T., Cassem, N. H., and Raker, J.: Patient delay in cancer, N. Engl. J. Med. **289:**14-20, 1973.

32. Hardy, J. D., Wolfe, H. G., and Goodell, H.: Pain sensations and reactions, Baltimore, 1952, The Williams & Wilkins Co.

33. Harwood, A.: The hot cold theory of disease: implications for the treatment of Puerto Rican patients, J.A.M.A. **216:**1153-1158.

34. Jackson, J., and Greenstick, M.: The worried-well revisited, Med. Care **12:**659-667, 1974.

35. Kasl, S., and Cobb, S.: Health behavior, illness behavior, and sick-role behavior, Arch. Environ. Health **12:**246-266, Feb. 1966.

36. Kent, D.: Social and family contexts of health problems of the aged. In Crawford, C., editor: Health and the family, New York, 1970, Macmillan, Inc.

37. Kessel, R.: Price discrimination in medicine, J. Law Econ. **1:**20-23, 1958.

38. Kirscht, J., Haefner, D., Kegeles, S. S., and Rosenstock, I.: National survey of health beliefs, J. Health Soc. Behav. **7:**248-254, 1968.

39. Kobb, B., et al.: Patient responsible delay in seeking care for cancer, Cancer **7:**920-926, 1954.

40. Kobb, B., et al.: Delay and diagnosis and treatment of cancer, J. Health Human Behav. **3:**171-178, 1961.

41. Koos, E.: The health of Regionville, New York, 1954, Columbia University Press.

42. Kutner, B., and Gordon, G.: Seeking care for cancer, J. Health Human Behav. **2:**171-178, 1961.

43. Lewis, C., Fein, R., and Mechanic, D.: A right to health: the problem of access to primary care, New York, 1976, John Wiley & Sons, Inc.

44. Lyons, R.: Surgery on poor is found higher, New York Times, Sept. 1, 1977.

45. McKinlay, J.: Help seeking behavior of the poor. In Kosa, J., and Zola, I., editors: Poverty and health: a sociologic analysis, Cambridge, Mass., 1976, Harvard University Press.

46. McKinlay, J.: Social networks, lay consultation and help seeking behavior, Soc. Forces **51:**275-292, 1973.

47. Marmor, T. R., and Marmor, J. S.: The politics of Medicare, Chicago, 1973, Aldine Publishing Co.

48. Mechanic, D.: The concept of illness behavior, J. Chronic Dis. **15:**189-194, 1962.

49. Mechanic, D.: Response factors in illness: the study of illness behavior, Soc. Psychol. **1:**12, 1966.

50. Mechanic, D.: Response factors in illness: the study of illness behavior. In Jaco, E. G., editor: Patients, physicians & illness, New York, 1972, Free Press.

51. Melzack, R.: Perception of pain, Sci. Am. **204:**41-49, 1961.

52. Miller, M.: Seeking advice for cancer symptoms, Am. J. Public Health **63:**955-961, 1973.

53. Monteiro, L. A.: Expense is no object: income and physician visits reconsidered, J. Health Soc. Behav. **14:**99-115, 1973.

54. Morsell, J.: Motivation of the volunteer VD patient, J. Soc. Hygiene **39:**41-42, 1952.

55. Moss, A., Wyman, B., and Goldstein, S.: Delay in hospitalization during the acute coronary period, Am. J. Cardiol. **24:**659-665, 1969.

56. National Analysts: A study of health practices and opinions conducted for the Food & Drug Administration, D.H.E.W. Contract FDA 66-193, Washington, D.C., 1972, National Technical Information Service.

57. National Center for Health Statistics: Differentials in health characteristics by color: United States, U.S.D.H.E.W. Publication no. 56, Washington, D.C. July 1965-1967, U.S. Government Printing Office.

58. Rosenstock, I.: Why people seek health services, Milbank Mem. Fund Q. **44:**94-124, 1966.

59. Roth, J.: The treatment of the sick. In Ross, J., and Zola, I., editors: Poverty and health: a sociological analysis, Cambridge, Mass., 1976, Harvard University Press.

60. Satin, D. G.: Help: life stresses and psycho-social problems in the hospital emergency unit, Soc. Psychiatry 7:1-8, 1972.
61. Satin, D. G., and Duhl, F. J.: Help? The hospital emergency unit as community physician, Med. Care 10:248-260, 1972.
62. Sheldon, S.: National Center for Health Statistics health resources statistics, health manpower, health facilities, 1972-3, U.S. Department of Health, Education, and Welfare publication no. 73, Washington, D.C., 1973, U.S. Government Printing Office.
63. Simmons, C. C., Daland, E. M., and Wallace, R. H.: Delay in the treatment of cancer, N. Engl. J. Med. 208:1097-1100, 1933.
64. Sloan, F.: Access to medical care and the local supply of physicians, Med. Care 15:338-346, 1977.
65. Snow, L.: Folk medical beliefs and their implications for care of patients, Ann. Intern. Med. 81:82-86,
66. Suchman, E. A.: Socio-medical variations among ethnic groups, Am. J. Sociol. 70:319-331, 1964.
67. Suchman, E. A.: Social patterns of illness and medical care, J. Health Human Behav. 6:2-16, 1965.
68. U.S. Department of Health, Education, and Welfare: National Health Survey data, health of the disadvantaged, U.S.D.H.E.W. Publication no. 77-628, Washington, D.C., 1970, U.S. Government Printing Office.
69. U.S. Social Security Administration: Your Medicare handbook, U.S.D.H.E.W. Publication no. SSA 77-10050, Washington, D.C., 1978, U.S. Government Printing Office.
70. Wan, T. H., and Soifer, S. J.: Determinants of physician utilization: a causal analysis, Ill. Med. J. 146:100-108, 1974.
71. Wardwell, W.: A marginal professional role: the chiropractor. In Scott, R., and Volkart, E., editors: Medical Care, New York, 1966, John Wiley & Sons, Inc.
72. Weikel, M. K., and Leamond, N. A.: A decade of Medicaid, Public Health Rep. 91:303-308, 1976.
73. White, K.: Life and death and medicine, Sci. Am. 229:22-33, 1973.
74. Zborowski, M.: People in pain, San Francisco, 1969, Jossey-Bass, Inc., Publishers.
75. Zola, I. K.: Culture and symptoms: an analysis of patients' presenting complaints, Am. Sociol. Rev. 31:615-630, 1966.
76. Zola, I. K.: Studying the decisions to see a doctor, Adv. Psychosom. Med. 8:226-227, 1972.

Chapter 4

Entering the medical system: health, illness, and ambulatory care

Once a person decides to obtain medical care for symptoms or other problems, what are the responsibilities of medical care providers to that person? What constitutes health, and what constitutes illness? Does being healthy or ill involve more than an individual's biologic status? And, if so, to what extent do medical care providers have a duty to deal with the panorama of factors—personal, social, and environmental—that may contribute to, be defined as, or result from illness? Does the provider's responsibility to care for illness also include an outreach function to locate those who are ill but who have not sought medical care and secure their entrance into the medical system?*

In this chapter we will address these questions about the boundaries, content, and responsibilities of medical care. Such questions, to some, may seem too abstract and philosophic to be of much relevance for students or practitioners in the medical care professions. But in fact how such questions are answered by the professions and by various other segments of our society has a very practical bearing. It affects the nature of medical professionals' training, their responsibilities in practice, the way that they are viewed by patients, and the way that the medical care delivery system more generally is structured.

Our focus will be on the nature of ambulatory care, which is the point of entrance into the medical system for most persons and constitutes the largest part of clinical practice. To appreciate both the frequency and nature of contact with medical care providers, we first will review some data on the use of ambulatory care services. Second, we will explore some ideas about what constitutes health and illness, including concerns that ours is an "overmedicalized" society as well as views about the rights and responsibilities of the individual in relation to health and

---

*Various data suggest that a large percentage of those who a physician would define as ill do not seek medical care. In a widely cited 1961 study, for example, White[62] and his colleagues reported that 33% of the population who had an illness episode in a given month sought health care, whereas 67% did not seek care in the presence of symptoms or illness.

health care. Third, we will consider some of the ways that two major fields of ambulatory care, primary care medicine and family medicine, are being defined in terms of their content and boundaries and the related responsibilities of both providers and patients. Finally, we will examine what is termed the "medical model" in relation to views about what conditions do and do not constitute appropriate grounds for seeking and receiving medical care. In this context we will briefly consider issues about the diagnosis of behavior as "deviant" in terms of the physician's role as a definer of illness and the attendant role as an agent of social control.

The utilization of ambulatory care

Following the recognition of symptoms, an individual may follow various courses of action, as discussed in the preceding chapter. An individual may decide, for instance, to "do nothing" or "wait and see," to self-medicate, to consult an alternative healer, or to seek care from an "orthodox" provider, most often a physician. Every sign, symptom, perceived illness, or other type of life problem thus does not lead a person into the medical care system.

Nonetheless, the American people annually make a vast number of contacts with physicians for a wide variety of reasons. Based on data from the Health Interview Survey[26] of the civilian noninstitutionalized population of the United States, there were approximately *1 billion contacts with physicians* during 1977, excluding inpatient hospital visits.* This figure translates into an average of 4.8 physician contacts per person in a given year, with some 75% of the civilian noninstitutionalized population seeing a physician at least once in a 12-month period.

Since most contacts with the medical care system involve ambulatory care, it is important to have some knowledge about the composition of that care. Although data from utilization studies need to be interpreted with caution, they nevertheless give us a general sense of the disorders for which people seek and receive ambulatory care.†

From utilization studies such as the National Ambulatory Medical Care Survey (NAMCS), one can *characterize ambulatory care as a high volume area of medical practice that deals with a wide range of organic, psychiatric, and psychosocial*

---

*In the Health Interview Survey physician *contact* or *visit* is broadly defined to include seeing or talking with physicians or their representatives in person or by telephone in any setting except inpatient hospital care (e.g., physician's office, clinic, emergency room, home). In contrast, The National Ambulatory Medical Care Survey limits physician *visit* to a personal encounter with a physician or representative in the office.

†In looking at utilization studies it is important to realize, first, that research in this field has many methodologic problems that make comparisons between studies and generalizations difficult. Second, different types of morbidity patterns and reasons for seeking medical care can be developed depending on the types of disease classification and data sources one uses and how they are arrayed and interpreted.[12,61] Third, most utilization studies use disease or disorder classifications that focus on specific organic conditions. These conditions, many authorities feel, do not reflect the range of undifferentiated syndromes and psychosocial problems seen in ambulatory care.[37,39,47,51]

problems. The majority of organically diagnosed problems are self-limiting and viewed by physicians as not serious or only slightly serious. Only some 20% of visits overall involve serious problems as defined by physicians.

Looking first at some *general patterns of office-based care*, the 1975 NAMCS[41] reported that there were an estimated 567.6 million office visits or an average of 2.7 visits per person.* Of the office-based specialties surveyed, the highest volume of visits (2 out of every 5) was to general and family practitioners. The vast majority (85%) of the office-based ambulatory care was return visits by patients. Moreover, 62% of the visits were for consultation or treatment of "old problems" for which the patient had seen the physician at least once before. These include medical or surgical aftercare, prenatal care, and management of chronic disorders such as hypertension, heart disease, diabetes, and arthritis. Overall, the physicians surveyed planned no follow-up for 13% of their patients and planned to refer only 2.8% to another physician or agency and to hospitalize another 2%.

Another portion of the NAMCS data looks at the *reasons patients gave for seeking care.*† In terms of their principal or first-listed complaint problems *not* directly related to illness or injury are prominent reasons for seeing an ambulatory care provider. These include nonspecific physical examinations, pregnancy examinations, and well-baby checkups. Other major reasons for seeing an ambulatory care physician include nonspecific symptoms or complaints such as a sore throat, abdominal pain, cough, fatigue, or headache.

As one might expect from the reasons listed by patients for seeking care, ambulatory providers characterize the majority (80%) of their practice as involving self-limiting and/or medically "not serious" problems. In looking at NAMCS data on *diagnoses most frequently recorded by physicians*, one also finds appropriately that the relatively unspecified problems cited by patients reappear as more specific diagnoses by physicians. For example, the leg and back problems that were the fourth and fifth most frequently cited complaint by patients may be defined by the physician as involving synovitis or bursitis, osteoarthritis, unspecified arthritis, or back pain or strain.

Utilization data on what patients and physicians respectively define as the

---

*The 1975 NAMCS results were based on a random sample of some 60,000 patient visits to 2472 participating physicians (MDs and osteopaths); data include general utilization patterns and utilization by physician practice and specialty characteristics, the patient's presenting problems, and the physician's diagnosis. When this chapter was written, the complete data from the 1977 survey were not available. An advance data release from the National Center for Health Statistics, however, noted that the results of most data items were similar in 1975, 1976, and 1977.

†In the National Ambulatory Medical Care Survey definitions of illness or injury are those provided by the International Classification of Diseases (ICD). The ICD, which originated as a pathologist's classification of causes of death, has been revised many times chiefly with reference to causes of morbidity among *hospitalized* patients. Many ambulatory care authorities believe that the ICD code is unsatisfactory for characterizing the content of ambulatory care.

patient's chief problem also show some interesting differences. In the NAMCS, for instance, physicians ranked essential benign hypertension as the third most common patient problem, whereas high blood pressure ranked nineteenth among the principal complaints cited by patients. Since people in part visit physicians to have the latter provide more specific diagnoses of their problems, many of the differences between physician and patient definitions of patient problems are unremarkable. As we will discuss more fully in Chapter 5, however, the frequent *lack of congruence* between why a person visits a physician and what the physician defines as the patient's problem and how it should be treated is an important source of tension in the doctor-patient relationship.

Although the data just reviewed above represent only a small portion of studies on the use of health care services in the United States, they do provide a good general picture of the demand for and content of ambulatory care as defined by patients and physicians. With some variations smaller studies provide comparable characterizations of the content of ambulatory care in both the United States and other countries.*

Perspectives on health and illness

In part because the content of ambulatory care practice is so varied and broad, it is very difficult to achieve any consensus about what should constitute its legitimate scope and boundaries. Yet how that scope is defined by and for medical and nursing educators, students, ambulatory care and other providers, patients, health care planners, and third-party payers is of central importance. How the "proper" scope of ambulatory care is defined, for example, (1) partly structures the content of graduate and postgraduate training programs in terms of the competencies thought necessary for providing medical care; (2) influences what students concentrate on learning; (3) shapes the providers' judgments of "appropriate" careseeking behavior and their responsibilities as providers; (4) shapes the lay person's perception of what problems should be brought to a provider and how the patient and provider should deal with them; (5) influences the nature of interrelationships between providers; (6) plays a role in determining the types of services provided at community, state, regional, and national levels; and (7) plays a role in determining the types of services that will be reimbursed by third-party payers.

In this section our goal is to suggest some of the types of complex issues that need to be considered in defining the proper content and boundaries of ambulatory care and of medicine more generally. We will do so first by examining views of what constitutes health and illness. Second, in relation to these views we will look at increasing calls for a greater assumption of individual responsibility for one's health and for health and/or health care to be provided as "rights."

---

*References 12, 19, 25, 37, 38, 39, and 47.

Health and illness

Most of us individually can tell when we feel healthy or ill. But we may find it hard to articulate exactly what we mean by those terms or to explain how we differentiate between various degrees of feeling well or unwell. The difficult task of defining health and illness has occupied generations of researchers, clinicians, philosophers, sociologists, and assorted other "experts" and filled volumes of books and journals. Medically health usually is thought of as meaning the absence of distress, disease, disability, morbidity, or mortality. Health status measures often are presented in terms of statistical fluctuations around ideal norms, as in the measurement of high or low blood pressure. In part because health and illness involve cultural and social views as well as biomedical parameters, however, the concept of health can assume a far broader meaning than just the absence of a given medically defined condition.

However health is defined, most people believe that its attainment and maintenance are an integral part of medicine's role in our society. For example, we speak commonly of health care providers and health care delivery, and various codes of ethics for physicians and nurses refer to these professionals' responsibilities for the health of their patients, not for the treatment or care of their illnesses.[3,64]

Consequently, how health is viewed has enormous implications for the competencies and responsibilities of medical professionals. The more broadly health is defined, the more we are apt to expect that medical professionals *can and should* deal with the many social and psychologic precursors and consequences of illness at both individual and societal levels as well as with a range of psychosocial problems that are viewed as "illnesses."

The problem of what boundaries, if any, we should set on medicine's role in relation to health begins to be evident if we consider one of the most frequently cited modern definitions of health. In the preamble to its 1946 Constitution the World Health Organization (WHO)[63] stated that *"health is a state of complete physical, mental and social well-being and not merely the absence of disease or infirmity."* Should it be the task of medical care providers to help their patients attain "a state of complete physical, mental, and social well-being?" If so, what expertise is required, and can it be achieved? If not, how should we limit the responsibilities of physicians, nurses, or medical social workers?

The WHO definition does have the virtue of recognizing that both illness and health have many nonbiologic dimensions. But it has been strongly criticized because by implication it makes the medical profession "the gatekeeper for happiness and social well-being" or "the final magic-healer of human misery."[9] Such a view of health may tempt one to view all sorts of social problems as matters of health or illness and thereby tend to increase the power, authority, and responsibility of the medical profession. By this type of reductionism health becomes a normative concept, "that which human beings must and ought to have if they are to live in peace with themselves and others."[9]

Illness and medicalization

One of the main reasons that many people are uneasy about a WHO-type concept of health is that it leads us to define more and more problems and conditions as *illnesses* and thus part of medicine's province. This process of "medicalization," as we pointed out in Chapter 1, is due as much or more to social and cultural forces as it is to what some critics see as "territorial expansion" by the medical profession itself.[27]

For whatever reasons it has occurred, however, there is growing concern from many quarters that American society has become "overmedicalized." Those who share this view believe that particularly during the past two decades we have defined too many personal and social problems as "illnesses," and turned to medicine for their prevention, cure, or palliation. These concerns also have refocused attention on older questions about the nature of what we call "illness." To what extent is illness "an objective reality, a subjective state, or a societal construct that exists chiefly in the minds of its social 'beholders'?"[17]

Many critics within and without medicine have detailed their concerns about the growing pervasiveness of health-illness concepts. In part our expanding notion of what constitutes illness is due to the increasing capability of biomedical science to detect a range of biochemical and physiologic states that are viewed as abnormal, presymptomatic, or otherwise indicative of possible, impending, or existing illness. In the newborn, for example, metabolic screening tests can detect a variety of biochemical abnormalities that may or may not prove to be clinically significant; adult screening tests increasingly can detect what are thought to be presymptomatic changes in various cells and tissues that signal the onset of conditions such as coronary artery disease or cervical cancer. Many asymptomatic persons also find through various types of routine tests that they suffer from previously unsuspected conditions such as hypertension or diabetes. As Zola[65] notes, "It seems that the more intensive the investigation, the higher the prevalence of clinically serious but previously undiagnosed and untreated disorders. . . . Instead of it being a relatively infrequent or abnormal phenomenon, the empirical reality may be that illness, defined as the presence of clinically serious symptoms, is the statistical *norm.*"

Another prominent focus of medicalization concerns is what Kittrie[31] calls the "continuing process of divestment" away from sin and crime and toward illness as the explanatory concept for various types of deviant or abnormal behavior. Similarly, Sedgwick[57] has expressed his concern about "the progressive annexation of not-illness into illness," that is, our tendency to define more and more behavior and problems as due to illness rather than nonmedical causes. The legitimacy of these types of medicalization concerns in turn needs to be assessed in terms of the social history surrounding earlier religious and criminal explanations for and efforts to deal with problems such as mental illness, alcoholism, and sexual deviancy.

Physicians recognize that their patient population is an expanding one in terms of the types of problems brought to them for advice, treatment, or care. Garfield[20] has coined the term *the worried well* to describe those who cannot be clinically defined as "ill" but who seem to legitimately feel in need of therapeutic aid. And Kass[30] has colorfully observed that "all kinds of problems now roll to the doctor's door, from sagging anatomies to suicides, from unwanted childlessness to unwanted pregnancy, from mental difficulties to learning difficulties, from genetic counseling to drug addiction, from laziness to crime. . . ."

Defining boundaries

Many sorts of factors can help to shape how medical professionals and patients deal with boundary issues about what problems or conditions constitute an illness. One set of factors that we see as important involves the interrelationship between how proficient medicine is in dealing with a particular problem and the degree of social consensus on whether that problem is a medical one. As summarized in Fig. 2, there tend to be few problems for providers or patients in deciding how to respond to a problem in cell 1; there is a high degree of consensus, for example, that a broken bone or infectious disease is a medical problem, and medicine can deal with these problems very effectively. There are also relatively few difficulties with problems falling into cell 4, those things that we generally agree are not medical problems and that medicine cannot deal with effectively (e.g., financial problems). Boundary problems are apt to be most severe, as cell 2 suggests, in those areas where medicine has developed an effective diagnostic or treatment modality but society is not sure whether its use is for a legitimate medical problem (for example, should prenatal diagnosis be used to identify fetal gender when gender is not important for detecting a genetic defect). In cell 3 boundary problems arise when society feels that a problem is at least partly medical but medicine cannot deal with very effectively, as in alcoholism or child abuse.

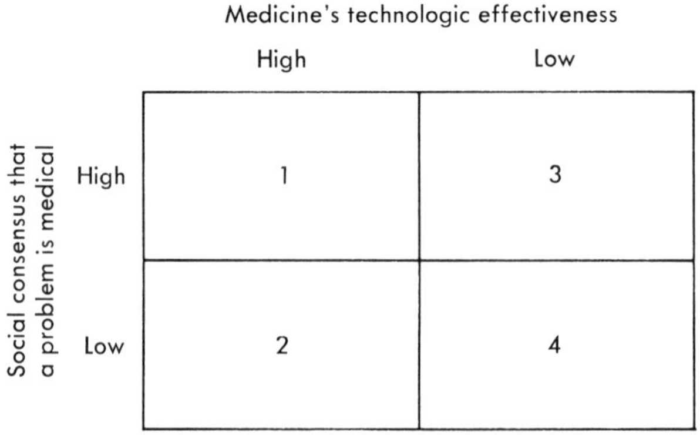

Medicine's technologic effectiveness

	High	Low
High	1	3
Low	2	4

Social consensus that a problem is medical

Fig. 2. Areas of boundary problems for providers and patients.

Another example of boundary problems is seen in the social and environmental factors that are recognized as contributing to the development of medical conditions or impeding their management. To what extent, for example, is the individual provider responsible for dealing with the poor housing conditions that are affecting the patient's recovery from a myocardial infarction? Should the provider be a real estate agent who helps the patient find new housing or adopt a broader role as an agent of social change for problems such as housing that affect health? Or should the provider do nothing? Our own view is that medical care providers as citizens and as professionals should be concerned with the social problems and conditions that relate to illness. At the same time, however, they should recognize that most of these problems are not most effectively remedied by clinical interventions and in many instances can be addressed by political and economic actions outside of the immediate context of provider-patient interactions.

Caring for health and illness: rights and responsibilities

Another important part of our society's perspective on health and illness is how we view the provision of health care (which we think is usually a misnomer for medical care). In this section we will briefly examine two increasingly shared beliefs in our society, both of which bear directly on what is expected of providers who must deal with a widening range of problems that are being defined as "medical."

The first of these beliefs is that health and/or health care is a *right* that a just society through its government is obligated to ensure to the fullest extent possible for its citizens. The second belief is related to the first because arguments about rights usually also involve arguments about the *reciprocal responsibilities* of those who have certain rights. Thus many increasingly believe that as individuals we have *responsibilities for our health.*

Health and health care as rights

The language of rights is a complex one philosophically, legally, and politically. As a number of books and articles on the subject make clear, discussions and actions by individual patients and providers, groups, and government agencies must start by separating and clarifying what is meant by a "right" to health and health care and what this in turn implies for the provision of health or medical care services.[5,23,48,60]

With reference to health and health care, the word "rights" refers to *moral rights,* a subject that is part of moral philosophy. This point is an important one to bear in mind because for most Americans the word "rights" usually is taken to mean certain freedoms or entitlements guaranteed under the Constitution or by legal statute.

In addition to being careful about how we use the word "rights," we also need to think carefully about what it means to assert that we have a *right to health*, as opposed to a *right to health or medical care*. There are those who believe that we do have a moral right to health, which in turn implies that our government has a duty to ensure our health. For example, following its famous definition of health, The WHO Preamble[63] declares that "the enjoyment of the highest attainable standard of health is one of the fundamental rights of every human being . . .", and that "governments have a responsibility for the health of their peoples which can be fulfilled only by a provision of adequate health and social measures."

In moral philosophy rights are usually discussed in terms of theories of justice. The idea of a right to health then can be rephrased as a principle that in a just society everyone should get the resources needed to be healthy. This indeed seems to be the meaning of the WHO statement about health as a fundamental right. As many commentators on rights and justice in health care have noted, however, "healthiness," even if we agreed on what the term means, would seem to be something that society cannot completely ensure. To assert a blanket "right to health" thus seems to many to be a sloganistic exercise. It makes the language of rights and justice meaningless because it makes impossible demands on society in the name of moral rights.

Both philosophically and in the practical realm of public policy decisions, therefore, it makes more sense to ask what it means to discuss *health or medical care* as a right. In this discussion ideas about the allocation of resources based on concepts of distributive justice take on particular importance. To begin with it is important to distinguish between efforts to be just about *things being distributed* (such as treatments for specific diseases) and their *mode of distribution* (that is, the systems by which the medically related goods are distributed).

Second, we need to consider which *principles of distributive justice* we would like to use as the bases for distributing medical care goods and services. Whether or not we believe that health care is a right, we need to deal with this question because in the real world resources are finite, and we must make decisions about how to allocate many different things.

Thus at the broadest level of social policy we must make decisions about how to divide up the pie of our economic and noneconomic resources. Apart from idiosyncratic political actions, on what bases should we decide how much of our resources to allocate to, for example, medical care versus defense versus welfare programs versus education? And within any given slice of the pie such as medical care how should we decide to allocate those limited resources among many important and competing needs? Then once we have decided to give X amount to one area and Y amount to another, how do we decide who receives X or Y if the demand exceeds the available supply of funds, facilities, equipment, or personnel?

To illustrate both the importance and difficulty of making these types of allocation decisions, we will look briefly at one particular treatment, *renal dialysis*.[18] This is only one of many examples of how different medical care services have been allocated according to different principles of social justice, even though the principles may not have been explicitly formulated at the time allocation decisions were made.

From the time that chronic dialysis for patients with end-stage renal failure was developed in 1960 until the early 1970s, the artificial kidney machine was a very scarce lifesaving medical resource. There were many more terminally ill patients than there were dialysis machines, and these patients had only three options: a kidney transplant, limited in availability by the supply of histocompatible donor kidneys; dialysis; or death from uremia.

Throughout the 1960s individual physicians, patient selection committees, and hospitals thus had to deal with an agonizing medical-moral problem: Who should receive chronic dialysis, and who should be refused treatment and die? Moreover, who should make such awesome decisions, and how?

If you were a member of the selection committee at your hospital, how do you think such an allocation decision should be made? That is, what principle or principles of social justice would you use as the bases for dealing with the following classic dilemma: *This month, your hospital has dialysis machines available for only three patients, but there are seven medically eligible candidates. How do you select the three dialysis patients?*

Six major principles of social justice are presented here.[60] The physicians and committees who had to allocate dialysis machines at hospitals used selection methods that involved one or more of these principles.

1. A *utilitarian "ethometrics"* principle allocates care to achieve the greatest good or benefit to the greatest number of persons. It is the principle underlying efforts to perform quantitative cost-benefit analyses for various components of health care services. In the case you must deal with, you would try to calculate which three of the seven dialysis candidates would provide the "greatest good" (economic, personal, or social) to the greatest number if chosen for treatment.

2. A *meritarian* concept of social justice would allocate care to individuals on the basis of their merits or deserts. In using this principle to select the three dialysis patients, you can define merits or deserts in many ways, such as conduct, achievement, or societal contribution.

3. An *ability* principle provides for care on the basis of various ability criteria. For example, in a fee-for-service system ability to pay is a determinant of who receives care, and you might eliminate from the pool of seven candidates those who cannot afford the high costs of chronic dialysis.

4. A *needs* principle attempts to allocate health care justly in terms of the essential needs of individuals, leaving open questions about how one defines "essential needs" and who defines them.

5. A principle of *compensatory justice* would allocate resources first to those who have previously suffered social wrongs that deprived them of the resources.

In choosing among the seven candidates, for example, you might opt in favor of those whose previous medical care had suffered because of their lower socioeconomic status.

6. In American society probably the most popular concept of social justice as a basis for distributing things like medical care is an *egalitarian* concept. Egalitarian principles, however, also can be formulated in various ways. For example, in terms of medical care we should "provide similar treatment for similar cases." (In acting on this principle we should be aware that it is not easy to define exactly what we mean by "similar treatment" or "similar cases.") During the 1960s several dialysis centers selected patients by a random lottery. Physicians at such centers believed this method provided the most egalitarian way of trying to provide similar treatment or a chance of treatment for similar cases.

As this brief discussion of principles of social justice suggests, allocation decisions pose very complicated medical, ethical, and socioeconomic issues. All participants in medical care have a stake in how these issues are addressed and resolved, whether in particular instances such as the distribution of renal dialysis or more broadly in terms of the overall provision of medical care services. If our society accepts medical care as a right instead of a privilege in more than a rhetoric or sloganistic sense, we need to think carefully about how we want to and can act on that right. As a first step beyond decisions based on political lobbying, we need to consider the various principles of social justice and decide which of them we want to underlie the provision of medical care.

Health, health care, and individual responsibility

Rights, as we have noted, usually are held to involve reciprocal responsibilities. Thus the growing emphasis on the responsibilities of individuals for their health and/or health care is the reciprocal value to health and/or health care as a right. In its modern form the calls for individual responsibility also in part stem from a reaction to the perceived overmedicalization of our society and in part from a recognition of the limits of medicine in preventing, palliating, or curing various diseases and disorders.[10,24]

As Dubos[15] reminds us, however, the view that man can do much to live a healthy life is ages old. From the fifth century BC on in ancient Greece, Dubos observes, the cult of the healing god, Asclepius, gained ascendancy. In earlier days throughout the classical world, however, the predominant cult was that of Hygeia, who "was probably a . . . personification of Athena, the goddess of reason. Although identified with health, she was not involved in the treatment of the sick. Rather, she was the guardian of health and symbolized the belief that men could remain well if they lived according to reason."[15]

In their modern dress followers of Hygeia are calling for, among other things, a greater reliance on self-care of many preventive and treatment regimens for which people commonly seek professional medical care. Some proponents of individual responsibility further affirm that we have a social *duty or obligation* to engage in self-help and other behaviors and practices that will promote our health.[30,32] Most prominently, the individual responsibility movement asserts that we can do far more to achieve and maintain health by altering individual habits and environmental conditions than we can by focusing our energies on illness care or curative medicine. Medicine too, some feel, can more effectively help to produce health if it accepts the responsibility of moving into what Haggerty[24] calls "the boundaries of health care," joining social medicine and public health with its traditional biomedical research and clinical practice domains. One of these boundary areas, which we discussed in Chapter 2, is the engagement of providers in health education activities that will better equip individuals to assume more responsibility for their health.

One of the best known and most articulate advocates of individual responsibility for health was the late Dr. John Knowles, whose career included positions as Director of Massachusetts General Hospital and President of the Rockefeller Foundation. "Control of the present major health problems in the United States," Knowles[32] asserted in a widely cited 1977 essay, "depends directly on the individual's behavior and habits of living." For Knowles, "prevention of disease means foresaking the bad habits which many people enjoy—overeating, too much drinking, taking pills, staying up at night, engaging in promiscuous sex, driving too fast, and smoking cigarettes. . . ."*

Knowles' arguments were more sophisticated and complex than they appear in the brief quotation above. He recognized that there are many barriers to the assumption of individual responsibility, including educational and economic handicaps and a too great reliance on the "beneficient state." He also acknowledged that the environment and workplace constitute major health problems of a far different nature and call for very different remedies than changes in one's habits or life-style.

To critics of the individual life-style school of thought, however, the analysis of writers like Knowles is basically flawed by "the assumption that the individual controls his or her health" and the consequent view that "simple meliorist approaches" can do much to improve the health of the individual or the population.[40] The focus on individual habits, many have observed, tends to ignore occupational and environmental risk factors. For reasons such as these Crawford[11] attacks individual responsibility as an ideology of blaming the victim, which in part seeks to "justify the retrenchment from rights and entitlements for access to medical services," and to "divert attention from the social causation of disease. . . ."

---

*Knowles and other advocates of individual responsibility have drawn heavily on studies such as those by Belloc and Breslow,[6,7] which document the common sense viewpoint that sound basic health habits are important for good health. As we discussed in Chapter 2, the "rules for healthy living" defined by this research include three meals a day, moderate exercise, adequate sleep, moderate weight, no smoking, and no or only moderate alcohol consumption.

Summary

How health and illness are being or should be defined, we have seen, is a controversial and unsettled question. There are differing views of what constitutes health and illness and of what the role and responsibilities of medical professionals and lay persons should be in dealing with health and illness. And, we have suggested, these views depend as much or more on their proponents' social and political ideologies as they do on any body of scientific, epidemiologic, and clinical data relating to the nature of health, disease and illness.

We also have noted that the ways health and illness are defined shape our judgment as to what constitutes the legitimate sphere of medical or health care. Despite calls for and some signs of "demedicalization," utilization data and other studies support the notion that our society is adopting an expansionist view of health and illness. Because of this expansion the borders of medicine are unsettled ones, as are judgments about the numbers, types, and skills of the "troops" needed within those borders. One emerging pattern, however, is that a broadening definition of health and illness is placing greater expectations and responsibilities on providers.

These issues about the boundaries, content, and responsibilities of medicine are confronted most sharply by those in ambulatory care because this is the entry point and major source of treatment for most patients. To illustrate boundary and content issues we will examine briefly two major fields of ambulatory care: primary care and family medicine.

Primary care and family medicine
Definitional issues

As a 1978 manpower policy study for primary health care noted, "The idea of primary care in health is well-known and widely supported, but there is considerable disagreement about the meaning of the term."[28] This disagreement makes it difficult to reach any consensus about *what* primary care should consist of, *who* should provide it, and *how* it should be delivered. In this section we will consider only the *what* question, recognizing that it is closely interwoven with the questions of who and how. The latter questions include the roles and interrelations of physicians, nurses, and others involved in solo or team care, the manpower needs for various types of providers, and the merits of various types of primary care organizations and settings, each of which is the subject of a growing body of literature.*

One of the most widely cited definitions of primary care is that of Alpert and Charney. They point out first that "primary medicine is within the personal health system rather than the public health system and, therefore, is focused on the health needs of individuals and families."[1] Next, they define what they see as the three major components of primary care. First is *first-contact medicine*, which includes

---

*References 1, 2, 4, 13, 28, 33, 42, 47, and 50.

(1) the care patients receive when they first decide to enter the health-service system, as distinguished from secondary or tertiary care; (2) an *outreach and follow-up* function; and (3) the task of *"helping the patient define the conditions under which entry to professional services and continuation in care are appropriate."*

Second, primary care involves a *"longitudinal responsibility* for the patient regardless of the presence of absence of disease." It is not limited to a single illness episode, but continues over time and involves negotiating a *"contract"* between provider and patient about their respective and mutual expectations and responsibilities.

Third, primary medicine has two sorts of *integrationist* functions closely related to its continuity of care aspect. The primary provider serves as the patient's *coordinator* when the patient receives other health care services and manages "to the limit of [the provider's] capability the physical, psychological, and social aspects of patient care." The integrationist concept, as Alpert and Charney note, is hard to define with precision and there is much disagreement about its limits. It also is the facet of primary care that to many in the field calls for the skills and resources of a primary care *team* rather than a single provider.

Alpert and Charney's definition of primary care was one of 38 that were reviewed by the Institute of Medicine[28] in a 1978 study of primary care manpower needs. The Institute task force in turn defined primary care in terms of five "essential attributes."

1. Good primary care requires *accessibility of services*, including physical location, internal facilities, and cost, availability, and acceptability to patients. In assuring accessible services, moreover, it is the *"responsibility of the provider team* to assist the patient or potential patient to overcome the *temporal, spatial, economic,* and *psychologic barriers* to health care."
2. Good primary care requires *comprehensiveness of services*. Primary providers must be willing and able "to handle the great majority of the health problems arising in the population it serves."
3. Primary care requires *coordination of services*.
4. Primary care requires *continuity of services* in much the same way as defined by Alpert and Charney.
5. Primary care providers, like other health care professionals, must be *accountable* for the process and outcome of the care they give.

Primary care somewhat confusingly is used both as a generic term that is analogous to ambulatory care or general practice and as a designate of a particular specialty area within ambulatory care (e.g., the primary care nurse or physician). When used generically, the term *primary care* can refer to several academic disciplines and related practice specialties that are considered to fall within its sphere, most commonly including internal medicine, pediatrics, obstetrics and gynecology, and family medicine-family practice.

Considered as an academic discipline, *family medicine* has been defined most fully in a 1978 textbook by one of the field's leading authorities, Dr. J. H. Medalie. Drawing on definitions of primary care Medalie[39] views family medicine and its practice as involving first-contact, longitudinal, and integrative care. It is also concerned not just with the individual patient, but with the family as society's basic social unit and with the relationships between the members of that unit.

Providing primary care

The definitions of primary medicine and family medicine mean that the providers of primary care can have an almost open-ended set of responsibilities, conditioned largely by the type of longitudinal care contract they set up with their patients, to deal with health and illness in the broadest sense of those terms. Outreach, education, prevention and health maintenance, knowledge about the care of the whole person and the whole family, a responsibility to assist persons in overcoming all the many barriers to seeking and receiving acceptable care—the list ramifies far beyond the diagnosis and treatment of the acute and chronic illnesses and injuries that constitute most morbidity, mortality, and utilization data and that are the core subject matter of training for work in medicine.

To many exponents of primary care the ultimate content of care and the attendant duties of providers are defined at least initially by whatever the *careseeker* defines as a *need*. "Need," asserts Pellegrino,[46] "must be interpreted, at least at the time of contact, broadly enough to embrace what the *patient* perceives as a need, not the physician." "Moreover," he argues, "the *moral center* of primary care . . . *is first contact care*. This is the moral fulcrum on which all rights and obligations in health care ultimately must balance."

Such a view of the scope and responsibilities of primary care in turn has obvious implications for the *competencies* required of primary care providers and thus for the nature of their professional *training*. In terms of providing longitudinal care the magnitude of what can be expected of the ambulatory care provider is exemplified by the recommendations of Breslow and Somer[8] for a "lifetime health monitoring program." To achieve more "health-effective" and cost-effective preventive health care they propose a lifetime monitoring program that "uses clinical and epidemiologic criteria to identify specific health goals and professional services appropriate for 10 different age groups." The types of comprehensive "preventive efforts" they call for are illustrated by the goals and services for the young adulthood group.

Young adulthood (18 to 24 years)*

Health goals

1. To facilitate transition from dependent adolescence to mature independent adulthood with maximum physical, mental and emotional resources

---

*From Breslow, L., and Somers, A. R.: The lifetime health-monitoring program: a practical approach to preventive medicine, N. Engl. J. Med. **296:**601-608, 1977. Reprinted by permission from The New England Journal of Medicine.

2. To achieve useful employment and maximum capacity for a healthy marriage, parenthood and social relations

Professional services

1. One professional visit with the healthy adult, including complete physical examinations, tetanus booster if not received within 10 years, tests for syphilis, gonorrhea, malnutrition, cholesterol and hypertension, and medical and behavioral history (This visit may be provided upon entrance into college, the armed forced, or first full-time job, but should be before marriage.)
2. Health education and individual counseling, as needed, for nutrition, exercise, study, career, job, occupational hazards and problems, sex, contraception, marriage and family relations, alcohol, drugs, smoking and driving
3. Dental examinations and prophylaxis every two years

Educators in the primary care disciplines believe that to accomplish these and other tasks the provider must be trained and recognized as a *specialist*, not as a jack-of-all-trades.

> Primary-care physicians, too often viewed as low-level generalists, are most appropriately thought of as specialists whose work demands specific skills. These physicians function as managers, advocates, educators and counselors for their patients while also serving as co-ordinators of other professionals involved in primary care.
>
> The basis for education in primary care should be a recognition of the specialized nature of the work that primary-care physicians perform.*

The knowledge and skills deemed necessary for primary care medicine make such textbooks as Medalie's[39] *Family medicine* or Noble's[42] *Primary care and the practice of medicine* into volumes very different from standard texts on clinical medicine. Medalie's text, for example, end with a short (1½ pages) but daunting chapter on the knowledge and skills needed for family practice. The following list consists of some of the "contributory subjects" he cites as relevant to the work of a family physician: basic sciences; behavioral sciences; laboratory sciences; clinical medicine; natural history of disease; epidemiology, probability diagnosis; anthropology; psychology; sociology; psychiatry; genetics; school health; occupational health; community dynamics, organization, and resources; public health (e.g., pollution, radiation, and other environmental hazards); housing standards; the medical care system; changes in society and its effect on health and medical care; community resources and organization; business and practice administration; evaluation procedures; group dynamics.[39]

A list such as the foregoing, and comparable ones in other works on primary care, is a formidable one for students, educators, and practitioners. Authorities such as Proger and Williams[47] recognize that their concept of primary care— "everything that a patient needs and expects as a person and a member of a family

---

*From Draper, P., and Smits, H. L.: The primary-care practitioner—specialist or jack-of-all-trades, N. Engl. J. Med. **293**:903-907, 1975.

and community when he or she decides to call a doctor"—is diffuse and seems to require omnicompetence. They maintain that the primary physician is *not* "a generalist who specializes in everything."[47] But it is difficult to deny that ambulatory care providers need an extraordinarily broad range of competencies if they are to meet the mandate contained in the intertwined views of health, illness, and the scope of primary care.

Diagnosis and the medical model: the physician as social control agent

In our society physicians are "the principal agents responsible for certifying, diagnosing, treating, and preventing illness."[17] If we consider these functions of the physician in relation to ambulatory medicine's mandate to care for a broad range of psychosocial as well as biomedical problems, we begin to see a series of important issues about the expertise and authority of the physician. For how society responds to the behaviors a person or group of people engage in depends on whether we view the behavior from a religious, legal, or medical perspective. As more and more behaviors and activities are viewed from a medical perspective, the authority of the physician to determine what happens to an individual or a group of people for exhibiting a range of behaviors has also grown. Physicians have become increasingly important agents of social control, not only in determining how society responds to some groups of individuals who engage in "deviant behavior" but also in influencing what society considers to be deviant behavior.

To gain a perspective on why this is an increasingly important facet of the physician's role, we need first to examine the concept of the *medical model*. The traditional medical model was focused on *disease*. As the modern concept of disease evolved from the end of the eighteenth century on, a disease was defined as "a destinct entity, the presence of which is verifiable objectively; it has a cause, and if we can identify the cause the physician can either cure or prevent it, or the means for its cure or prevention inevitably will be developed by the biomedical researcher. This view of disease presupposes that it is something distinct from the person who contracts it and that if rid of it the person will be normal (healthy)."[35]

Traditionally then the clinician's diagnostic, treatment, and prevention role centered on dealing with an organic disease or illness entity. "In the traditional medical model, a person who feels ill initiates contact with a physician with the hope . . . that he or she will be treated and consequently rendered healthy. The physician first makes a diagnosis, naming the disease that is causing the patient to feel ill. Based upon this diagnosis the physician can perform the other functions expected of him or her. The physician can provide a prognosis, predicting what will become of the patient, and therapy designed to cure the disease; to either delay the progress of, or compensate for its disabling manifestations; or to relieve symptoms. Finally, the physician is expected to care for the patient with all that the word 'care' implies."*

The social implications of the traditional medical model were formulated by Parsons[36,43,44] in his concept of the sick role, which we will discuss more fully in Chapter 5. As summarized by Fox,[17] the sick role involves two interrelated sets of exemptions and obligations.

> A person who is defined as ill . . . is not held morally accountable for the fact that he is sick (it is not considered to be his "fault"), and he is not expected to make himself better without the help of others. In addition, he is viewed as someone whose capacity to function normally is impaired, and who is therefore relieved of some of his usual familial, occupational, and civic activities and responsibilities. In exchange for these exemptions . . . the sick individual is expected to define the state of being ill as aberrant and undesirable, and to do everything possible to facilitate his recovery from it. In the case of illness of any moment, the responsibility to try to get well also entails the obligation . . . to confer with a medically trained person, usually a physician, and to undergo the modes of diagnosis and treatment that are recommended, including the ministrations of other medical professionals and hospitalization. Upon entering this relationship with institutionalized medicine and its professional practitioners, an individual with a health problem becomes a patient. By cooperating and collaborating with the medical professionals caring for him, the patient is expected to work toward recovery, or, at least, toward the more effective management of his illness.†

In the traditional medical model, as Levine[35] points out, "individuals diagnosed as having functional [nonorganic] illness may be regarded as illegitimate petitioners for the entitlements of the sick role." That is, their careseeking may be defined as inappropriate by a physician, who has the authority to legitimate illness, and they therefore may be precluded from assuming the exemptions or obligations of the sick role.

But the concept of illness, as we have seen, has grown far beyond the confines of the traditional medical model to include not only a range of psychiatrically defined functional disorders, but a broad mix of behaviors and psychosocial concerns. In turn, Fox[17] points out, "this medicalization of deviance and suffering has had a network of consequences. . . . The fact that the exemptions and the obligations of sickness have been extended to people with a widening arc of attitudes, experiences, and behaviors in American society means primarily that what is regarded as 'conditionally legitimate deviance' [i.e., being sick] has increased." Because more and more problems are defined as illness physicians have increasingly important social control functions. For as we began this section by pointing out, it is physicians who are charged with diagnosing, treating, preventing, and certifying illness.

---

*From Levine, R. J.: Foreword: the traditional medical model. In Miller, M. G., and Schworn, M. B., editors: Mental illness and the problem of boundaries, Washington, D.C., 1979, Medicine in the Public Interest, Inc.

†From Fox, R. C.: The medicalization and demedicalization of American society, Daedalus **106**:9, 1977.

As the gatekeepers of social and behavioral as well as biologic deviance, then, it is important for physicians and other providers to understand the social ramifications of defining patients for various reasons as "deviant." Physicians are empowered to define or diagnose a person as being deviant, that is, *as departing in some way from an ideal norm or standard of behavior.*[29,58] They also are charged with treating or caring for that deviance either themselves or by making referrals to other institutions or agencies, and these processes usually impinge strongly not only on the individual patient but on family and other close associates as well.

As Scott[56] points out, most people have strong if often unconsciously held views about the causes and nature of deviance.* There are numerous theories as to what constitutes and causes deviant behavior.[34] Statistics abound on the estimated incidence of various types of socially deviant behavior, such as crime, drug abuse, alcoholism, child abuse, and mental illness. Added together such figures suggest that the majority of the American population engages in one or more forms of deviant behavior. Cumulatively, many researchers believe there thus are serious credibility problems with data on deviance in terms of the ways that deviance is being defined and measured.

In research and in social policy formulations deviance traditionally has been defined in terms of *norm or rule violation:* we (society or certain segments of society) are a group with norms or rules, and those who violate the rules are deviant. Until the 1970s most research on deviance focused on *who breaks rules* and *why rules are broken.*

The causal question "why are some people deviant?" traditionally rested on the presumption that deviance is a personal quality that some people have and some do not. The many variables proposed and studied over decades to account for the *why* fall into two main categories. First, various types of deviance have been attributed to *biologic causes*, such as genetic defects or biochemical abnormalities. Second, deviant behavior has been explained in terms of *environmental causes*, either psychologic or social in origin.

Part of the difficulty in establishing or accepting either biologic or environmental explanations for deviance lies in the fact that it is difficult to draw a clear and invariable distinction between people who are and are not deviant. Additionally, if one looks at responses to the question "what is deviance?" one finds that they vary among societies and change over time within a society.

More recently attention has been directed to two other questions that have yielded an alternative perspective on deviance: *when* is norm violation held to constitute deviance, and *who makes such decisions?* Sociologists such as Scott have

---

*Portions of this section are adapted from lectures on deviance by Professor Robert A. Scott in the Socio-Medical Sciences Course, Boston University School of Medicine.

argued that *to understand deviance we must understand the nondeviant group.* In support of this contention consider the proposition that *rule breaking is endemic in society.* Most of us, with varying frequency, violate many types of norms or rules; we break traffic laws, engage in tax evasion, smoke marijuana, or skip school or work. Yet most of us do not regard ourselves and are not regarded by others as "deviant." This suggests, first, that we need to pay closer attention to informal social rules and their violation, as opposed to formal rules, in understanding how deviance comes to be defined. Second, if most of us are violating norms, but most of us think we are not, we must be ignoring most norm violations; *we explain them away* or normalize them (e.g., Joe is acting "that way"—talking to himself—because he's not himself today) *or literally do not see them* (e.g., Joe is a professor and we do not notice that he often "thinks aloud").

One must then ask why do we sometimes *not* ignore norm violations. That is, why are some behaviors defined as deviant? One extreme answer advanced by Szasz[53,59] and others in works such as *The Myth of Mental Illness* is termed the *labeling theory* in sociology. This view in essence holds that deviance is purely a social construct: there is no such thing as deviance "out there" in society in any objective sense, but rather only behaviors that certain groups choose to label as mental illness or other types of deviance.

Without accepting the labeling theory we believe there are strong arguments for accepting the relativistic thesis that a society's view of deviance at a given time is related to the forces that make social organization possible. According to this argument social norms exist only by agreement among members of the group as to what constitutes ideal or appropriate behavior. We *define and recognize our norms,* the argument holds, *by reference to the nonnormative.*

In this sociologic view of deviance, then, determinations of *when* rule breaking constitutes deviance are made by a nondeviant social group in terms of the degree to which behaviors and attitudes are congruent with or threatening to their norms. Studies such as the analysis by Erikson[16] of deviance in Puritan New England further suggest that the definition or labeling of behaviors or attitudes as deviant is particularly likely to occur at those points where a group's normative boundaries are blurred or breaking down. For the physician this means that diagnostic decisions will be strongly influenced by social norms that may actually have little to do with health or illness as usually defined by medicine.

As the last point suggests, the above sociologic perspective on deviance has an important bearing on the physician's gatekeeping and social control roles as the diagnostic certifier and treater of deviance. It also has implications for the management of patients with more strictly biomedical illnesses or conditions that involve social ascriptions of "being different" such as having physical handicaps.

As the source of first-contact care, primary care providers see many individuals or members of their families who are concerned that a particular constellation of behaviors, such as drinking or eating patterns, drug use, sexual activities, or thought processes, mean that a person is "sick" in the sense of "suffering from" social deviance. The process of *clinical judgment* through which a physician reaches a diagnosis and formulates a treatment plan involves complex combinations of knowledge and clinical and interpersonal skills.[54] The physician, Pellegrino[45] observes, asks and attempts to answer three generic questions: *What is wrong with this patient? What can be done?* And *what should be done?*

When physicians have patients with psychosocial or behavioral problems, the view of deviance presented above suggests that the process of clinical judgment needs to incorporate an awareness of the individual's personal, family, and community background, as well as broader cultural views of normatively appropriate behavior. Physicians also need to recognize and analyze their own beliefs about what constitutes deviance and why deviance occurs, for their own beliefs and attitudes can strongly affect their clinical decision making in this area. Given the social context of deviance, physicians need to guard against using their diagnostic power as a lever to shape what is considered to be socially appropriate behavior when what is deemed "appropriate" is based more on personal group preferences than on any medical reality.

Furthermore, when assessing deviance, as in all areas of medical diagnosis and care, physicians confront problems of uncertainty that they deal with in various ways. Uncertainty may be particularly pronounced with a patient whose problems are psychosocial or behavioral in nature.

Examining the decision rules or norms that govern medical diagnosis, Scheff[52] argues that physicians in part deal with uncertainty by making what statisticians call *type 2 errors* and avoiding *type 1 errors*. A *type 1* error is *rejecting a hypothesis that is true*, whereas *type 2* is *accepting a hypothesis that is false*. In medicine a type 2 error is to judge a healthy person as sick; conversely a type 1 error involves judging a sick person as healthy and dismissing that person as a patient.

"Most physicians," Scheff comments, "learn early in their training that it is far more culpable to dismiss a sick patient than to retain a well one. This rule is so pervasive and fundamental that it goes unstated in textbooks on diagnosis." Thus, Scheff argues, "Physicians follow a decision rule which may be stated, 'when in doubt, diagnose illness.'"

Physicians need to think carefully about the consequences of type 2 errors when they are assessing deviance. Because of the *stigma* attached to mental illness and other forms of deviant behavior, we would agree with Scheff that diagnosing a healthy person as sick may be more harmful than missing a diagnosis of illness for a person with seemingly deviant behavior.

Goffman's[21] concept of *putative social identity* underlines the potential negative impact of such stigma. By this term Goffman refers to the way that we structure relationships with persons we do not know well by giving them a *social identity* and then structuring or interpreting their behavior in terms of that putative identity. For example, we meet Ms. A, are told that she is a surgeon, and then interpret her behavior as due to her "being a surgeon," or we define Mr. B's behavior, when we learn he is a policeman, in terms of his "being a policeman."

As Goffman and others have pointed out, putative identities related to deviant labels are powerful and enduring.[49] We tend to define or explain the behavior and indeed the entire life of a person in terms of his or her putative identity as a deviant. Thus we think of Mr. X or Ms. Y as "an alcoholic," "a criminal," or "a mental patient" and are apt to use this putative identity indefinitely, even if the person has been cured or rehabilitated. Mr. X or Ms. Y is socially defined as "an ex-alcoholic," "an ex-convict," or "a former mental patient."

Physicians and other medical professionals also need to recognize that in our society many types of illnesses or disorders besides deviant behavior carry with them imputations of deviance and through social norms become organizing vehicles for a person's life. Medical professionals in particular are apt to define and relate to people with chronic disorders or physical handicaps *in terms* of their disorder or handicap, as will be discussed more fully in Chapter 7. For example, Ms. D is defined by her physicians as "a diabetic" rather than as "a person with diabetes" and is expected to organize her life around her chronic illness; Mr. E is viewed as "a paraplegic," and his caregivers talk with him about the "disease-appropriate behaviors" he should engage in; Mr. F, suffering from severe low vision, is labeled prematurely as "a blind person," is referred by his physician to an agency for the blind, and is treated by that agency, as well as his family, as "a blind person." Such putative social identities are particularly apt to be given to those with visible *stigma*, either physical or behavioral in nature. Persons closely associated with the stigmatized in turn are apt to acquire *courtesy stigma*, social identities defined in part by their relationship to the stigmatized individual.[22]

Finally, physicians should learn about the views and activities of *agencies* for the physically or socially deviant to which they may refer patients. For as Scott[55] has shown in his important study of agencies for the blind, how such agencies perceive "deviance" and deal with their clients are important determinants of how clients view themselves and how they are treated by others. These assessments of patients and their social backgrounds, of you as a provider, and of referral agencies can be difficult and time-consuming. But they are important parts of reaching a decision, as a clinician whose judgments will powerfully affect the patient's life, about what is wrong with and what can and should be done for the patient.

In sum, as persons with nonorganic problems and organic disorders as well enter the medical care system and providers decide whether they will acquire the status of "patient," clinical judgments need to incorporate an understanding of how society views and responds to health and illness. The facet of health-illness that we have explored in this section, deviance, is a controversial one that has extensive implications for the role of physicians as agents of social control and for the patients who seek their care.

Suppose, for example, you find that your patient is engaging on a regular basis in what the patient admits is "excessive drinking" and that this drinking is beginning to affect his or her health, work, and family relationships. As a primary care provider, you feel that your patient has a problem that you should help with medically and psychosocially. The question then becomes how should you deal with it, and what could be the consequences for the patient and the patient's family of various possible courses of action? Should you legitimate the behavior by defining the patient as sick and placing him or her in the sick role? If not, how will you account for the problem and suggest the patient deal with it? If you do define the patient as sick, how will you explain the etiology of the illness? Is it due to biologic, psychologic, or social factors? What bearing does your etiologic view have on possible courses of treatment? If you diagnose your patient as an alcoholic, what will be the consequences of this putative social identity for the patient and his or her family? These are difficult questions—for which there are no simple right or wrong answers—that providers need to be aware of and think through in their social role as the diagnosers and certifiers of deviance.

Summary

Proceeding from the discussion of decisions to seek care in Chapter 3, this chapter has explored various aspects of a person's entrance into the medical system. Our focus has been on examining the content of ambulatory care in relation to issues about the nature of health and illness and in relation to the role of medicine in attaining or maintaining health and preventing or treating illness.

In briefly reviewing utilization data we saw that there is an enormous demand for ambulatory care, which constitutes the bulk of clinical medicine. Ambulatory care is broad and varied; people seek the help of first-contact ambulatory care providers for many different reasons—biologic, behavioral, and social in nature—that they define as falling within the scope of medicine.

The content of ambulatory care, then, frames questions about what constitutes health and illness. How these questions are answered by various segments of society has important implications for the training and practice of medical professionals. If, as seems to be the case today, health is broadly defined as encompassing psychologic and social as well as physical well-being and if medicine's role is to deal with the achievement of health and the prevention or care of illness, medical care providers will be expected to have a broad range of competencies that will enable them to handle the many dimensions of health and illness.

The broadening definition of health and illness, we have seen, has given rise to concerns that American society is "overmedicalized," that is, more and more problems are being defined as illness and being brought to medicine for their resolution. We also are in the midst of calls, on one hand, for a greater assumption of individual responsibility for one's health and, on the other hand, for health and health care to be viewed as rights that society has an obligation to meet. These messages are complicated ones. They arise from varied sources and have many different implications for the role and responsibilities of ambulatory care and other providers.

Finally, we briefly explored the concept of the medical model in relation to the broadening concept of health and illness and the role of the physician as the diagnoser and certifier of illness. In a boundary area such as social deviance, we pointed out, the physician is in a difficult professional role, one in which he or she potentially has great power as a social control agent. It thus is important for physicians and all other medical professionals to understand what they mean by "deviance" and what the implications are for patients and their relatives when the patient is given the putative social identity, deviant.

References

1. Alpert, J. J., and Charney, E.: The education of physicians for primary care, D.H.E.W. Publication no. (HRA) 74-3113, Washington, D.C., 1973, U.S. Government Printing Office.
2. American Academy of Nursing: Primary care by nurses: sphere of responsibility and accountability, Kansas City, 1977, American Academy of Nursing.
3. American Nurses' Association: Code for nurses with interpretive statements, 1976.
4. Andreopoulos, S., editor: Primary care: where medicine fails, New York, 1974, John Wiley & Sons, Inc.
5. Beauchamp, T. L., and Childress, J. F.: Principles of biomedical ethics, New York, 1979, Oxford University Press, Inc.
6. Belloc, N. B., and Breslow, L.: The relation of physical health status and health practices, Prev. Med. 1:409, 1972.
7. Belloc, N. B.: Relationship of health practices and mortality, Prev. Med. 2:67-81, 1973.
8. Breslow, L., and Somers, A. R.: The lifetime health-monitoring program: a practical approach to preventive medicine, N. Engl. J. Med. 296:601-608, 1977.
9. Callahan, D.: The WHO definition of 'health,' Hastings Cent. Stud. 1:77-88, 1973.
10. Carlson, R. J.: The end of medicine, New York, 1975, John Wiley & Sons, Inc.
11. Crawford, R.: You are dangerous to your

health: the ideology and politics of victim blaming, Int. J. Health Serv. 7:663-680, 1977.
12. Dingle, J.: The ills of man. In Life and death and medicine, San Francisco, 1973, W. H. Freeman & Co. Publishers.
13. Dorsey, J. L., editor: Essays in medicine: in search of primary care, Morris Plains, N.J., 1974, Warner/Chilcott.
14. Draper, P., and Smits, H. L.: The primary-care practitioner—specialist or jack-of-all-trades, N. Engl. J. Med. 293:903-907, 1975.
15. Dubos, R.: Mirage of health, New York, 1971, Harper & Row, Publishers, Inc.
16. Erikson, K.: Wayward puritans: a study in the sociology of deviance, New York, 1966, John Wiley & Sons, Inc.
17. Fox, R. C.: The medicalization and demedicalization of American society, Daedalus 106:9, 1977.
18. Fox, R. C., and Swazey, J. P.: The courage to fail: a social view of organ transplants and dialysis, ed. 2, rev., Chicago, 1978, University of Chicago Press.
19. Fry, J.: Profiles of disease: a study in the natural history of common diseases, London, 1966, E. & S. Livingstone.
20. Garfield, S. R.: The delivery of medical care, Sci. Am. 222:15-23, 1970.
21. Goffman, E.: Stigma, Harmondsworth, England, 1968, Penguin Books Ltd.
22. Goffman, E.: The presentation of self in everyday life, London, 1969, The Penguin Press.

23. Gorovitz, S., Jameton, A. L., Macklin, R., et al, editors: Moral problems in medicine, Englewood Cliffs, N.J., 1976, Prentice-Hall, Inc.
24. Haggerty, R. J.: The boundaries of health care, Pharos 35:106, 1972.
25. Haight, R. O., McKee, C. A., and Barkmeier, J. R.: Morbidity in the first year of a family practice and its comparison to the Virginia study, J. Fam. Pract. 9:295-299, 1979.
26. Howie, L. J., and Drury, T. F.: Current estimates from the health interview survey, DHEW Publication no. (PHS) 78-1554, Washington, D.C., 1979, National Center for Health Statistics.
27. Illich, I.: Medical nemesis, London, 1975, Calder & Boyars Ltd.
28. Institute of Medicine: A manpower policy for primary care, Washington, D.C., 1978, National Academy of Sciences.
29. Jones, R. K., and Jones, P.: Sociology in medicine, New York, 1975, John Wiley & Sons, Inc.
30. Kass, L. R.: Regarding the end of medicine and the pursuit of health, The Public Interest 40:11, 1975.
31. Kittrie, N. N.: The right to be different: deviance and enforced therapy, Baltimore, 1971, The Johns Hopkins University Press.
32. Knowles, J. H.: The responsibility of the individual, Daedalus 106:57, 1977.
33. Lee, P. R., LeRoy, L., Stalcup, J., and Beck, J.: Primary care in a specialized world, Cambridge, Mass., 1976, Ballinger Publishing Co.
34. Lefton, M., Skipper, J. K., and McCaghy, C. H., editors: Approaches to deviance, New York, 1968, Appleton-Century-Crofts.
35. Levine, R. J.: Foreword: the traditional medical model. In Miller, M. G., and Schworm, M. B., editors: Mental illness and the problem of boundaries, Washington, D.C., 1979, Medicine in the Public Interest, Inc.
36. Levine, S., and Kozloff, M. A.: The sick role: an assessment and overview, Annu. Rev. Sociol. 4:317, 1978.
37. Mann, K. J., Medalie, J. H., Lieber, E., Groen, J. J., and Guttman, L.: Visits to doctors, Jerusalem, 1970, Academic Press, Inc.
38. Marsland, D. W., Wood, M., and Mayo, F.: A data bank for patient care, curriculum, and research in family practice: 526,196 patient problems, J. Fam. Pract. 3:25-28, 1976.
39. Medalie, J. H., editor: Family medicine, Baltimore, 1978, The Williams & Wilkins Co.
40. Miller, L. G.: Healthy, wealthy, and wise: an essay review of doing better and feeling worse: health in the United States, Soc. Sci. Med. 12:429, 1978.
41. National Center for Health Statistics: The national ambulatory medical care survey: 1975 summary, D.H.E.W. Publication no. (PHS) 78-1784, Washington, D.C., 1978, U.S. Government Printing Office.
42. Noble, J., editor: Primary care and the practice of medicine, Boston, 1976, Little, Brown & Co.
43. Parsons, T.: The social system, Glencoe, Ill., 1951, The Free Press.
44. Parsons, T.: The sick role and the role of the physician reconsidered, Milbank, Mem. Fund Q. 53:257-278, 1975.
45. Pellegrino, E. D.: The anatomy of clinical judgments: some notes on right reason and right action (unpublished manuscript).
46. Pellegrino, E. D.: The social ethics of primary care: the relationship between a human need and an obligation of society, Mt. Sinai J. Med. 45:593-601, 1978.
47. Proger, S., and Williams, G.: A career in primary care, Cambridge, Mass., 1976, Ballinger Publishing Co.
48. Reiser, S. J., Dyck, A. J., and Curran, W. L., editors: Ethics in medicine, Cambridge, Mass., 1977, Massachusetts Institute of Technology Press.
49. Rosenhan, D. L.: On being sane in insane places, Science 179:250-258, 1973.
50. Roueche, B., editor: Together: a casebook of joint practices in primary care, Chicago, 1977, National Joint Practice Commission.
51. Royal College of General Practitioners: Present state and future needs, London, 1970.
52. Scheff, T. J.: Decision rules, types of error, and their consequences in medical diagnosis, Behav. Sci. 8:97, 1963.
53. Scheff, T. J.: Mental illness and social process, New York, 1967, Harper & Row, Publishers, Inc.
54. Schwartz, W. B., Gorry, G. A., Kassirer, J. P., et al.: Decision analysis and clinical judgment, Am. J. Med. 55:459-472, 1973.
55. Scott, R. A.: The making of blind men, New York, 1969, Russell Sage Foundation.
56. Scott, R. A.: Lecture on deviance, Boston University School of Medicine, May 1978.

57. Sedgwick, P.: Illness—mental and otherwise, Hastings Cent. Stud. 1:19, 1973.

58. Shuval, J. T.: Primary care and social control, Med. Care 17:631-638, 1979.

59. Szasz, T.: The myth of mental illness, London, 1972, Paladin Books.

60. Veatch, R. M., and Branson, R., editors: Ethics and health policy, Cambridge, Mass., 1976, Ballinger Publishing Co.

61. White, K. L., Williams, T. F., and Greenberg, B. G.: The ecology of medical care, N. Engl. J. Med. 265:885-892, 1961.

62. White, K. L.: Life and death and medicine. In Life and death and medicine, San Francisco, 1973, W. H. Freeman & Co. Publishers.

63. World Health Organization: Preamble to the constitution of the World Health Organization, Basic Documents, ed. 26, Geneva, 1976, World Health Organization.

64. World Medical Association: Declaration of Geneva, World Med. Assoc. Bull. 1:109, 1948.

65. Zola, I. K.: Culture and symptoms: an analysis of patients' presenting complaints, Am. Soc. Rev. 31:615-630, 1966.

Part II

PHYSICIANS AND PATIENTS

Chapter 5

The doctor-patient relationship

The delivery of medical care in the United States today takes place in many different settings. At one extreme we find desperately sick patients, surrounded by sophisticated medical technology and a cadre of experts, receiving treatment in an intensive care unit in a large medical center. At the other extreme medical care consists of a physician or other provider and a layman coming together in a small, private setting. They are brought together by a problem that is usually not life-threatening and for which there is often little relevant technology. Regardless of the setting or the medical problem, however, provider-patient interactions are at the core of medical practice. These interactions or relationships* take many forms, involve increasingly a variety of providers, and focus on an ever-expanding array of human ills, biologic, psychologic, and even social.

Many contemporary discussions of medical practice, its successes, and problems tend to focus either on the technology of modern medicine or on the systems of medical care delivery that have evolved in our society. In this chapter we take a more microscopic view of medical care and examine provider-patient relationships, relationships that are at the "hub" of medical care regardless of the technology involved or the specific system of delivery.

Students in medical school today may find a few lectures and occasionally a seminar devoted to the topic of "the doctor-patient relationship." But in general the central vehicle for the delivery of medical care in our country—the doctor-patient relationship—is given little attention in most medical schools. This may be the case for several reasons. First, some assume that doctors will naturally learn to establish effective doctor-patient relationships without any specific training or effort. Second, others assert that since effective doctor-patient relationships involve more art than science, it is difficult if not impossible to teach such skills to students.

---

*It is customary in writing about medical care providers and those seeking such care to speak of the "doctor-patient relationship." Such a title is too narrow, however, to describe the variety of parties that can be involved in the delivery of medical care today. Also, as will become evident in this chapter, sometimes a "relationship" exists, but often the encounter is simply an exchange or short encounter, with little of the involvement suggested by the term "relationship." Nevertheless we will often use the term "relationship" because of its familiarity, but restrict our use to mean a meeting of a provider and a lay person without any assumption about the permanency or involvement of provider and patient.

Regardless of the merits of such assumptions, which many would challenge, Americans frequently are not satisfied with the encounters they have with their physicians. In particular, they are dissatisfied with the interpersonal and educative skills of their providers. Such skills apparently do not come naturally nor for that matter even with experience. And, as this and the following chapter will make clear, patient satisfaction is not the only outcome dependent on a doctor's knowledge about and skill in developing effective doctor-patient relationships.

For example, a provider's understanding of the provider-patient relationship and skill in understanding, motivating, and educating patients can play a decisive role in determining a patient's medical status. And it is a patient's medical status, not simply the medical knowledge of the providers or the technology at their disposal, that is one important criterion by which we should judge the effectiveness of our medical care system.

We begin our discussion with an analysis and critique of traditional views of doctor-patient relationships in medicine in the United States. Next, we review a variety of studies on doctor-patient encounters, attempting to locate what appear to be recurring problems in doctor-patient encounters that impede the realization of the potential inherent in these relationships. Finally, we conclude this chapter by exploring several developments in our society, such as the consumer movement, increasing legal pressure for informed consent, and the changing organizational base of medical care, considering how such developments may be providing new frameworks for doctor-patient encounters.

As is evident, this chapter will have a selective focus. It deals exclusively with doctor-patient relationships that take place within the formal, institutionalized medical care system, and we focus more on doctor-patient encounters in ambulatory care than in institutional settings. Also, we discuss relationships between doctors and patients, with only limited attention given to nurse-patient and doctor-nurse-patient relationships. We provide no discussion of lay encounters with medical or health care providers outside the formal medical system (e.g., faith healers). This selective focus is suggested both by the centrality of the doctor-patient relationship in the formal medical care system and by the fact that much of the research in this area has been on doctor-patient encounters, with relatively little attention given to other provider-patient encounters.

Visiting the doctor

In the previous chapter we learned that in 1977 there were an estimated 570 million visits made to office-based, nonfederally employed physicians in the conterminous United States. This means that on average each person in the United States made about three visits to physicians' offices during that year. Almost 60% of these visits were to physicians in solo practice and the remaining 40% were to physicians in partnerships and group practices.[22]

A summary of the types of physicians visited in 1977 is presented in Table 10.

Table 10. Number and percent distribution of office visits by physician specialty and type and location of practice: United States, 1977*

Physician characteristic	Number of visits in thousands	Percent distribution
All visits	570,052	100.0
Physician specialty		
General and family practice	222,919	39.1
Medical specialties	155,501	27.3
Internal medicine	64,959	11.4
Pediatrics	54,762	9.6
Other	35,780	6.3
Surgical specialties	167,927	29.5
General surgery	36,124	6.3
Obstetrics and gynecology	49,273	8.6
Other	82,530	14.0
Other specialties	23,705	4.2
Psychiatry	16,197	2.8
Other	7,508	1.3
Type of practice		
Solo	335,261	58.8
Other†	234,791	41.2
Location of practice		
Metropolitan	434,739	76.3
Nonmetropolitan	135,313	23.7

*From Koch, H., and McLemore, J.: Advancedata **48**:3, 1979.
†Includes partnership and group practices.

As can be seen, 39.1% of visits were to general and family practitioners, 11.4% were to internists, and 9.6% were to pediatricians. These constitute the core primary care "specialties" and together account for about 60% of visits to physicians' offices.

Of the estimated 570 million visits in 1977 almost 60% were for an "old" problem. About 85% of the visits were return visits to a physician the patient had seen previously, and 95% of the time the patient was self-referred.

The National Ambulatory Medical Care Survey, from which the preceding data are taken, suggests that although Americans visit their physicians about three times a year, they spend relatively little time with physicians at each of these visits. For example, the mean duration for an average office visit in 1977 was 15.4 minutes in actual face-to-face contact between the patient and the physician. A more refined breakdown reveals that about 17% of office visits lasted 5 minutes or less, 47% lasted 10 minutes or less, 74% lasted 15 minutes or less, and 94% lasted 30 minutes or less; only 6% lasted more than 30 minutes.[22]

The observation that almost 50% of doctor-patient encounters take up to only 10 minutes and 75% take 15 minutes or less suggests that most encounters are very focused and must deal with a rather limited number of problems or concerns. In light of this it is interesting to recall from Chapter 4 the wide array of responsibilities, including not just diagnosis, prognosis, and treatment but patient education, counseling, and advice giving, that are being ascribed by some to medicine. It is difficult to see how such a wide assortment of activities could be accomplished in such relatively short periods of time. Moreover, it would also appear difficult for both providers and patients to get to know each other or to establish a relationship on the basis of such short encounters, even if they recur periodically over time. What is clear is that doctor-patient encounters are usually relatively brief, and if a doctor is to be effective, he or she must be skilled at using this time to provide the patient with the best medical care.

A reading of any of the numerous National Ambulatory Medical Care Survey reports would reveal many more statistical generalizations about physician office visits.

But statistical summaries provide only a skeleton view of doctor-patient encounters. A more detailed view requires exploring a variety of cultural, social, and medical factors as they affect doctor-patient relationships.

From Greek pantheon to consumer magazines

The authority that doctors can exercise in doctor-patient encounters, and even in society at large, has been termed *Aesculapian authority*.[37] Aesculapius, the first physician according to Greek legend, was eventually elevated to the Greek pantheon of gods and, along with Hygeia and Panacea, ruled over health and illness in Greek mythology.

Associating the authority of physicians with that of the gods reflects an attitude about physicians seen in much writing concerning physicians and what transpires when physicians and patients meet. Clearly, physicians have been viewed as a powerful, influential class in our society, a group of highly educated experts whose activities involve life and death decisions and whose motives and activities are often assumed to be technically and ethically beyond question or assessment by lay people.

However, alongside this view one must place an increasing chorus of voices that talk about doctors and doctor-patient encounters from a much different viewpoint. For example, a 1978 issue of a consumer magazine carried an article on how to select physicians, how to relate to them, and what to expect.[20] In addition, numerous books have appeared recently, some written by physicians such as *Managing Your Doctor*,[13] that attempt to educate the public about contemporary medicine, its benefits and pitfalls. Often these books give the distinct impression that a wise patient should approach physicians carefully and use their counsel and ministrations judiciously.*

---

*The subtitles to various sections in Freese's book, *Managing Your Doctor*, clearly suggest that a patient must exercise caution in seeking and using medical advice. For example, three section subtitles in his book read: "What you must know to protect yourself in dealing with doctors, hospitals, dentists, and medical emergencies;" "Special problems in managing your doctor: how to keep yourself safe from medical mayhem;" and "Doctor talk and what it really means to you."

Such examples suggest that public expectations of medicine generally, and of physicians in particular, are becoming more complex and perhaps less idealistic and sanguine. As such, the physician entering the medical care marketplace over the next few years can expect to find a mixture of positive and negative beliefs among patients about medicine and physicians. To operate effectively in such a complex environment the physician must be increasingly sensitive to patients' values and expectations.

Whether viewed simply as purveyors of a "consumable" service who must be approached with suspicion or as relatives of a distant mythical Greek god or both, however, there are regularities in how physicians relate to patients when they meet about a medical problem. A number of sociologists have attempted to describe regularities in doctor-patient encounters, and in so doing they have provided us with a perspective on how doctor-patient encounters may vary depending on factors such as the ethnicity of the patient, the nature of the medical problem involved, and the setting in which the encounters occur.

Sick patients and active physicians

Certainly one of the most common, if not the most idealized, views of the doctor-patient relationship in our society is that of an acutely sick person seeking out a knowledgeable doctor who provides necessary medical care and advice to return the patient to health. Such a view underlies one of the earliest and most influential formulations of doctor-patient interactions in sociologic literature.

In a treatise in which he was attempting to present a formal, conceptual view of society and the professions generally, Parsons[30] used medical professionals and their relationships to their patients as the basis for developing a model view of how professionals relate to lay people. Parsons found it useful to view the patient and the physician as occupying social roles that have certain expectations about obligatory behavior associated with them, as well as privileges that the role occupants could enjoy.

Parsons argued that patients can be seen as occupying a "sick" role and physicians a "professional" role. The sick role, Parsons held, imposes on the patient the obligations shown in Table 11—namely, the patient must be motivated to get well, must seek technically competent help, and must trust that the physician will do what is in the best interests of the patient. At least two "privileges" go along with these obligations. First, the patient will be exempted, under some conditions, from performing certain aspects of normal social obligations. For example, the person will not be expected to go to work or perform certain chores around the house. Second, it is assumed that patients are not ill because of some action on their part but because of events beyond their control. In short, patients are not held responsible for their sick status.

Looking at the professional role Parsons suggested that the physician is expected

Table 11. Parsons' view of the patient and professional roles comprising the doctor-patient relationship*†

Patient	Doctor
Sick role	**Professional role**
Obligation to	Obligation to
Be motivated to get well	Act for the welfare of the patient
Seek technically competent help	Be guided by the rules of professional behavior
Trust the doctor or to accept the competence gap	Apply high degree of achieved skill and knowledge to problems of illness
	Be objective and emotionally detached
	Engage in professional self-regulation
Privileges	Privileges
Exemption from performance of normal social obligations	Access to physical and personal intimacy
Exemption from responsibility for one's own health state	Professional dominance

*From Parsons, T.: The social system, New York, 1951, The Free Press. Copyright 1951 by Talcott Parsons. Reprinted by permission of The Free Press.
†Premise: "Modern medicine is organized about the application of scientific knowledge to the problems of illness and health and to the control of disease."

to (1) act for the welfare of the patient; (2) treat all patients in a professional manner; (3) apply professional skills and knowledge as competently as possible; and (4) not get emotionally involved with the patients.

In terms of privileges a physician is granted access to the complete person, both physically and psychologically, for medical purposes, can exercise a large degree of autonomy in applying expertise, and, because of technical expertise, can exercise dominance over other types of professional medical care providers.

One could, of course, list additional assumptions that seem to apply to doctor-patient relationships, for example, patients should not become emotionally involved with physicians and patients should tell doctors the truth, even if it is embarrassing.

Underlying Parsons' view is the position that physicians have technical competencies that they will employ and that patients lack this expertise. In other words there is a "competency gap" between the expert physician and the lay patient. This competency gap serves, first, to establish the relationship in that the patient seeks out the more knowledgeable physician for advice and help. And the competency gap also serves to shape in part how the interaction between physician and patient proceeds. More specifically, Parsons held, the competency gap produces a basic asymmetry in doctor-patient relationships.

Because physicians know more about illness, its etiology, development, and treatment, they tend to dominate or control the relationship with a patient, defining what the problem is and deciding what should be done.

And, as Parsons and some of his students have argued, the asymmetry found in the doctor-patient relationship rests not just on the assumed knowledge gap

Table 12. The three basic models in the Szasz-Hollander conceptualization of the doctor-patient relationship*

Model	Physician's role	Patient's role	Clinical application of model	Prototype of model
Activity-passivity	Does something to patient	Recipient (unable to respond or inert)	Anesthesia, acute trauma, delirium, coma, etc.	Parent-infant
Guidance-cooperation	Tells patient what to do	Cooperator (obeys)	Acute infectious processes, etc.	Parent-child (adolescent)
Mutual participation	Helps patient to help himself	Participant in "partnership" (uses expert help)	Most chronic illnesses, psychoanalysis, etc.	Adult-adult

*From Szasz, T. S., and Hollander, M. H.: Arch. Intern. Med. **97:**585-592, 1956. Copyright 1956 by the American Medical Association.

between doctor and patient. There is an emotional basis for the more powerful position of the physician as well.[31] Parsons and Fox claim illness itself can make a person dependent. Not only is the person often incapacitated by illness, but our culture teaches us that "regression" to a state of dependency is, within limits, not only acceptable but to some degree expected of those who are seriously ill.[31]

Some examples of situations in which the doctor-patient relationship can have many of the attributes Parsons claims it has are provided by Szasz and Hollander.[42] These authors have suggested three basic behavioral models of the doctor-patient relationship, as shown in Table 12. The first two situations seem to reflect very much a Parsonian view. At one extreme the doctor-patient relationship may consist of *activity* on the part of the doctor and total *passivity* on the part of the patient. An example they give is that of a patient in a coma being treated by a physician. Clearly the patient cannot participate, and the physician totally controls the events, providing a diagnosis and initiating therapy.

The second Szasz and Hollander model is called the *guidance-cooperation* model. Here the patient is conscious, as in the case of a person with an acute infection, and is active by cooperating with the physician in following a prescribed regimen.

Finally, Szasz and Hollander, going somewhat beyond Parsons, posit a *mutual participation* model. Here, as illustrated by the case of diabetes, the physician is viewed as entering into a partnership with a patient to control a medical problem, one usually of a chronic nature that requires the patient to actively pursue a life-style or regimen that only he or she ultimately can control.

The Szasz and Hollander models are interesting in two respects. First, all three models reflect to some degree a view of the fundamental asymmetry in these encounters that Parsons asserted. For example, in all three models the physician is active in defining and regulating the encounter, even in the third model in which the patient "participates."

Second, Szasz and Hollander do not seem to entertain the possibility that a patient may be as active as and at times exercise as much or even more power than the physician. This view of asymmetric power is consistent with a Parsonian position.

In short, Parsons offers a conceptual picture of doctor-patient relationships in which there is a fundamental imbalance in power, with the doctor largely controlling the interaction. This asymmetry rests on the difference in knowledge, as well as emotional factors. And added to this is a complementarity in the attitudes and motivations of the patient and the physician as they approach encounters. As Table 11 suggests, patients theoretically approach the encounter with expectations and values that complement the values and expectations of the physician.

If the picture Parsons provides of the doctor-patient relationship is accurate, then we would expect most doctor-patient encounters to work well and the doctor and patient to cooperate. Patients would be motivated to get well. They would readily provide all the necessary information about their illness to the physician and trust and follow the advice and admonitions of their physician. The physician in turn would always be able to do something about the patient's problem and could count on the patient to disclose all relevant facts.

As might be expected, however, this is not always the case. Doctor-patient encounters are far more complex. Nevertheless, the Parsonian view of doctor-patient encounters, or major elements of it, has stimulated much social and behavioral science research on doctor-patient relationships. These studies suggest that major changes in or additions to the view put forth by Parsons must be made if we are to understand the diversity and richness of contemporary provider-patient interactions.

First, Kassebaum and Bauman[21] suggested that Parsons' model has more applicability for acute disease episodes than for chronic diseases. Clearly, in the case of such things as appendicitis, pneumonia, or severe bodily trauma, many of the characteristics Parsons attributed to the sick role seem to be important. For example, acutely ill patients are dependent on physicians for immediate, intensive care that they would be hard pressed to find outside the formal medical care system. And in such situations there is little that patients can do for themselves. Also, of course, in the examples given the physician can in fact actively intervene in the patients' behalf in very effective ways.

On the other hand, for nonacute or chronic conditions the sick role as defined by Parsons seems to have less applicability. For example, in chronic conditions such as diabetes the patient must become responsible for much of his or her medical care.[5] Accordingly, the physician must provide the patient with medical knowledge that is not as necessary when the patient is acutely ill. The patient thus acquires some technical competency and in so doing becomes less dependent on the physician than Parsons' view would seem to suggest.

In other types of medical conditions or situations, not necessarily chronic, some of the characteristics Parsons attributed to the role of the patient do not seem as applicable. For example, people who are labeled mentally ill vary markedly in the degree to which they are willing to view themselves as sick and adopt the patient role.[33] Also, there is variation in the extent to which mentally ill people are viewed by society as responsible for their illness[24] and hence are accorded the privileges accruing to those "legitimately" sick.

Likewise there is variation in our society in beliefs about whether a number of conditions like drug abuse and alcoholism are or are not diseases and whether individuals who have such conditions or exhibit such behaviors are or are not sick.[24] Again it is not clear whether alcoholics or drug abusers are held responsible for their problem and, accordingly, both society and physicians respond in a variety of ways to people with such problems.

Another class of disorders for which the patient role delineated by Parsons does not seem fully applicable is physical disabilities. For example, a number of studies* suggest that people do not view the physically disabled in the same ways in which they view people who are acutely sick. More specifically, the physically disabled may be viewed as occupying an impaired role, and there is often considerable pressure on the impaired to live normal lives and perform normal activities within certain limits.[19]

In short, there is extensive literature that suggests that, on one hand, Parsons' notions about the social role of the sick patient have utility, especially for individuals who are acutely ill. On the other hand, it is equally clear that Parsons' formulation has limited ability to be generalized. Physicians and patients meet over a large and ever-expanding array of diseases, disorders, and problems. Sometimes the patient is ill but at other times is not or has a problem or concern that is not clearly a "medical" problem. As such, depending on the disease or disorder, physician and patient may be approaching their respective roles in a variety of ways, sometimes reflecting the asymmetry in power and complementarity of expectations suggested by Parsons and sometimes not.

Research also suggests that conditions other than the nature of the disease or disorder may affect both lay and professional approaches to the doctor-patient relationship. In reviewing the literature on lay perceptions Levine and Kosloff[25] suggest that there is much variability in how the public views the sick role and, concomitantly, the patient role. They suggest that it may not be useful to view people with various problems as either sick or not sick but rather to view them as occupying various positions between being sick and being well. In fact, they suggest that we view the movement between these two end points as a temporal process in which a person may move back and forth among at least five "stages" between being sick

---

*References 4, 19, 27, 43, and 44.

or well.[25] First, there is a "well" state, the meaning of which may vary among different cultural or social groups. Second, a person may move into a transition state in which the person or others around him may perceive an illness, impairment, or disability. These perceptions also can vary by social and cultural group.[48]

Third, the person so labeled or self-described as such may respond or "cope" in various ways, ranging from denial to seeking nonprofessional help to contacting a physician.[25] Once again cultural factors are important in shaping various responses to illness. For example, looking again at different ethnic groups, research suggests that Italians are likely to seek help when a health problem interferes with their interpersonal lives, whereas Anglo-Saxon Protestants are more likely to seek help when a problem interferes with their work and/or physical activities.[49]

Fourth, the person may perform a sick role and become a patient, but the exact nature and duration of this role will depend on many factors, including the nature of the disorder and the patient's social and cultural background. And finally, the person will either get better and return to the well state or may establish a permanent sick or impaired role.

For the physician the preceding discussion suggests that, although there are a few general notions about illness and a socially acceptable response to it, in our society there is considerable diversity in the ways in which members of society and various groups within society respond to illness and enact the patient role. As a corollary, when a patient appears in a physician's office, that appearance may be at any point in the several stages suggested, from a routine visit for a "well" person to one in which the patient has self-diagnosed and self-treated a longtime problem. As such, the physician may be the first or only the latest in a long list of sources of help the patient has sought. And the way in which the patients relate to the physician and in turn expect the physician to relate to them will be very much shaped by these prior experiences.

In sum, it may be useful to think of there being many "sick roles" instead of a common society-wide sick role. And one consequence is that the expectations and attitudes of patients, which Parsons thought defined in part the doctor-patient encounter in our society, may in fact not be as consistent as Parsons would have us believe.

Given that different lay people approach the role of being sick and being a patient differently, what about medical care providers? Do different providers approach their role as provider similarly, or is there variation? This issue has been studied far less extensively than the issue of how lay people vary in their approach to the patient role. The research that has been done suggests that in fact there is variation, which may condition the manner in which the provider goes about enacting the provider-patient role with the patient.

Perhaps one of the more sustained efforts to understand and describe factors conditioning how professional health care providers approach their work has been in the efforts of Freidson,[14-16,18] the medical sociologist. Looking in particular at how the setting in which physicians work conditions how they practice, Freidson has drawn our attention to the importance of organizational and setting factors in shaping physician activities. At the same time, Freidson's work encompasses a general critique of the model of the doctor-patient relationship provided by Parsons. Moreover, Freidson has suggested important modification of at least four major points in Parsons' work.[3] First, Freidson argues, Parsons' view gives ascendency to the physician's perspective at the cost of ignoring the often varying expectations of the patient, the patient's family, and other health care providers. The model assumes too much complementarity in expectations between physician and patient.

Second, the expectations Parsons posits are just that—expectations. They do not necessarily describe what actually transpires when physician and patient meet. Third, the situation in which doctor and patient meet, solo versus referral-based practice, for example, is important in shaping doctor-patient behavior, not just the expectations of the two parties involved.

Fourth, Freidson claims that the view put forth by Parsons ignores the almost necessary conflict that exists when two parties meet, each with its own definition of the situation and views about what should or should not be done.

In short, Freidson, unlike Parsons, emphasizes the potential for a "clash of perspectives" in the doctor-patient relationship.[3] Freidson argues as though the physician and patient are from two cultures instead of one, as Parsons would assert, and a necessary corollary is that physician and patient must work out or negotiate their interaction.[1]

Freidson and others like him who emphasize the potential for conflict or disagreement in this social encounter do not assert that conflict or disagreement is always present. Rather the occurrence of conflict depends on a variety of situational factors growing in part out of the different values and perspectives that physician and patient bring to the encounter, as well as features of the situation in which physician and patient meet.

For example, in a study titled *Patients' Views of Medical Practice*, Freidson[15] described what he calls the "lay referral structure," the sources of information, advice, and support that a lay person may use prior to actually seeing a physician. The perspective that a person may acquire in this lay referral structure may or may not coincide with the prevailing cultural conceptions of the sick role and may or may not correspond with the perspective of the physician.

A second source of potential conflict resides in the very structure of how medical care is organized. For example, Freidson has drawn a distinction between "client-dependent" practices and "professional-dependent" arrangements. A patient-dependent practice, typified by a physician in solo practice, is one in which a physician is dependent on patients seeking his or her services. As such, Freidson argues, there is considerable pressure on the physician to provide not only good technical medical care but also a strong incentive to structure services to please patients generally. Satisfying patients means that patients are more likely to return for additional medical services and thus become part of the physician's established practice. In such a situation one would assume that physicians would try to please patients and in so doing reduce the potential for conflict or disagreement over a diagnosis or therapy.

Conversely, Freidson has identified a second, less frequent, but growing type of practice arrangement: a professional-dependent practice. In these situations, typified by a specialty or subspecialty practice, the physician is not totally dependent on patients to seek him or her out. Instead the physician is often dependent on other physicians to provide patients via referrals. Accordingly, the incentive for doctors in these practice arrangements, Freidson argues, is to be perhaps less concerned with the nontechnical aspects of the doctor-patient encounter, that is, pleasing patients, and more with what the referring doctors might think of the services provided. In short, this would imply great concern with the technical aspects of care. As such, there would appear to be a greater potential for conflict or disagreement with the patients in such relationships because the physician is oriented more to the referring physician than to the patient directly.

In short, Freidson and others[28,36,39] suggest, in opposition to Parsons, that there are cultural, structural, and even organizational arrangements in the delivery of medical care that make conflict or disagreement between professional and client in the doctor-patient relationship more or less likely. Patients and physicians do not always share a common cultural set of expectations and at times they may have significantly different interests in what transpires when they come together for medical care.

Although there is considerable literature on the doctor-patient relationship that we have not discussed, much of this literature reflects the major themes that we have already covered. From the perspective of the physician in training, the previous discussion suggests that physicians can expect only some very general similarities in the ways in which patients will approach the sick role and the role of being a patient. What this implies in turn is that only within certain broad limits can the physician in practice assume that a variety of patients, under varying circumstances and in different settings, will share a common perspective on what physicians should or should not do and correspondingly what patients should or should not do. Accordingly, each encounter presents something new as well as something old to the medical practitioner, who must be prepared to understand this novelty to provide effective medical care.

Communication in doctor-patient relationships

The discussion so far has provided us with some perspective on how lay people and professionals as well may vary in their views of the doctor-patient relationship.

What happens now when lay person and physician bring their particular perspectives into the doctor-patient relationship? What types of problems emerge, and what appear to be the sources of most problems? In this next section we turn our attention to communication in the doctor-patient relationship, a topic that permits us to explore the doctor-patient relationship in even more detail.

There is considerable evidence that Americans have much confidence in their physicians, particularly in physicians' technical skills. And most Americans assume that physicians will attempt to do whatever will benefit the patient. For example, a 1973 national survey of noninstitutionalized adults revealed that more than three out of four of those questioned agreed with the statement: "Most doctors put helping the patient above everything else."[9]

But at the same time the survey disclosed that about half the people questioned agreed with the statement: "The medical profession concentrates too much on science and not enough on people." In part the response to these statements reveals what numerous other studies have revealed. Although Americans are usually satisfied with the technical aspects of their medical care, there is often dissatisfaction with the nontechnical aspects and in particular with the relationships patients establish with their medical care providers.

In reviewing such studies it seems that patients are looking for at least two things when they meet with a physician. First, of course, they want a physician who is technically competent. Accuracy in diagnosis and implementation or recommendation of an effective treatment regimen is the sine qua non of medical care. At the same time, however, patients are seeking physicians who are considerate, sensitive, and, above all, interested in the patient and the problem.

Not only do patients hold these expectations for their encounters with physicians, but they often make decisions to continue or discontinue seeing a particular physician on the basis of whether or not the physician meets these expectations. For example, in one community-based study of women by Mechanic it was found that among the people sampled, about one third reported having changed their medical care provider or clinic because of dissatisfaction with the provider. Among the most frequently given reasons for dissatisfaction were (1) the patient sensed a lack of interest by the physician in the problem and (2) the physician made an incorrect diagnosis or instituted an unsuccessful treatment.[29]

Clearly, this study suggests patients want both technical competency and interest by the physician in their problems.*

The Mechanic study turned up an additional observation, however, perhaps

---

*The word "interest" is, of course, vague and can refer to multiple behaviors. Mechanic asked the participants in his study what they meant when they talked about a doctor who is interested in his patient. Among the items listed were: cares about you and your family; gives you sufficient time; calls you or asks you to call him; is respectful; sympathetic; thoughtful; listens; explains; and knows your history.

even more important than documenting that patients want more than technical proficiency from their providers. The reason most frequently given by patients in this study for being dissatisfied with a physician and seeking care elsewhere was that the physician "failed to do what seemed indicated."[29] This response suggests that a significant number of patients, at least in this study, came to their physician with a diagnosis, however tentative, and perhaps even some tentative notions about what should be done. And, regardless of the accuracy of such lay diagnoses, when the physician's diagnosis, prognosis, or treatment did not match and presumably when the patient was not educated as to the reasons for the difference, there was marked patient dissatisfaction.

Studies of this kind suggest that a not uncommon problem in doctor-patient relationships is lack of communication between patient and provider about each other's expectations and a mutual failure to explain the assumptions and rationales underlying their own behavior.

It is important to emphasize that effective communication leads to more than patient satisfaction. In analyzing the role of effective doctor-patient communication Waitzken and Stockle[47] have outlined at least four major consequences of effective communication on the delivery of effective medical care.

First, they note, effective communication can increase the accuracy and hence the value of history taking. Certainly history taking is one of the more important aspects of clinical medicine. To the extent that the physician is not capable of obtaining accurate and complete information, there is the chance that the physician cannot benefit the patient as fully as possible.

Second, effective communication can lead to more useful medical records. As medical care shifts from a one-on-one model to more group practice arrangements where a patient may be seen by not one but several different providers across time, the medical record takes on increased importance as a method of communication among the various providers involved. Accurate information gathered in each provider-patient encounter and accurately entered in patient records can increase the level of knowledge among providers and improve the effectiveness of their joint efforts.

Third, effective communication of information in doctor-patient encounters can lead to better patient compliance with therapeutic regimens. As will be discussed in detail in Chapter 6, of what value is the training, sophistication, and technology of modern medical practitioners if patients, or a substantial number of them, do not follow through on the physician's advice or directives? More effective communication in doctor-patient encounters can improve patient compliance.

Fourth, as we will see, there is evidence that effective communication not only increases patient satisfaction and compliance but, in certain situations, it appears to improve patients' psychologic and even physiologic reactions to certain medical interventions.

Finally, as the mandate of medicine has broadened to encompass not just acute, life-threatening disease or injury episodes but care of chronic disease and even prevention of illness as well, the role of communication with patients has broadened. To be effective today the physician must be an *educator* as well as a *diagnostician* and *healer*. And to be an effective educator requires skill in communication.

A recent discussion of doctor-patient relationships referred to the "two cultures" that may constitute this interaction.[45] Emphasizing the basis for potential conflict, disagreement, or dissatisfaction, this discussion draws attention to the fact that an effective, satisfying doctor-patient relationship takes effort on the part of both the doctor and the patient.

The basis for problems developing in the doctor-patient relationship resides in more than ethnic and sociocultural differences between doctor and patient discussed previously. In focusing more specifically on doctor-patient interactions we find it useful to build on this theme of "two cultures," a *professional* as well as a *patient culture*.

Professional culture refers to the attitudes, values, and behaviors that physicians bring with them or have reinforced by the situation in which they deliver medical care. The values and behaviors of providers reflect their personal beliefs and experiences, but perhaps even more so the impact of their professional training, particular experiences, and professional situations. There are inherent in patient and professional cultures, then, as we are viewing them here, the grounds for developing both effective as well as ineffective communication. And, paradoxical as it may be, the very thing that usually brings a patient and a physician together, the competency gap between the two, may result in ineffective communication.

To explore these ideas a little further we need to examine doctor-patient relationships in more detail. In the opening section of this chapter we discussed how sociocultural factors and the lay referral system can shape patients' responses to illness episodes and in turn help to define their concerns and expectations if and when they contact a physician. Drawing our observations together they suggest that many patients approach their physicians with what we may call an "agenda." Included in this agenda will be culturally and socially shaped expectations about how physicians should behave generally. In addition, there will be concerns of the patients about their problems or reasons for seeing a physician as well as, sometimes, a lay or self-diagnosis about what the problems are, their origins, and what should be done. With the exception of encounters involving routine physicals and follow-up visits, patients will not usually seek the help of medical care providers unless they are experiencing problems that disrupt their lives in one way or another. Hence patients will have varying levels of emotional involvement in and concern about their problems. Clearly, the agendas patients bring to their doctor-patient encounters are very complex.

Doctors also will approach the doctor-patient relationship with an agenda, though undoubtedly there will be considerable variation in the agendas of different types of medical care providers and even among different types of medical specialists. However, when we consider physicians providing primary care, we may nevertheless highlight some of the more salient issues that we suspect are common to most physicians' agendas.

The ways in which doctors approach the doctor-patient relationship reflect many things. Certainly professional socialization instills some attitudes and values about what is important and what is unimportant in meeting with patients. Likewise there are legal requirements that shape their behavior and time demands, particular organizational or setting characteristics, and even personal attitudes that condition their behavior in encounters with patients.

Perhaps one of the most pervasive aspects of professional culture physicians bring to patient encounters grows out of the orientation to their work acquired in much of their training. In 1910 Flexner[11] published a report on the quality of medical education in the United States. This report was significant not only for the severe critique it offered of extant medical education; more importantly, it provided a blueprint for medical education that has shaped it up through today. The Flexner Report provided both a mission and a method for American medical educators. The mission was to make physicians scientists. The method was to model American medical education after the German and British models.

The specifics of this reform are not important for us here. What is important is that this reform took hold, and the mission of medical education—the physician as scientist and medicine as applied science—became the dominant organizing principle for American medical curricula. Basic science became the first and most pervasive aspect of a physician's training and, accordingly, physicians came to look on medicine largely as applied science. The model of being a physician was to treat each patient and each patient's problem as a scientific problem and to proceed or search for solutions in a scientific manner. The more narrow and precisely defined the problem, the more likely one could be scientific in solving it.

Added to this has been the movement toward specialization within medicine.[41] Although specialization unquestionably has the potential for making physicians competent in a technical sense, it reinforces an even narrower view of the physician as clinician in the problems patients bring to physicians.

Together the scientific emphasis in medical training (in particular, the view that medicine is largely if not exclusively applied science) combined with specialization gives rise to an agenda among medical practitioners that may not match that of patients. This agenda would seem to meet patient demands for technical proficiency. However, we would expect, as in fact we find, problems in meeting patients' demands for professional interest and involvement in their problems beyond their purely technical boundaries.

A number of studies have looked in depth at communication in various types of doctor-patient encounters and documented some of the problems to which we have alluded. Although it is not possible to review this literature in detail, we can summarize several findings that appear with some consistency.[47]

For example, in a study of a pediatric outpatient clinic, Korsch[23] and her colleagues discovered that ordinary civilities such as introductions were rare in the doctor-patient exchanges they studied. In addition, an analysis of the types of topics that patients and physicians talked about showed that the discussions were largely technical and information-oriented. For example, there was little expression of friendliness or hostility by either the physicians or the patients involved. Most of the discussion involved the giving and receiving of information, particularly the asking of questions by the physician and the providing of answers by the patients. The picture one gets from such an analysis is that of doctor-patient relationships as highly technical or task-oriented, with relatively little attention given to the expression or discussion of social or emotional topics, including expressions of concern, worry, or anxiety.

Not surprisingly the Korsch study showed that, at least in the setting studied, physicians dominated the exchange.[23] Moreover, doctors tended to be overly technical in their communication with patients. The Korsch study and others as well report other findings that reflect even more serious problems in some doctor-patient relationships. For example, although Korsch and her colleagues report that about 76% of the patients were satisfied with the encounter with their physicians, almost 20% reported they had not been given a clear statement of what was wrong with their infants. And about half of the mothers reported that when they left the physician, they felt they did not have a clear understanding of what had caused their children's illnesses.[23] As Korsch and her colleagues point out, such knowledge is very important, particularly in pediatric settings where mothers often want to know not only what is wrong but why, so they can prevent the problems from recurring.

This same study also revealed that, interestingly, fully 26% of the mothers reported after their visit that they had not mentioned their greatest concern to the physician, saying that they did not do so because either they did not have an opportunity or they felt they had not been encouraged. At the same time these authors found that the most common and most critical complaint among these mothers was that the physician did not show interest in their concerns about their children. In particular, many felt that the physician totally disregarded their diagnoses about what was ailing their children. In a striking finding Korsch and her colleagues noted that almost 70% of the mothers who felt their concerns were not appreciated by the physician reported they were dissatisfied with their visit. Conversely only 17% of the mothers who felt the physician understood their concern were dissatisfied. And patient satisfaction was significantly related to a mother's complying with the treatment regimen given by the physician.[23]

The study from which we have drawn several of our examples and findings is a single study, of course, and in one type of medical setting—pediatrics. Thus we should be careful in extending those observations to all medical encounters. Yet it would seem that pediatrics is a setting in which particular care would be given to many of the issues we have raised here. We suspect that if studies were conducted in a variety of other medical settings, what we would find would be not so much change in the nature but rather in the degree of communication problems that surfaced in the Korsch study.

Turning to other sources of problems students are told that treatment-management decisions must rest on "knowing the patient." Yet studies of doctor-patient interactions such as that just reviewed suggest that this "knowing" appears to often be limited to a strict biologic-technical domain. And with most physician encounters lasting only 15 minutes or less, it would seem to be difficult for a physician to get to know much about the patient other than just the specifics of the medical problem that brings them together.

In addition studies have shown that patients do not always ask the questions they want to nor do they sometimes even voice what concerns them the most.[35] At the same time physicians sometimes underestimate the actual medical knowledge that patients have[34] and in so doing assume that the patient cannot absorb or use additional medical knowledge, thus creating a vicious cycle that maintains the patient's ignorance about the medical condition and precludes discussion of related concerns.

As for the doctor-patient relationship being a learning experience for the patient, the literature presents a very mixed picture. A number of studies suggest that it is not uncommon for only between one half to two thirds of patients to be able to remember after a visitation what their physician told them.[26,40]

Our discussion of doctor-patient exchanges so far has focused almost exclusively on such encounters in rather routine ambulatory care. If one looks at doctor-patient exchanges in hospital settings, we see many of the same problems but, in addition, several new ones. For example, Duff and Hollingshead[7] found that hospitalized patients were often exposed to inconsistent and disorganized information from the various medical care providers.

In addition, a number of studies suggest that medical care professionals will sometimes deliberately limit the amount of information available to a hospitalized patient, controlling the information in such a way as to make the patient more tractable to the requirements of institutional life.[6,32,38] And for a variety of reasons the past decade has witnessed the rise of the patient advocate or patient representative in many hospitals, whose task is to better integrate the needs of the patient and the hospital in the delivery of effective health care.[46] Such positions reflect the fact that doctor-patient or more generally provider-patient relationships in hospital settings often leave a lot to be desired.

These studies, while noting some of the problems in effective communication in doctor-patient relationships, at the same time record the importance of such communication and suggest ways in which communication can be made more effective. For example, a number of studies have shown that the more a patient knows about his or her illness or condition, the greater the compliance of the patient with suggested medical regimens.[47] This topic will be discussed at length in Chapter 6. There is even one study that suggests that the adjustment of patients postoperatively, and in particular their need for pain-relieving medication, is significantly related to what they have been told to expect subsequent to their operation.[8]

Strategies for improving doctor-patient interaction

From a practical standpoint it is important, of course, to note not only the problems in communication in doctor-patient relationships, but to suggest strategies for making such communication more effective. Although the specifics of a particular doctor-patient relationship impose certain constraints, it would appear that several strategies are available for a doctor to employ to increase effective communication with patients.

The first is not to assume that effective doctor-patient relationships occur naturally; they do not appear to. Rather, they take work and effort by both the professional and the lay person.

Second, it appears important for the doctor to attempt to learn the agenda or the concerns that a patient brings to the doctor-patient encounter. It is understandable why a physician does not want to rely solely on the intuitions and speculations of a patient as to the nature and reasons for a particular medical complaint. Yet as several studies reviewed previously suggest, it is not uncommon for patients to formulate their own ideas as to what is wrong, how it happened, and what should be done about it. And many patients evaluate the advice and recommendations of their physicians in terms of their personal diagnoses and prognoses.

Third, and in the same vein, it would appear that the physician cannot always assume that the patient is going to voice all or even the most important of his or her concerns. Yet we have seen that a patient's satisfaction and often willingness to follow a prescribed therapy rests on the physician's knowing what the patient thinks and taking this perspective seriously. Accordingly, it is of some use to the physician to understand these lay perceptions and to engage not only in education but at times in reeducation of the patient if necessary.

Fourth, it appears that some of the communication problems in doctor-patient relationships rest in part on the use of esoteric language and medical jargon by doctors and other medical care providers. It would seem that more effective communication would result if effort were devoted to assuring that patients did in fact understand what had been said to them and that physicians take particular pains to avoid the use of technical language. If, as is sometimes necessary, technical language must be used, then care should be taken to assure that patients comprehend what is being said.

Fifth, as medicine moves from a one-on-one mode of medical care delivery to the delivery of care by multiple providers, it seems increasingly important that patients not be left with contradictory and confusing information. As we suggested, this has perhaps always been something of a problem when patient care is delivered in a hospital or clinic setting where there are several professionals involved.

Finally, perhaps one of the most difficult problems confronting the physician is to maintain adequate interest and concern in the problems that patients bring. One way we may view the activity of physicians is to see them as professionals who routinize other people's medical and health problems, concerns, and emergencies. In fact, much has been written about the necessity of physicians developing a sense of "detached concern" about the medical problems they will become involved in.[12] This detachment enables physicians to function in situations in which others would be immobilized by the drama of human medical emergencies. Although detached concern may be one thing that is in fact necessary to the delivery of effective medical care, too much may be a disadvantage. If a physician sees the same types of problems day in and day out, it is understandable that at a certain point this repetitiveness may serve to lessen dramatically or even extinguish interest and involvement. However, for the patient involved who may be experiencing the problem for the first and only time, the novelty, uncertainties, and emotional concern may be very great. If in such situations the physician, although competent, appears disinterested or unconcerned, the patient may be very dissatisfied with the physician and hence may lack an important incentive to pursue the advice and suggestions of the physician.

It seems useful, in light of such consideration, for physicians to remember that what for them as professionals may be simple, routine problems may for patients symbolize a threat to their existence and to the plans they have developed for their lives. Understanding this and entering this into encounters with patients would seem to be a necessary ingredient if a physician is interested in developing effective communication with patients.

The changing context of doctor-patient relationships

Up to this point we have discussed what transpires when doctor and patient meet and factors that may make lay people and professionals approach the doctor-patient encounter in various ways. In addition, we have focused on communication in doctor-patient relationships and reviewed studies that have identified problems that can occur repeatedly in this particular type of lay-expert encounter. In this final section we stand back somewhat from the specifics of doctor-patient exchanges and consider several developments, some internal and some external to the domain of medicine, and explore very briefly implications of these changes for doctor-patient encounters in the near future.

The changing scope of medical care

At several places in this book we have pointed out that the mandate of medicine is changing. Of particular importance is the observation that medical care is increasingly encompassing not only biologic problems but a wide assortment of psychologic and even social problems as well. For example, although alcoholism was once considered a moral, criminal, or psychologic problem, many today advocate that it is the proper concern of medicine. Likewise some family problems such as child abuse, although previously viewed as beyond the pale of medicine, are today being viewed by some as of medical interest, that is, problems that physicians should understand and be able to help families handle or solve.

Such observations underscore the simple point that medicine is, in essence a social undertaking. What is viewed as a medical problem in one culture or society may not be so viewed in another. Likewise what is viewed as a medical problem today may not be considered a problem tomorrow in the same culture or society, although our culture seems to be viewing more and more problems as medical. One of the things that practitioners in the future have to consider is this changing social mandate of medicine. What society views today as a medical problem of the first magnitude may tomorrow move outside the boundaries of accepted medical practice. And what a physician is trained to practice today may not be adequate for the practice of medicine in the future. For the individual practitioner this means that some patients will be willing to discuss some problems and others will not. It will also mean that the practitioner must be willing to view continual education as part of the prospects of being a physician, not only formal continuing medical education but continuous education from patients as to their needs, views, and expectations.

Also, related to the changing scope of medicine is the observation that the mandate of medicine is growing such that physicians today, and certainly physicians of the future, will have to concern themselves with not just a larger and larger variety of problems. In addition, the work of physicians increasingly seems to include not just the traditional tasks of diagnosis, prognosis, and treatment but also prevention. And directly related to prevention is the skill to educate, that is, teach patients what they need to know to remain healthy. This means that to the degree that medicine generally and physicians specifically adopt a preventive role, they must become as concerned with educating patients as they presently are with the accuracy of their diagnosis and the efficacy of a prescribed regimen.

Changes in public views of medicine and role of doctors

Physicians still occupy a position of high status in the United States. At the same time the past decade has witnessed the growth of distrust in experts of all kinds and the development of consumerism in various facets of American life, including the medical and health care areas.

It would be easy to overstate the degree to which consumerism has in fact penetrated the world of medicine. There is, nevertheless, mounting evidence of increased concern by many groups and organizations in the United States with patients' rights,[2] emphasis on physicians' obligations,[17] and, in general, a questioning of the authority physicians have traditionally exercised over medical and health issues, both with respect to their own patients and with regard to such problems on a societal level as well.[18]

One implication of such developments for medicine is that increasingly physicians may find patients not only demanding more out of their contacts with physicians but at the same time increasingly questioning the advice and expertise of physicians. In particular, physicians may find patients wanting a larger say in how a particular medical problem should be handled.

Added to this and contributing to it is the fact that over the past decade more and more medical procedures have been submitted to carefully controlled clinical trials to assess their efficacy.[10] The public, realizing that convention perhaps as much as scientific demonstration is important in determining what is considered "good medical practice," is becoming increasingly skeptical of many facets of medical practice. Accordingly, physicians in the future should expect to find patients demanding much more information than in the past about the advisability of many medical procedures. Physicians should not be intimidated by this. If physicians are willing to accept and respond positively to this, patients may gain a greater understanding of their illnesses and treatments and may gain a greater trust in medicine, because there will be fewer misunderstandings and unexpected surprises for the fully-informed patient.

Changes in the delivery of medical care

Elsewhere in this book we discuss some of the major changes in the delivery of medical care that have occurred in the past and some that may occur in the future. For example, it is increasingly clear that in the not too distant future many health professionals other than physicians will be involved in the delivery of medical and health care. Already there are various types of physician's assistants, expanded nursing roles, and even highly specialized auxiliary personnel who assist physicians in the delivery of specialized medical services. Such developments mean that physicians are and will be relating to patients in different and perhaps very complex ways. Certainly the days of a one-on-one relationship that lasted over many years, with extensive opportunity for patient and physician to get to know each other, are ending. Physicians must learn to share certain types of responsibility with other health care providers, and patients must learn to obtain adequate medical care in a medical care system that is complex, variegated, and, from the patient's perspective, not always highly integrated. Such situations will put new pressures on provider-patient relationships.

Summary

Our intention in this chapter has been to examine in some depth the hub of the medical care delivery system, the provider-patient relationship. Our focus has been selective, with particular attention given to noting communication problems in doctor-patient relationships and in providing a limited perspective on the directions this relationship may take over the next few years.

By way of conclusion we want to return briefly to the notion of Aesculapian authority, which we discussed at the start of this chapter. Aesculapian authority consists of three kinds of authority—sapiential, moral, and charismatic. It is interesting to close our discussion of doctor-patient relationships by examining briefly each of these bases of authority as they relate to contemporary medical care and to possible developments in the future.

The first basis of the classical, almost-God-like, authority of physicians was their knowledge. Sapiential authority refers to the entitlement to be heard by right of expert knowledge. If anything it would seem that this basis of the authority of physicians has increased right up to the present, with medicine becoming ever more science based. Yet on reflection this is probably not the case. The public, now more so than previously, realizes the limits of medicine and is beginning to appreciate the role of judgment and tradition, as well as science and facts, in the making of medical decisions. Although it is the case that there is much science in medicine, the public is increasingly aware that medicine is not just science. This may be particularly true for the more educated segments of society, but with increasing public discussion of the limits, errors, and mistakes in medicine the public at all levels is sensing the limits of medicine as science. Clearly, physicians have much expert knowledge and much technology. But the use of that knowledge is not science, and although the public may be retaining much of its respect for the knowledge base of medicine, there seems to be increased awareness of the problems and issues in using that knowledge. In short, the sapiential authority of physicians may be decreasing and with it some decrease in the traditional power and authority of doctors over lay people in doctor-patient encounters.

The second basis for Aesculapian authority was moral authority. Moral authority rests on the entitlement to be heard by the rightness or inherent goodness of an activity. As we have seen, there is considerable evidence that many Americans believe that most physicians will try to do what is of benefit for their patients. At the same time it is interesting to note that an almost equally large percent of the population holds the opinion that physicians, although not necessarily doing something of harm to their patients, believe that physicians do not always act in ways that benefit the patient financially. And with the very high costs of medical care today this is a significant issue for many lay people. When viewed in light of the recent consumer movements it would seem that the moral basis of authority of the physician may also be on the decline.

Finally, Aesculapian authority rests in part on charismatic authority. The latter is the entitlement to be heard by reason of God-given grace. This authority reflects the early association of religion and medicine. In addition, it reflects the fact that medicine and medical practitioners are engaged in an activity that carries high symbolic importance for almost everyone. In particular, medicine and medical practitioners are involved in activities that involve birth, life, and death, that is, events that define the meaning of most lives and hence carry tremendous symbolic significance. Of the various types of authority underlying Aesculapian authority, it would seem that this element, the "charisma" of medicine and medical practice, may have decreased the least over the past few decades and in fact may increase somewhat as the boundaries of medicine expand, permitting more control of the creation, maintenance, and termination of life.

Physicians training for the future face a changing, complex situation. Not only is the scientific and technologic base of medical practice changing but what society and patients want from medicine is changing also. And with these changes the role of the professional and the lay person in the doctor-patient relationship will change. The doctor-patient relationship will remain, in various forms, nonetheless an important relationship in most people's lives. And the competent physician of the future will be one who understands the complexities of this relationship, using such understanding to further the effectiveness of the medical knowledge and technology available for improving the health and happiness of patients.

References

1. Anderson, W. T., and Holm, D. T.: The physician-patient encounter: a process of reality negotiation. In Jace, E., editor: Patients, physicians, and illness, ed. 3, New York, 1979, The Free Press.
2. Annas, G.: The rights of hospital patients, New York, 1975, Avon Books.
3. Bloom, S. W., and Wilson, R. N.: Patient-practitioner relationships. In Freeman, H., Levine, S., and Reader, L., editors: Handbook of medical sociology, ed. 3, Englewood Cliffs, N.J., 1979, Prentice-Hall, Inc.
4. Bynder, H., and New, P. K. M.: Time for a change: from micro to macrosociological concepts in disability research, J. Health Soc. Behav. 17:45, 1976.
5. Cogswell, B., and Weir, D.: A role in process: the development of medical professionals' role in long term care of chronically diseased patients, J. Health Soc. Behav. 5:95, 1964.
6. Davis, F.: Passage through crisis: polio victims and their families, Indianapolis, 1963, The Bobbs-Merrill Co., Inc.
7. Duff, R., and Hollingshead, A.: Sickness and society, New York, 1968, Harper & Row, Publishers, Inc.
8. Egbert, L., Battit, F., Welch, C., and Bartlett, M.: Reduction of postoperative pain by encouragement and instruction of patients, N. Engl. J. Med. 270:825, 1964.
9. Final Report: a study of health practices and opinions, Washington, D.C., 1972, National Technical Information Services, U.S. Department of Commerce.
10. Fineberg, H., and Hiatt, H.: Evaluation of medical practices: the case for technology assessment, N. Engl. J. Med. 301(20):1086, 1979.
11. Flexner, A.: Medical education in the United States and Canada, Bulletin no. 4, Carnegie Foundation for the Advancement of Teaching, 1910.
12. Fox, R.: The medical student's training for detached concern. In Lief, H., Lief, V., and Lief, N., editors: The psychological basis of medical practice, New York, 1963, Harper & Row, Publishers, Inc.
13. Freese, A. S.: Managing your doctor, New York, 1974, Briarbooks.
14. Freidson, E.: Client control and medical practice, Am. J. Sociol. 65:375, 1960.
15. Freidson, E.: Patients' views of medical practice, New York, 1961, Russell Sage Foundation.
16. Freidson, E.: Profession of medicine, New York, 1970, Dodd, Mead & Co.
17. Freidson, E.: The limits of professional autonomy. In Profession of medicine, New York, 1970, Dodd, Mead & Co.
18. Freidson, E.: Professional dominance, New York, 1970, Atherton Press.

19. Gordon, G.: Role theory and illness: a socio-logical perspective, New Haven, Conn., 1966, College & University Press.
20. Howorth, B.: Your physician and you, Consumers' Research Magazine 11:11, 1979.
21. Kassebaum, G. G., and Baumann, B. O.: Dimensions of the sick role in chronic illness, J. Health Human Behav. 6:16, 1965.
22. Koch, H., and McLemore, T.: 1977 summary: national ambulatory medical care survey, Advancedata 48:3, 1979.
23. Korsch, B., Gozzi, E., and Francis, V.: Gaps in doctor-patient communication, Pediatrics 42:864, 1968.
24. Kurtz, R., and Giacepassi, D.: Medical and social work students' perceptions of deviant conditions and sick role incumbency, Soc. Sci. Med. 9:249, 1975.
25. Levine, S., and Kozloff, M.: The sick role: assessment and overview, Ann. Rev. Sociol. 4:317, 1978.
26. Ley, P., and Spelman, M.: Communication in an outpatient setting, Br. J. Soc. Clin. Psychol. 4:114, 1965.
27. Litman, T. J.: The influence of self-conception and life orientation factors in the rehabilitation of the orthopedically disabled, J. Health Human Behav. 3:249, 1962.
28. Lorber, J.: Good patients and problem patients: conformity and deviance in a general hospital, J. Health Soc. Behav. 16:213, 1975.
29. Mechanic, D.: Medical sociology, New York, 1968, The Free Press.
30. Parsons, T.: The social system, New York, 1951, The Free Press.
31. Parsons, T., and Fox, R.: Illness, therapy, and the modern urban American family, J. Soc. Issues 8(4):31, 1952.
32. Pericci, R.: Circle of madness, Englewood Cliffs, N.J., 1974, Prentice-Hall, Inc.
33. Petroni, F. A.: Correlates of the psychiatric sick role, J. Health Soc. Behav. 13:47, 1972.
34. Pratt, L., Seligmann, A., and Reader, G.: Physicians' views on the level of medical information among patients, Am. J. Public Health 47:1277, 1957.
35. Reader, G., Pratt, L., and Mudd, M.: What

patients expect from their doctors, Mod. Hospital 89:88, 1957.
36. Rosengren, W. R., and Tefton, M.: Hospitals and patients, New York, 1969, Atherton Press.
37. Siegler, M., and Osmond, H.: Aesculapian authority, Hastings Cent. Stud. 1:41, 1973.
38. Skipper, J. K., Mauksch, H., Tagliacozzo, D.: Some barriers to communication between patients and hospital functionaries, Nurs. Forum 2:14, 1963.
39. Sorenson, J. R.: Biomedical innovation, uncertainty, and doctor-patient interaction, J. Health Soc. Behav. 15:366, 1974.
40. Sorenson, J. R., et al.: Volume I: the impact of genetic counseling: an empirical assessment, final report to the National Foundation—March of Dimes, Boston University School of Medicine, October 1979. (Unpublished manuscript.)
41. Stevens, R.: American medicine and the public interest, New Haven, Conn. 1971, Yale University Press.
42. Szasz, T., and Hollander, M.: A contribution to the philosophy of medicine: the basic models of the doctor-patient relationship, AMA Arch. Intern. Med. 97:585, 1956.
43. Thomas, E. J.: Problems of disability from the perspective of role theory, J. Health Human Behav. 3:249, 1962.
44. Titley, R. W.: Imaginations about the disabled, Soc. Sci. Med. 3:29, 1969.
45. Twaddle, A. C., and Hessler, R. M.: A sociology of health, St. Louis, 1977, The C. V. Mosby Co.
46. Ver Steeg, C. F., and Croog, S.: Hospitals and related health care delivery settings. In Freeman, H., Levine, S., and Reeder, L., editors: Handbook of medical sociology, ed. 3, Englewood Cliffs, N.J., 1979, Prentice-Hall, Inc.
47. Waitzkin, H., and Stockle, J. D.: The communication of information about illness, Adv. Psychosom. Med. 8:180, 1972.
48. Zborowski, M.: Cultural components in response to pain, J. Soc. Issues 8:16, 1952.
49. Zola, I.: Culture and symptoms, Am. Sociol. Rev. 31:615, 1966.

Chapter 6

Patient compliance with medical regimens

Problems presented by noncompliance

After a physician examines a patient, conducts laboratory tests, and reaches a medical diagnosis, a critical moment in medical care is reached. From the standpoint of the medical profession all the efforts of medical education, medical research, and medical technology to understand and diagnose illness and determine a therapy are finally offered to the patient. Much of the extent to which these efforts will be efficacious is now largely in the hands of the patient.

From the patient's point of view, he or she has now gone through a number of events and behaviors. These may include having (1) recognized physiologic symptoms or an altered body state, (2) consulted with friends, (3) considered past experiences with illness, especially as these involved interactions with medical personnel, (4) obtained an appointment with a physician, (5) spent considerable time in a waiting room, and (6) submitted to physical examination and probably a wide variety of auxiliary laboratory and radiology tests. The patient now awaits the climax of all this activity: diagnosis and treatment. All these efforts offer testimony of the patient's feelings of *need* on one hand and *trust* in medicine on the other.

All too often a seemingly illogical behavior then occurs: the patient who needed and trusted the physician fails to comply with the medical regimen that so many people, visible and not visible to the patient, worked hard to produce. According to one review, although some published reports claim 100% compliance by patients with medical regimens, other studies have indicated that as few as 4% of patients comply.[36]

If any one conclusion can be reached from the spate of articles that have been published on this topic, it is that medical care providers cannot expect all patients, or even a majority of patients, to adhere to the medical and other therapeutic regimens they prescribe.

Noncompliance can take many forms.* One study of diabetes and congestive heart disease patients examined by a random sample of physicians in an Indiana community is typical. Among the 357 patients in the study (1) only two thirds were rated as fully compliant when a patient home interview was compared with medical records and physician reports of what the patient had been asked to do, (2) 19% were not taking any of the prescribed medications, whereas an equal percentage were taking drugs other than those prescribed, and (3) 17% took prescribed medications but in incorrect doses or sequences.[27] As these figures suggest, of those who were noncompliant, most were noncompliant in more than one way.

The problem is exacerbated because many physicians have considerable difficulty in ascertaining which patients comply and which patients do not. Berkowitz,[7] in a study of physicians in 55 clinics, and Caron,[8] in a study of 27 physicians and 525 patients, reported that over three fourths of the physicians studied overestimated the degree to which their patients comply. Caron also reported that the physicians in his study were unable to distinguish which patients were good compliers and which patients were poor compliers. Inability of physicians to distinguish between patients who comply and those who do not and to assess the extent to which patients comply poses a serious problem in the management of illness. Without such knowledge physicians cannot assess the value of specific therapies for a noncompliant patient's recovery. On a broader scale the value of specific regimens for patient recovery in general may be called into question if those assessing the treatments do not know which persons treated in fact followed the regimen as prescribed.[14]

Factors influencing compliance

In the past few years numerous descriptive studies have compared compliant and noncompliant patients. From this research we have learned a great deal about the ways that characteristics and attitudes of the patient, characteristics of the treatment regimen, and the nature of the doctor-patient interaction influence compliance.

Characteristics of the illness

Briefly summarized this research informs us that noncompliance can pose a problem regardless of the severity of a patient's disorder in terms of painfulness, disability, or threat to life. Noncompliance is particularly high when the disorder being treated is asymptomatic or psychiatric in nature.[23] However, numerous studies have

---

*"Compliance" is perhaps not the best term to use in describing the degree to which patients carry out treatment recommendations; it makes one think possibly of pulmonary compliance and thereby suggests a view of the provider-patient relationship in which the patient is a passive element acted on by and resisting the application of outside forces. As we shall see, this conception of the role of the patient will do little to promote compliance. We use the word "both" because the alternatives that have been proposed, such as "adherence," are no more attractive and because "compliance" is the term employed by most researchers in the field.

shown that the severity of a disorder as measured by a physician's evaluation or prior hospitalizations or diagnoses generally is unrelated to compliance.

Although one would think that people with more severe problems would be more motivated to comply, such disorders often require more complex, difficult regimens. Persons with severe disorders may find compliance difficult because of limitations imposed on them by their illnesses and may also be discouraged by the failure of their previous efforts to prevent or cure their ailments. The fact that a person's illness is serious, painful, or even life-threatening, then, does not ensure a high level of compliance.

Patient background

A patient's demographic characteristics also do not consistently predict whether or not the patient will be compliant. Studies that report *no* relation between patient compliance and social class, age, sex, education, occupation, and marital status outnumber those that do report some relation between compliance and these demographic characteristics by almost three to one.[23,39]

Surprising as such a finding may seem, the lack of association between demographic characteristics and compliance has been observed for a variety of disorders and in a variety of medical settings, using a variety of measurement techniques. Though this does not mean that such demographic characteristics as social class never predict compliance, it does mean that noncompliance can be a problem with any patient population regardless of social class level, age composition, or racial and ethnic background.

Patient knowledge

Although common sense tells us that knowledge about one's illness and understanding of how to follow the regimen are necessary for a patient to comply, they are not always sufficient. Becker[3] has argued that some medical care providers mistakenly assume that their patients are like empty vessels into which they can pour knowledge and recommendations and assume compliance will follow. Evidence has now accumulated indicating that this assumption is often false.

This point is graphically illustrated by a study by Bergman and Werner[6] in which 59 families of children with streptococcal pharyngitis were observed. When questioned at home 95% of the respondents correctly recalled the appropriate regimen. By the sixth day of a 10-day course of treatment, however, pill counts and urine assays revealed that only 30% of the patient had received the prescribed penicillin.

More recently Sacket et al.[43] conducted a randomized controlled trial to increase patient compliance with antihypertensive regimens among more than 230 men. Although the experimental group receiving intensive instruction did show greater increases in knowledge about hypertension than the control group, the experimental group was no more compliant than the control group. Measurements of patient knowledge at intake and 6 months follow-up in both the intervention and control groups were not related to compliance.

Nature of the regimen

More consistently predictive of compliance is the nature of the regimen offered to patients.[37] The more complex a regimen (e.g., the greater the number of medications, the more times per day that medications must be taken) the less likely is full compliance. Compliance also tends to diminish as the duration of treatment increases over time. *Proscriptive* regimens, which require marked changes in behavior, especially abandoning established behaviors like smoking or drinking or certain dietary habits, are less likely to be followed than *prescriptive* regimens, which require patients to initiate new behaviors, especially behaviors that do not disrupt their normal routines. Regimens that produce adverse side effects for the patient are also less likely to be followed.

Patient beliefs about illness and treatment

A number of studies have demonstrated rather consistently that one's beliefs about one's illness and its treatment can influence compliance independently of knowledge about the illness and treatment, the actual nature of the illness and treatment, or the characteristics of the regimen. These studies have explored the impact of the beliefs outlined in the *Health Belief Model* originally proposed to explain preventive health behaviors, such as obtaining chest radiographs or immunizations.[42]

Applied to compliance this model suggests that patients will be more likely to follow regimens offered to them if (1) they feel *susceptible* to problems or complications because of their illnesses or susceptible to further attacks of the illnesses, (2) they believe that their illnesses could pose *severe* consequences for their health and daily functioning, (3) they believe that the proposed treatment plans will be highly *effective* in treating their illnesses, and (4) they do not foresee major *obstacles* to compliance, such as adverse drug effects, high cost of the regimen, or perceived lack of safety of a medication. More recent research also suggests that people's general health motivation, that is, their feelings of control over health matters and their overall confidence in medical care, may influence their compliance.[5]

Although very few studies have systematically explored all the major features of the model, a number of studies have examined individual beliefs. Not every study has found all the beliefs in the model associated with compliance,[10,24] but in the most thorough review of literature on the model and compliance[2,10,19,24] to date, Becker[4] concluded that most studies have produced internally consistent findings in the predicted direction that, taken together, yield relatively strong support for this conceptual model.

Provider-patient interactions

The provider-patient interaction can be an emotionally charged encounter that is a difficult learning situation for both the patient and the physician.[45] Patients may be worried about what their symptoms mean or whether pain and discomfort can be alleviated and may have concerns about the physician's or nurse's opinion of them as persons. Similarly, providers may not only wonder about what the patient's symptoms mean or what treatment is best but may be anxious about how their diagnostic and treatment skills will be viewed by colleagues or the patient. A patient who has had a lengthy, tiring trip to the clinic or a frustrating wait on arrival may be upset even before the interaction begins. Similarly, a busy clinic, late appointments with patients the day before, or even a missing patient record may make the provider appear brusque, distracted, and perhaps insensitive to the patient.

Given the observed relationship between patient beliefs about illness and its treatment with compliance, one would suspect that the provider's ability to identify those patient beliefs would increase compliance.

Although giving appropriate instructions and molding beliefs of patients do not sound like difficult tasks, many physicians have found that achieving these objectives is difficult in practice. Perhaps one reason is that in the emotionally laden provider-patient interaction there often is considerable misunderstanding and even mistrust.

Some of this misunderstanding and mistrust may come from physicians. For example, when over 100 physician faculty members at a major medical school in New York were asked why patients fail to comply with medical regimens, over two thirds of those responding blamed noncompliance on the uncooperative personalities of patients.[11] In a more recent article McKinlay[34] cites a number of studies that suggest that many physicians have difficulty accurately estimating how much medical information patients are capable of comprehending.

Pratt[41] and her colleagues sought to examine the impact the physician's underestimating patient knowledge has on patient behavior. They compared doctor-patient interactions in situations where doctors underestimated patient knowledge and those in which doctors made efforts to give their patients full information about their disorders. They reported that:

When a doctor perceives the patient as rather poorly informed, he considers the tremendous difficulties of translating his knowledge into language the patient can understand, along with dangers of frightening the patient; the patient, in turn, reacts dully to this limited information, either asking uninspired questions or refraining from questioning the doctor at all, thus reinforcing the doctor's view that the patient is ill-equipped to comprehend his problem. Lacking guidance, the patient performs at a low level; hence, the doctor rates his capacities as even lower than they are.*

*From Pratt, I., et al.: Physician views on the level of medical information among patients, Am. J. Public Health **47:**1281, 1957.

In contrast, patients who were given more thorough explanations were found to participate somewhat more effectively with the physician and were more likely to completely accept the physician's formulation than were patients who received very little explanation.

Research on provider-patient interaction and compliance has further revealed that patients are less likely to comply (1) if they believe they are not held in adequate esteem by their physicians,[13] (2) if their physicians actively seek information from them without providing feedback about either why that information is being gathered or on the patients' conditions,[12] (3) if tension emerges during a doctor-patient interaction and is not addressed or resolved, or (4) if patients believe that their expectations are not being met or that their physicians are not behaving in a friendly manner.[17,30] In general, the more satisfied patients are with their providers and the settings in which care is provided, the more likely they will comply.

Though given less attention than the actual encounter with the physician, the entire clinic environment to which patients are exposed can influence their interaction with the clinician. Inconvenient hours, lack of adequate translators, and block appointment systems where all patients are asked to arrive before a clinic session, as opposed to an individual appointment system, can all produce an atmosphere in which the patient feels less important and less respected.[15,20]

The compliance-oriented history

As with other problems in medicine, the importance of history taking in addressing the problem of noncompliance cannot be overstated. The extension of the medical history to include information on the patient's health-related beliefs can be of use to the practitioner in two distinct ways: (1) Understanding of these beliefs on the part of the practitioner can help to predict the degree to which a patient is at risk for poor compliance. (2) Investigating the issues raised by the Health Belief Model can contribute to the development of a relationship with the patient that will most likely foster compliance. A systematic exploration of these beliefs can offer the physician more compliance-related information than is obtained in any other facet of the medical encounter. The model implies that the following areas merit attention.

Beliefs about the illness itself

The provider can ascertain beliefs the patient may have about a disorder, which include beliefs about the seriousness of the disorder and if applicable about the likelihood of suffering future episodes, by asking questions such as "What is it that worries you the most about having developed high blood pressure?" "How likely do you think it is that your pain will return?" "What do you think is causing the problem you describe?" "Have you known anyone with a rash such as yours? How did things turn out for that person?" These questions can identify misconceptions on the part of the patient that may be predictive of poor compliance. Such misconceptions, it has been found, may involve either underestimates or overestimates of the seriousness of the disorder and the likelihood of recurrent episodes.[33]

Depending on the disorder in question, it may be beliefs about the symptom rather than about the illness itself that must be investigated. Most women, for example, would be fearful of cancer on detecting a breast mass. Even when the diagnosis of a benign lesion is made, the fear of cancer may remain. In the case of symptoms with considerable meaning to patients it is reasonable to ask questions about perceived seriousness and susceptibility early in the visit at the time when historical material is customarily elicited. With other disorders, including those that present systematically, the practitioner must bear in mind that the relevant beliefs about the illness may only surface once the patient has been informed of the diagnosis. This requires that the questioning of the patient not be confined, as is often the case, to the early part of the visit. Rather, it must be reintroduced at various times throughout the encounter as information is provided to the patient.

Beliefs about the treatment plan

The Health Belief Model implies that patients undertake something like a cost-benefit analysis in deciding whether or not to follow medical instructions. Those patients who perceive many or serious costs associated with the treatment plan, while anticipating little benefit, are at risk for poor compliance. The costs of adhering to a therapeutic regimen may be more than just financial. They may also entail the abandonment of familiar behavior patterns or the acquisition of new ones, the involvement required of family members, the anticipated adverse effects of treatment, and the abandonment of other remedies from which the patient may have been deriving real or placebo benefit. A practitioner can assess perceived costs by asking such questions as "What have you been doing for the pain on your own?" "Can you think of any problems you might have in taking these pills an hour before meals?" "Is there anything that worries you about having these monthly blood tests?" "Are you concerned about any particular side effects of the medication?"

The patient's perception of the benefits of the proposed treatment includes notions about the efficacy of the regimen as well as ideas about what problems might be avoided if treatment is carried out as recommended. These beliefs may be discerned by asking questions such as "How effective do you think the injections will be for you?" and "What do you think would happen if you forgot to take your medicine one night?"

In implementing the suggestions offered here, the physician or nurse must recognize that a patient's beliefs can change markedly from visit to visit. It is unusual for an individual to employ the provider as the sole source of medical information. Friends, relatives, books, magazine articles, and other providers may be consulted between the time the diagnosis is made and the time the treatment is completed. The type of information obtained from such sources can have as much or more influence on compliance as that given by the provider. Experimental evidence is now available that indicates that to ensure optimal compliance with an ongoing treatment plan, the provider would be well advised to *repeatedly* assess the status of the beliefs discussed previously over the duration of a particular episode of illness.[35]

Also, in asking these questions it is important not to rush the patient's answers. We can learn from psychiatry in this regard. Psychiatrists point out that all of us have a tendency to be frightened by silence during conversations, and physicians are no exception. If a physician starts to fill in information for patients or interrupts patients before they have an opportunity to voice their true opinions or muster the courage to tell the physician what they believe, that physician may close off valuable information that later could be used to foster compliance or reduce barriers to compliance.

One can hypothesize that merely by routinely asking the series of questions about patient beliefs concerning illness and treatment and allowing the patient time to answer these questions adequately (1) the doctor-patient interaction will be improved, and (2) information will come to the physician's attention that can be used to more adequately encourage or foster compliance. By attempting to determine salient beliefs the physician can gain fuller insight into exactly what patients do or do not understand about their illnesses and treatments. Consequently underestimation of patient knowledge will be less likely to occur. By earnestly seeking to understand patient concerns regarding illness and treatment physicians may also reduce beliefs among some patients that they are not respected by their physicians, which also has been reported to inhibit compliance. By discussing patient concerns some of the tensions that impede doctor-patient interactions may be reduced. Most probably, if patients can voice their concerns, fewer will feel that they have given information to the physician about their illnesses without receiving feedback concerning the worries their illnesses produce.

Interventions to improve compliance

Once the physician has explored a patient's perceptions of the illness and its treatment, several different steps can be taken to encourage the patient to follow the prescribed regimen. The information elicited during the compliance-oriented history can be most useful in this regard.

Information

Providing the patient with a clear description of the condition, its treatment, and the implications of the illness for the patient when treated and untreated probably constitutes the most frequently used way to promote compliance. Although useful, however, merely presenting information does not always ensure compliance. One recent study has further suggested that not merely describing a regimen but also discussing the specific purpose and function of the prescribed medications will enhance compliance.[28] Most observers, additionally, believe that a patient is more likely to follow a medical regimen when the provider conveys a personal belief in the worth of the treatment.[29]

To be sure that the patient understands what is said the physician can ask the patient to repeat key parts of what he or she has been told, especially how to follow the prescribed regimen. Clearly written or typed instructions are also useful.[9] And whenever presenting new information to a patient the physician should ask if there are any questions.

Reinforcing or changing beliefs

Patients will generally hold some beliefs, correct or incorrect, about their illnesses before contacting their physicians. Together with these old beliefs, which will have been held for varying lengths of time and with varying degrees of intensity, new beliefs will emerge during the course of treatment. If physicians think that patients' beliefs are appropriate, they should attempt to reinforce them. This may be done by indicating that the patients seem to have understanding of their situations, and by asking patients to telephone if any problems emerge during the course of treatment. Alternately, asking patients to write down questions or concerns as they come up may help patients remember them at follow-up visits.

A much more difficult situation exists when patients hold erroneous beliefs about their illnesses or treatment plans. Several options are available to change such beliefs. Perhaps the most overused option is fear arousal. So many health care providers have attempted to scare their patients into complying that the literature about this approach is particularly extensive. Review articles on the use of fear arousal have all reached the same fundamental conclusion: *fear arousal is not consistently successful and, in some situations, may actually hinder compliance.*[25,31] Fear arousal techniques seldom work with highly educated populations, and even when fear appeals have success, it is generally short-lived.[5]

Fear arousal techniques can falter for several reasons.[26] Patients exposed to a fear arousal message may perceive the threatened outcome as improbable, inapplicable, unimportant, or remote in time. Patients advised to stop smoking because of its adverse health consequences, for example, can deny or rationalize the advice away. Moreover, even if a fear appeal succeeds in arousing sufficient anxiety, it may fail to produce the intended behavioral change because the physician's recommendation may not be regarded as very effective.

If the patients are already anxious about their disorders, use of scare techniques may actually make thinking about the illness and treatment so painful that any action on the issue is avoided. If a patient is already deeply anxious about the illness, a fear appeal may be immobilizing. A far more helpful approach is one that attempts to allay fears by pointing out the promises held by treatment. Although appeals to other emotions may not have been given the same attention as fear arousal, they may actually prove more effective in altering beliefs and behavior. For example, appeals to love, career plans, or parental responsibility can be powerfully motivating in some individuals.

Pointing out any inconsistencies that may exist in the structure of the patients' stated beliefs may also be helpful. A patient's ambivalence about an illness or its treatment often needs to be addressed before the patient will comply. A patient may be reluctant to follow a particular regimen that is consciously or unconsciously in conflict with other desired goals, which may be work-related, recreational, or family-oriented.

Another alternative is to appeal to sources of information in which the patient has or can develop considerable trust. It may be difficult, for example, for a seriously ill patient to fully trust the physician who has never experienced the problems associated with having the disorder in question. In such a situation it is frequently useful to have the patient speak with other individuals with similar conditions who have benefited from the suggested therapy. To the patient such individuals, though not so technically knowledgeable, may appear more credible than the physician.

Social pressure and support

The use of social pressure and social support can also be of help to patients. Such strategies have long been used with behavioral problems such as obesity, smoking, and alcohol abuse. More recently, Avery[1] examined the use of such techniques with asthmatic patients. Comparing asthmatic patients placed in discussion groups focusing on ways to prevent asthma attacks with controls drawn from the same emergency room population, they found that visits to the emergency room during the next 4 months by patients in the discussion groups were but half the number of visits made by controls.

A feature of social pressure strategies that is used in Alcoholics Anonymous is the testimonial speech where a member vows in front of others to not drink again. People are reluctant to break commitments they have made in front of their peers. A recent study suggests that the obtaining of a verbal commitment from patients may even promote compliance in a one-to-one provider-patient relationship.[32]

When social support or social pressure is being invoked to promote compliance, patients with similar problems need not be the only resource. In many circumstances family members, employers, and friends can be invaluable in helping patients follow their regimens and informing their physicians if the patients appear to be having difficulties.

Memory aids

Another approach has been tested to overcome patient memory problems. In addition to providing instructions about medication one study compared the relative impact of a daily reminder chart that patients filled out at home each time they took their medication. The chart included typed information about the drug, its dosage, and times of administration. Comparison of two randomized groups of hypertension patients in which only one group was given the charts to use revealed that the group given the charts had one third less noncompliance 2 months later. At that point the control group was given charts to fill out and by the third month of the trial their compliance rose to the same level as the group initially given the charts.[18]

Patient involvement

This approach not only points to the importance of reminders but suggests that increasing *patient involvement in monitoring treatment* may affect compliance. This hypothesis has been more directly tested in an experimental study that divided into two groups a sample of patients who at 6 months after the initiation of antihypertensive therapy were not compliant. The experimental group was given instructions about how to take and record home blood pressures and chart their medication consumption. With each patient ways were discussed to tailor the regimen to habitual daily activities. Six months later 80% of those in the experimental group were compliant, which was twice the percentage of compliant control group patients.[21] Involving patients in a decision-making capacity and teaching them how to observe the impact of their illnesses seems to have provided incentives for compliance that these patients had previously not experienced.

Treatments plans

A further set of interventions to improve compliance revolve around the treatment plan itself. One general principle of compliance-oriented prescribing is to *simplify the regimen* as much as possible. This may be done in a variety of ways. One of the most consistently successful strategies in this regard is the use, when available, of long-acting injectable pharmaceuticals. The use of such preparations has been found to enhance both compliance and clinical outcome in streptococcal laryngitis, rheumatic fever prophylaxis, schizophrenia, and tuberculosis.[22]

A related approach involves the scheduling of oral medication. In general, the physician would be well advised to avoid divided doses of medication when once-a-day administration would be equally effective. Although in many cases the possibility of implementing this strategy hinges on product availability, the pharmaceutical industry's increased attention to the problem of noncompliance has resulted in the recent introduction of a variety of products designed for once-a-day oral administration. These can often be used to good advantage in those patients for whom noncompliance is suspected to be a problem.

The principle of keeping down the number of pills per day applies particularly in the case of *multiple drug regimens*. This principle dictates the avoidance on the part of the physician of *routine* prescription of such medications as vitamin supplements, bowel preparations, and tranquilizing drugs. The addition of such drugs may increase both errors in medication and noncompliance. Consideration should be given to the use of such preparations once the appropriate ratio of the drugs involved has been determined by separate administration.

There are further ways in which the physician can simplify the treatment plan. Questioning patients about their daily routine has been found to be beneficial. When behavior changes that are more difficult to comply with are involved, such as dietary habits, exercise habits, or smoking, the principles of behavior modification[38] suggest the introduction of such changes gradually over the course of several visits rather than all at once. Changes in behavior in these difficult areas will come more easily by reinforcing compliance as it occurs and only then adding a new task.

The occurrence of *side effects* also has been found to hinder compliance. If a medication has common side effects, the physician should indicate this in advance to the patient and add, when appropriate, that the side effect may be unpleasant but is not serious. When initially describing a regimen to a patient, moreover, the provider must be careful to avoid promising better results than the patient has a right to expect. Although slight exaggeration may appear tempting when trying to coax a skeptical patient along, such an approach is not only misleading and unethical, it is illegal.[44]

It is also important to keep in mind that the *monetary cost* of following a regimen may interfere with compliance. The physician alert to the problem of noncompliance will investigate or delegate the investigation of the patient's health insurance coverage to ensure that the patient receives all due benefits. Prescribing by generic name often can significantly reduce the cost of medication. Furthermore, patients should be informed that prescription prices can vary widely from pharmacy to pharmacy and that a pharmacy offering the best price on one product may *not* offer the best price on others. Patients should therefore be encouraged to request price information on a prescription before having it filled and be supported in the notion that there is no onus to comparative shopping for pharmaceuticals.

Finally, after initial formulation of a treatment plan and its presentation to the patient, *physician follow-up* can prove most important in promoting good compliance. The use of mailed appointment reminder cards and follow-up telephone calls have been found to be successful in encouraging patients to keep appointments with providers.[16,40] Similarly, there is evidence that home visits by nonprofessional workers to help arrange transportation and baby-sitting and to schedule convenient appointment times can improve clinic attendance. Patients receiving written instructions concerning the proposed regimen have been found, as has been noted, to be more compliant than control groups.

Summary and conclusions

There are a number of factors known to be related to compliance that clinicians can identify when they initially interact with patients and when they prescribe a medical regimen. If physicians focus attention on identifying factors that might impede compliance among their patients, they will be better able to identify potential noncomplying patients, and the information gathered in the process may prove useful in reducing noncompliance.

In particular, the beliefs a patient brings to a provider-patient interaction about an illness and the effectiveness and difficulties of treatment can affect the extent to which medical recommendations are followed. Therefore to identify potential noncomplying patients and forestall noncompliance physicians and other providers need to systematically undertake the task of exploring the beliefs and motivations of each patient with regard to illness and treatment. At a minimum each patient should be asked:

1. Have you been taking anything for this problem already?
2. Does anything worry you about the illness?
3. What can happen if the recommended regimen is not followed?
4. How likely is that to occur?
5. How effective do you feel the regimen will be in treating the disorder?
6. Can you think of any problems you might have in following the regimen?
7. Do you have any questions about the regimen or how to follow it?

One can hypothesize that by routinely asking this series of questions about patient beliefs concerning illness and treatment and allowing the patient time to answer these questions adequately (1) provider-patient interactions will be improved, and (2) information will come to the provider's attention that can be used to more adequately encourage or foster compliance.

First, by attempting to determine salient beliefs the physician can gain fuller insight into exactly what patients understand or do not understand about their illnesses and their treatments. Consequently, underestimation of patient knowledge will be less likely to occur.[41] By earnestly seeking to understand patient concerns regarding illness and treatment, the physician also may reduce beliefs among some patients that they are not respected by their physicians, which has been reported to inhibit compliance.[13] If patients believe physicians respect and are concerned about their feelings, they may be less likely to think that physicians have negative perceptions of them. By discussing patient concerns some of the tensions that impede doctor-patient interactions may be reduced. Most probably, if patients can voice their concerns, fewer will feel that they have given information to physicians about their illnesses without receiving feedback concerning the worries their illnesses produce.

Also, the information gleaned by these questions can be helpful to physicians in adjusting regimens or encouraging compliance. For example, patients may not be aware of the potential ramifications of noncompliance or may not understand the seriousness of their disorders or exactly how to comply. Missing information can be supplied by physicians and incorrect beliefs addressed. Moreover, physicians may not be aware of the potential difficulties some patients encounter in compliance. Efforts to accommodate or simplify regimens may be the result of physicians actively attempting to uncover patient-perceived obstacles to compliance. Finally, when compliance may eliminate or reduce the source of patients worries about their illnesses, that fact can be underscored by physicians in an effort to encourage compliance. In short, if providers have more information with which to work, they will be better able to foster compliance.

In some instances patients will not follow medically proposed regimens no matter how carefully physicians and other medical care professionals explore patient beliefs and attempt to address those beliefs by tailoring their proposed recommendations for regimens to patient needs. Most frustrating of all, some patients will assert that they are following medical advice even when they are not.

This undoubtedly is one of the most discouraging situations for providers. Although some may feel tempted to confront these patients or recommend that they seek care elsewhere, providers should be careful not to so fixate on patients' refusals to comply with particular medical recommendations that it interferes with the larger purpose of care. Recommending that a patient with heart disease seek another provider because of the patient's unwillingness to stop smoking or lose weight may only make the patient delay or fail to seek care in a cardiac emergency. Expressing anger or disrespect to a patient who will not stop drinking despite medical complications may only heighten the patient's problems.

Physicians and other providers must be cautious not to have patient compliance become an end in itself. If providers adopt the philosophy of whatever works, try it, then the strategies we have listed to foster a more effective provider-patient relationship will degenerate into psychologic manipulation of patients. Though a patient's adherence to prescribed regimens can promote health, compliance with a particular regimen should be secondary to patients and providers in developing a relationship of mutual respect where they can work together in the interest of the patient's health and psychologic well-being.

References

1. Avery, C., et al.: Reducing emergency room visits of asthmatics: an experiment in patient education—testimony, Pittsburgh, 1972, President's Committee on Health Education.
2. Becker, M., et al.: Predicting mother's compliance with pediatric medical regimens, J. Pediatr. 81:843, 1972.
3. Becker, M.: Lecture on patient compliance presented at Boston University School of Medicine, 1976.
4. Becker, M.: Socio-behavioral determinants of compliance. In Sackett, D. L., and Haynes, R., editors: Compliance with therapeutic regimens, Baltimore, 1976, The Johns Hopkins University Press.
5. Becker, M., et al.: The health belief model and prediction of dietary compliance: a field experiment, J. Health Soc. Behav. 18:348-366, 1977.
6. Bergman, A. B., and Werner, R. J.: Failure of children to receive penicillin by mouth, N. Engl. J. Med. 268:1334, 1963.
7. Berkowitz, N.: Patient follow through in the outpatient department, Nurs. Res. 12:16-22, 1963.
8. Caron, H.: and Roth, H.: Patient cooperation

with a medical regimen, J.A.M.A. 203:922-926, 1968.

9. Colcher, I., and Bass, J.: Penicillin treatment of streptococcal pharyngitis, J.A.M.A. 222:657, 1972.

10. Croog, S., and Richards, N.: Health beliefs and smoking patterns in heart patients and their wives: a longitudinal study, Am. J. Public Health 67:921-931, 1977.

11. Davis, M.: Variations in patient's compliance with doctor's orders: analysis of the congruence between survey responses and results of empirical investigation, J. Med. Educ. 41:1037-1040, 1966.

12. Davis, M.: Variations in patients' compliance with doctor's advice: an empirical analysis of patterns of communication, Am. J. Public Health 58:274, 1968.

13. Elling, R.: Patient participation in a pediatric program, J. Health Human Behav. 1:183, 1960.

14. Feinstein, A.: Compliance bias and the interpretation of therapeutic trials. In Sackett, D., and Haynes, R., editors: Compliance with therapeutic regimens, Baltimore, 1976, The Johns Hopkins University Press.

15. Finnerty, F.: The problem of non-compliance, Resident and Staff Physician 100:23-32, 1979.

16. Fletcher, S. W., Appel, F. A., and Bourgois, M.: Improving emergency room patient follow-up in a metropolitan teaching hospital, N. Engl. J. Med. 291:385-388, 1974.

17. Francis, V., Korsch, B. M., and Morris, M. J.: Gaps in doctor-patient communication, N. Engl. J. Med. 280:535, 1969.

18. Gabriel, M., Gagnon, J. P., and Bryan, C. K.: Improved patient compliance through use of a daily drug reminder chart, Am. J. Public Health 67:966-968, 1977.

19. Gordis, L.: Why patients don't follow medical advice: a study of children on long term prophylaxis, J. Pediatr. 75:957, 1969.

20. Hartz, P., and Stamps, P.: Appointment keeping behavior re-evaluated, Am. J. Public Health 67:1033-1036, 1977.

21. Haynes, R., et al.: Improvement of medication compliance in uncontrolled hypertension, Lancet 1:1265, 1976.

22. Haynes, R.: Strategies for improving compliance: a methodologic analysis and review. In Sackett, D. L., and Haynes, R., editors: Compliance with therapeutic regimens, Baltimore, 1976, The Johns Hopkins University Press.

23. Haynes, R.: A critical review of determinants of patient compliance with therapeutic regimens. In Sackett, D. L., and Haynes, R., editors: Compliance with therapeutic regimens, Baltimore, 1976, The Johns Hopkins University Press.

24. Heinzelman, F.: Factors in prophylaxis behavior in treating rheumatic fever, J. Health Human Behav. 3:73, 1962.

25. Higbee, K.: Fifteen years of fear arousal: research on threat appeals, Psychol. Bull. 72:426, 1969.

26. Hovland, C., et al.: Communication and persuasion, New Haven, Conn., 1953, Yale University Press.

27. Hulka, B., Kupper, L., Cassel, J., and Efird, R.: Medication use and misuse: physician-patient discrepancies, J. Chronic Dis. 28:7-21, 1975.

28. Hulka, B. S., Cassel, J. C., and Kupper, L. L., et al.: Communication, compliance, and concordance between physicians and patients with prescribed medications, Am. J. Public Health 66:847, 1976.

29. Komaroff, A. L.: The practitioner and the compliant patient, Am. J. Public Health 66:833-835, 1976.

30. Korsch, B. M., Gozzi, E. K., and Francis, V.: Gaps in doctor-patient communication I: doctor-patient interaction and patient satisfaction, Pediatrics 42:855, 1968.

31. Leventhal, H.: Effect of fear communication in the acceptance of preventive health practices, Bull. NY Acad. Med. 41:11, 1965.

32. Levy, R. L., Yamashita, D., and Pow, G.: The relationship of an overt commitment to the frequency and speed of compliance with symptom reporting, Med. Care 17:281-284, 1979.

33. Ley, P., and Spelman, M.: Communication in an outpatient setting, Br. J. Soc. Clin. Psychol. 4:115, 1965.

34. McKinlay, J.: Who is really ignorant? J. Health Soc. Behav. 16:3-12, 1975.

35. McKinney, J. M., et al.: The effects of clinical pharmacy services on patients in essential hypertension, Circulation 48:1104-1111, 1973.

36. Marston, M. V.: Compliance with medical regimens: a review of the literature, Nurs. Res. 19:312-323, 1970.

37. Matthews, D., and Hingson, R.: Improving patient compliance: a guide for physicians, Med. Clin. North Am. 61:879-889, 1977.

38. Meyer, V., and Chesser, E.: Behavior therapy

in clinical psychiatry, Baltimore, 1970, Penguin Books Ltd.

39. Mitchell, J.: Compliance with medical regimens: an annotated bibliography, Health Educ. Monogr. **2**:75, 1974.

40. Nazarian, L. F., Mechaber, J., and Charney, E., et al.: Effect of a mailed appointment reminder on appointment keeping, Pediatrics **53**:349, 1974.

41. Pratt, I., et al.: Physician views on the level of medical information among patients, Am. J. Public Health **47**:1281, 1957.

42. Rosenstock, I.: Why people use health services, Milbank Mem. Fund Q. **44**:94, 1966.

43. Sackett, D. L., Haynes, R. B., and Gibson, E. S., et al.: A randomized clinical trial of strategies for improving medication compliance in primary hypertension, Lancet **1**:1205, 1975.

44. *Sullivan vs O'Connor*, 296 N.E. 2d 183 (Mass, 1973). *Guilmet vs Campbell*, 188 N.W. 29 601 (Michigan, 1971).

45. Zola, I.: Taking your medication: problem for doctor or patient. In Barofsky, I., editor: Medication compliance: a behavior management approach, Thorofare, N.J., 1977, Charles B. Slack, Inc.

Chapter 7

Physical disability and rehabilitation

More than 18 million American adults have some type of chronic illness that limits their physical abilities.[56] At least 1 million of these people are in either chronic disease hospitals, institutions for the physically or mentally disabled, or nursing homes. People with disabilities account for 37% of physician visits and 41% of hospital days.[57] Although physical disability is most common among the elderly and the poor, it can be found in every social stratum.[45] Moreover, one can expect the prevalence of disability in the population to increase in the future as medical science increases its ability to prolong life.

The problems associated with disability pose a challenge not only to patients and their families but also to providers, who can and should play a crucial role in fostering rehabilitation. But at least by some accounts the performance of many clinicians, most notably physicians, in helping the disabled has been inadequate. Johnstone and Miller[30] have commented that "rehabilitation, while embodying the noblest ideas of the medical profession, requires a wide range of services, many quite beyond the scope of medicine. Too frequently in the past have the surgeon and medical practitioner dropped the patient as soon as their personal services to him were completed, leaving the patient confused and dejected, not knowing *where* to turn for further help." In this chapter we will discuss some of the problems disabled people encounter, including the social and psychologic barriers to rehabilitation. We will also offer some suggestions for providers to help patients adjust socially and psychologically to their disabilities.

Problems encountered by disabled persons

What is it like to be disabled? Imagine for a moment that you are one of the 6000 people paralyzed each year from the waist down with a spinal cord injury or that you are one of the 200,000 people crippled each year by stroke. What would a typical day be like? How would you go about getting out of bed in the morning, showering, dressing, making breakfast, and traveling to school? Once in school would people interact with you as they do now? What about dating? Would that be different? When you finish school, what would your employment prospects be like? Would you be able to pursue the career you have in mind? Would you find obtaining a job more difficult? What about marriage and having a family?

Even a brief consideration of these questions makes one realize that besides directly limiting a person's physical activities disability can also precipitate economic, interpersonal, and psychologic problems, which in turn further impede full functioning. Physical incapacity can affect virtually every aspect of daily life; disabled persons are *more likely to experience difficulties in employment, friendship, courtship, sex, travel, recreation, and education.* As we shall see, their experience in some of these respects is *similar* to that of *disadvantaged minority groups* in our society. It is similar in that many of the problems of disabled people arise not from the disability or from themselves but from the insensitivities and lack of understanding of society at large.

Social and psychologic adjustments

Individuals with *congenital* disabilities face the lifelong task of interacting with people yet (1) know that they cannot do all the things others can do, (2) know that others may not be fully aware of their capabilities and incapabilities, and (3) know that their *disabilities*, not their abilities or other attributes, are frequently the focus of attention or the feature by which they are distinguished in others' minds. As we noted in Chapter 4, disabled people often are identified in terms of their disabilities, such as "the kid with a cleft palate" or "the blind guy."

Persons who *acquire* disabilities during the course of their lives face other difficulties as well. They must come to terms with the limitations imposed on their activities and the modifications that must be made in their life-styles. Beyond this is the diminished self-esteem that may result from feelings of being less physically attractive and/or less useful in family and occupational roles. When one acquires a disability, one's whole conception of self may change profoundly.[41] How people shape this new self-image can affect rather strikingly the extent to which they can function to the limits of their physical capabilities.

Moreover, *the problems of the disabled affect those close to them.* The development of a disability by a married person may contribute to marital problems and, ultimately, to divorce. Parents of disabled children have been found to agree less on how to handle their children, to experience less closeness as a couple, and to have greater marital conflict.[9] The impact of disability on a family can also be felt by siblings, who may feel that the disabled child is being given preferential treatment.[14]

Most people with physical disabilities are medical patients at some point. In general, as was discussed in detail in Chapter 5, patients are expected to adopt the obligations of the *sick role.*[44] As traditionally formulated, largely in terms of an acute illness, the sick role concept holds that society places certain expectations or obligations on people who are sick, and their conduct as patients is closely watched. Persons who are ill are expected to relinquish or abandon many of their normal activities and concentrate on the task of regaining health as quickly as possible. Patients are expected to depend on the medical staff, comply with their orders, and put aside, to some degree, the external power and prestige of their normal social roles. They are expected to endure suffering and pain with as much grace and as little complaining as possible. In short, patients should admit they are sick, should want to get well, and should do everything possible to aid the process.

Role expectations for the disabled

Role expectations become more difficult to fulfill when one acquires a long-term impairment.[31] Overcoming disability can be a far more arduous task than complying with a short-term medical plan when full recovery is expected. The rewards for the disabled are not as immediate and dramatic; the disabled person may never again be able to fully resume the various activities in which he or she was once able to engage. And after a while those *privileges* included in the sick role come to be withdrawn and *different role expectations emerge.*[18]

First, the individual is expected to *accept the full extent of the disability.* For some, however, the prospect of permanent disability can be so psychologically devastating that the defense mechanism of denial is used to cope. Croog, Shapiro, and Levine surveyed 345 men who had been hospitalized 3 weeks earlier for an unequivocal myocardial infarction. All of the men were asked, "From what you know about your own illness, do you think you had a heart attack?" Of the 345 men, 12% replied "No" and 8% indicated that they did not know.[12] Difficulty in acceptance can be heightened if family members also employ denial as a defense. Parents, perhaps because of feelings of guilt and responsibility, are especially likely to view their disabled child's prospects with unrealistic optimism. One study of handicapped children suggests that the greater the personal attachment parents feel toward a child, the less realistic are the appraisals that they make of the child's abilities.[67]

Second, once a person has accepted the nature and extent of the disability, it is incumbent on the person to attempt to develop at least a partial repertoire of behaviors that can substitute for those lost as a result of the physical impairment. The person must learn to be what has been called a *handicapped performer.* Learning to read Braille, use sign language, read lips, or use ambulatory aids is not easy. The motivation to engage in such training must come from the realization that without it the person will not be able to engage in many normal activities and may in fact hinder others. The risk that the person will give up in despair, however, is also high.

Losing hope of further improvement is itself a frequent problem encountered by those who develop a disability. In some cases when the patient also experiences such symptoms as a disordered sleep pattern, anorexia, or weight loss, the despair shades into clinical depression. Depression following disability occasionally becomes severe; it can include serious suicidal feelings and/or frank psychotic delusions. Although such severe problems merit psychiatric attention, in most cases the despair experienced by the newly disabled is a normal psychologic response to an extremely stressful life event, and psychiatric care is not indicated. As we shall see, however, the responses of all those caring for the disabled patient can strongly influence the patient's state of mind.

Third, the disabled person often is required to become an *active participant in decisions concerning the development of a life-style consistent with both impairment and rehabilitation.* Disabled persons generally must take part in determining the goals, methods, and pace of their treatment and in evaluating its effectiveness. Here again denial may result in patients becoming overly optimistic in framing rehabilitation plans or cause them to attempt activities well beyond their physical capacities. Conversely, the patients experiencing despair may withdraw from participation in rehabilitation entirely, having no hope for success.

Fourth, disabled persons must adjust to being continually *helped persons,* helped by both therapists and the other people with whom they have contact. Disabled persons are likely to require more than usual amounts of personal assistance and consequently may develop feelings of inferiority, excessive obligation to others, or guilt because they cannot repay their helpers. As a result, they may feel uncomfortable any time they receive assistance. Also, the disabled are frequently the object of assistance they do not need, that is, they are at times *treated as more disabled than they actually are.* The disabled person, therefore, faces the task of either accepting unneeded help ungrudgingly or declining it in such a manner as not to offend the offerer.

Finally, disabled persons need to develop *strategies for engaging in social interactions* with people who are not intimately familiar with their disabilities. Interactions between nondisabled and disabled persons are often awkward because most people are unsure about how to interact with someone who is visibly disabled. All of us have probably noticed some increased strain on first meeting such a person. Such questions arise as, "Should I ignore his missing leg?" "Should I mention it?" "Should I even talk freely about it?" Seeing another person with a disability is a reminder of the hazards all of us face in life. We may wonder, "Why him and not me?" The apparent inequity in who acquires disability makes some people feel both guilty and leery about how the disabled person will react to them; they may fear that the person will exhibit bitterness or contempt.[48] Many nondisabled persons simply have difficulty understanding the needs, capabilities, and emotions of the disabled.

Disabled individuals often complain about the ineptness of the nondisabled in their behavior toward them. Complaints range from being stared at to being ignored, from being offered help that is not needed to being overlooked when it is needed, and from being attributed with unnatural insight to being considered intellectually as well as physically disabled. Davis[13] argues that the strains and inhibitions resulting from such interactions often deny the disabled person the status of social normalcy.

Employment, transportation, and housing

In addition to the sorts of psychologic and interpersonal problems we have discussed, people who are disabled encounter serious difficulties in employment, transportation, and housing that also seriously jeopardize the quality of their lives.

Disabled people in general experience considerably more *unemployment* than the population at large. The Massachusetts Rehabilitation Commission, for example, estimated in 1978 that 60% of the disabled in that state were unemployed.[29] One study of over 500 spinal cord injury patients in five United States hospitals reported that only one third of all paraplegics and only one half of all quadriplegics return to work and that only 10% to 15% of either group return to their former jobs.[51] Once the disabled find jobs, it is also more difficult for them to maintain them. For example, in northern California a survey of vocational rehabilitation clients with a variety of disabilities revealed that less than 45% remained employed for 1 year after receiving training and job placement by the state's rehabilitation services.[66]

In considering these employment difficulties it should not be forgotten that in the life of an individual, work is more than a means of earning income. It determines the pattern of interpersonal associations of individuals and is a critical determinant of their life-styles. It serves as a core element around which activities in the lives of individuals are organized. The opportunity to be productive in a working setting gives meaning to the lives of many individuals, and the loss of employment may have serious effects on personal adjustment and mental health.[11]

Lack of *accessibility to buildings and transportation* and *of architecturally altered housing*[54] poses further problems for many disabled people. Despite the recent promulgation of regulations requiring access for all persons, including the disabled, to all public buildings, it is unlikely that most buildings and public transportation will in fact be made accessible before the late 1980s. This in turn places a great financial burden on many of the disabled because it restricts where they can work and where they can shop.

In general, *disabled people spend far more each year to survive than do the nondisabled.* For example, estimates of the yearly costs of living for individuals with spinal cord injuries compared to individuals in the general population suggest that paraplegics spend from $1500 to $5000 more each year.[7,51] Included in these estimates are such extra expenses as buying medications and/or appliances necessary for the management of the disability, architecturally altering one's home, and additional transportation costs. These additional expenditures can erode the motivation of patients to participate in rehabilitation programs or to return to work if in so doing they render themselves ineligible for financial benefits that absorb such costs.

Factors influencing adjustment to disability

How successful are most disabled persons in coping with these problems? What factors influence whether or not a person will successfully adapt? The answers to these questions are not clear, for little systematic research has been undertaken in the area of disability. Most studies in the area have been *retrospective* analyses of single patients or small groups of patients. Only a handful of studies have *prospectively* examined even moderate-sized populations, attempting to isolate the social and psychologic factors that assist or impede successful rehabilitation.

Nonetheless some findings have emerged that provide insights into the rehabilitation process and that suggest a number of research questions requiring future attention. In the next few pages we shall review selected studies about how the rehabilitation process is affected by the nature of the disability, the characteristics of the disabled person (e.g., social class, age, home situation, and beliefs about illness and its effect on him or her), and the nature of the services offered to the disabled.

The nature of the disability

The nature and characteristics of a disability can have considerable impact on the success of people's efforts to perform to the utmost of their capacities. There is some evidence suggesting that people with more severe disabilities exhibit more motivation in rehabilitation.[42] Predictably, however, *the greater the number and variety of daily living activities restricted by a disability, the fewer activities the individual will be likely to regain.*[64] Moreover, the fewer the activities a person can perform, the lower the chance of survival. Daily living activities that have been examined include self-feeding, dressing and undressing, bathing, toilet activities, bladder and bowel control, and a variety of ambulation measures.

If the disability is *highly visible* and/or if the person's *ability to communicate with others* is impaired, adjustment to a disability becomes particularly difficult. Visible disorders are generally unattractive and often evoke feelings of discomfort and pity among the nondisabled. In questioning several student and working populations about how they feel toward people with various disabilities, Tringo[55] found that respondents were much less disposed to interact with those whose disabilities are highly visible (e.g., hunchbacks, cerebral palsy victims, and paraplegics) than with those with less visible disabilities such as arthritis or heart disease. This negative posture toward the visibly disabled appears to be stronger in adults than in children; studies of children at various ages shows that as they grow older, they are more likely to be repelled by the sight of body and facial disfigurement.[28] Consequently, people with highly visible disabilities encounter greater difficulty in interpersonal relationships.[65]

Interpersonal relationships may not only be affected by the *visibility* of a disorder but also by the degree to which one's *ability to communicate* is affected. Aphasic stroke patients, for example, frequently experience considerable difficulty in this regard. A disabled patient, for example, needs to communicate with the therapist about the disorder, the rehabilitation program, and the progress being made. A disabled patient also needs communication skills to overcome the other barriers to interaction that we have considered. It should not be surprising, then, that loss of communication skills has been found to seriously hamper successful rehabilitation.

The patient's social class

The rehabilitation process is a very expensive one, requiring the efforts of many professionals over a long period of time. Consequently, people with low incomes and those without insurance coverage are frequently unable to obtain needed rehabilitation services. In fact, the disabled frequently experience difficulty in obtaining insurance to pay for *any* of their health needs.

Many people with marginal incomes are reluctant to begin rehabilitation for fear that they will lose workmen's compensation payments. Johnstone and Miller[30] have noted that "to them compensation, although a pittance, offers a sure thing. So they wait for a final settlement of their claim. Soon indifference, fear, and apathy overcome the patient. Final settlements are delayed until maximum improvement has been reached or until the patient's disability is stationary and can be rated equitably. In this long lag the patient loses his will to work; his self-discipline oozes away and he despondently, even docilely, accepts an unhappy life of dependency."

Although it is clear that lack of income may reduce one's ability or motivation to obtain rehabilitation services, it is less certain that a person's actual performance once in a rehabilitation program is directly affected by income. Some studies suggest that when given the opportunity poor people do just as well in rehabilitation programs as those of greater means. But beyond success in specific rehabilitation programs, the picture again becomes gloomy for people with low incomes.

Employment problems for lower-income people are especially severe because they more often have held jobs that disabled persons cannot fill. Manual labor, even in highly skilled or specialized forms, is frequently difficult or impossible for physically disabled persons. On the other hand, white-collar employees may have held jobs that are not so greatly jeopardized by a physical handicap.[33] The experience of cardiac patients illustrates this problem. Studying men under 65 who had suffered a myocardial infarction, Sharland[50] found that lower-class men were more likely to change jobs after their infarction than upper-class men. In a study of 24- to 54-year-old enrollees in the Health Insurance Plan of Greater New York who suffered a myocardial infarction, Shapiro similarly found that blue-collar workers were much slower to return to work than white-collar workers.[60] In Croog and Levin's study of 292 heart attack patients, only 2% of persons with white-collar jobs were unemployed when interviewed 1 year later. In contrast, 26% of semiskilled or unskilled workers were unemployed.[10]

In short, lower-income, less educated blue-collar workers who acquire a disability have less motivation to seek rehabilitation services and experience more difficulty in obtaining them. Moreover, even though such people may respond to therapy as well as middle- and upper-income people, their subsequent employment prospects may be more limited because of the more strenuous physical demands of their jobs.

The patient's age

Most studies have supported the intuitive notion that as one ages, the chances of being successfully rehabilitated for a disability diminish for both physical and psychologic reasons.* Sometimes, however, the psychologic reasons outpace the physical reasons. After interviewing a national sample of noninstitutionalized disabled individuals in the United States, Haber[24] concluded that older people with disabilities are generally not rehabilitated to their fullest capacities because jobs are least accessible to them, thus reducing their motivation, and they are more likely to devalue their own capabilities. Expectations among the elderly about how well they might be able to function may be unrealistically limited because of the common assumption that reduced capacity is an inexorable product of aging. There is an obvious need to prevent elderly persons from unnecessarily underestimating their physical potential in the face of disability.

The patient's psychologic state

The findings we have just reviewed underscore the extent to which a disabled person's self-perception can affect progress during and adjustment after rehabilitation. *Fear, denial, and despair* can all impede successful adjustment to a disability.

It is only natural for people who acquire disabilities to be *fearful.* A common fear is that the condition is only the first symptom of a deteriorating course. A disabled person is likely to wonder, "Will I lose more vision? Experience more pain? Be able to do even less? Die?" Such fears, of course, may prompt some people to make appropriate changes in their life-styles and follow professional recommendations more closely. However, other people may so overprotect themselves that they do *not* engage in activities that they are capable of doing. The overly apprehensive postmyocardial infarction patient who adopts an unnecessarily sedentary life is an example of such a reaction.[6]

To make the adjustments to a disability described earlier, it is important for disabled persons to accept the full extent of their disability without despairing about their self-worth. Patients who fail to fully accept their disabilities are, in general, less likely to take steps considered necessary for recovery. Croog, Shapiro, and Levine[12] in their study of cardiac patients reported that those who denied their illnesses were less likely to follow their physician's advice about smoking, work, rest, and weight reduction. Moreover, Fogel and Rosillo,[19] studying over 100 pa-

*References 19, 32, 35, 37, 40, and 52.

tients with a variety of disabilities, reported that those who recognized and most realistically assessed their problems made the most progress in rehabilitation. Unless disabled patients can squarely face the full extent of their disabilities, they may not be willing or able to take the arduous steps necessary for rehabilitation.

On the other hand, although accurately appraising one's disability may be necessary for rehabilitation, it also increases one's likelihood of being overwhelmed by its nature or magnitude. A number of studies reveal that the *loss of self-esteem and feelings of stigma* associated with a disability *reduce the likelihood of successful rehabilitation.*[26,27,40] Kemp and Vash found that the patients most successful in coping with hemiplegia and paraplegia were those who had a forward-looking, goal-setting outlook characterized by an orientation away from the actual physical losses brought about by the injury. More successful patients expressed goals in the vocational, social, and family areas; less successful patients' goals concerned only regaining bodily functions. A major problem for those working with the disabled is how to prevent them from concluding "What's the use? I'll never be normal again, and I'll never be able to do what others can do."

In addition to loss of self-esteem and feelings of stigma, feelings of isolation and loneliness may contribute to poor progress in rehabilitation.[1,26,28] The hemiplegic and paraplegic patients in Kemp and Vash's study who made the *least* progress were the least outgoing, scoring lowest on measures of sociability.[35] Hyman similarly found that patients who felt lonely and isolated made the least progress in rehabilitation. Not only were their *feelings* of loneliness related to rehabilitation but measures of their *actual degree* of social isolation were related to rehabilitation progress.[26,28]

The patient's family

Since feelings of isolation inhibit successful rehabilitation, it is not surprising that the families of disabled people have been found to play a crucial role, with those patients given strong family encouragement and acceptance showing the best performance.[37,39,52] Studying patients with multiple illnesses and disabilities after hospital discharge Kelman[34] found that people who lived alone without such supports were more likely to be rehospitalized than persons living with supportive families.

It follows from our earlier discussion, however, that if a person's friends and family hope to be supportive, they must realistically accept the disability and provide *realistic* support and encouragement. If a family underestimates the capacities of its disabled member, they may be overprotective and impede rehabilitation. On the other hand, should family members deny the disability or refuse to accept all of its implications, the disabled person may be confused and hindered by unattainable and hence frustrating expectations.

Beyond the information presented above, little is known about the factors associated with the successful rehabilitation of the disabled. This may be due in part to certain methodological problems surrounding research in this area. For example, there is no consensus as to what actually constitutes "successful rehabilitation." Some studies emphasize morbidity, mortality, and physical functioning. Others attempt to examine such indicators of "quality of life" as ability to perform various activities of daily living, psychologic adjustment, marital status, successful attendance and completion of rehabilitation programs, or job status after leaving such a program. As a result, comparability between studies is low.

Also, there are many different kinds of disabilities with a variety of prognoses; this has made it difficult to develop a body of knowledge applicable to all. As new medical and surgical techniques develop, for example, new types of disability arise. The uncertainties experienced by a heart transplant patient, for instance, may be much greater than those experienced by a paraplegic accident victim. In the latter case, the extent of the person's disability and the steps to optimal functioning are relatively clearly established. In the former the prognosis may not be clear and to a certain extent the responsibility for rehabilitation may rest with new medical developments rather than with the effort of the patient.

The medical care system

In addition to the above concerns it has become clear that the way in which medical services are organized and caregivers are trained influences the quality of research in the field and, more importantly, the kind of treatment offered to the disabled. One might say, then, that one of the most important social factors in patient rehabilitation is the emphasis given it by the medical establishment.

Research into both the rehabilitation process and the care of the disabled requires the combined efforts of many professional groups. In our era of highly specialized medicine, however, the care provided by physicians to disabled patients is essentially divided up according to the specific location of the physical disability (cardiologists care for heart patients, urologists care for kidney patients, ophthalmologists care for low-vision patients, etc.). The result has been that little attention has been systematically devoted to developing a core of knowledge and training techniques concerning the management of problems common to all patients with long-term disabilities.

Moreover, delivery of care to the disabled requires physicians to work closely with nonphysicians yet, as many clinicians and researchers have noted, interdisciplinary cooperation in the delivery of care is often difficult to achieve.[17,53,61] Questions frequently arise as to who should assume or coordinate responsibility for diagnosis, selection of treatment, and actual rendering of care. All too often professionals working with the same patient will explicitly or implicitly convey different messages about prognosis and treatment progress because of differences in philosophies among professional groups. Despite this few teaching institutions devote curriculum time to issues involved in developing teamwork among members of different professions. Very few medical schools, for example, expose future physicians to even rudimentary instruction about the roles of other disciplines serving disabled persons, particularly social work and occupational and physical therapy.

Clinical training. Although the problems and progress of disabled persons extend over a period of years, and the results are usually not dramatic, the clinical training of almost all medical professionals is divided into brief "electives," "affiliations," or "rotations." Even year-long internships are normally subdivided into rotations through various wards and ambulatory clinics so that few interns have the opportunity to follow the progress of a disabled person over an extended period of time. One might argue that residency programs in physical medicine and rehabilitation would be the place where physicians can best be trained in long-term care. But there are less than 50 such programs in the United States, hardly enough to meet the needs of the growing number of disabled persons. In general, compared to other specialties rehabilitation medicine may be perceived by young physicians as an unattractive career choice. Although there are over 300,000 active practicing physicians in the United States, only 1500 are primarily engaged in rehabilitation medicine.[58] Young physicians may regard the potential for patient rehabilitation as too limited to be rewarding or find too many psychologic and social factors that interfere with the progress that can be made. An additional problem is that even those training institutions that do offer residencies in physical medicine and rehabilitation may have only a limited impact on trainees in the many other medical specialties and professional disciplines dealing with the disabled.

Even psychiatry, a medical specialty devoted almost exclusively to long-term care and with psychologic concerns as its central focus, has devoted little attention to the problems of the disabled. Less than 5% of the articles published between 1970 and 1977 in the *American Journal of Psychiatry* (the specialty's most prestigious journal) specifically address the psychologic problems of the physically disabled. This may have resulted from a combination of American psychiatry's attention to those "purely" psychologic problems seen as originating in early life experiences and the profession's relative isolation from the concerns of other medical specialties.

Agencies and organizations

Just as cooperation and communication among individual professionals are important factors in the rehabilitation process, so too are cooperation and communication among the various agencies and organizations that may be involved in the provision of rehabilitative services. Although there are a sizable number of such agencies in most communities, their services are rarely coordinated to prevent overlap in some areas and service gaps in others. In many communities it appears that potential clients are often literally lost in a confusing network of independent agencies.[11,34] Unless disabled persons are knowledgeable about the pathways of the network, they may simply be unable to apply for services that might be available.

Even the person who is aware of available services needs to be persistent and aggressive in seeking them out.

Part of this problem has arisen from the continuing needs of rehabilitation agencies for financial support while the priorities of funding services fluctuate. Until recently most federal and state monies in rehabilitation were directed toward those agencies that could demonstrate that the services they provided made people *economically productive members of society.* This contributed to the practice within agencies of accepting only those people who were the least disabled and could most easily be helped to return to work.

The passage of Public Law 93-112 in 1973 has prompted a marked increase in assistance provided to the most severely disabled.[36] The law provides financial support for rehabilitation programs to assist individuals who, due to the severity of their disabilities or other factors such as age, could not reasonably be expected to be vocationally rehabilitated but who might be able to live independently or function normally within their families and communities with rehabilitation services.

The disabled person seeking help, however, is likely to be unaware of financial aid variations and consequently may incorrectly assume that rejection by one agency means that all agencies will refuse to provide assistance. As a result, many disabled persons have been discouraged from seeking the help they need and could receive. Moreover, even though funding priorities have changed, the varying selection procedures still employed by rehabilitation agencies continue to make it difficult for even the most sophisticated person to judge how successful a particular agency or institution may be in dealing with a specific disability at a certain level of severity.

This situation is made even more difficult for the prospective helpseeker by those organizational needs that impede appropriate referral. Some organizational reformers feel that if one can get the leaders of various voluntary organizations together, they will better understand one another's eligibility requirements to other agencies. Unfortunately, however, having a lengthy patient waiting list remains important to many agencies because it demonstrates to funding sources a need for the services the agency offers and because it provides a continuous supply of patients. Consequently, interagency communication does not always help in assuring appropriate referrals.[38,63]

Another important feature of rehabilitation agencies is that they differ in philosophy of care. Some emphasize helping patients accept their disabilities so that they can learn substituting accommodating behaviors. Although such acceptance is generally desirable, it can pose problems if the patient has some residual ability that is overlooked by the agency staff. For example, many persons classified as legally blind do have some vision. Teaching such people to read Braille or use Seeing Eye dogs would be inappropriate if low-vision corrective lenses and optical aids would enable them to read and move around safely. This philosophy can also pose problems if it fosters excessive dependence on the agency. Scott argues that many agencies serving the blind operate on the assumption that only a few highly gifted individuals are capable of achieving independence from an agency. With clients who do not fit into this category, these agencies adopt an accommodative approach that trains people to function effectively only within the confines of the agency itself: clients are rewarded for trivial things and praised for performing tasks in a mediocre fashion. "This superficial and overly generous reward system makes it impossible for most clients to assess their accomplishments accurately. . . . many come to believe that the underlying assumption must be that blindness makes them incompetent. . . . the blind person learns skills and behaviors that are necessary for participating in activities and programs of the agency, but which make it more difficult to cope with the environment of the larger community."[49]

One benefit to the agency of adopting an accommodative approach is, of course, that it will always have clients who need its services.

Helping disabled persons to adjust psychologically and socially
Informing the patient

A crucial element in rehabilitation, as we have emphasized, is the acceptance by the patient of the diagnosis and prognosis. Although it is most often a physician who initially presents this information, all professionals working with the patient convey overt or covert messages about the disability and the meaning of day-to-day changes in functional status during rehabilitation. It is important, then, that all those involved in the care of a disabled person communicate regularly so that the patient is not given contradictory information. Failure to do this only serves to make acceptance more difficult and painful and promotes patient distrust of *all* team members trying to help.

When informing patients of diagnosis and prognosis full candor is the desired norm. News must be given, however, in a way that does not unnecessarily extinguish all hope. For example, even though patients with a spinal cord injury may have lost the functioning of their legs, they may be told that one cannot absolutely preclude the development of techniques within the patient's lifetime that could restore functioning. The reality that the patient must come to accept is only that needed to maximize function in the *proximate* future.

Also, disclosure should not be done so rapidly that it emotionally traumatizes the patient. Corcoran[8] has argued for the use of "successive approximation" in disclosing bad news. By giving patients information gradually over time with deliberate hints that more information is coming, one allows them to shore up psychologic defenses before receiving each new piece of information.

Strategies to prevent despair

Once diagnostic and prognostic information has been disclosed, the problem for those providing help is how to prevent *excessive* anxiety, denial, or despair. A variety of strategies have been developed by rehabilitation programs to grapple with this problem. In some agencies patient and provider jointly set a number of *short-term, achievable goals* with designated rewards for their accomplishments that, at times, *take the form of "contracts."* Asking the patient to keep personal charts and records of progress in meeting these goals often helps to instill feelings of participation and increased control over the environment.[20]

Having the patient meet people with similar disabilities who have shown good adjustment and who are functioning well outside the hospital can also prove helpful. Such lay individuals are often more credible than professionals who themselves have not experienced the disability. Also, they may have developed strategies not envisioned by the professional staff to deal successfully with problems their disabilities pose.[47]

In enlisting the aid of such individuals certain points should be kept in mind. First, those chosen to interact with the patient should be carefully screened; being instructed by someone who has even a slightly different disability or prognosis can be discouraging and misleading. Second, those who undertake this task must be sufficiently sensitive to the patient's fears and concerns to provide empathy and support as well as information and a practical demonstration of the possibilities offered by rehabilitation. In initiating such interactions one of the provider's goals should be for the patient to understand that when other people evaluate him or her they consider not only the disability but also how well he or she *responds* to the disability.

Some programs also try to have patients take *limited forays outside the institutional setting* even before they are ready to do so on an extended basis, for example, taking patients to a restaurant near the hospital. Not only does this expose patients to some of the problems they may encounter outside the institution but it can also provide relief from the feelings of institutional confinement. In addition to these measures *psychologic* interventions such as biofeedback, relaxation training, hypnosis, autosuggestion, and specific behavior modification techniques have also been introduced to some patients and are currently under study.[2]

Inquiry into patient concerns

Most important of all, providers should *anticipate and be open to hearing the concerns of patients about their disabilities.* Such matters as occupational prospects, sexual functioning, costs of rehabilitation, transportation and housing needs, the understanding of the condition by friends and family members, communication and interaction with other people, and problems with agencies or other professionals may be broached by patients on their own, but may also remain unaddressed. Consequently, it is incumbent on professionals working with disabled individuals to raise each of these issues at some point during rehabilitation.

Working with family and friends

An initial assessment must be made of the level of understanding of and amount of emotional support possible from family and/or close friends. As has been mentioned, accurate understanding and consistent support by such people can play an essential role in rehabilitation. Families and friends can help to combat the despair associated with the development of a disability, and they can often be of assistance in helping the professional staff take care of the patient's physical needs, such as feeding, washing, and positioning in bed. It is also useful for members of the rehabilitation staff to acknowledge to the family that providing such support can, at times, be difficult and frustrating. If family members make sacrifices to help a disabled person, they should be recognized and commended. If, on the other hand, family members feel obliged to make inordinate sacrifices, members of the staff can provide guidance as to what most people consider sufficient and appropriate support.

At times feelings of guilt on the part of either the patient or a family member may compromise a supportive relationship. When disability arises suddenly (as from a stroke, accident, or heart attack), patients and family members often attempt to attribute it to something they did or did not do. Occurrences immediately prior to or following the event may take on disproportionate importance in people's minds. To the extent that a member of the rehabilitation team recognizes and attempts to correct overreactions of this sort, both patient and family may be spared personal suffering and interpersonal recriminations.

Assisting with employment problems

Helping patients who desire to return to work is a key feature of most rehabilitation programs. Professionals working with disabled patients should fully discuss their work experience and occupational aspirations so that realistic plans can be made and patients can be directed to the most appropriate agencies. As has been pointed out, the employment prospects of disabled persons do not compare favorably with those of the rest of the population. All too often this has prompted both disabled individuals and the professionals involved in their care to underestimate the potential for future employment. An unfortunate consequence of this underestimation is that many disabled people become unnecessarily discouraged or find themselves being trained for inappropriately menial or otherwise unenjoyable jobs. This in turn lowers their motivation to complete the vocational programs in which they are enrolled or to remain with the jobs in which they are subsequently placed.

The Federal Rehabilitation Act of 1973 may effect some improvement in the employment prospects of disabled persons by requiring any employer holding federal contracts of $2500 or more to actively recruit, hire, and promote disabled persons. Under the act any persons who feel they have been discriminated against may file a complaint with the Department of Labor. Although a constructive step this legislation does not apply to many businesses and places the burden of legal action on disabled people themselves.[47] Nonetheless during rehabilitation patients should be informed of their legal rights as prospective job applicants.

Sexual counseling

In recent years, growing out of a realization that even disabilities that alter sexual functioning do not necessarily alter sexual expectations, there has been an increased awareness of the need to provide counseling on sexual matters to disabled persons.[3] Yet of all the social and psychologic issues that should be addressed during rehabilitation, sexuality is one of the most sensitive and difficult for the disabled and their sexual partners and also for clinicians. Sexual counseling of the disabled can take many different directions, depending on the nature of the disability and the characteristics of the disabled person as an individual. Obviously the concerns vary according to the patient's sex, age, marital status, degree of past sexual experience, sexual orientation, and range of sexual preferences. Because of the number of factors it is necessary to take into account, it is not possible to consider sexual counseling in any detail. A few points, however, have broad applicability.

First, *merely broaching the topic* of sex with disabled patients and their sexual partners in a way that lets them know that it is all right to discuss their concerns with a professional and with each other is an extraordinarily important step.[7] Second, the clinician can be of considerable help in reducing feelings of *guilt* or *insecurity* when patients have to *alter* their usual sexual practices to satisfy themselves or their partners. Although genital intercourse that leads to orgasm is possible for most disabled people, for example, it is not possible for all. Consequently, counseling may need to break down the tendency of many disabled people to consider sex as an all-or-nothing activity that can acceptably be done in only one way. Body contact and foreplay of various types are possible for most individuals, and stimulation of secondary erogenous zones proves gratifying and pleasurable whether or not genital functioning is possible. Also, prosthetic appliances help many disabled persons increase the satisfaction they offer to partners.[25] While being sensitive not to impose one's own morality on the disabled, the professional can strive to "realign the performance expectations and capabilities so that the only allowable criteria for concern are based on what the couple or the individual prefers within their abilities. . . . It must be made clear that what one does in the privacy of the bedroom is of concern only to the individuals involved. Persons should be encouraged to maximize the use of functions that remain rather than bemoan the nonuse of those functions that are lost."[15]

Communication and interaction with other people

As has been pointed out, social interactions between disabled and nondisabled persons are frequently strained and laden with ambiguity because most people do not understand the abilities, needs, and emotions of the physically disabled. It is important that disabled people be forewarned about the types of reaction their disabilities may provoke and the strengths and limitations of the strategies other disabled persons use to deal with them. The style of many disabled people is to pretend to be "normal" to avoid having the attention of another person focused on their disability during an interaction.[22] This is exemplified by those blind persons who look directly at the person with whom they are speaking even though they see nothing or by those deaf persons adept at lipreading who pretend to hear.[13] Although pretense may be effective in many instances, the disabled who try to hide their disabilities run the risk of exposure and can never be sure what the observer's reaction might be.

Although the effectiveness of any particular strategy will depend on the nature of the disability and the personality of the individual employing it, *professionals should be wary of encouraging efforts to pass as "normal."* Not only does this strategy place its user at the risk of seriously embarrassing both the user and other persons but it also may contribute to feelings of low self-esteem by introducing an element of disingenuousness into the interaction: the disabled person may rationalize that he or she is accepted by the other person only because of the deceit. In other cases the user of this strategy may contribute to a patient's inability to acknowledge, even to himself or herself, the nature or extent of the disability, which may in turn compromise other facets of the rehabilitation process.

Two other strategies seem preferable. First, one can attempt to *educate the nondisabled* about one's disability.[23] This may include explaining its nature, extent, and the plan of rehabilitation or management or providing information about the implications of the disability for the individual's life as well as clarification about the types of personal assistance that the individual does and does not need.

The second strategy that the disabled can employ has been called *breaking through*.[13] Its purpose is to help others realize that, outside of a specific disability, the disabled person is like other people and possesses similar beliefs, values, aspirations, and problems. Individuals who are breaking through project images, attitudes, and concepts of self that encourage the nondisabled to identify with them.

Breaking through may sometimes require the disabled to consciously present themselves as the same as nondisabled and at other times to voluntarily withhold themselves from those situations in which the nondisabled would find it difficult to see them as normal. They have to make a special effort to demonstrate to others that they have interests and concerns about matters (other than those pertaining to disability) that are the same as those of nondisabled individuals.

Managing the costs of rehabilitation

Given the extra expenses incurred by disabled persons both during rehabilitation and after, those offering care should raise the issue of finances with the disabled person and actively explore ways to meet the costs.

The federal government supplies financial assistance to many disabled persons through its Social Security Disability Insurance Program* and the Supplementary Security Income Program.† Other major sources include Medicare, veteran's benefits, private insurance, workmen's compensation, Medicaid, and other state-run welfare benefits.

Referrals to rehabilitation agencies

In addition to being aware of the resources mentioned above, it is extremely important for those involved in rehabilitation to be familiar with the private and public agencies within their communities that provide financial support and other services for the disabled.

Before any provider makes a referral to a rehabilitation agency the provider should not only assess the patient's need for service but also investigate the characteristics of the agency to which referral is being considered. The person making the referral should learn:

1. The agency's eligibility criteria
2. Who pays for the services
3. The rehabilitative goals of the agency
4. The agency's definition of the problem
5. Who staffs the agency
6. The specific types of treatment or assistance the agency offers
7. How the agency evaluates patient progress
8. Whether it feeds back information to the referring health care provider
9. How well its staff believes it accomplishes its goals
10. What types of persons staff believe do best and worst in their program
11. What people who have used the agency think about the services they were offered

Without this information it is difficult for providers to adequately assess and compare the suitability of different agencies for their patients. Perhaps more importantly, knowledge about these points helps the provider to *avoid* referring to agencies with an accommodative approach to those patients who have residual abilities or who, if sent to a program with a different philosophy, might be able to achieve functional independence.

Beyond the efforts of the provider

As can be seen from the preceding discussion, many of the improvements that might be effected in the care of the disabled would derive from changes in the

---

*A program for persons who in the past have contributed to the social security fund through their work and who have a substantial disability that will extend over 12 months and interfere with their capacity to work.

†Persons of any age may qualify for SSI. Monthly payments are determined by standard formulas, including marital status, income, living situation, and savings.

medical care system itself rather than from the efforts of individual clinicians. In the area of professional education, for example, it is important that additional attention be paid to the needs and problems of long-term care. Acute care generally permits the patient to accept a passive role vis-á-vis the caregiver. The patient explains what he or she feels, a diagnosis is reached, treatment is prescribed, and the patient is expected to comply. Rehabilitation work necessitates a provider-patient relationship of a different sort. Rather than placing emphasis on diagnostic and therapeutic procedures, rehabilitation focuses on restoration of normal functioning, adjustment to disability, and relearning of lost skills. For optimal progress to occur, patients must assume *an active role in informing the clinician* of both progress and setbacks. Rehabilitation therefore often requires more sharing of both information and decision making between provider and patient than in acute care.[62] Moreover, long-term treatment often requires the clinician to pay greater attention to the feelings, needs, and beliefs of the patient's family to facilitate the patient's successful return home. Working with disabled patients thus requires considerable sociologic and psychologic sophistication, the development of which has traditionally been given little attention in the training of medical providers.

Similarly, more systematic efforts must be made to bring the problems of disabled patients to the attention of students in the medical professions. Because long-term follow-up is normally essential in rehabilitation, new strategies must be employed that will give students an exposure to disabled patients over longer periods of time. Alterations in curricula and increased student contact with community rehabilitation programs are needed. Since the process of rehabilitation demands interdisciplinary efforts, it is essential that educational programs include extensive exposure to members of the entire medical team. Only in this way can students effectively learn of the contributions members of professions other than their own can make to patient care. Further, issues of interdisciplinary cooperation in long-term management should be explicitly addressed in health science curricula.

Beyond the educational arena our medical care system must support greater research efforts into understanding the social and psychologic barriers to successful rehabilitation. There is still considerable ambiguity about what constitutes successful rehabilitation, and additional efforts are needed to establish standard criteria so that the various professionals dealing with different forms of disability can share their knowledge. Once again interdisciplinary cooperation and communication are essential. Researchers have tended to publish their results only in their own specialty journals, causing concepts that have long been in use in one field to be proposed by another as representing new and important contributions.

Moreover, research is needed that goes beyond comparing the social and psychologic characteristics of patients who are successfully rehabilitated and those who are not. The development and evaluation of specific interventions to overcome the social and psychologic barriers to rehabilitation are urgently needed. To date, systematic interventions have been directed largely toward individual patients in rehabilitation settings. Evaluations of such programs have provided fruitful leads, but the multitude of social processes affecting rehabilitation implies that we also need efforts aimed at those individuals who affect the disabled patient's life. For example, would offering financial incentives to employers to hire or train disabled individuals be an effective means of increasing self-sufficiency on the part of the disabled and reducing overall public expenditures on their behalf? Would providing special training to family members enhance the adjustment of disabled individuals to home life? Would it decrease their need for relying on therapeutic agencies? Would public education about the problems associated with common disabilities increase the ease with which disabled individuals interact with others? Answers to these questions will be yielded only by studies that conceive of disability as a social as well as a medical phenomenon.

In the area of provision of services to the disabled, efforts are needed either to increase coordination among rehabilitation agencies or to develop strategies for identifying and circumventing the problems created by their lack of coordination. We know, for example, that rehabilitation agencies have varying eligibility and payment requirements. We also know that hospitals, the source of referral of many disabled patients to such agencies, experience considerable staff turnover. Yet few hospitals expedite referrals by providing staff members with an up-to-date guide to community rehabilitation agencies and their eligibility and payment requirements.* Unfortunately, new staff in most hospitals are forced to learn about referral agencies on their own, leaving open the possibility that many patients will not be appropriately referred.

Finally, during the last few years the disabled have become increasingly willing to organize politically and to lobby for legislation in their own interest. In so doing many groups of disabled people have succeeded in overcoming barriers posed by the social stigma attached to their disabilities. Groups representing different disabilities are now joining forces to bring greater political weight to their causes. Medical professionals can play useful political roles by recommending and supporting needed changes in our society's programs for the disabled. Not only can professionals provide technical guidance as to which measures might achieve the greatest benefits for the disabled, but they can also lend the considerable prestige of their professional status and the power of their organizations to the advocacy of such programs.

We have mentioned but a few of the steps that can be taken now to improve the lot of disabled persons in the United States. In the future as medical science in-

---

*An excellent example of what could be offered is the *1978 Resource Directory: a guide to services for spinal cord injured persons and others with severe physical diabilities* by the New England Spinal Cord Injury Foundation of Newton, Mass.[43]

creases its ability to preserve and prolong life, parallel efforts must be made to ensure that the lives saved will not be overwhelmed by the problems of disability.

References

1. Anderson, T., Boureston, N., Greenberg, F., and Heldyard, V.: Predictive factors in stroke rehabilitation, Arch. Phys. Med. Rehabil. **55:** 545-553, 1975.
2. Barsky, A.: Patient heal thyself: activating the ambulatory medical patient, J. Chronic Dis. **29:**585-597, 1976.
3. Berkman, A., Weisman, R., and Frielich, M.: Sexual adjustment of spinal cord injured veterans living in the community, Arch. Phys. Med. Rehabil. **59:**29-33, 1978.
4. Butler, R.: Why survive? Being old in America, New York, 1975, Harper & Row, Publishers, Inc.
5. Carpenter, J. O.: Changing roles and disagreement in families with disabled husbands, Arch. Phys. Med. Rehabil. **55:**272, 1974.
6. Cassem, N., and Hackett, T.: Psychological aspects of myocardial infarction, Med. Clin. North Am. **61:**711-721, 1977.
7. Cole, T.: Sexuality and the spinal cord injured. In Green, R., editor: Human sexuality: a health practitioner's text, Baltimore, 1975, The Williams & Wilkins Co.
8. Corcoran, P.: Lecture presented at Boston University Medical School, May 1978.
9. Crain, A., Sussman, M., and Weil, W.: Effects of a diabetic child on marital integration and related measures of family functioning, J. Health Human Behav. **7:**122-127, 1966.
10. Croog, S., and Levine, S.: The heart patient recovers, New York, 1977, Human Sciences Press, Inc.
11. Croog, S., Levine, S., and Zifre, L.: The heart patient and the recovery process, Soc. Sci. Med. **2:**141, 1968.
12. Croog, S., Shapiro, D., and Levine, S.: Denial among heart disease patients, Psychosom. Med. **33:**385-397, 1971.
13. Davis, F.: Deviance disavowal: the management of strained interaction for the visibly handicapped, Soc. Problems **9:**120-132, 1961.
14. Davis, F.: In The family: role performance and relationships. Passage through crisis, Indianapolis, 1963, The Bobbs-Merrill Co., Inc.
15. Diamond, M.: Sexuality and the handicapped, Rehabil. Lit. **35:**34-49, 1974.
16. Diamond, M., Weiss, A., and Grynbaum, B.:
The unmotivated patient, Arch. Phys. Med. Rehabil. **49:**281, 1968.
17. Duff, R., and Hollingshead, A.: Sickness and society, New York, 1968, Harper & Row, Publishers, Inc.
18. Edwin, T.: Problems of disability from the perspective of role therapy, J. Health Human Behav. **7:**6-7, 1966.
19. Fogel, M., and Rosillo, R.: Correlations of psychologic variables and progress in physical rehabilitation: the relation of body image to success in physical rehabilitation, Phys. Rehabil. **51:**227, 1970.
20. Fordyce, W. E., Fowel, R. S., Jr., Lehmann, J. F.: Operant conditioning in the treatment of chronic pain, Arch. Phys. Med. Rehabil. **54:**399-408, 1973.
21. Ghatit, A., and Hanson, R.: Outcome of marriages existing at the time of a male's spinal cord injury, J. Chronic Dis. **28:**383-388, 1975.
22. Goffman, E.: Stigma notes on the management of spoiled identity, Englewood Cliffs, N.J., 1963, Prentice-Hall, Inc.
23. Gussom, Z., and Tracy, G. S.: Status ideology and adaptation to stigmatized illness' study of leprosy, Human Organization **27:**316-325, 1968.
24. Haber, L.: Age and capacity devaluation, J. Health Soc. Behav. **11:**167-183, 1970.
25. Holman, G.: Reactions of the individual with a disability complicated by a sexual problem, Arch. Phys. Med. Rehabil. **56:**9-10, 1975.
26. Hyman, M.: Social psychological determinants of patient performance in stroke rehabilitation, Arch. Phys. Med. Rehabil. **53:**217, 1972.
27. Hyman, M.: Social psychological factors affecting disability among ambulatory patients, J. Chronic Dis. **28:**199-216, 1975.
28. Hyman, M.: Social isolation and performance in rehabilitation, J. Chronic Dis. **25:**85-89, 1972.
29. Johnston, M.: Report on the Massachusetts Rehabilitation Commission, Boston Region CETA, Feb. 1, 1978.
30. Johnstone, R., and Miller, D.: Occupation diseases and industrial medicine, Philadelphia, 1960, W. B. Saunders Co.
31. Kassebaum, G., and Bauman, B.: Dimensions

of the sick role in chronic illness, J. Health Human Behav. **6:**16-27, 1965.

32. Katz, S., Ford, A. B., and Heiple, K. G.: Studies of illness in the aged: recovery after fracture of the hip, J. Gerontol. **19:**285-293, 1964.

33. Katz, S., Jackson, B., Jaffe, M., Little, A., and Turk, C.: Comparison study of rehabilitated and non-rehabilitated patients with fracture of the hip, J. Chronic Dis. **15:**979-984, 1962.

34. Kelman, H., Miller, J., and Lowenthal, M.: Post hospital adaptation of a chronically ill and disabled rehabilitation population, J. Health Human Behav. **5:**108-114, 1964.

35. Kemp, B., and Vash, C.: Productivity after injury in a sample of spinal cord injured patients: a pilot study, J. Chronic Dis. **24:**259-275, 1971.

36. La Vor, M. L., Duncan, J. G.: Vocational rehabilitation—the new law and its implications for the future, J. Rehabil. **42:**20-28, 1976.

37. Lehmann, J. F., DeLateur, B. J., Fowler, R. S., Jr., et al.: Stroke rehabilitation: outcome and prediction, Arch. Phys. Med. Rehabil. **56:**383-389, 1975.

38. Levine, S., and White, P.: Exchange as a conceptual framework for the study of interorganizational relationships, Adm. Sci. Q. **5:**583-601, 1961.

39. Litman, T.: The family and physical rehabilitation, J. Chronic Dis. **19:**211-217, 1966.

40. Litman, T.: The influence of self conception and life orientation factors in the rehabilitation of the orthopedically disabled, J. Health Soc. Behav. **3:**249-257, 1962.

41. Litman, T.: Physical rehabilitation: a social and psychological approach. In Jaco, E. G., editor: Patients physicians and illness, New York, 1976, The Free Press.

42. Ludwig, E., and Adams, S.: Patient cooperation in a rehabilitation center: assumption of a client role, J. Health Soc. Behav. **9:**328-336, 1968.

43. 1978 Resource Directory: a guide to services for spinal cord injured persons and others with severe physical disabilities, Newton, Mass., 1978, New England Spinal Cord Injury Foundation.

44. Parsons, T., and Fox, R.: Illness, therapy and the modern urban family, J. Soc. Issues **8:**31-44, 1952.

45. Profile of American health—1973, Public Health Rep. **89:**509-514, 1974.

46. Richardson, S. A.: Age and sex differences in values towards physical handicaps, J. Health Soc. Behav. **11:**207-214, 1970.

47. Romano, M.: Social skills training with the newly handicapped, Arch. Phys. Med. Rehabil. **57:**302-303, 1976.

48. Rothschild, C. S.: The sociology and social psychology of disability and rehabilitation, New York, 1968, Random House, Inc.

49. Scott, R.: The making of blind men, New York, 1969, Russell Sage Foundation.

50. Sharland, D. E.: Ability of men to return to work after cardiac infarction, Br. Med. J. **5411:**718-720, 1964.

51. Smart, C., and Saunders, C.: The costs of motor vehicle related spinal cord injuries, Washington, D.C., 1976, Institute for Highway Safety.

52. Smits, S.: Variables related to success in a medical rehabilitation setting, Arch. Phys. Med. Rehabil. **55:**449-454, 1974.

53. Strauss, A.: The hospital as a negotiated order. In Friedson, E., editor: The hospital in modern society, Glencoe, Ill., 1963, The Free Press.

54. Thompson, M. M.: Housing and handicapped people, presented to the President's Committee on Employment of the Handicapped, Washington, D.C., 1976.

55. Tringo, J.: The hierarchy of preference toward disability groups, J. Special Educ. **4:**295-306, 1970.

56. U.S. Department of Health, Education, and Welfare: Health of the disadvantaged, Health Resources Administration D.H.E.W. Publication no. HRA 77-628, Washington, D.C., 1977, U.S. Government Printing Office.

57. U.S. Department of Health, Education, and Welfare: Health—United States 1976-1977, Health Resources Administration, National Center for Health Statistics, D.H.E.W. Publication no. HRA 77-1233, Washington, D.C., 1977, U.S. Government Printing Office.

58. U.S. Department of Health, Education, and Welfare: Health resources statistics—National Center for Health Statistics, D.H.E.W. Publication no. HSM 73-1509, Washington, D.C., 1973, U.S. Government Printing Office.

59. U.S. Department of Health, Education, and Welfare: Characteristics, social contacts and activities of nursing home residents, D.H.E.W. Publication no. HRA 77-1778, Washington, D.C., 1978, U.S. Government Printing Office.

60. Weinblatt, E., Shapiro, S., Frank, C. W., et al: Return to work and work status following first myocardial infarction, Am. J. Public Health **56:**169, 1966.
61. Wessen, A.: Hospital ideology and communication between ward personnel. In Jaco, E. G., editor: Patients physicians and illness, New York, 1958, The Free Press.
62. Wessen, A. F.: The apparatus of rehabilitation: an organizational analysis. In Sussman, M., editor: Sociology and rehabilitation, Washington, D.C., 1966, American Sociological Association.
63. White, P., and Vlasak, G.: Exchange as a conceptual framework for understanding interorganizational relationships: application to nonprofit organizations, Baltimore, 1970, The Johns Hopkins University Press.
64. Wylie, C., and White, B.: A measure of disability, Arch. Environ. Health **8:**834-839, 1964.
65. Zahn, M.: Incapacity, impotence and invisible impairment: their effects on interpersonal relations, J. Health Soc. Behav. **14:**115-123, 1973.
66. Zelle, J. A., and Taranto, K.: Health care utilization by persons with chronic disabilities who have been vocationally rehabilitated, Arch. Phys. Med. Rehabil. **57:**282-290, 1976.
67. Zuk, G. H.: Autistic distortion in parents of retarded children, J. Consult. Clin. Psychol. **23:**171-176, 1959.

Chapter 8

The dying patient

The problems associated with the treatment of the terminally ill patient are more distressing personally and professionally to members of the medical profession than virtually any others that they encounter. When and how to give the patient "the bad news," how to interact with the dying patient and the family, how to handle the patient's denial, anger, or withdrawal, how to decide whether or when treatment efforts should give way to comfort measures only, and how, as a provider, to accept the inexorable fact of death are some of the complex facets of caring for the dying patient.

We believe that the first step in dealing with these extraordinarily difficult problems is to attempt to understand the process of *dying*, the ways in which this process has changed over the last 2 or 3 decades, and the ways in which social institutions have responded or, in some instances, failed to respond to these changes. In this chapter we shall explore some factors that have led to the surge of interest in the dying patient. We shall separate and compare in our discussion the different problems posed to society by death and dying. Social responses to each will be described, and we shall conclude by taking stock of the current state of the art of medical care for the terminally ill.

The death and dying movement

In 1969 Dr. Elisabeth Kübler-Ross[29] published her important book *On Death and Dying*. In the previous 30 years only a few such works had been published and still fewer of these were well known.[13,15,21,35] It was not uncommon for those who wrote about terminal patients to point out, with some validity, that death and dying appeared to be a taboo topic in America. For example, in an introduction to *The Dying Patient* Freeman[17] wrote:

Death in the twentieth century has replaced sex as the socially taboo topic. It has become the fashion in youth-idolizing America to focus attention on living, on a longer life, on a better life, on 'living it up.' People turn their backs on death as much as possible, symbolically taking out and renewing all the life insurance they can get. They cannot help but note that others die, a reason perhaps for turning the music up, but on the whole there now seems to be a tendency in American society to regard death as a technical error, to write off the dying as if they were a business loss. . . .*

However, since Kübler-Ross's trailblazing book appeared in 1969, it seems as if a dam has burst. There has been a flood of books and articles on death and dying in both the professional and popular literature. Movies, television, and the theater have all produced works focused on the dying patient. In academia courses on death and dying have proliferated from the elementary school level through graduate and professional schools. So intense has the interest in death and dying been during the last decade indeed that it has generated its own occupational niche—thanatology.

Is this wave of concern a passing fad? Probably not. Having denied death for so long, has America suddenly become obsessed with death? Again, probably not, although there are concerns that we have become overly preoccupied about learning how to die "correctly," how to interact with the dying person, and how to grieve "properly" for the newly dead. A brief look at the magnitude of the phenomenon and at concomitant changes in medicine's technologic capabilities and in American society may help us understand the powerful upsurge of interest in the dying patient.

Numbers

The first explanation for current interest in the dying patient is perhaps the easiest, for it has to do with simple numbers. As populations have increased worldwide, so too have deaths. In 1977, for example, there were approximately 54 million deaths in the world.[10] In 1978 there were 1,924,000 deaths in the United States.[43] Consider that each person who dies has significant relationships with numerous other people: spouses, parents, children, siblings, close friends, employers, and others. The death of almost 2 million people thus has a powerful impact on perhaps another 10 to 20 million people. And if we add to this figure the estimated 1 million people, at any time, who are alive but who are diagnosed as having a terminal disease, we see that a "critical mass" of people are involved in death and dying.[44]

From what we know about the attitudes of the American people toward death and dying, they are concerned not so much about the fact of death as about *the manner of their dying.* Given the sheer numbers of those each year who die or are associated with dying persons, there is a large constituency to challenge, publicly and privately, those aspects of the dying process and the medical care in which it is embedded that they find worrisome or unacceptable.

Advances in medical technology

Even more fundamental than numbers in explaining the rising interest in and concern about death and dying have been the effects—both positive and negative—

*From Freeman, H.: New dimensions in dying. In Brim, O., Freeman, H., Levine, S., and Scotch, N., editors: The dying patient, New York, 1970, Russell Sage Foundation.

of advances in medical technology. This century has seen dramatic changes in morbidity and mortality patterns due in part to medical achievements such as the control of infectious diseases. Today, as we pointed out in Chapter 2, the likelihood is that most people will die from cardiovascular disease, cancer, or the effects of a chronic illness such as diabetes or kidney disease. One by-product of these leading causes of death is that dying tends to be a lingering process rather than a rapid event and that the majority of those who die in a given year are age 65 or over.

In terms of a more immediate impact on the dying patient, medicine has developed an array of drugs, devices, and procedures capable of temporarily arresting and sometimes indefinitely prolonging the moment of death. In part because these technologies, in many instances, can save or meaningfully extend life, in contrast to prolonging the dying process, decisions about whether or how they should be employed are complex ones. Such decisions, for individual patients, classes of conditions, and in terms of resource allocations, involve not only clinical factors such as a patient's medical status and prognosis but also a variety of ethical, social, legal, and economic considerations.

For many persons—medical professionals as well as lay people—one of the most disturbing or frightening prospects about dying is the thought of being sustained for weeks, months, or years by "machines," an image used most profitably by physician-author Cook[6] in his best-selling novel *Coma*. In the judgment of many participants in and observers of the care of dying patients medicine too often succumbs to a "technologic imperative." Efforts to cure or care for patients slip, often imperceptibly, into a fruitless prolongation of life. In these instances, it is believed, technology has captured its users: in the absence of proven humane benefits it is used *because* it exists or because not to use it implies that "everything" that can be done is not being done.

Who, then, should decide whether, by what means, or for how long efforts to sustain the life of dying patients should be made? Such questions are relatively new ones. For until very recently decisions to use life-prolonging technologies lay, virtually unquestioned, not in the hands of those most affected (the patients) but in the hands of the technologies' possessors (the physicians). Today, however, the belief that patients should control or at least participate in decisions about their treatments has made decision making far more complex. Does the competent adult patient have an unqualified right to refuse treatment, even if that refusal will result in death? Who should make treatment or nontreatment decisions for incompetent adults, for comatose patients, for children, or for critically ill newborns? And on what bases should such decisions be made? Although not new these "dilemmas of dying" have been given very real urgency by modern medicine's technologic capabilities.[45] They are a major reason for the mounting interest in and concern about death and dying over the last decade and have made the care of dying patients a major topic in the interfaces between medicine, ethics, and law.

Changes in American society

Technologic developments in medicine have been accompanied by profound social changes in American society, many of which impact on or reflect issues in terminal care. One aspect of the growing concern about providing *equality of opportunity*, in large part due to the civil rights movement, has been concern that all members of society have equal access to medical care. Even among the terminally ill there are some patients who are not as well served as others by medical facilities. As in other areas of medical care, it tends to be the elderly, poor, and minorities who experience delay or other inequalities in treatment. Moreover, terminal patients as a whole, regardless of their social background, may receive less medical attention than other patients.[41]

Another concept that has gained prominence in the last decade is that of *quality of life*. Included in this far-reaching concept are beliefs that "meaningful" life must include, for example, human dignity, a good physical environment, and reasonable access to opportunity and social and economic rewards. In medicine the acceptance of "quality of life" as an important value is reflected in the attitude of most physicians that the biologic life of critically or terminally ill patients should not be maintained *per se* simply because it is within medicine's ability to do so.[8,37] Rather, most believe that the patient's potential "quality of life" is an important consideration in treatment decisions, with debate centering on how "quality" is assessed and by whom.[42]

Currently there is also a growing *questioning of science and technology*. During the post-Sputnik years, triggered by the Soviet Union's launching of the first space satellite in the 1950s, our society devoted much of its resources to a vast array of scientific and technologic endeavors, ranging from the "conquest of space" to its medical analogue, the "war on cancer."[40] For a variety of reasons, however, large segments of society in the past few years have begun to question the worth and consequences of our enormous investment in science and technology. Alarm about the possible consequences of recombinant DNA research, fears over the safety of nuclear power, cutbacks in biomedical research funding, and concerns about the mounting costs of medical technology and about how decisions governing its uses are made are but a few examples of the shifting climate of public opinion. No longer is there an unfettered social acceptance of the value of basic research and its applications. Rather, those who engage in these activities must be prepared to deal with questions about the proper allocations of public funds and other resources, provide assurances that new technologies are both safe and efficacious, and demonstrate that as many short- and long-term consequences as possible have been anticipated.[22,30]

An outgrowth of questions raised about the value of science and technology has been a growing demand for more comprehensive assessments of the safety, efficacy, and cost-effectiveness of innovations before they diffuse into the marketplace. In the area of medical care, for example, the 1970s saw the establishment of the U.S. Congress' Office of Technology Assessment, the Department of Health and Welfare's National Center for Health Care Technology, and legislation empowering the Food and Drug Administration to regulate the development and marketing of medical devices.

This demand for greater accountability in developing, assessing, and using medical technologies has been felt by individual practitioners as well as researchers. Their use of, or decision not to use, particular technologies, for example, may be questions by recipients (patients), their relatives, colleagues, and, in the event of serious uncertainty or dissatisfaction, the courts.

Decisions about using a given medical technology with a critically or terminally ill patient are particularly problematic because life and death may hang in the balance. The situation is made more complex by the development of new, experimental procedures that often are first tested clinically with terminal patients and by the rising concern with what is seen as the "unnecessary" use of technology in the face of hopeless medical situations. As we shall discuss more fully, the physician treating the terminal patient often finds himself in the untenable position of "damned if you do, damned if you don't," caught between pressures to do *everything* possible to save and extend life and pressures to humanely avoid using costly, painful, and, ultimately, nonbeneficial treatment.

Another development in American society that bears on death and dying has been the *decreasing importance of religion* in favor of a more secular philosophy. The less a society adheres to a sacred philosophy and concomitantly the more a secular philosophy becomes dominant, the more change there is in the balance of how moral questions are asked and answered. Thus as a society dominated by a "rational-scientific" orientation, we ask and can often obtain precise answers to certain questions about the nature of the universe. At the same time to the extent that various religious philosophies are ignored, other questions about the nature of the universe tend to be asked, at least publicly, much less. In consequence the meaning of life and, more important, the meaning of death become at once less "known" and more existentially anxiety provoking. For many Americans who no longer embrace a religious philosophy, death is not seen as a transitional state from life on earth to life in the "hereafter." Death becomes an *end state*. It is viewed as a "meaningless" event or as the "absolute end" and therefore an extraordinarily disturbing prospect.[39] A need to fill the void left by traditional western religion is one explanation for the current popularity of pseudorational and pseudoreligious books and other accounts of "life after life."

Lastly, in relation to religious-secular changes in society, we must note the charismatic contributions of major figures who have called our attention to the dying patient. Chief among these is Elisabeth Kübler-Ross, whose books and lectures throughout the world have called attention to numerous problems in the services provided the terminal patient. Another major figure is Cicely Saunders,[35] whose development of the hospice as an enlightened institution devoted to dealing uniquely with the emotional and social needs of dying patients has gained worldwide recognition and emulation.

Death and social institutions

As we suggested in the last section, several recent medical and social changes have (1) raised our awareness of death and dying as major personal and societal issues, (2) made the process of dying more difficult, (3) raised new ethical and legal issues, and (4) generated new attempts to remedy or ameliorate some of these problems.

The process of dying has changed profoundly in numerous ways, but social responses have not always kept pace with technical change. As a result, our society finds itself in a situation in which old responses no longer deal adequately with a social-biologic process that has metamorphosed into a rather new phenomenon. Social scientists use the term *cultural lag* to describe the phenomenon of social system falling behind in its efforts to develop adequate means for dealing with new social problems. In an industrial society such as ours there has been a long-term tendency for technology to outstrip social institutions in terms of major change. This seems to be the case with the process of dying. Currently our society is in a transitional "muddling through" phase of developing appropriate social mechanisms for dealing with the major *new* problems presented by dying. For those such as physicians and nurses caught up in the complexity of providing services for the dying, it is important to develop a perspective that permits them to understand the nature of the social and moral conflicts in which they find themselves involved. Such a perspective may help reduce their own personal and professional conflicts and in so doing assist them in providing more thoughtful and beneficial care to those who are dying.

All social systems develop institutional mechanisms for dealing with repetitive life cycle developments and problems to *reduce* (1) the emotional pain they cause and (2) their disruption of the social system. Thus all societies develop procedures (institutions) for dealing with birth, education, decision making, and death and dying. An examination of how our society, as well as others, deals with death as distinct from how it deals with dying illustrates cultural lag, particularly in the latter area. This analysis also will alert us to key problems that death and dying pose for medical personnel.

The death of most individuals produces common problems for most societies. Particular characteristics of the dead person may add further problems, for example, the death of children, of leaders, or of highly unusual "irreplaceable" people. In other circumstances the death of extremely old, sick, or isolated persons may be seen as "solving" rather than introducing problems.

The major, universal problems created by death include first the emotional response to loss felt by relatives, friends, and colleagues. Second, there is the problem of how to handle the transitional period, with rites such as mourning and burial, before the ordinary activities are resumed. Third, the work the dead person can no longer produce must be dealt with. Finally, the economic disposition of the deceased's property and status must be handled.

All societies have institutionalized methods of dealing with such problems to minimize the social, emotional, and economic disruptions of death. However, the particular institutional responses to death reflect the culture in which that death occurs.

Because social institutions in the United States have strong bureaucratic, organizational characteristics, such qualities can be found in our society's response to death. The disposal of the deceased, for example, is typically handled by large mortuaries, often with assembly line precision. Morticians are so skilled at taking over the whole burial process that the remaining family members often find themselves essentially playing a spectator role. Clergymen sometimes are not familiar with the departed and therefore may huddle briefly with the family, take a few notes, and construct an "appropriate" eulogy that contains some facts about the departed in the midst of stock phrases.

Regardless of the strength of religious beliefs or membership in a particular religion, the mourning period typically is one in which social supports are provided by friends and relatives of the departed to closest family members. Mourning usually takes place in a religious framework. It is remarkable how many different ethnic and religious groups in American and other societies provide similar social supports, for example, the Irish wake and the Jewish "sit shiva."

A number of mechanisms have been developed in the United States to reduce the economic disruption to the family caused by the death of a wage earner. These include social security benefits, insurance, and retirement benefits. Wills are used to provide for an orderly transfer of the property of the deceased (other societies have formal rules such as primogeniture). At the workplace, which is characteristically bureaucratic, workers are seen as interchangeable and thus are easily replaced. This seems as true of presidents as of laborers.

Thus death produces well-defined social responses from a variety of sources—religious, professional (morticians), business (insurance), and governmental (social security). All of these are effective, to some degree at least, in reducing the disruptive consequences of death.

Predictably institutionalized responses and bureaucratic activities used by our society to help with death also may produce their own problems. In a bureaucracy it is not unusual to find particular types of problems arising, such as those produced by rigidity, impersonality, and "foul-ups."

Impersonality, a major attribute of bureaucratic organizations, may be troublesome in death in several ways. The falseness in the eulogy of a clergyman who did not know the deceased may strike some as hypocritical. Mortuaries have been known to mix up funerals, especially when they are processing several in 1 day, as when a casket is placed before the wrong mourners. And in the hectic pace of urban settings the processing of the funeral in an "efficient" manner may cause an expected sacred and dignified ceremony to become a charade. For example, Epstein[14] has poignantly written:

> There is a newer road which now leads from the pleasant resorts of Eastern Long Island into the city: a highway eight lanes wide over which one speeds through the city's brutal outskirts in a hermetic trance, interrupted from time to time by streams of headlights, incongruously glowing in the daylight. There are cars of mourners following hearses that come out of the city each morning to the immense new graveyards that ring New York, perhaps thirty or forty miles from the center. There is no time on this road for stately travel. The hearses race along, sometimes two or even three abreast, at the speed of other traffic or even faster, past the roaring trucks and lines of casual travelers. One watches and wonders how often, in this frightful race, a car of mourners, falling behind, becomes detached from the proper object of its grief and follows a stranger to his grave. Perhaps it doesn't matter. You die here as you live, more or less irrelevantly, and you grow accustomed to losing your way.*

As we have pointed out in earlier chapters, additional major unsolved problems associated with death in America pivot around inequality. Though life expectancy has increased significantly since the turn of the century, large disparities still exist between whites and ethnic and racial minorities and between the poor and the middle and upper classes. These differences are reflective of numerous factors— poor nutrition, housing, hazardous jobs, and inadequate medical care. Fortunately some progress has been made in reducing the gap; hopefully more progress will be made in the years ahead.

Dying in America

The methods used by our society to deal with dying are in a greater state of transition than those used to deal with death. As the process of dying in America has changed in numerous significant ways over the last 3 decades, new problems have emerged for which institutionalized responses have not yet been developed. There also are a number of older problems associated with dying that continue to prove difficult for our society to deal with. In discussing both old and new problems, our focus will be on the *hospitalized* dying patient, for this now is the place where death occurs for most people in America.

---

*From Epstein, J.: Living in New York, New York Review of Books **5:**14, 1966. Reprinted with permission from The New York Review of Books. Copyright © 1966 Nyrev, Inc.

Old problems

The most glaring unresolved problem in dying, *inequality*, is not limited to life expectancy but is also found in the ways in which medical care providers respond to the terminal patient. Sudnow[41] carefully studied how personnel in two hospitals responded differently to patients with different *perceived social values*. He observed that young, middle-class patients obtained more sympathetic care than the elderly or the poor. Those whom hospital staff perceived as having "no social worth," such as the very old, alcoholics, drug abusers, and suicides, were not as likely to be as well-treated as, for example, a child. A dying child is universally regarded as tragic, and therefore hospital staff, understandably, mobilize great technical and social resources in an effort to minimize discomfort and maximize prolongation of life.

Similarly, there are numerous instances of an incredible marshaling of medical resources for VIPs such as President Kennedy, President Franco in Spain, Nobel Prize winner Landau in Russia, and others.

In addition to care varying according to social differences among terminal patients, the care of terminal patients as a class often differs from that given to other types of patients. In general, terminal patients tend to be viewed as having lost social value as well as symbolizing the limits, if not the failures, of medical care. As such, they tend to get considerably less attention from hospital staff than do "viable" patients. Nurses, for example, usually take much longer to respond to calls from terminal patients than from other patients, and house staff and other physicians often find various reasons to avoid seeing dying patients.[41]

A second enduring problem associated with care of the terminal patient lies in the *lack of sufficient training* found in medical and nursing schools for this difficult task. To be sure, most schools now devote a few hours of curricula time to this problem, but from all reports of recent graduates this hardly has been sufficient. As an example, although most medical schools expose students to arguments about whether or not to inform dying patients of their diagnosis and prognosis, no medical school curriculum with which we are familiar helps students learn to give "bad news." Though clearly more is done today than before in training, considerably more is needed.

New problems

Many of the newer problems associated with dying are interconnected, and in some cases one problem area is largely responsible for another. In this section we will focus on five such problems that have emerged: (1) increased time between dying and diagnosis, (2) the cost of dying, (3) the issue of candor, (4) the issue of prolongation *versus* termination, and (5) interpersonal problems.

Time. Since the leading causes of death in the United States are now chronic rather than acute diseases, we can readily appreciate that the process of dying has been lengthened. In a study in New Haven, Connecticut, for example, Duff and Hollingshead[11] found that among terminal patients the mean time between diagnosis and death was 29 months. In part the often lengthy period between a terminal diagnosis and death, as we have noted, is due to treatment advances that can palliate or produce temporary remissions in the course of a fatal condition.

Why should we view such "added" time as problematic rather than as primarily beneficial to the patient and family? To be sure, in many instances added time *is* beneficial, permitting the patient to take part in family activities or fulfill unfinished business.

At the same time, however, a wide array of problems may appear or existing ones become exacerbated by the lengthened process of dying. For example, medical costs may increase, or physical pain and suffering may be extended. The patient who knows he or she is dying may find the increased time filled with greater anxiety and depression rather than happiness. Further, the relatives of the patient find themselves in a state of suspended animation, unable to live their usual lives, delaying decision making, and generally suffering from emotional turmoil. There are no clear guidelines for action. Relationships between the living and the dying are frequently painful and awkward and tend to become more so as time passes. Well-meaning employers often experience conflict about whether or not to replace a worker with a terminal illness, wanting on one hand to be supportive and loyal and on the other hand obliged to see that work gets done and that a replacement is properly trained.

Some patients with a terminal diagnosis spend much of their time in a frantic search for a cure. After exhausting possibilities within orthodox medicine they may turn to questionable treatments found outside of traditional medicine, such as the current controversial treatment for cancer known as laetrile.

The lengthened course of dying poses problems for professionals as well. Difficult decisions become drawn out. Patients often ask physicians to predict how long they will live and question the competence of physicians when they refuse to make predictions or give ones that prove incorrect. A lengthy period of dying often means that the draining emotions of family and patient during the process must be dealt with in an institutional setting, often upsetting other patients and staff. Finally, a prolonged period of dying is, for a physician, like a failure that will not go away. Not only must medical staff face the frustration of not being able to save a person's life; they must face that same realization and the person they cannot save often for a period of months.

Costs associated with dying. Somewhat ironically, dying has become one of life's most expensive activities. Veatch,[44] for example, describes the case of a patient for whom there was no possible hope who was kept alive for a short period of time at a cost of about $160,000. Other comparable examples abound. In 1968 the first heart transplant in the United States was provided for Mike Kasperak at a cost of $28,000. He lived for 16 days.

A study by Cullen[8] of critically ill patients treated in the intensive care unit of the Massachusetts General Hospital from June 1972 to June 1973 focuses on the costs of such care. For 10 patients in the recovery room of the acute care unit costs were calculated to be $600 to $800 a day, and "when blood and blood products were needed, the cost ran as high as $2000 for that 24-hour period." The most critically ill patients in the total study numbered 226, for whom total costs were estimated to be $3,232,647, or $14,304 per patient. These figures did not include physician fees or the cost of blood. Cullen[8] raises serious questions regarding this allocation of scarce resources, including physicians and other hospital personnel, blood, and related treatment outlays. He writes:

> Intensive care medicine is extraordinarily expensive, yet results in only a small number of patients surviving to useful and productive lives. Far more likely is death or survival with poor functional recovery. High quality intensive care resulted in a one year survival rate of 27%. Only 12% of the entire study group were fully recovered and functioning as productively one year later as they had prior to their critical illnesses. This was accomplished as a total cost of $3,232,647. . . .*

These data are indicative of the high costs that can be incurred by dying in the increasingly costly labor and equipment intensive setting of the hospital. Because most deaths now occur in hospitals, often after extensive periods of care, the rising costs of hospitalization mean that the costs of dying have mounted steadily. Some 80% of deaths in the United States now occur in hospitals, compared to only 37% in the late 1930s.[27]

When the often extraordinarily high costs of terminal care are covered by third parties such as private insurance or Medicaid, there is little outcry by those affected. But many people are not covered or are only partially covered and find such costs a major financial burden. Because of these costs and other factors to be discussed later in this chapter, there has been some effort to decrease hospital stays of terminal patients, and indeed a movement toward home deaths or alternative settings such as hospices is underway.

Providers usually have not concerned themselves about the costs to patients of hospitalization and other forms of treatment or even have been very aware of them. Their appropriate role customarily is defined as providing the "best" care regardless of cost. However, when the benefits of such care might be questionable and the costs high, it would seem appropriate for physicians in particular to enlarge the scope of their concern for their patients. Certainly the costs of various alternatives as well as the possibility of significant benefits ought to be assessed and conveyed to patients, and decisions should be made jointly.

Candor

For a physician, informing a patient that he or she has a terminal illness must be more emotionally stressful than virtually any other task a physician is expected

*From Cullen, D. J.: Results and costs of intensive care, Anesthesiology 17:203-216, 1977.

to perform. There is no easy way out, no matter how sensitive and skilled the physician. Hence some physicians have tried to deal with the problem by being flatly untruthful, by obscuring the prognosis with medical jargon, or by bending the truth just enough to leave the patient hopefully uncertain, while not exactly lying.[44]

Historically, physicians' attitudes toward informing patients about terminal diagnoses have shifted back and forth like a pendulum, reflecting changes both in societal values and medical norms. The most recent shift has occurred between the 1950s and 1970s in large part as a response to the growing belief in the rights of patients to participate in decisions about their treatments.

Several surveys conducted during the 1950s and 1960s indicated that a majority of physician respondents believed that it was not appropriate to inform patients of terminal diagnoses. Most of the reasons given pivoted around protecting patients from "needless" and "cruel" information about which little could be done. Moreover, disclosure was awkward and abrasive to the physician's ego, involving a confession of professional helplessness and often relative ignorance about when death will occur.[44] In 1953, for example, Fitts and Ravdin[16] conducted a mailed questionnaire survey of 444 physicians serially selected from alphabetic lists of physicians in Philadelphia. Of the 90% who responded, 70% reported that they never or usually did not inform their patients of diagnoses of cancer. Comparably, in the early 1960s Oken[32] surveyed 219 staff members at Michael Reese Hospital in Chicago (a private nonprofit teaching hospital).[32] Over 95% of the staff returned their questionnaires. When questioned about informing patients of cancer diagnoses with grave prognoses, 90% said their usual policy was never to tell patients. Although most of the physicians indicated they acquired their approaches through clinical experience, only 14% claimed to have tried a policy different from their current one, and only 29% said their personal policies might be swayed by future research on the question. In opposition to their own posture on informing patients, however, some 60% of the physicians stated they personally *would* want to be told their diagnoses under similar circumstances.

Despite physician and even family secrecy patients often learned their diagnoses or prognoses. In a study at Yale University Hospital in the 1960s Duff and Hollingshead[11] reported that in 73% of expected deaths among the patients they studied, the physician and families conspired to keep the patient uninformed. Only 20% were directly told of their impending death, and these were all men, predominantly from upper income groups. Nevertheless a full 45% of those ostensibly deceived were aware that they would die. Similarly, Saunders[36] reported that over 50% of her small sample of 45 patients at St. Joseph's Hospital knew they were dying and were willing to talk about it despite the fact that very few were informed on arrival at the hospital.

One reason frequently cited by physicians for not telling patients of their forthcoming death was that most patients did not want to know. Nonetheless the studies available at that time seemed to indicate that more terminal patients preferred to know their diagnoses and prognoses than were actually given that information. Kelly and Frieson[28] asked 100 cancer patients, most of whom had inoperable conditions, whether or not they preferred to know whether or not they had cancer. Of those patients 89% said they preferred to know their conditions, even though only 73% believed people in general should be told if they have cancer. From a study of nonpatients and patients with somatic disorders in Canada, Cappon[5] reported that a majority of his study subjects, either healthy or ill, wanted to know if they would die. Those who were actually dying were the least likely to want such information. However, a majority of dying persons still wanted to know not only whether they would die but also when they would die and how they would feel while dying. Moreover, few variables appeared to affect this desire for information. Persons with parents, a wife, a husband, or children, who were loved and valued, wished for no more information than those persons who had no one to love. Age and other variables like income and education similarly had no differential impact.

Despite the often assumed potential negative responses of patients to disclosure physicians in the last decade have increasingly come to recognize that failure to disclose impending death may have several deleterious consequences.[19] First, failure to disclose may undermine the confidence of patients in their physicians. For despite a cheery, optimistic front by physicians patients may learn that death is impending through a variety of sources. They may realize that their conditions are progressively worse, contrary to the verbal observations of physicians. Relatives may purposely disclose patients' fates to them without the physician's knowledge, or patients may accidentally overhear conversations about their cases among staff or between staff and family. Under any of these conditions patients may come to feel that physicians are not telling them either all they know or the truth.

Second, failure to disclose impending death may prevent patients from putting their affairs in order. On one hand patients may want to alter their wills or make decisions about their affairs that will smooth the transition for others after their deaths. On the other hand, informing patients that they are dying may allow them time to reach personal, psychologic closure in terms of the meaning of their lives.

Third, informing patients of impending death may help physicians to explain changes in treatment. It may also reduce the dissonance physicians encounter when they misrepresent the meaning of treatments or the patient's future to the patient.

Fourth, failure to disclose the truth forces a wedge between patients and their relatives and friends, who would normally be candid and honest with each other. Although some relatives and friends may feel that secrecy should be preserved, others may find such a masquerade distasteful. Moreover, they may disagree about the reasons for secrecy. Under such conditions the possibility is high that someone will purposely or accidentally inform patients. If disclosure in fact occurs, patients may easily come to feel that they have been betrayed or treated as irresponsible by those for whom they care the most.

In brief, failure to tell patients that they are dying subtracts from what little remaining consciousness, self-control, and decision-making powers they may have left in their lives. During the late 1960s and the 1970s the tendency not to tell patients the truth subsided. Using the same questionnaire Oken used in the early 1960s when he reported that 90% of physicians preferred not to disclose terminal diagnoses, Novack et al.[31] in 1979 reported that 97% of 278 physicians interviewed at Strong Memorial Hospital preferred to tell patients the truth.

But although the pendulum has shifted, the policy of withholding truth has left an unfortunate legacy for medicine. Many people, for example, no longer believe the diagnosis physicians give them after performing a biopsy when the information is favorable. How ironic it is that some patients feel they are being protected or deceived by their physicians when indeed there is nothing to be protected from. We see in this example that the behavior of one generation of physicians has consequences for the next.

The issue of candor, of course, transcends informing terminal patients of their diagnoses and prognoses and indeed is a central element in the doctor-patient relationship. Currently, reflecting both ethical and legal principles about the rights of patients, the prevailing philosophy is that patients should be told by their physicians about the nature of their disorders, their prognoses, and the risks and benefits of various treatment alternatives. Physicians in general are no longer viewed as benevolent, paternalistic experts who have the duty and right to make decisions on behalf of their patients. Rather, patients too have become decision makers about their medical care, and to exercise their right of giving *informed voluntary consent* to treatment, they need to be knowledgeable about their conditions.

The basic *moral principle* that underlies the belief that physicians have a duty to disclose and patients a right to receive information is that of *autonomy*, the freedom of an individual to choose and execute his or her own course of action. A second principle underlying the belief in candor is that of *utility*. On this principle truthfulness is important in part because it helps to maintain *relationships of trust* between providers, patients, and the public more generally.

In the language of philosophy these are some of the major reasons for following a *principle of veracity*, that is, candor or truthfulness.[3] For a variety of reasons, however, such an ethical prescription sometimes is easier to hold than to follow. Many argue, with various degrees of conviction, that physicians often *should or can* only follow a policy of *limited disclosure*. Among the reasons candor can be difficult is the fact that the prognosis of any disease is always somewhat uncertain, and even those with a very bleak outlook have been known in rare cases to enter into a long remission. There understandably is a natural inclination to search for any ray of hope in an otherwise dismal picture, and emphasizing the positive and de-emphasizing the negative aspects of a prognosis appeals to most physicians as the most humane approach. Similarly, the possibility that research will produce new treatment and possibly a cure tends to be exaggerated.

Second, some providers continue to argue that some patients are not emotionally strong enough to handle a terminal prognosis. Physicians mention depression or suicide as likely outcomes of candor with some patients and thus maintain that they employ "benevolent deception," withholding the truth because it is in the patient's "best interests." To the extent that physicians feel able to identify such patients, and this itself is open to question, they may use any of a number of techniques to "protect" the patient, from withholding the truth entirely to obfuscating the truth with jargon.[44] There is no evidence, however, that patients tend to commit suicide or become psychotically depressed when told they are terminally ill. In any case questions arise regarding the "right" to be depressed, and indeed the right to choose the time and manner of one's death.

A third reason offered for avoiding full disclosure is that patients who know they have a terminal illness may be difficult for medical staff to deal with. Kübler-Ross, for example, has described what she calls the *stages of dying*, holding that most patients pass through a sequence of responses to knowledge of their impending death that include (1) anger, rage, or resentment that they will die while others live; (2) bargaining and attempts to gain reprieves for good behavior; (3) depression at impending death, foregone dreams, and hospital costs; and (4) acceptance and resignation.[29] During the anger response patients become hostile to family and relatives. Frequently they wonder, "Why me?" "Why not someone else who is less deserving than me?" Hostility also may be displayed to physicians and other staff. Patients may question the quality and quantity of the care they receive.

Finally, with some patients, such as children or the very old, communication is usually with relatives or surrogates. With many other competent patients, however, family members may interject themselves between physician and patient, or the physician may choose to inform a family member rather than the patient about the latter's terminal prognosis. Usually the rationale is one of protecting the patient from the "bad news." Often, though not always, these efforts are misguided and rather than protecting the patient the family and physician take on themselves the right to make decisions, which really belongs to the patient.

Although we strongly advocate honest disclosure, we recognize that there is no perfect or simple answer to this issue. Given the arguments we have discussed, medical professionals now usually face a choice of either (1) adopting a single hard-and-fast rule to always disclose or (2) deciding about disclosure on a case-by-case basis. It would be naive to assume that in every single instance every person treated with full candor will suffer less pain and unhappiness than if information about a terminal illness had been withheld, at least for a while. Similarly, serious problems can arise if decisions are made on a case-by-case basis. It is difficult to know what criteria to use in making the case-by-case decision, and mistakes of judgment are inevitable. Moreover, in deciding on a case-by-case basis providers can be influenced by their own values, their perhaps limited knowledge of their patients as people, their own personal fears and dislike for having to break bad news, or their anticipated emotional discomfort in dealing with the patient after the disclosure has been made.[44]

As a duty to disclose becomes more normative among physicians, more attention needs to be given to *how* disclosure should be handled. With the shift toward telling the truth, some physicians have become almost brutal in their honesty, an approach that is both unnecessary and unhelpful.

In the difficult and stressful job of "giving the bad news," the physician should strive to be gentle and sensitive, should stress whatever may be hopeful regarding treatment, and, as part of good communication, should maintain eye contact with the patient. One strategy that physicians can employ is the technique of "successive approximations." The method involves giving information gradually in a series of steps, so that the patient has time to marshall his or her psychologic defenses. Few patients fail to ask for an estimate of how much time they have left. Here physicians are on solid ground when they are vague, given the usual lack of definite and accurate knowledge about the timetable of a fatal illness. Since most patients are concerned with how they will die, they will need to be told about what to expect and to be assured that there are many ways to reduce, and in some cases eliminate, the physical pain and suffering that is so feared by most patients.

Dying is a traumatic event for both the patient and even the most experienced physician. When a terminal prognosis has been given, there must be providers *willing* and *able* to care for a patient with all that the word *care* implies until death. They should provide support and avoid gestures that inhibit full ventilation of the patient's feelings or that lead to feelings of alienation or abandonment.

Finally, it should be remembered that it is the patient who has the right to information first and not family members. The patient should be given the prerogative, if at all possible, as to how other family members are to be informed.

Prolongation/termination

For many years techniques have existed for physicians to prolong life when acute life-threatening episodes occur. Most often such procedures were used with viable patients who, if they could be resuscitated, had a reasonable prospect of resuming functional life. From time to time the issue arose as to whether to use such techniques—often referred to as "heroic treatment"—when the patient was terminally ill.[4]

Though never carefully studied physician accounts indicate that, in general, if the patient was terminally ill but death was not imminent, heroic treatment would be employed. Under certain circumstances heroic treatment might be withheld such as when death was imminent, particularly when the patient was very old or comatose. Of course, the personal values of the physician or the norms of the hospital often helped to shape the nature of the response to acute life-threatening episodes.

These kinds of situations and medical behavior were rarely discussed in textbooks or medical literature, nor were they part of medical school training. They were simply quietly carried out. Young physicians developed their own preferences by watching others during their training.

In recent years the development of numerous medical technologies has provided a wide array of options for dealing with major life-threatening situations such as cardiac arrest or coronary fibrillation, but also with slow failure. Cardiac and respiratory aids also make it possible to keep some patients alive when major organs, including the brain, have ceased to function.

The use of such techniques among terminally ill patients has come under increasing criticism from a variety of sources and for a variety of reasons. Among the reasons for criticism are that life prolongation tends to be costly, painful, and nonbeneficial for the patient. Moreover, when scarce resources such as the time and efforts of medical personnel, drugs, blood, and hospital beds are used with hopelessly ill patients, they may be seen as diverted from other more needy and viable patients.

Beyond issues having to do with the allocation of resources, there is a widespread feeling that in the modern hospital one can no longer "die with dignity." When people are asked to associate the term *dying patient*, they frequently talk about comatose, intubated patients surrounded by oxygen tents, with eerie monitoring machines emitting strange bleeps and casting weird lights from electronic tracings. Such images of death occurring in intensive care settings are accurate only part of the time, but critics of American medicine such as Illich[24] have charged that because of the "medicalization of death," "Western man has lost the right to preside at his act of dying."

In part because of current legal uncertainties and ethical debates about withholding or ceasing treatment for various classes of critically or terminally ill patients, there are examples of what Glantz and Swazey[18] describe as, "sad, horrifying, and sometimes ghoulish" efforts to avert death. They write:

> We have learned, for example, of the implantation of a cardiac pacemaker in a brain-dead "patient," of a terminally ill woman who was defibrillated 70 times in a 24-hour period before succumbing to her disease, and of nurses in intensive care units exhausted from attempting to resuscitate patients that could not be saved.*

Some areas of nontreatment decisions, such as the issuance of "do not resuscitate" (DNR) orders for patients whose conditions cannot be helped further by medical interventions, slowly are being clarified medically, legally, and ethically.[26,38]

---

*From Glantz, L., and Swazey, J.: Decisions not to treat: the Saikewicz case and its aftermath, Forum Med. **2:**22, 1979.

Decisions about whether to continue or to cease treating critically ill patients, however, involve a far wider and more complex range of options and issues than whether to employ cardiopulmonary resuscitation or to "pull the plug" on the respirator. Less dramatic but more common types of decisions, for example, include whether to institute or continue intravenous feeding, to treat a patient's pneumonia, or to "snow" a patient in severe pain with heavy doses of drugs that may hasten the moment of death as well as relieve pain.

Beyond anecdotal reports it is difficult to determine *how often* and on *what bases* physicians decide to withhold either ordinary or "heroic" treatments from critically ill patients or how often such patients elect not to be treated when given an option.

In one of the few studies of patient decision making a series of 24 patients at Los Angeles County UCLA Medical Center, whose burns were so extensive that there had been no recorded instances of survival, were informed of their conditions and prognoses. When asked whether they wished the team to engage in heroic treatment or instead to be offered merely pain medications, 21 of the 24 opted for no treatment, and all 24 died.[25]

The most detailed study of physician attitudes about the treatment of critically ill patients was conducted by Crane[7] from 1970 to 1971. A large sample of internists, neurosurgeons, pediatricians, and pediatric heart surgeons completed questionnaires built around detailed case histories with various treatment options. Crane's study tells us a great deal about physician *attitudes* toward treating critically ill patients in relation to medical variables such as a patient's prognosis, social variables such as patient and family attitudes and social class, and professional variables such as physician training and type of hospital. As Crane herself recognizes, however, there is not a perfect correlation between questionnaire responses and actual behavior in a clinical setting.

To briefly summarize some of Crane's extensive data, she found that a physician's decision to withhold or terminate *ordinary* medical treatment is influenced by several factors. Legal requirements for consent notwithstanding, the consent of the patient or, if incompetent, the patient's agent was only one factor, and often not primary, in deciding whether or not to treat. To the physicians in Crane's study there were two other major considerations. *First, is a patient "salvageable?"* That is, if the patient survives an acute, life-threatening crisis, can he or she be maintained at a "reasonable" level of functioning for a "substantial" amount of time? *Second, is the patient's condition impairing mental as well as physical functioning?* It cannot be emphasized too strongly that both of these considerations are not just questions of medical "facts." Rather, they involve as much, if not more, *value judgments* on the part of the physician and whoever else is involved in treatment/nontreatment decisions.

In terms of how actively they would treat critically ill patients by their criteria of salvageability and physical or mental deficits, in sum, the physicians sampled by Crane ranked patients in the following order: (1) salvageable patients with only physical deficits, (2) salvageable patients with severe mental deficits, (3) unsalvageable patients with only physical deficits, and (4) unsalvageable patients with mental deficits.

Although the distinction between "ordinary" and "extraordinary" treatments often are blurred ones, the use of life-sustaining equipment such as respirators generally is discussed in terms of extraordinary interventions. Decisions to withhold or terminate such extraordinary treatment for terminally ill patients also involve a mix of medical, value, and legal considerations by physicians and other staff and patients or families. Legally and ethically there is uncertainty and debate about whether (1) a conscious, competent patient can order the life-supporting respirator disconnected and (2) whether such a decision can be made for an unconscious or otherwise incompetent patient.[2,18] The latter situation is so complex in part because it involves the issue of *involuntary euthanasia* and questions about the moral and legal differences between *active* and *passive euthanasia*.[4] Should disconnecting a respirator, for example, be considered a passive act that "lets a patient die," in contrast to "killing" a patient by injecting air bubbles into a vein or administering a lethal dose of narcotics? Or what are the distinctions to be drawn between *not* putting a patient on a respirator and withdrawing him *from* the respirator?

The history of the euthanasia debate is a long and involved one that has extended far beyond the original meaning of euthanasia—a "good death." In recent years euthanasia in the sense of a "good death" or "death with dignity" is a cause that has attracted many followers. National organizations such as the Euthanasia Educational Society, for example, have been active in public and professional educational efforts. And legislation has been introduced in many states, and passed in several, that gives legal force to documents such as the "living will," which permits people to indicate their treatment preferences and/or appointment decision-making agents should they become incompetent.[33,34]

It appears likely that more and more pressures will be exerted against excessive treatment for terminal patients. Problems, however, will continue to arise in numerous types of situations, particularly involving patients who, medically and legally, are incapable of participating in decisions about their treatment. But even with competent patients the prognosis is not always certain, and it is difficult not to treat those for whom there is some hope of extending life even for a few months. Glaser and Strauss[19] in their study of terminal patients emphasize how often patients die before hospital personnel expect, as well as how often they live well beyond predictions, and point out how such situations are problematic for staff, each in different ways.

As our discussion of prolongation/termination issues suggests, these situations are likely to be difficult and emotionally distressing to all involved. In the next sections of this chapter we shall examine how prolongation and other issues associated with dying tend to involve several deeply held but conflicting values that in part account for the interpersonal difficulties faced by patients, families, and providers.

Interpersonal relationships and the dying patient

Relationships involving terminal patients, relatives, physicians, and nurses have always been difficult. As a consequence of the new issues we have been discussing, such as increased time between diagnosis and death, problems with candor, rising hospital costs, and questions regarding prolongation, interpersonal relationships have become exacerbated. At the same time, possibly because these problems are so troublesome to so many people, they are being more carefully examined and receiving explicit attention, and some problems such as candor are in the process of being reduced.

The relationship between physician and dying patient has always had its difficult aspects. When the primary physician refers a patient to a specialist for diagnosis, for example, the role of each physician is not always carefully worked out as to who gives information and counseling to the patient and family. By and large the norm appears to be that unless the primary physician "hands" the patient over to the specialist, the specialist is expected to relay diagnostic and prognostic information back to the primary physician. The primary physician, presumably familiar with the patient and his or her emotional strengths and weaknesses, then meets with the patient to discuss the diagnosis, prognosis, and treatment alternatives. Even when this norm is carefully followed, many patients experience intense anxiety, have to wait a longer period of time for the diagnosis, and are puzzled or hurt by the impassive quality of the specialist's interaction.

We have already discussed the issue of candor in informing patients about their diagnoses and prognoses. It is extraordinarily difficult to have to give patients tragic and catastrophic news, and there is little to recommend that would make the task easier. Cancer patients, for example, commonly experience what Prout* calls "the crisis of diagnosis." When informed of their conditions, she observes, they usually react in one or more patterned responses, which physicians need to learn to "diagnose and manage" along with their disease states. These responses include denial, feelings of guilt and/or fear, initiating a frantic search for a negative diagnosis from another provider, or overly passive acquiescence with the physician's views.

As times goes on and the patient begins to fail, most physicians find their inability to halt the inexorable progress of the disease painfully frustrating, for their medical training begins to fail them, and the limits of medicine and the inevitability of death become starkly apparent. During this time, physicians must

---

*Personal communication, Marianne Prout, MD, Section Chief, Medical Oncology, Boston City Hospital, January 1980.

cope with their own frustrations and anxieties as well as the medical and psycho-social dimensions of their patient's dying.

For older physicians trained during a time when information was withheld from terminal patients and for those younger physicians for whom candor is so personally difficult, it is tempting to try to circumvent many of these interpersonally difficult aspects of caring for a dying patient by not honestly discussing their diagnoses or prognoses with them. Lack of disclosure, however, can be as problematic, or more so, than candor. In the face of irreversible disease and increasing symptomatology, it is not easy to maintain an optimistic outlook nor is it easy to explain why predicted improvement fails to occur or when medication has been increased.

The scenario is more complicated when the family knows the expected prognosis, because family members are also expected to act cheerful while awaiting the patient's "recovery." Other hospital staff may or may not be informed of their expected roles and many may or may not go along willingly with the script. Even when they are not explicitly informed about their conditions, moreover, most patients sooner or later draw appropriate conclusions. In either case all involved appear to experience considerable discomfort as a consequence of their duplicity.

In addition to their physical deterioration terminally ill patients may also go through a process that has been called *social dying*, in which behaviors usually directed toward a living person diminish. The socially dying person becomes increasingly isolated from human interaction. This may be prompted by the patient or by those around the patient. In the former case persons close to the patient may (1) underestimate a patient's ability to interact or comprehend or (2) interaction on a meaningful level may be so difficult emotionally that interactions decrease or degenerate to discussion of nonthreatening trivia.

For the dying patient decreasing the amount of meaningful communication with others may serve several functions.[9,20] For example, it may (1) be merely a continuation of the process of disengagement with society common among the aged, (2) give the patient time to reassess and perhaps reformulate his or her self-identity, or (3) protect the patient from an emotional crisis caused by recognizing that normal interaction soon will be taken away. When patients impose isolation on themselves, questions emerge as to whether or not they really wanted to be treated as though they are no longer alive. Efforts need to be made to distinguish between patients who sincerely want to be left alone and those whose calls for solitude may in fact be misunderstood pleas for understanding and compassion.

Moreover, medical staff should be alert to their own social withdrawal from a dying patient and to the withdrawal of family members. If part of the "pain" of death is the loss of loved ones and of human interaction more generally, a major task of those caring for the terminally ill is to provide the social support that will prevent patients, to the extent possible, from suffering this pain before they die.

Relationships between the medical personnel involved with a dying patient also can be difficult. In teaching hospitals, for example, the patient's attending physician can differ from house staff who actually provide day-to-day care for the patient as to what constitutes appropriate treatment. The attending physician, perhaps complying with the patient's or family's wishes, or with his or her own treatment philosophy, may continue to order aggressive treatment when the house staff feel that all that can reasonably be done has been done. Or the reverse may hold true: the experienced attending physician "knows" how useless more treatment would be, whereas the young physician has not yet come to terms with the ultimate limits of medicine and technology. When such disagreements occur, they usually are resolved in terms of the hierarchical relationships traditional in medicine, with the senior physician's position prevailing.

Of all areas of potential strain between physicians and nurses, and there are many, those involving the terminal patient are likely to lead to considerable bitterness and despair for the nurse. For whatever approach the physician takes with the patient (honest or dishonest; aggressively heroic or palliative), it is the nurse who provides by far the bulk of care for and interaction with the patient. To the extent that nurses who are responsible for day-to-day care disagree with the physician's approach either in terms of professional or personal values, conflict will be generated. Since the power of the physician in decision making is considerably greater than that of the nurse, once again the physician's orders presumably will be followed, however, reluctantly, by the nurse.[12,45]

When there are disagreements and tensions between attending physicians and house staff and between physicians and nurses, the terminally ill patient is the one most apt to be affected by the conflict. Thus the attending physician may not have been totally truthful concerning prognosis, the patient senses that he or she is not recovering but becoming more ill, and turns to the house staff or the nurse for an explanation. If the subordinate physician or nurse implies, however indirectly, that the situation is other than that described by the attending physician to the patient, the patient begins to doubt everyone and everything.

In the milieu of the hospital a major problem that negatively affects both relationships among providers and between provider and patient is the failure to identify a *responsible physician* for a given patient.[45] This a *generic problem* in hospital care, particularly in large teaching hospitals; it becomes particularly acute when crucial decisions, such as a shift from active treatment to comfort measures only or DNR orders, are being made and implemented. The patient, who sees a procession of house staff and specialists, may desperately ask, "Who is *my* doctor?" "Who can *I* discuss my problems and the decisions I must make with?" Too often the answer is not forthcoming, for no single physician has been designated to serve, in effect, as the patient's primary caregiver. Staff, too, can be equally bewildered as to who is "in charge" of a given patient. As a result, conflicting messages, or no messages, are relayed among caregivers and from them to the patient, various treatment actions are implemented, or an agreed-on policy such as a DNR is not carried out. Nursing staff are most apt to be placed in a bind by such conflicts, unsure as to whose orders they should carry out.[12] When Mr. Jones has a cardiac arrest, for example, what should his nurse do when three different doctors have ordered her to (1) do nothing, (2) respond with a "fast walk" (i.e., attempt to resuscitate Mr. Jones), and (3) respond with a "slow walk" (i.e., give the appearance of trying to resuscitate Mr. Jones)?

Thus it is critically important that all members of the medical team attempt to develop some consensus regarding the care of a terminal patient and that one person be identified as the patient's "responsible physician." There will be times when disagreement is pronounced, for example, on DNR orders. At such times, more than any others, all personnel must attempt to understand the various positions, reach a consensus, and accept and implement the dominant position in the interests both of patient comfort and of medical team cohesion.

Relationships between medical staff and the patient's family also have great potential for conflict as well as for agreement and cooperation. Much will pivot on the characteristics of the patient and, to a lesser extent, on the relatives. Any one of a large range of possibilities might occur: if the patient is old and has been a burden to his or her children perhaps because of some senile dementia, a quick and painless end may be welcomed; conversely, if the patient is young and vigorous, pressure will likely be exerted to do everything possible and use all type of heroic or experimental procedures. Or, as often happens, family members may disagree with one another, with medical staff, or with the patient. All of these situations plus others too numerous to describe present serious problems to the staff, and they are difficult to ignore.

To the extent possible the physician is on excellent grounds when dealing with the family of a competent dying patient if the physician can honestly say, "I have discussed the situation fully with the patient. We have both examined all the alternatives, and it is the patient's wish that we follow the procedure that I have already instituted." Such a stance puts decision making in the hands of the person to whom it belongs. It also protects the medical staff and provides a buffer against undue family pressure. It is another argument in favor of an honest relationship between physician and patient.

In the case of the critically or terminally ill patient who is incompetent—the infant or young child, the senile aged patient, or the comatose—one can expect relationships between family and staff to be considerably more complex. If there is disagreement between staff and family about the type of treatment that should be given or whether active treatment should be given or withheld or terminated, whose wishes should prevail, and why? And in the case of decisions not to treat, even when staff and family agree, should these decisions be made and carried out privately? Or should they be exposed to public scrutiny and be made by a presumably more dispassionate agent such as a judge? Should nontreatment decisions on behalf of incompetent patients be made *only* on the basis of what the decision makers think are that patient's "best interests?" If so, how do we decide what those interests are? If not, what sorts of other interests should be allowed? As a number of recent publicly debated cases of this sort have made clear, these questions involve far more than medical judgment. They involve matters of society's laws and morality and deeply held personal values. *How* decisions should be made for "voiceless patients" and by *whom* are perhaps the most problematic, conflict-producing questions generated by the dying patient's care.[45]

Impact of the dying patient on the physician

Throughout this chapter we have made numerous comments regarding how troublesome the death of a patient is to medical personnel. We need not repeat these here. But some of the more profound aspects of the difficulties with terminal patients do warrant further discussion.

Aside from equating death with either personal or professional limitation, other factors add further difficulties. The overwhelming thrust of the training of physicians, whether in medical school or in residency, is toward the technologic. Trained for what sociologists call an *instrumental* role, physicians often find themselves ill-equipped for those situations in which they need to play an *expressive* role, as in caring for the terminally ill. Put more simply, physicians engaged in the instrumental behaviors for which they are trained are doing what they know and do best: ordering diagnostic tests, interpreting such tests, and devising and administering appropriate therapy. But with the terminal patient, especially near the end, few instrumental actions are required other than those involving comfort measures such as the administration of pain medication. In lieu of technical skills the physician now needs to exercise the interpersonal skills called for by the expressive role, for which there has been little training. The physician has to talk to the patient and the patient's family not about diagnosis, prognosis, or treatment but about dying and death. The ability to empathize with the patient, to share the poignancy, to talk, to listen, and to avoid a false cheerfulness is what is required and yet is so difficult. Whether explicit training for the expressive role aspects of such *supportive* medical care would be helpful is difficult to assess, since so little training has yet been tried and evaluated.

Finally, the deaths of patients create enormous strain for the physician and other medical care personnel because such deaths often involve fundamental value conflicts that are difficult to resolve. The impact of *value conflict* on those who experience it cannot be minimized. The eminent psychiatrist Karen Horney[23] in her classic monograph *The Neurotic Personality of Our Time* asserted that the value conflicts endemic in a pluralistic society such as the United States contribute significantly to the development of neurotic behavior. She pointed out that many major values conflict with one another so that following one set of values means violating others. For example, the basic democratic value that one person is no better than another clashes with the values of achievement and success, inherent in which is the notion that some people are indeed better than others.

Without further pursuing a psychodynamic framework, there are many facets of caring for dying patients that can create severe value conflicts within and among staff, patients, and families. As illustrated by many nontreatment decisions, these conflicts are so stressful and so difficult to resolve because they involve *fundamental moral dilemmas.*[3] And it is inherent in the nature of such dilemmas that no one answer or action is obviously correct.

For example, within medicine two major values that are expected to guide the behavior of physicians are the sanctity of life and the principle of doing no harm. As pointed out several times earlier, these values often conflict with each other in treating the terminal patient, and one value must given way to the other. There are times when allegiance to the sanctity of life value will violate the humanitarian value that calls for the prevention of suffering and in the end result in doing harm. Thus placing a pacemaker in a failing 90-year-old semicomatose woman, a recent case brought to our attention, seems difficult to justify medically or morally. Conversely, standing "idly" by while a patient slips away without doing something, "anything," violates perhaps the most basic norm in medicine—to do everything possible to save lives. Such value conflicts do not arise in every case or indeed in many cases. But when such conflicts do arise they cause considerable anguish for those who experience them.

Other value conflicts, which we shall note only briefly, also affect those involved with the dying patient. Some of these are not exclusively medical but rather reflect issues in the larger American society. These include tensions between *social differentiation* vs. "all are created equal" (e.g., young people "deserve" better or more treatment than the old); *utilitarianism* (e.g., scarce resources should be allocated to benefit those who will live rather than those who are dying or more for important people, less for the unimportant); *scientific advancement* (e.g., lives prolonged not to save people as much as to learn more about the disease or the treatment); and the value of *success* (e.g., extending life for even a few days in part to display or learn technical skills).

There is no easy answer to the question of how to deal with the clash of incompatible values. To try avoid such potentially distressing conflicts some physicians, not uniquely, adopt a rigidly consistent approach from which they rarely deviate. With regard to disclosure they might say, "I always tell the patient the full truth," or they might say the opposite, "I never tell the patient that his situation is hopeless." Or regarding prolongation: "I always do everything possible to keep the patient alive." This is an economical position for the physician that protects him or her from having to develop a different position for each and every patient. However, the rigidity of this position presents problems when the opposite of the physician's firm rule seems called for, and the physician needs to bend to the prevailing values of others or admit personally that an alternative approach is called for.

But the alternative on closer inspection seems little better. Here the physician says, "I have no fixed rules but make whatever decision is appropriate based on my assessment of the situation." Although this approach has a surface rationality, it assumes that the physician can and will accurately assess each situation and understand completely the needs of the patient and family and numerous other aspects of the case. At the conclusion the physician may be apt to wonder, "Did I do the right thing?"

If neither of these alternatives is very satisfactory, what is left? Not much in terms of guides to physician behavior. What is important is that the physician understand that the situation may be a "no win" situation no matter what he or she does. Such a perspective is important for the caregiver's own mental health. It reduces defensive rigid behavior on one hand and wallowing in guilt on the other. It permits the physician to work in the best interests of the patient, to the extent that this is known, and to accept the limits of available alternatives.

Conclusions

We have described a number of new problems, in addition to enduring ones, associated with dying in America. We have argued that as new problems arise in a society, a period of trial and error tends to follow as the society searches for appropriate solutions. The United States, we would further argue, is far enough into this transitional period so that we are on the verge of producing a coherent series of acceptable options for many situations. The existence of the whole array of problems has been recognized, and sufficient concern with certain problems has led to action.

Death and dying are seen as depressing and tragic. This need not be so. Death is part of life and always has been. So long as human beings are assisted in dying with dignity and emotional support, society is fulfilling its requirements. Describing the course of his own terminal illness in his book *Stay of Execution*, Alsop[1] wrote:

> A dying man needs to die, as a sleepy man needs to sleep, and there comes a time when it is wrong, as well as useless, to resist . . . that time has not yet come for me. But it will. It will come for all of us.*

---

*From Alsop, S.: Stay of execution, Philadelphia, 1973, J. B. Lippincott Co.

References

1. Alsop, S.: Stay of execution, Philadelphia, 1973, J. B. Lippincott Co.
2. Annas, G.: Reconciling Quinlan and Saikewicz: decision making for the terminally ill incompetent, Am. J. Law Med. 4:367, 1979.
3. Beauchamp, T., and Childress, J.: Principles of biomedical ethics, New York, 1979, Oxford University Press, Inc.
4. Behnke, J., and Bok, S., editors: The dilemmas of euthanasia, New York, 1975, Doubleday & Co., Inc.

5. Cappon, D.: Attitudes of and towards dying, Can. Med. Assoc. J. **87**:693, 1962.
6. Cook, R.: Coma, New York, 1977, New American Library.
7. Crane, D.: The sanctity of social life: physicians' treatment of critically ill patients, New York, 1975, Russell Sage Foundation.
8. Cullen, D. J.: Results and costs of intensive care, Anesthesiology **17**:203-216, 1977.
9. Cumming, E., and Henry, W.: Growing old: the process of disengagement, New York, 1961, Basic Books, Inc., Publishers.
10. Demographic Yearbook—1977, New York, 1978, United Nations.
11. Duff, R., and Hollingshead, A.: Sickness and society, New York, 1968, Harper & Row, Publishers, Inc.
12. Earle, A., Argondizzo, N., and Kutsches, A., editors: The nurse as caregiver for the terminal patient and his family, New York, 1976, Columbia University Press.
13. Eissler, K.: The psychiatrist and the dying patient, New York, 1955, International Universities Press, Inc.
14. Epstein, J.: Living in New York, New York Review of Books **5**:14, 1966.
15. Feifel, H.: The meaning of death, New York, 1959, McGraw-Hill, Inc.
16. Fitts, W., and Ravdin, I.: What Philadelphia physicians tell patients with cancer, J.A.M.A. **153**:901, 1953.
17. Freeman, H.: New dimensions of dying. In Brim, O., Freeman, H., Levine, S., and Scotch, N., editors: The dying patient, New York, 1970, Russell Sage Foundation.
18. Glantz, L., and Swazey, J.: Decisions not to treat: the Saikewicz case and its aftermath, Forum Med. **2**:22, 1979.
19. Glaser, B., and Strauss, A.: Awareness of dying, Chicago, 1965, Aldine Publishing Co.
20. Gustafson, E.: Dying, the career of the nursing home patient, J. Health Soc. Behav. **13**:26, 1972.
21. Hinton, J.: Dying, Baltimore, 1967, Penguin Books.
22. Holton, G., and Morism, R., editors: Limits of scientific inquiry, New York, 1979, W. W. Norton & Co., Inc.
23. Horney, K.: The neurotic personality of our time, New York, 1937, W. W. Norton & Co., Inc.
24. Illich, I.: Medical nemesis, London, 1975, Calder & Boyars Ltd.
25. Imbus, S., and Zawacke, B.: Autonomy for burned patients when survival is unprecedented, N. Engl. J. Med. **297**:308, 1977.
26. In the matter of *Shirley Dinnerstein*, 380 NE 2d 134 (Mass. Appeals Court, 1978).
27. Katz, B., Zdeb, M., and Therricault, G.: Where people die, Public Health Rep. **94**:522, 1979.
28. Kelly, W., and Frieson, S.: Do cancer patients want to be told? Surgery **27**:822, 1950.
29. Kübler-Ross, E.: On death and dying, New York, 1969, Macmillan, Inc.
30. Nelkin, D., editor: Controversy: politics of technical decisions, Beverly Hills, 1978, Sage Publications, Inc.
31. Novack, D. H., Plumer, R., Smith, R. L., et al.: Changes in physicians' attitudes toward telling the cancer patient, J.A.M.A. **241**:897, 1979.
32. Oken, D.: What to tell cancer patients, J.A.M.A. **153**:1120, 1961.
33. Relman, A.: Michigan's sensible "living will," N. Engl. J. Med. **300**:1270, 1979.
34. Rubin, H.: Death with dignity in California, The New Physician, p. 26, May 1978.
35. Saunders, C.: Care of the dying, London, 1959, Macmillan, Inc.
36. Saunders, C.: Moment of truth: care of the dying patient. In Pearson, L., editor: Death and dying, Cleveland, 1969, Press of Case Western Reserve University.
37. Shaw, A., Randolph, J., and Manard, B.: Ethical issues in pediatric surgery: a national survey of pediatricians and pediatric surgeons, Pediatrics **60**:588, 1977.
38. Spencer, S.: "Code" or "no code": a nonlegal opinion, N. Engl. J. Med. **300**:138, 1979.
39. Spiegel, J.: Cultural variations in attitudes towards death and disease. In Grossner, G., Wecksler, H., and Greenblat, M., editors: The threat of impending disaster, Cambridge, Mass., 1964, Massachusetts Institute of Technology Press.
40. Strickland, S.: Politics, science, and dread disease, Cambridge, Mass., 1972, Harvard University Press.
41. Sudnow, D.: Passing on, Englewood Cliffs, N.J., 1967, Prentice-Hall, Inc.
42. Swazey, J.: To treat or not to treat: the search for principled decisions. In Abernethy, V., editor: Frontiers in medical ethics, Cambridge, Mass., 1980, Ballinger Publishing Co.
43. U.S. Department of Health, Education, and

Welfare: Monthly vital statistics report, annual summary 1978, D.H.E.W. Publication no. PHS 79-1120, vol. 27, no. 13, Aug. 13, 1979, National Center for Health Statistics.

44. Veatch, R.: Death, dying, and the biological revolution, New Haven, Conn., 1976, Yale University Press.

45. Wong, C., and Swazey, J., editors: Dilemmas of dying: policies and procedures for decisions not to treat, Boston, 1981, G. K. Hall & Co.

Part III

THE MEDICAL DOMAIN

■ In Chapters 3 through 8 we have looked in a roughly temporal
sequence at various aspects of provider-patient interactions.
Our orientation in these chapters, as we pointed out in Chapter 1,
has been that of sociology *in* medicine: using the knowledge
and skills of the social sciences to help medical professionals
understand and deal more effectively with problematic aspects of
their work. Chapters 9 to 12 also draw from a sociology
in medicine perspective but include, more than previous chapters,
the second major focus of medical sociology, termed the
sociology *of* medicine. That is, they involve a more detached,
academic analysis of three aspects of what we term the
"medical domain"—the institutional, professional, and societal
contexts of medicine in the United States.

■ This is a large topic, one that we cannot thoroughly cover even in
four chapters. Thus in developing this final section we have
been highly selective, aiming at enduring issues in the "medical
domain." Even with this in mind it is important to note that
the "medical domain" is changing, and a description of current
complexities is likely to be soon out of date.

Chapter 9

Becoming a physician

The institutional context of medical training

Formal organizations play an important role in the careers of all professionals. For example, organizations comprise the context in which people acquire most of the knowledge and skills and many of the attitudes and values that make them professionals. And once trained, professionals perform a significant proportion of their work, some spending entire careers, in complex organizations. Organizations formally structure a professional's authority and accountability. By placing people in authority hierarchies, organizations structure whom professionals interact with, many of the features of those interactions, and the professionals' responsibilities.

Complex organizations, just like individuals, have their own needs and create demands. Organizations facilitate many human activities, such as education and the delivery of human services, including medical care. But at the same time they can hinder and inadvertently impose constraints and in fact interfere with their very reason for existing.

In Chapters 9 and 10 we focus on some of the dominant institutions and practice settings in the lives of medical care providers—medical schools, hospitals, and various ambulatory care settings. We explore some of the ways in which these organizations and settings both facilitate and hinder the training of physicians and the delivery of medical services. As will become apparent, it is sometimes difficult to live with complex organizations. But, as is also apparent, it has become impossible to live without them.

Medical school: past and present

In several ways the first year of medical school does not live up to . . . expectations. [Students] are disillusioned when they find that they will not get near patients at all, that the first year will be just like another year of college. In fact, some feel that it is not even as good as college because their work in some areas is not as thorough as courses in the same fields in undergraduate school. They come to think that their courses (with the exception of anatomy) are not worth much because, in the first place, the faculty (being Ph.D.s) know nothing about the practice of medicine and, in the second place, the subject matter itself is irrelevant, or, as the students say, "ancient history."

The freshmen are further disillusioned when the faculty tells them in a variety of ways that there is more to medicine than they can possibly learn. They realize it may be impossible for them to learn all they need to know in order to practice medicine properly. Their disillusionment becomes more profound when they discover that this statement of the faculty is literally true. Experience in trying to master the detail of the anatomy of the extremities convinces them that they cannot do it in the time they have.*

This quote, from a classic study on medical education now nearly a quarter of a century old,[1] yet still often applicable, highlights some of the enduring problems and concerns of first-year medical students.

For most students entrance to medical school marks an end to one set of experiences and the beginning of another. The struggle to merely gain entrance is over. Real professional training is about to begin. Students look forward to developing skills and mastering medical knowledge, in essence becoming competent professionals with unique responsibilities to care for the sick. Yet there is little question that many students find their introduction to becoming a physician not what they expect.

What factors have contributed and are contributing to the nature of the medical school experience today? And what changes have been and are being planned with respect to medical education? Though incoming medical students may understandably anticipate that the major focus of *medical school* activity will be to train them to be physicians, the goals and activities of medical schools are far more complex and often are influenced by social, economic, and historical forces completely extraneous to the training of medical students. After all, medical schools are centers of research and sources of new medical knowledge, gatekeepers of medical licensure, providers of patient care, centers of continuing education for graduate physicians and other medical care providers, sites where other graduate and doctoral students are trained, battlegrounds for decisions about what is appropriate patient treatment and medical practice, and the settings in which medical providers as well as numerous types of nonphysicians carry out their professional careers and attempt to inform others of their ideas and orientation. As we will see, medical education in this country is still powerfully shaped by historical developments. But at the same time it is beginning to show important changes, developments reflecting not only discontent with the methods of medical education but with the very goal of this enterprise as well.

Since its inception medical education in the United States has undergone only one major revolution, which provided medical educators with both a goal and a means of achieving that goal. For analytic purposes we can point to 1910 as the year of the revolution and the publication of bulletin number 4 of the Carnegie Foundation, titled *On Medical Education in the United States and Canada*, as the manifesto of the revolution.[8] The "Flexner Report," as this publication has come

---

*From Becker, H., and Geer, B.: The fate of idealism in medical school, Am. Sociol. Rev. 23:51, 1958.

to be known, dealt a death blow to much of medical education as it was then known and set the stage for many of the major features of medical education that developed over the next several decades and that still persist today. A brief look at medical education prior to the Flexner Report will help us understand the importance of this event in the history of medical education.

From the beginning of the settlement of this country until the mid-1700s medical education for most consisted of preceptorships. This meant spending time, usually up to 3 years, with a practicing physician, reading, studying, and seeing patients. For better or worse the quality of the education received necessarily depended heavily on the particular preceptor one studied with.[5]

Beginning in the mid-1700s and extending into the late 1800s this preceptorship was increasingly associated with some "formal" medical school training. Although there were a few university-affiliated schools, such as the University of Pennsylvania and Harvard University, many schools were private and proprietary.[5] One of the first activities of the American Medical Association (AMA) when it was formed in 1847 was to undertake reform of medical education, a move based in part on concern about the growing numbers of physicians and in particular about the quality of training many physicians were receiving, especially in the rapidly expanding proprietary schools.

Although the AMA established a committee on medical education as early as 1842, it was not until the turn of the century that significant reform took place.[5] From 1908 to 1910 a nonphysician, Abraham Flexner, under the auspices of the Carnegie Foundation and with the support of the AMA, visited virtually all medical schools in the United States and Canada. He reported in colorful and uncompromising detail what he found.[16]

> . . . Kentucky was delineated as "one of the largest producers of low-grade doctors in the entire Union;" Chicago "the plague spot of the country." The most devastating invective was reserved for the small proprietary schools: schools such as Bennett Medical College, a "stock company practically owned by the dean of the school;" and Jenner Medical College an "out-and-out commercial enterprise." The National Medical University, also in Chicago, was distinguished by giving a free trip to Vienna to any student who paid fees regularly, in cash, for three years. Although the school occupied a badly lighted building, "containing nothing that can be dignified by the name of equipment," it claims its top floor, where there were "two lonely patients," as a hospital. Terms such as "very weak," "wholly inadequate," "miserable," "dirty," and "utterly wretched" appear on almost every page of the Flexner Report. Only Harvard, Johns Hopkins, and Western Reserve received clean bills of health.*

The Flexner Report had both a rapid and a long-term impact on the nature of medical education in the United States. Many proprietary schools closed soon after publication of the report. Perhaps more importantly Flexner provided medical

---

*From Stevens, R.: American medicine and the public interest, New Haven, Conn., 1971, Yale University Press.

education with both a mission and a method. Medicine to Flexner was very much an applied science, and his mission was to make physicians scientists.

Using the curriculum of Johns Hopkins University as his model, which in turn had been established along the lines of medical education in Germany, Flexner suggested five major changes.[5] First, Flexner advocated adoption of a 4-year curriculum, a curriculum that until recently was highly standardized in an almost lockstep progression. Second, he recommended the introduction of laboratory teaching into medical school, especially during the first 2 years, emphasizing the scientific basis of medicine. Third, he wanted expanded clinical exposure, especially during the latter phase of education. Fourth, to improve teaching he suggested bringing medical schools into the framework of universities, and fifth, he supported the incorporation of research into medical schools.

The reform growing out of the Flexner Report may have extended beyond its author's original intentions in that a scientific focus came to overly dominate the medical school curriculum.[3] In addition, developments have occurred since Flexner's report, giving new shape and meaning to his suggestions. For example, the scientific basis of medical education has expanded dramatically since the early 1900s. Whereas at one time the science deemed relevant to the training of a physician was limited largely to biology, this is no longer the case. The expansion of the content of the curriculum without any significant change in the amount of time has resulted in much pressure on both faculty and students, especially during the preclinical years. Teachers are confronted with the problem of selecting what should be taught from all that could be taught. And, correspondingly students are often confronted with a similar problem of selecting what to learn from all that is presented. In such a situation neither party may feel satisfied, continuously confronting the questions "Has enough been taught?" or "Have the important things been learned?"

Another development shaping the nature of medical education today is the changing function of medical schools. Increasingly medical schools are part of, or affiliated with, large medical centers where education is but one goal, along with research and service. Federal and private funding for biomedical research and more recent efforts to increase the number of primary care physicians have influenced the size and composition of medical school faculty.[6] As such, the faculty who students meet in medical school today is a mixed group of professionals, for example, some MDs, some PhDs, some more interested in research than in teaching, some devoted to clinical medicine, or some never having contact with patients. What this means is that not infrequently the interests of the faculty and students do not coincide, giving rise to an educational experience that from both points of view is less than desirable. Students often feel overwhelmed and disappointed by their training to be a physician, especially during the first 2 years.

And the faculty, particularly preclinical faculty, often feels frustrated as well. Not only does teaching compete with educators' need to do research, but they must teach students who most often do not share the interest and investment in their material that they would find among graduate students. Moreover, the growing mandate of medicine and the rapid expansion in scientific knowledge has created a situation where a curriculum does not derive purely from rational planning; instead much of its form results from interdepartmental politics and from the contingencies of federal funding programs.

In many ways, then, the medical school as an institution for training tomorrow's physicians has undergone significant change since Flexner gave medical educators their mandate just after the turn of the century. Medical schools are now complex organizations that serve various functions, only one being the education of physicians. Viewed from this perspective it is understandable why medical schools have and continue to experience some of the problems they do and why medical students do not always find the medical school experience to be what they expect. It is clear that medical schools will continue to experience such problems as they and their complex mandate evolve over the next decades.

The medical school experience

The discussion so far has highlighted some of the larger historical and social forces that are shaping medical schools today. For students, however, these forces are apt to be much less salient than their day-to-day experiences. What problems do students typically confront? And how do they attempt to cope with them? A number of sociologic studies have looked at the process of medical education or, as sociologists would phrase it, the socialization of medical students. These studies provide a rich and varied comment on the medical school experience both in terms of how students acquire the skills and knowledge required to be a competent physician and how students learn some of the values and attitudes that are part of the professional culture of medicine. We will examine a few of these.

First, because of the high prestige of the profession, the perceived value of the work it performs, and the high level of the rewards, intellectual and financial, many students want to attend medical school and are strongly encouraged by family and friends. Consequently, as everyone knows, gaining entrance to medical school is a difficult task. Between 1978 and 1979 there were 36,636 applicants for approximately 16,500 openings. The average candidate completed over nine different applications. Those accepted had remarkable undergraduate records: 50% had grade point averages of 3.6 or higher on a 4-point scale, and nearly 10% already had some type of graduate degree.[12]

In addition to the competition to enter medical school, being a medical student carries special concerns and problems. For example, being in medical school, somewhat in contrast to law school and perhaps even more in contrast to graduate school, reflects an investment that has what may be referred to as *relatively low convertible value*. That is, law students who withdraw from law school may convert their experience in law school into various professional activities other than law. For example, they may go into business, accounting, or any of a large number of fields where this experience can be put to use. From a professional perspective they may in fact do as well without a law degree as they would have with one.

Even more so perhaps PhD graduate students who fail in one area may switch areas or even academic disciplines or use their advanced training for entrance into a large number of occupations and professions, many with similar rewards to the professions they originally planned.

It would appear, however, that the opportunity to convert an incomplete medical education experience into another professional career even approximately equal to that of medicine is much less. This may be so for a variety of reasons, including such things as the high prestige and incomes of physicians, which are difficult, if not impossible, to match in any other health profession. In addition, if a student leaves medical school for any reason, it is often very difficult for family and friends not to view it as a failure on the part of the student. People often do not understand that even given a choice, some students would prefer to be in a field other than medicine.

This low training convertibility and the atmosphere and attitudes it fosters regarding the importance of, or even more so, the necessity of becoming a physician are important pressures students bring to medical school. And even though comparatively few students fail or withdraw from medical school (between 1% and 2% in any given year),[12] the value and necessity of becoming a physician and the lack of what many view as acceptable career alternatives are present as the medical student undertakes the difficult task of learning to be a physician. Such pressures, of course, help to create strong desires to succeed, which the educational experience may frustrate in various ways.

For at least the first 2 years at most medical schools medical education is a group experience in which students often put in 8-hour classroom and laboratory days. Unlike doctoral programs in graduate schools, medical school individual faculty members do not closely supervise and guide the development of individual students over the course of several years of training. Rather, large groups of students at the same level are seen by each faculty member for short periods during their training. Though some students and some faculty do informally establish relationships that go beyond the specific course instruction where they meet, by and large medical school, particularly during the preclinical years, is an impersonal experience for students.

The preclinical years, in particular the first year, are largely science focused, with limited, if any, contact with patients. The learning required of students is predominantly memorization and comprehension. Unlike law students, medical students are rarely verbally grilled, and the seminars and writing of papers and essays, so common in graduate school, comprise only a small fraction of medical student effort. Most of the evaluation of students is based on performance on short answer and multiple choice examinations.

Many students not infrequently find that the demands and experience of the preclinical years are overwhelming. For students, most of whom have known nothing but academic success, the medical school experience can be extremely threatening. This is especially so when, for the first time in their academic lives, some students find themselves not in their accustomed place at the top of the class but at the bottom.

Moreover, students are constantly reminded by faculty that the training they receive in each basic science area is only a fraction of what there is to learn. Thus students do not experience the gratification of a sense of mastery over the content of a given discipline.

Students cope with the amount of information they must learn in several ways. One study found that many students begin by attempting to learn everything. When they find this impossible, they attempt to learn only what they think will be important for the practice of medicine. When this too fails, they fall back on attempting to learn only what they think their instructors want them to learn, even if its perceived relevance to medical practice is low.[1]

There are problems with these approaches, of course. With respect to the second tactic, selecting out what they think is important for the practice of medicine, students do not yet really know what is important for the practice of medicine. They are unable, because of lack of experience, to know what they should know. With respect to the third tactic, it is not always clear what the instructor thinks is important, and thus students find it hard to know what to learn.

Given such experiences many students become disillusioned early in their medical school education to the point where some of the initial enthusiasm and idealism they may have brought with them to medical school turns into cynicism.[1] As students progress into the clinical years, some of this cynicism and disillusionment may lessen, however, with increasing contact with the clinical aspects of medicine.

In addition to learning the scientific and clinical knowledge requisite for practicing medicine medical education involves other types of learning. Becoming a physician, for example, involves acquiring sets of attitudes about the human body as an object of investigation, developing the capacity to handle life and death situations, and learning to be concerned, but not overly so, about people and their medical problems. In regard to such developments, research on the medical school experience in the 1950s suggested a number of stress points in the attitudinal evolution of students, stress points that we suspect are as salient today as they were then. These "attitude learning sequences" are interesting, for they suggest, as Fox[10] has noted, that in confronting certain professional issues and activities students are not infrequently confronted with the problem of "blending" counter attitudes. For example, in relating to patients, students learn to balance "concern" for the patients with a certain amount of "detachment" as well. Hence, developing the capacity for "detached concern" is one task confronting students throughout medical school, especially as their involvement with and responsibility for patients increase.[10]

In a similar vein students learn to cope with certainty and uncertainty in providing care, to temper idealism with realism in judging their own limits as well as the limits of medicine, and to assess their self-interests in terms of the broader social-humanitarian ideology of the medical profession.[9]

Experiences that shape such attitudes begin early in medical school with anatomy and dissection of the human body. These experiences become more intense as the student begins to see patients and becomes acquainted with the human body and how it functions in illness and injury.[1] In the process of their education students learn to confront death and disability both personally and as professionals, and they learn to pick, probe, and explore the human body not just in fantasy but in fact.

In some respects the development of professional attitudes is as important in becoming a competent physician as are technical knowledge and skills. As perhaps is the case in most professional education, however, the primary attention of educators and the structure and content of the educational curricula in most medical schools are focused almost exclusively on the acquisition of technical knowledge and skills. Students handle attitudinal learning and associated problems on a personal basis, or they handle them among themselves often with little formal assistance from their faculty. Thus in a sense socialization for the physician's role is only partially provided for formally in medical school. Medical education in terms of curriculum and content remains a largely technically focused experience, although learning to be a physician entails many human problems, the exercise of values, and the development of many attitudes, as does the very practice of medicine itself.

Yet despite its frustrations and difficulties, the first 2 years of medical training actually expose medical students to an enormous amount of information and a wide range of medical experiences. Though many students may not fully perceive the transformation, their knowledge and many values and attitudes as well are dramatically changed.

As students move into the last two more clinically focused years of medical school, the nature and the structure of the educational experience change. Whereas the first 2 years were largely a group experience, learning is more individual in the last 2 years. Students learn in small groups in which student membership is constantly changing as students switch clinical rotations. Medical students comprise a relatively small part of the clinical groups they rotate through and hold the lowest status in the clinical hierarchy. Consequently, the social structure of the clinical environment heightens the pressure on students to adopt the norms and culture of their superiors, even beyond their desire to learn clinical medicine.

It is during these years that students begin to have significant contact with patients and begin to actually perform work on patients. Many of these tasks, however, are hardly "medical" in a narrow technical sense. More often they involve such things as obtaining lab reports and running after lost charts and records, which is referred to as "scut" work.[2] Students do perform some medical tasks such as taking histories and drawing blood, which initially are exciting but soon become routine.

During the clinical years of medical school the mechanism for student evaluation also changes. Though most students will take national board examinations, the primary mode of evaluation shifts to their participation in clinical conferences, the thoroughness and appropriateness of their patient history taking, and their ability to learn and retain the details of the case history of patients to whom they are assigned. It is also during this time that medical students begin to learn the unwritten but important standards of comportment by which they will be judged as interns and residents.

Intellectually the clinical years pose a somewhat different task than the preclinical years. That is, in some respects the preclinical years are largely science oriented, wherein the emphasis is on acquiring scientific facts and learning to exercise rational empirical decision making. This experience may foster a view of medical practice as one of simply applying the relevant facts in a given situation. With clinical exposure comes a somewhat different emphasis. Although scientific fact and rational-empirical skepticism are still important, development of clinical skills and personal judgment takes on increasing importance in the clinical years. For example, students will witness discussions, sometimes very heated ones, in which physicians attempt to integrate personal clinical experience with "scientific reports" in literature. When there is congruence between clinical experience and published report there is no problem, of course. But when there is a difference, complex judgments must be made, often on the spot, concerning the immediate care of a patient. This introduction to integrating science and experience is the beginning of a problem that physicians will experience throughout their careers.

In many respects, then, the clinical years provide a different set of learning situations, experiences, and challenges than the preclinical years. Students, through clinical rotations, are exposed to the complex but often exciting worlds of the various medical specialties, and in the process they begin to formulate and develop career interests. At the same time through such clinical experiences, interacting with patients, and adopting the words, dress, and deportment of their profession, students, however hesitatingly, in various ways begin to conceive of themselves as physicians. Graduation from medical school will, of course, bring formal conferral of the medical degree. And the internship will provide a demanding test of young physicians, not only of their knowledge and skills but of their own conceptions of themselves as "real" physicians.

Residency: from student to physician

Students bring to medical school many concerns, anxieties, and even fears, as we have seen, about the experience they are undertaking. As physicians, at least by degree and title, young residents begin their residencies with many concerns, anxieties, and again even fears about the experience they are undertaking. But the anxieties and fears this time involve not only concern about personal performance and achievement but worry over the patients they will be responsible for, for now they are physicians. Concern over knowing what to do or, perhaps even more so, knowing enough so as not to injure a patient are highly salient anxieties as residents don the full garb and responsibility of the physician.

Given the nature of graduate medical education, how well founded are such fears and anxieties? Before discussing this topic specifically let us begin with a brief description of the organizational and institutional nature of residency training in the United States. This will shed some light on the ways in which the graduate experience permits a young, largely inexperienced physician to both provide care and to learn, perhaps not without errors or problems but often with considerable back-up and support.

The hospital as school

Under the Flexner model of medical education graduation from medical school was tantamount to preparation for practice. In the years since Flexner, with the broadening of the scientific and clinical bases of medicine, graduation from medical school is no longer viewed as adequate preparation for the practice of medicine. In general, medical school has slowly become a form of undergraduate training.

Some form of graduate medical education was available in the United States even before the turn of the century. Up to about 1900 a select group of physicians, usually only those trained in one of the few university-affiliated medical schools, obtained some graduate hospital training.[11] This experience, referred to as the *internship*, came more and more into acceptance. By the mid-1940s, however, it was becoming apparent that even internship was not adequate. In fact as early as 1928 residencies were established, graduate experiences that took the physician into a longer and more intensive exposure to medical care than the more limited 1-year internship.[11]

In 1966 a report on the status of graduate medical education in the United States called for abandonment of the internship and institution of the residency.[11] This has in effect become the policy today, with virtually all medical school graduates entering a residency program for varying lengths of time (Table 13).

Just as the dominant, but not sole, location for undergraduate medical education is the medical school, the hospital in its various forms becomes the dominant, but not exclusive, site for residency training at the graduate level. Other locations

Table 13. Length of graduate training programs*†

	GMF year					Entering	Finishing
	1	**2**	**3**	**4**	**5**		
Family practice – 13%	←———————→					1,820	1,820
Pediatrics – 10%	←——————→					1,400	1,400
Internal medicine – 45%						6,300	
General (20%)	←——————→						2,800
Specialties (18%)			←————→				2,520
Neurology (2%)		←————→					280
Dermatology (1%)		←————→					140
Psychiatry (4%)		←————→					560
Obstetrics – 7%	←————————→					980	980
Surgery – 15%						2,100	
General (6%)	←——————————→						840
Neurosurgery (1%)		←—————————→					140
Ophthalmology (2%)		←—————————→					280
Orthopedic surgery (3%)		←—————————→					420
Otorhinolaryngology (1%)		←—————————→					140
Urology (2%)		←—————————→					280
General – 10%						1,400	
Anesthesiology (3%)		←—————→					420
Pathology (3%)		←————→					420
Physical medicine (1%)		←———→					140
Radiology (3%)		←—————→					420
						14,000	14,000

*Reprinted with permission from Becoming a physician: development of values and attitudes in medicine. Copyright 1979, Ballinger Publishing Co.
†Length determined primarily by the requirements for certification by the appropriate specialty boards. Abscissa: years of residency training.

include state medical examiner offices, blood banks, ambulatory clinics, and mental health agencies.[12]

From an organizational perspective the structure of graduate medical education is much different from that of medical school. In the first place medical schools generally have strong university ties, and accordingly are controlled almost exclusively by the academic medical community. In contrast the 4630 accredited residency programs take place in a variety of institutions. As a consequence, decisions about residency programs, their structure, content, and the experiences they offer trainees is less under the control of the academic medical community than is the medical school experience.

It is the case, of course, that residency programs are accredited by various professional bodies. This means that certain minimum experiences, training, and activities are provided for the trainee. However, on a day-to-day basis, given the variety of hospitals, their varying academic medicine ties, and especially the necessity of their maintaining significant control over the patient care that takes place under their auspices, the organizational setting for residency training is very complex. One result of this is that there is perhaps less standardization among residency programs than among medical schools in the educational experiences provided.

A related point is that in part due to varying links to academic medicine hospitals in which residency programs occur differ greatly in how they endorse and mix three goals: service, teaching, and research. For example, some residency programs are located in large university hospitals, with major commitment to research and innovation in medical care. Other programs are located in small local hospitals with virtually no research. In the former type of setting the residency experience and patient care will be largely, but not exclusively, under the control of the university hospital medical school faculty. In such a setting the young resident will be exposed to academically oriented norms regarding patient care and the roles, rights, and responsibilities of the physician and patient. In a small local hospital with less of an academic commitment primary authority over patient care will reside in local private practitioners who admit patients to the hospital, and the young resident will experience less emphasis on research and academic medicine. In short, the nature of the residency experience, its emphases, and its norms of accountability vary markedly, depending on the particular type of hospital in which it occurs and the relative emphasis given to each or all of the goals of teaching, research, and patient care.

A second important organizational feature of graduate medical education is that it takes place, as we have noted, largely in hospitals. Hospitals generally expose physicians to only a select variety of medical problems and patients, those requiring the most intensive, specialized care available.

It is important to note that residents do spend some of their graduate time in various hospital clinics providing ambulatory care. However, the overall impact of hospitals being the dominant locus of graduate training is to provide trainees with a very select view of the range and nature of medical problems and patients. In general, the residency experience seems to provide an excellent opportunity to see secondary and tertiary level problems and patients. However, there is very limited opportunity to become familiar with the most frequent primary care problems for which patients seek medical care. For those physicians who go into non-hospital-based practice, which most do, this situation creates a real disjunction between their residency experiences and their subsequent day-to-day professional experiences.

Further, the organizational environment of a hospital residency and private practice, particularly solo practice, are also distinct. In a hospital residents are salaried, responsible to superiors, and supported by ancillary staff over which the physician has only partial authority. Hiring, firing, and promoting other professionals usually rest in their separate departments (e.g., nursing or social work). During residency training only a small part of the house officer's effort is devoted to coordinative and administrative tasks like appointments, record keeping, bill collection, and equipment and supply purchase and maintenance. However, once in private practice, particularly solo practice, the autonomy and administrative responsibilities of physicians expand enormously. Few residency programs provide any preparation for such responsibilities.

Finally, the residency period is a time during which many critical decisions are made by trainees about the type of medical care they ultimately want to practice. For example, trainees decide to be generalists within one of the recognized specialties or they subspecialize. In addition, important decisions are made about the type of career one wants—straight practice, academic, or mixed arrangement—and plans are formulated about the nature of the patient population to serve and the location of one's practice. The content and organization of the residency program, often powerfully shaped by its medical school affiliation, can have a dramatic impact on such decisions.[13]

Having highlighted a few major structural aspects of graduate medical education, we now turn to a discussion of the residency experience from the perspective of those going through these programs.

The residency experience: from the books to the bedside

The residency is a period during which young, knowledgeable, but largely inexperienced physicians learn to do the things physicians do. This is a difficult task. The residency experience, vividly described in a number of recent popular autobiographies and novels,[4,14,18] presents the young physician with many difficult personal as well as professional problems. The problems in some respect constitute "rites of passage." They define the flavor and nature of the residency experience and provide some insight into what it means to become a physician.

The experiences confronting residents can be variously described. One way suggests an almost temporal sequence of events confronting the young physician. These begin with *survival issues*—learning to cope with the demands, physical and otherwise, that the residency experience imposes. Occurring almost alongside survival issues, but increasing in importance as the resident progresses, are what we may call *competency-independence* issues. These include such things as learning to accept increasing responsibility for patient care or learning to be an autonomous, functioning, independent professional. Another set of problems confronting the new physician involves learning to establish *workable professional relationships* with other care providers. We will examine each of these topics briefly.

Survival

The residency imposes many burdens on the young physician. As in medical school, there is much to learn but only limited time in which to do it. There are conferences to attend, journals to read, and an almost limitless list of tasks to do, especially tasks that no one else wants to perform.

The residents' early experience as physicians "being on call" comes in large doses. For example, residents are sometimes on call for very long periods of time, sometimes extending for more than 48 hours. Patients and their crises come at all times of the day and night, and it can be extremely difficult for residents to bring structure and order to their lives. As a consequence, a common problem among residents is simply chronic, grinding fatigue. Finding time to sleep, eat, and rest becomes a major task.

The tempo and intensity of the early residency experience has both short- and long-term effects. One is that the resident, out of necessity, quickly learns to value time and its use. As a consequence of this, many residents begin to develop attitudes about patients based on how much time patients require. For example, "good" patients are those who present clear problems and symptoms and comply. Conversely, "bad" patients are the complainers, those with vague problems and symptoms, and those who return endlessly and use up valuable time. Such attitudes can be important in shaping physicians' future views of patients and the types of relationships they will establish with patients.

Outside of the immediate milieu of the hospital another consequence of the intensity and tempo of the residency experience is that any social life or commitments become very limited or nonexistent. If residents are married and have children, for example, the residency experience can pose particularly difficult strains on their family obligations.

Residency programs vary, of course, in the demands they place on physicians. Some specialties, such as radiology, psychiatry, or public health, provide more regular hours and routinization of work than other specialties, such as medicine or surgery. Likewise some hospitals, such as large, inner-city hospitals that serve large populations, offer residency experiences where the problems alluded to previously will be much intensified compared to the residency experiences found in small, suburban hospitals serving more affluent populations.[13] However, there is present in virtually all residencies the problem of learning to use time carefully and to cope with long hours of caring for patients.

Becoming competent: to err (once) is human

It is not just the long hours and chronic fatigue that makes the residency a trying experience, however. Imposed on top of all this, and in fact taking priority over it, is the new task of having responsibility, however limited, for patient care. Taking responsibility for patient care is, as we have noted, one of the initial anxiety-provoking tasks confronting residents. Yet in some respects the organization of the residency experience is such that young residents are not as much "on their own" as they may fear. This comes about in two ways.

First, although residents may be the initial on-line physicians a hospitalized patient has contact with, there is always available advice and counsel and, if necessary, the taking over of a patient by a more experienced physician. The young resident learns early that seeking assistance from the physician ultimately responsible when really necessary is a must and failure to do so brings severe repercussions.[2] At the same time, however, the resident, wanting to demonstrate competency especially to superiors, may feel reluctant to seek advice or assistance. Seeking help unnecessarily can reflect an inability to handle difficult situations. However, if a mistake is made by the resident, even if he or she failed to inform the attending physician, it is still the attending physician who is accountable. Failure to inform a superior of an impending problem places the superior at risk. It violates the implicit rule attending physicians have for residents in training, the rule of "no surprises."[2] The resident must weigh the desire to act independently and appear competent against the need to seek appropriate assistance and the obligation to keep attending physicians informed about developments in patient management. Balancing these two concerns takes time, experience, and, as most residents learn, a few bruises.

A second way in which the inexperience of the young resident is covered comes about through the fact that the resident will almost always deliver care in the presence of sometimes very experienced nurses and other care providers. As was the case in seeking assistance from superiors and hence demonstrating certain incompetencies, young residents are often reluctant to seek help from or accept the advice of nonphysicians, again admitting their incompetencies or, conversely, the superior abilities and experience of nonphysician providers. Yet most young residents learn rapidly the value of establishing trust in and accepting the advice and assistance of more experienced providers, whether they are physicians or not.[14]

Developing a sense of competency entails more than learning to both seek and accept advice. It entails a series of difficult tasks, including translating the book learning of medical school into bedside practice, mastering technical skills, and learning to make difficult judgments. Central to the development of residents' evolving sense of competency will be their experience and response to making mistakes. Residents learn that errors (certain types of errors) are expected, and one is expected to make them, but no more than once.

Bosk[2] in a recent study provides an in-depth view of some of the major professional norms and values surrounding "errors," at least as they occurred in a surgical residency. In examining errors on the surgical ward and the responses to them Bosk described two types of errors residents could commit, one he called *errors in technique* and the other *moral errors*. The first refers to errors in surgical techniques or misjudgments about how best to proceed technically with a given patient. Moral errors are violations of the code of conduct among physicians, not as to their technical proficiency but rather their norms about interpersonal behavior as professionals. Interestingly, Bosk reports that professional responses to moral errors were more immediate and severe than were responses to technical errors. In fact he suggests that whereas the thrust of responses to technical errors were restitutive in nature, responses to moral errors were more characteristically repressive. That is, the former responses were attempts to understand and provide for correction so as not to repeat the error, whereas the latter were attempts to divorce or isolate the offender from the group and its approval.

Bosk's observations, to the degree they are generalizable to other residency programs, are important. They suggest something of the environment in which residents learn, an environment that recognizes error and in fact provides support for certain types of technical errors, which it is believed almost all inexperienced physicians will commit. It is a learning environment, however, that at the same time punishes heavily mistakes that violate the code of conduct of physicians.

In short, a core problem for the resident is to learn to take increased responsibility for the life and limb of patients. This is a stressful and anxiety-provoking task that adds significantly to the intensity and burden of the residency experience. Yet the nature and culture of the residency experience provide support for the novice, as long as the resident reflects such professional values as recognition of superiors and their authority, cooperation, and not repeating mistakes.

Working with others

Residents learn rapidly that regardless of their own knowledge or skills they must learn to work with a large number of other medical care providers if they are to survive their residency and become competent physicians. In contrast to learning such things as skills and techniques, which will actually be taught and demonstrated, learning to establish working and workable relationships with colleagues is done informally and often through painful experience.

There are in reality four dimensions to such learning. First, the resident must learn to work with a variety of medical care providers other than physicians, such as nurses, technicians, aides, and hospital administrators. Nurses play a central role in helping inexperienced residents cope with patient care and learn how to be physicians. As noted previously, not infrequently young physicians will find themselves paired with a much experienced nurse who, from a practical and experiential perspective, knows much more about delivering care and treating patients than they do. Accepting this and learning to benefit from it are often important lessons for the new resident.

Second, residents need to cooperate with one another. Social forces can draw them together but also can pull them apart. On the one hand, residents must share responsibilities in patient care, experience similar crises and demands, and be mutually vulnerable to criticism from attending physicians. On the other hand, many residency programs are competitive and the desire to please faculty and to be given responsibility for challenging and interesting medical and surgical cases may draw residents apart. Further, although residents generally are sympathetic to one another when they make mistakes because mistakes are an inevitable part of training, repeated mistakes by a single or couple of residents in a program may impose staff criticism on all residents and may increase the work load responsibilities even of those who did not make the mistake. Such forces can obviously draw residents apart. Negotiating and coordinating efforts with fellow residents while maintaining high standards for patient care and pleasing faculty are not always simple tasks.

A third interpersonal problem confronting residents is assessing their situation in the medical hierarchy and learning to function within it. As alluded to previously, inexperienced residents must learn to seek help, in other words learn to admit incompetency to their superiors when necessary. Not doing so reflects bad judgment. The medical authority structure is fairly well defined in residency programs and learning how this structure works is another important part of the residency experience. An intriguing conflict that residents face as they progress through their residency is the move from being supervised to, at least in part, supervising other house staff. The change in authority position forces some senior residents to make decisions that they, as interns or junior residents, might have criticized as imperious or unfair.

Finally, during residency training many residents go through a trial and error process of learning what is expected of them by faculty. Though many enter with the idea that their aptitude and ability to diagnose and treat illness will be paramount to their superiors, most soon learn that of greater importance is their willingness to (1) work hard and be available when needed and (2) accept staff criticism without being defensive and adapt their behavior based on that criticism.[2] Residents who are defensive or antagonistic to staff or who show enthusiasm only for some portions of their work are generally less favorably rated by their faculty.

In coping with such interpersonal issues residents become more and more able to handle interpersonal problems and exercise authority appropriate to the situation. Clearly, such skills will be of marked utility to them in their careers, whether they go into private, patient-oriented practice or pursue a career in academic medicine.

Some current medical education issues

Medical education in the United States has come a long way since the pre-Flexner days. To a large degree Flexner established both the mission and the method for undergraduate medical school education. Since Flexner it is fair to say that with few exceptions there has been very little incentive or desire to change the fundamental definition of the physician as scientist as provided by Flexner. However, there has been considerable interest in changing or at least experimenting with the methods of medical school education. Yet even here major aspects of the curriculum advocated by Flexner still dominate.

At the graduate level the educational process is more complex and hence, in some ways, less amenable to generalization. There is interest in changing certain aspects of the graduate educational experience, and we will examine a few of these current developments.

As one looks at the status of medical education in the United States today, there does not appear to be an overriding concern about the efficacy of the medical education system to turn out reasonably competent practitioners. In this regard American medical educational institutions appear to be doing a reasonably competent job. There are, however, concerns that in the final analysis do bear on the quality of care delivered.

First, although it is the case that physicians educated today are by and large quite competent technically, there is growing concern about their expressive or interpersonal skills in relating to and managing patients.[7] Some assert that the medical education experience, both in medical schools and in residencies, is largely a technologic experience, whereas the practice of medicine is not or is only a partially technical one. Thus there is concern that medical education should broaden the exposure of physicians to the social and behavioral aspects of medical practice, a goal that is being adopted more and more, especially at the undergraduate level.

Second, and not unrelated to the first point, is the complaint that the educational experience of physicians today is limited largely to hospitalized, nonambulatory patients.[17] Although this training is important, such acute care patients do not constitute the bulk of day-to-day medical practice for most physicians. In a sense, then, there is a poor fit between the experiences provided by graduate medical education and the experiences of most practitioners. This problem, too, is being addressed in a limited fashion in that some residency programs are beginning to offer a variety of clinical experiences involving ambulatory patients.

Finally, perhaps the greatest concern about medical education revolves about what is termed the *maldistribution* of physicians in the United States. On balance it is felt that there are too many specialists and subspecialists and not enough generalists, leading to a call for more primary care providers in fields such as family medicine and general internal medicine.[15] In response to this perceived need a number of primary care and family practice residency programs were instituted in the 1970s, aimed specifically at educating physicians for ambulatory care.

A corollary concern is about where physicians decide to practice. Clearly, some geographic regions of the country have many more physicians than others and, in general, rural and inner city areas have far fewer physicians for their populations than do suburban and metropolitan areas.[15] The issue of the geographic maldistribution of physicians is a difficult one to attack, given the structure of medical practice in the United States. Nevertheless within the past few years federal interest in this problem has increased, and there are currently programs, such as Area Health Education Centers and the National Health Service Corps, aimed at increasing the supply of physicians to underserved areas.

In general, then, the concerns today about medical education are concerns not so much about the technical competency of physicians but rather about other skills and the geographic and specialty distribution of physicians. Whether or not the various programs designed to bring about changes in the specialty and geographic distribution of physicians can be effective and whether medical schools and residencies are the appropriate mechanisms for instituting such changes remain to be seen.

References

1. Becker, H., and Geer, B.: The fate of idealism in medical school, Am. Sociol. Rev. **23**:50-56, 1958.
2. Bosk, C.: Forgive and remember, Chicago, 1979, University of Chicago Press.
3. Chapman, C.: The Flexner report by Abraham Flexner, Daedalus **103**:105-117, 1974.
4. Cook, R.: The year of the intern, New York, 1972, Harcourt Brace Jovanovich, Inc.
5. Cooper, J. A. D.: Undergraduate medical education. In Bowers, J., and Purcell, E., editors: Advances in American medicine: essays at the Bicentennial, New York, 1976, Josiah Macy, Jr Foundation.
6. Ebert, R.: The medical school. In Life and death and medicine, San Francisco, 1973, W. H. Freeman & Co. Publishers.
7. Engel, G. L.: The need for a new medical model: a challenge for bio-medicine, Science **196**:129-136, 1977.
8. Flexner, A.: On medical education in the United States and Canada, Washington, D.C., 1910, Science and Health Publications, Inc.
9. Fox, R.: Training for uncertainty. In Merton, R., Reader, G., and Kendall, P., editors: The student physician, Cambridge, Mass., 1969, Harvard University Press.
10. Fox, R.: Is there a 'new' medical student? In Tancredi, L. R., editor: Ethics of health care, 1974, National Academy of Sciences.
11. Holden, W. D.: Graduate medical education. In Bowers, J., and Purcell, E., editors: Advances in American medicine: essays at the Bicentennial, New York, 1976, Josiah Macy, Jr Foundation.
12. Medical education in the United States: 1978-1979, J.A.M.A. **243**:841-923, 1980.
13. Mumford, E.: Interns from students to physicians, Cambridge, Mass., 1970, Harvard University Press.
14. Nolan, W. A.: The making of a surgeon, New York, 1968, Random House, Inc.
15. Rogers, D. E.: The challenge of primary care, Daedalus **106**:81-103, 1977.
16. Stevens, R.: American medicine and the public interest, New Haven, Conn., 1971, Yale University Press.
17. White, K.: Life and death and medicine. In Life and death and medicine, San Francisco, 1973, W. H. Freeman & Co. Publishers.
18. X, Doctor:Intern, New York, 1965, Harper & Row, Publishers, Inc.

Chapter 10

Medical practice: hospital and ambulatory care settings

In the United States medical care is delivered in a variety of settings. The diversity is often confusing to those trying to understand or assess the adequacy of medical care delivery in this country. It means that the care people receive is not uniform in nature and quality. In such a pluralistic system the problems and satisfactions of providers and patients vary according to the delivery setting in which they participate. The diversity of settings reveals that medical care delivery is in a period of change where many believe it is no longer adequate for the preponderance of care to be given in private solo practice arrangements. Yet there is little consensus as to what mix of settings is best.

In this chapter we discuss some of the more common settings in which medical care is delivered and outline some of the factors that facilitate and hinder the delivery of care in these settings.

Hospitals: the citadel of technologic medicine

Hospitals epitomize both the best and the worst of what modern medical care can be.[10] At one extreme, hospitals are the repositories of the technical side of medicine—the large machines, intricate intensive care, and often dramatic capacity to save and extend life. It is a comfort to know that such facilities are available and waiting for a medical emergency. At the other extreme, hospitals also can represent some of the worst features of medical care, such as impersonalized and dehumanizing patient care, unequal access, poor quality of care, and expenses that can be so great that they cannot be afforded by some individuals and, increasingly, so large that they are outstripping even our collective capacity to pay. As such, many have come to dread the idea of hospitalization and what it symbolizes financially.

However one views hospitals, they are a significant and expanding component of modern medical care. A few general observations reveal this dramatically. For example, from 1972 to 1977 the number of discharges from short-stay hospitals increased 11%, totaling about 36.8 million discharges in 1977. During this same period the number of days of care increased about 6% to some 291.9 million in 1977.

Surgical rates have increased over the past decade also. The rate per 1000 population from 1966 to 1967 was 78.4. This increased to 94.5 from 1976 to 1977. Finally, on the financial side hospital care accounted for approximately 40% of the nation's total health expenditures in 1978, up from 30% in 1950. Thus by a variety of measures the role of hospitals in medical care is expanding dramatically.[14]

In 1974 there were approximately 7100 hospitals in the United States. They can be categorized in a variety of ways, for example, there are short- versus long-term hospitals, general hospitals (hospitals that accept a wide variety of patients), and specialty hospitals. Some hospitals are private, whereas others are public, supported by local, state, or federal funds. Some hospitals are proprietary, whereas others are nonprofit. Most of the 7100 hospitals in the United States are nonfederal, short-term, general hospitals.[10]

The nature and organization of hospitals have changed substantially over the past several decades in the United States. For example, the number of short-term hospitals has increased, while the number of long-term hospital care facilities, primarily mental institutions, has decreased.[7] There has been an increase in the number of general hospitals and a corresponding drop in the number of specialized hospitals. Also smaller hospitals for various reasons are closing, giving way to larger and larger hospitals. And the number of hospital employees per patient is growing dramatically. In 1950 there were about 1.8 employees per patient and by 1973 this had increased to about 3.2 per patient. This increase is due in part to the rise in the number of various types of medical care providers and ancillary personnel such as technicians. It also is due to the evolution of modern hospitals as multiservice centers, which offer a wide variety of ambulatory care and associated social services as well as care for the acutely ill and injured.[7]

As medical care settings, hospitals offer both extraordinary opportunities and exceedingly difficult barriers to the delivery of quality care. In general, we can identify three types of issues that appear to be endemic to hospitals and that pose significant problems for these institutions in achieving their service goals.

The first set of issues concerns the complex and changing mandate of hospitals. Although some hospitals can pursue a single goal, such as patient care for general or specialized medical problems, increasingly hospitals are serving as complex health–medical care centers.[7] For example, the past few years have witnessed the rise of increased ambulatory services offered by many hospitals, particularly in the inner city. Clinics, which traditionally have run a poor second to ward facilities in hospitals, have been increased and with their advent and increased use hospitals have had to adapt to new sets of patient problems, demands, and needs. This has meant new staffing arrangements, new expenses, and new problems in meeting the ambulatory as opposed to the "hospitalized" needs of patients. University-affiliated hospitals today feel particularly beleaguered in trying to meet their mixed goals of patient service, physician education, and medical research.[10] The pursuit of these goals can create organizational dilemmas. For example, the hospital as a setting for the education of physicians as well as the care of patients faces certain problems. From a teaching perspective the more frequently residents performed tests and procedures and the more patients they see, the more likely they will become skilled and competent physicians. However, from a service perspective much routine testing may serve little or no medical benefit for the patients and thus may only add to the expense, and occasionally to the risks, of hospitalization for patients. Likewise the necessity of having "teaching material" constantly available may serve as a strong incentive to institutions to both admit and keep patients when in fact hospitalization is of questionable medical value.

In a similar vein joint pursuit of service and research goals may create tensions. For example, research often requires trying novel diagnostic or treatment techniques. Sometimes procedures already exist that are acceptable or satisfactory, but these may be passed over or played down in favor of experimental techniques.

In short, in pursuing mixed goals hospitals create situations in which at times it is difficult to adhere to any specific goal uncompromisingly. The medical care workers in these institutions become aware of such tensions, the resolutions of which can powerfully shape their attitudes and practices regarding patients, patients' rights, and the decision-making authority of the medical care provider and the hospital vis-á-vis the patient.

A second set of recurring problems in hospitals involves a tension between the needs of hospitals as bureaucracies and the interests and needs of medical care providers as professionals.[2] For both professionals and institutional administrative staff the tensions that occur between their respective methods and objectives can be made at minimum more tolerable by understanding the characteristics of bureaucracies. The public and many professionals alike have come to see "bureaucracy" as unresponsive, cumbersome, a roadblock to achieving important goals, and therefore without social value. It is the case nevertheless that bureaucracies solve numerous organizational problems and provide a means of coordinating the activities of sometimes dozens of highly specialized professionals. At the same time the bureaucracy is an organizational arrangement that enables large-scale organizations, such as the military or the telephone company, to efficiently accomplish a large number of tasks. The ideal bureaucracy's characteristics include (1) a large degree of job specialization, (2) vesting authority in the office rather than in the person holding the office (e.g., the office of the president), which permits interchangeability of organizational parts and provides for a continuity of the organization, (3) clearly defined lines of organization and communication and a hierarchy of command, (4) placing problems into categories rather than dealing with them individually, and (5) operating democratically in the sense of rewarding personnel for meeting the requirements of their jobs rather than for reasons of favoritism.[4]

In the real world, however, bureaucracies do not function in a totally ideal way. One characteristic of bureaucracies that is highly problematic for those work- ing within them and those who must deal with them from the outside is the fact that people in bureaucratic jobs often learn the rules of their jobs or organizations so well that they ignore the *ends* or objectives of their work. Instead they focus almost exclusively on the *means* of getting the job done. For example, in their concern with complying with Medicaid reimbursement regulations and filling out forms "bureaucrats" lose sight of the end of the job—providing financial assistance that will enable people to obtain needed medical services. This preoccupation with the rules of the game is sometimes referred to as "occupational deformity" or "trained incapacity."

In short, bureaucracies tend to become impervious to the outside world, making it hard for their customers or clients, and their employees as well, to break through organizational layers, exert leverage, and have their problems or needs dealth with to their satisfaction. Despite the truly impressive accomplishments that the bureaucratic form of organization makes possible, their often inflexible, rigid nature conflicts with professional norms of authority and autonomy.

When professionals such as physicians or nurses work in bureaucratic organiza- tions such as hospitals, they must deal with several lines of often conflicting bu- reaucratic and professional authority.[2] There is the institution's administrative staff and its chain of command, the medical staff, the nursing staff, and the social service staff, for example, each with its own needs, objectives, policies, and procedures. When a problem arises, for example, over patient care or the availability of supplies, a physician can become very frustrated with no formal control per se over nurses or social workers or no control over ordering and ensuring the availability of supplies. Likewise when a physician asks a nurse or orderly to do something prohibited by their superiors, tensions are created.

Problems arise not only from the formal bureaucratic and professional struc- tures but from the informal systems of power and friendships that invariably accom- pany the formal lines of authority and power. Newcomers to a large bureaucracy are faced not only with learning the formal system but they must come to under- stand the informal system as well and how it functions vis-à-vis the formal system.

A third set of problems revolves about the "bureaucratizing" of human services, which is a problem that is not peculiar to hospitals. It occurs in virtually all institu- tions that attempt to meet some human need. However, the hospital is a particu- larly striking example, for hospitals are concerned with meeting very immediate, sometimes life-threatening needs of patients, which to the patients may be some of the most important in their lives.

Most hospitals basically are crisis-oriented institutions geared to "process" people who are experiencing a significant emergency or serious acute illness. To perform these functions on large numbers of people hospitals must routinize emer- gencies and to the degree possible institute standard, uniform ways of coping with crises and the many other needs patients can present. It is, of course, in striving for routinization of patients, which brings not only an efficiency and economy of scale but the potential for increased effectiveness of treatment, that patients may experience some of the complaints of bureaucratization—impersonal care, insensitive treatment, and a general perception that no one cares or has an interest in their problems.

Examples of such events can confront the patients from their very entrance to the hospital. For example, on entrance, sometimes even when patients are seeking emergency care they are required to provide evidence of ability to meet any financial obligations; in essence, they must go through a financial means test before services are made available. Such an experience, although understandable from the organization's point of view, makes many patients question the nature of the institution's interest in them.

The routinization of services from food to sleeping pill dispensations emphasizes to hospitalized patients the nonuniqueness of their situations. The needs of the organization seem to dominant over the needs of individuals. Thus all patients are awakened in the early morning and certain activities, such as seeing family members or even seeing one's own physician, are often "scheduled" to meet the needs of the organization, not to reflect the changing needs, concerns, and questions of patients as they arise.

Another circumstance contributing to the sense of impersonalization felt by many patients grows out of the fact that from a technical point of view hospitals are staffed by professionals who even collectively have only a limited interest in the patient as a person. That is, physicians, nurses, and other medical personnel have a primary, if often exclusive, interest in the nature and control of the problem that brought the patient to the hospital. Interest in the patient beyond the specific medical problem often becomes costly for professionals. Professionals have many patients and many commitments and are often not particularly well trained to engage the patient on other than a disease-oriented plane.

An additional problem associated with the above is that hospitalized patients often experience discrepancies in what they are told by the various professionals with whom they have contact while hospitalized.[3] This situation grows out of the fact that providers do not always communicate fully with one another about patients, nor do they have identical interests in the same patient. Hence they may hold different impressions of the patients, their conditions, and situations. In talking to a patient they may thus create confusion and concern about the quality of care being received and even jeopardize care by making the patient uncooperative.

Conclusion

Hospitals have a long and varied history in the evolution of medical care. In the past 60 years Knowles[7] suggested the hospital ". . . has evolved from a house of despair for the sick poor to a house of hope for all social and economic classes. . . ." Although one may not agree entirely with this statement, particularly as to the idea of access for "all social and economic classes," there is no doubt that the hospital symbolizes much of the power, success, and charisma of modern medicine. But, as we have noted, it also symbolizes myriad problems—exorbitant costs, bureaucratization, and impersonalization. Hospitals will continue nevertheless to constitute a major vehicle for the dispensation of medical care and increasingly health care over the next few decades in the United States.

Ambulatory care settings

Medical care delivered outside of hospitals is usually called *ambulatory care* and is delivered in many different settings. The differences can be described along a variety of dimensions, such as the size of the facility, how many and what types of people staff it, how patients pay for services, how medical professionals are paid, and the nature of the services offered. Although some ambulatory care is actually provided in hospital clinics or emergency services, most ambulatory care is office based and is rendered by private practitioners in solo practice, partnership, or group practice on a fee-for-service basis. Office-based ambulatory care is also available in Health Maintenance Organizations (HMOs), Independent Practice Associations (IPAs), prepaid group practices, health department clinics, neighborhood health centers, occupationally based health services, and school, military, and prison services.

Indeed, as we pointed out in Chapter 4, the bulk of medical care offered is nonhospital-based ambulatory care. As can be seen in Table 14, well over half of the practicing physicians in the United States engage in office-based practices. Although most of these physicians have privileges in and offer some patient care in hospitals, most of their efforts are for ambulatory patients and are conducted in their offices.

Most physician-provided ambulatory care is delivered in private practice. Physicians in private practice provide a range of medical services limited only by the licensing laws of the state in which they may be operating as independent entrepreneurs. The physician contracts directly with patients (though almost never in writing) to provide a set of services in return for a fee (fee-for-service).[6]

Approximately 75% of office-based physicians are in specialties as compared to general practice (Table 14). While the absolute numbers in specialty practice are increasing, the numbers in general practice are decreasing.

Although most physicians offering office-based ambulatory care work independently, group practices have become an increasingly popular way of organizing ambulatory care. It has been estimated that the proportion of office-based practitioners in group practices has at least quadrupled in the last 20 years, and one estimate suggests that almost one third of office-based practitioners are now in a group practice arrangement.[5] By group practice we are referring to an association

Table 14. Physicians (MD) by type of practice: 1969 and 1978*

	MDs	
Type of practice	**1969†**	**1978‡**
TOTAL[1]	324,942	437,486
Active physicians[2]	302,966	401,364
Nonfederal	273,502	381,122
Patient care	247,508	325,783
Office-based practice	184,355	238,943
General and family practice	51,353	45,148
Other full-time primary specialty[3]	129,657	185,987
Hospital-based practice	63,153	86,840
Training programs[4]	45,744	57,205
Full-time physician staff	17,409	29,635
Other professional activity[5]	25,994	29,786
Not classified[6]	—	25,553
Federal	29,464	20,242
Patient care	23,229	16,931
Office-based practice	3,811	923
General and family practice	1,451	260
Other full-time primary specialty[3]	1,947	617
Hospital-based practice	19,418	16,008
Training programs[4]	6,072	3,405
Full-time physician staff	13,346	12,603
Other professional activity[5]	6,235	3,311
Inactive	19,895	26,831
Address unknown	2,081	9,291

*From Physician distribution and medical licensure in the United States, 1976. Reprinted with the permission of the American Medical Association.

†From Haug, J. N., and Roback, G. A.: Distribution of physicians, hospitals, and hospital beds in the U.S., 1969, Chicago, 1970, American Medical Association.

‡From Wunderman, L. E.: Physician distribution and medical licensure in the U.S., 1978, Chicago, 1979, American Medical Association.

[1]Includes nonfederal physicians (MDs) in the 50 states, District of Columbia, Puerto Rico, and other U.S. outlying areas (American Samoa, Canal Zone, Pacific Islands, and Virgin Islands), those with addresses temporarily unknown to the American Medical Association and federal physicians (MDs) in the United States and abroad. Excludes physicians (MDs) with temporary foreign addresses.

[2]Excludes inactive and address unknown.

[3]Excludes physicians reporting "no specialty" and "other specialties" not listed on AMA list of specialty designations.

[4]Includes interns and residents.

[5]Includes medical teaching, administration, research, and other activities.

[6]Not classified as to their specialty.

of three or more medical practitioners, made up of any combination of licensed physicians, engaged jointly in providing medical services. Group practices thus can include more than one physician in the same specialty or physicians from a variety of specialties. This does not include physicians who work in the same building and perhaps share a nurse or a secretary but rather those who integrate their services and practices.

Group practices have become increasingly popular among physicians for a vari-

ety of reasons. By pooling resources physicians are often able to obtain better facilities, technical support services, and equipment than they could alone. Practicing
in a group often means coverage of patients can be shared, allowing each physician
more controllable work hours. Peer support, such as sharing of knowledge and providing support through adversity, are additional benefits. From the patients' point
of view, if a group practice is multispecialty, it reduces the number of places they
need to go for care. Generally groups can provide more continuously available care
and for economic reasons often provide a wider variety of services, including more
preventive services.

On the other hand, some physicians do not like to forfeit the independence
offered by solo practice. They may not like sharing decision making with others or
having to meet certain requirements to join a group. Patients, for their part, may
believe that their care is less personalized because they are less likely to see the
same physician during each illness episode. Sometimes group practices can afford
to hire nurses or other nonphysician health professionals to provide services that
solo practitioners might offer themselves, and some patients object to being seen
by health professionals other than a physician. According to a national Gallup Poll
in early 1980 only one third of the public would prefer being treated by a group of
physicians to contain costs, and less than half approved of seeing trained assistants
for certain problems.[1] It also has been hypothesized that in a group practice, because
each physician is not solely dependent on his or her patients, physicians become
less concerned with meeting the practice standards of their physician peers.[8]

Though every form of patient payment and physician reimbursement can be
found in group practices, the most common forms are (1) fee-for-service patient
payment with fee-for-service physician reimbursement, (2) patient prepayment with
physician reimbursement by capitation, and (3) patient prepayment with physician
reimbursement by salary.

Although they constitute only a small minority of group practices, prepaid
group practices have received a great deal of attention in recent years. Prepaid
group practices accept responsibility for the organization, financing, and delivery
of health services for a defined prepaying population. The largest prepayment
groups are the Kaiser-Permanente group, with nearly 2 million enrollees mostly
on the West Coast, and the Health Insurance Plan of New York, with approximately 800,000 enrollees. People in such programs are charged a flat fee for their
medical services each year, and in turn the clinic or group agrees to provide all the
medical services a person may need (including fees to other specialists or institutions
outside the group if needed by a patient).[5] The prepayment arrangement means
that the immediate financial burden of each illness episode is shared by the group
of enrollees, minimizing a "catastrophic" financial impact on the person who is ill.
It also permits greater allocation of the group practice's resources beyond treatment
of medical problems into preventive services.

A further development in the prepaid group practice concept is the Health Maintenance Organization (HMO). HMOs are systems of health care that accept the responsibility of providing care, including health maintenance and treatment services, to a voluntary group of persons in a geographic area and are reimbursed in a fixed, prenegotiated payment made by or for each family enrolled in the plan. The HMO may be hospital based or based in a group of such facilities. Enrollment in HMOs has been estimated at 8 million people.[13] Under a federal law (P.L. 93-222) that provided federal start-up grants to help stimulate the development of HMOs, qualifying as an HMO requires that a wide variety of services be provided, including inpatient and outpatient hospital care, short-term and evaluative crisis intervention, mental health services, medical treatment and referral services for drug and alcohol problems, diagnostic laboratory, and diagnostic and therapeutic radiologic and preventive health services.

Because of the flat prepayment rate per year per enrollee rather than a case-by-case reimbursement, HMOs have a budget ceiling within any given year for their services. Because they also provide a wide array of prevention services, proponents believe that medical care costs can be reduced in the highly expensive treatment areas, especially hospitalization. In general, in the United States hospital costs have been the largest single area of increase in the health care expenditure. Thus far it appears that the HMO record does show reduced hospitalization rates of its enrollees, but lower hospitalization rates in HMOs may in part reflect the characteristics of enrollees.

HMOs are of such recent development that it is not possible at this time to provide a detailed statement as to their overall success, but accumulating literature on HMOs does provide some perspective. In general, it appears that although some HMOs have relatively high patient population turnover, reaching nearly 20% in some cases, patient satisfaction with the care they receive and the way HMOs are run is at least as good as patient satisfaction with the more traditional fee-for-service type of medical care. One complaint fairly frequently made by HMO patients is that they cannot use their own discretion in seeking a care provider but instead must go through the usual triage procedures of seeing their HMO primary care provider and letting the provider make decisions about seeing a specialist. Some patients like to go to specialists or, in general, shop around for their care providers. These patients are dissatisfied with the rigidity of most HMOs in terms of access to specialists.

In terms of quality of care a recent large review of numerous studies of patients in HMOs compared to patients in traditional fee-for-service arrangements revealed virtually no significant differences in terms of a large number of health outcome measures. It would appear that, at least to date, HMOs are as capable of delivering good care as are fee-for-service arrangements.[15]

Providers who work in HMOs find a number of benefits. One is that they can work more regular hours than physicians in traditional solo fee-for-service settings. In addition, HMOs can offer physicians professional colleagueship that is not as available in solo arrangements. A couple of common complaints to participation in HMO arrangements relate to lower income and to more or less continuous formal peer review. It also appears that as HMOs become larger, tensions between staff and management can develop, which have led to a variety of arrangements between HMO management and physician staff in negotiating such things as working hours and salaries. Such developments have led to the unionization of physicians in at least one HMO and concern by some, especially HMO management, that HMO physicians are exhibiting employee—as opposed to professional—mentality.

Whatever the problems and successes it appears that HMOs in multiple forms will be with us for some time. Whether they will be able to fulfill their complex mission, move beyond the traditional emphasis on clinical treatment services or clinical prevention endeavors, and fully adopt the goal of fostering the community health of the regions for which they have assumed responsibility is an important question for the 1980s.

Though this brief review of ambulatory care settings cannot provide even a short description of all the types of delivery settings, one other type that deserves mention is the neighborhood health center. Neighborhood health centers render only a small portion of the overall ambulatory care in this country, but they serve populations most in need of medical services and people whose health is a bench-mark for the health of the nation. Most neighborhood health centers developed during the 1960s to provide care of the medically underserved inner-city popula-tions in our country. As we have described in earlier chapters in this book, inner-city lower income populations had less access and accordingly had less contact with the health care system than any other portion of the population. A strong stimulant in the neighborhood health center movement was the Office of Economic Oppor-tunity, developed during the War on Poverty of the Johnson administration.

Neighborhood health centers have appeared in many forms and with a variety of funding sources. Nonetheless some common precepts are shared by most of these organizations. First, attention is given to community participation in the health center decision making. This varies from inclusion of token community mem-bers on the boards of trustees that make the center's decisions to neighborhood centers completely controlled by community boards of trustees.

Second, there is an attempt by many neighborhood health centers to focus not only on providing ambulatory medical services but to actively attempt to change the often deplorable public health conditions, such as poor sanitation, housing, and nutrition, in the communities they serve. The widely cited Tufts–Delta Mound Bayou in Mississippi is an example of a center that moved actively to improve the public health of the community it serves, often through programs that others would consider nonclinical in focus.[12]

Third, many neighborhood health centers have made an attempt to hire residents from the communities they serve. Although this goal has been strongly supported by many of the communities in which health centers operate, it has been a source of tension in communities where qualified health professionals are scarce. Indeed the emphasis on community involvement in decision making and pressures to hire local staff, coupled with disincentives attendant with working in low income areas, have contributed to high professional staff turnover in many neighborhood health centers.

Regarding balance, neighborhood health centers have at least in part filled an unfortunate gap in our health care systems. Though their administrations do not always run smoothly, as evidenced by the decline in their numbers during the 1970s, and although they have been criticized for representing a two-class system of health care, they help populations desperately in need of their services.[6] And at least in part their difficulties have derived from the rather tense and erratic funding situations that many have faced since their inception.

In addition to the various forms of ambulatory care that we have sketched, ambulatory services are also offered by health department clinics, occupationally based health services, school, military, and prison services, and programs like the Indian Health Service of the U.S. government. Although some applaud the diversity of medical services offered in this country, because they believe it allows people to choose the form most suited to their own personal preference and fosters a healthy competition among provider sources, the fact is that not all groups in the population have much choice about which services to use. The poor and the near poor are virtually locked into public clinics, hospital ambulatory care, or neighborhood health centers because of difficulties in paying for services and the absence of private practitioners and group practice arrangements in low income areas. Likewise persons in rural areas have little choice and generally must accept whichever services are geographically most proximate. Furthermore, the complexity of the system makes the choice of which services to use difficult, even for those in a financial or geographic position to exercise a choice.

The complex mosaic of ambulatory services also means that the system is difficult to evaluate, and efforts to improve ambulatory health care delivery are difficult to coordinate. Though the inequities of access and quality of care in the United States have diminished in recent years, there can be little doubt that inequities persist.[11] Services are not only difficult for policy planners to understand and coordinate but they can be difficult for individual practitioners. Figuring out eligibility requirements, coordinating patient referrals, and making sure that certain patient needs are not overlooked are but a few of the problems presented to individual practitioners by the present diversity in services and reimbursement plans available. Unquestionably, everyone entering the medical professions will be affected by government and private sector attempts to improve on the present organization and modes of ambulatory care delivery. The search for a more equitable, cost efficient, and effective system of care will no doubt produce strains on their practices. Hopefully providers will be flexible in adapting to anticipated changes and invest in the search for ways to improve on the inadequacies of our present approaches.

References

1. American Medical Association: Insights, J.A.M.A. **243:**23, 1980.
2. Croog, S., and Ver Steeg, D.: The hospital as a social system. In Freeman, H., Levine, S., and Reeder, L., editors: Handbook of medical sociology, Englewood Cliffs, N.J., 1972, Prentice-Hall, Inc.
3. Duff, R., and Hollingshead, A.: Sickness and society, New York, 1968, Harper & Row, Publishers, Inc.
4. Etzioni, A.: Complex organizations, New York, 1966, Holt, Rinehart & Winston.
5. Field, J.: Group practice development, Germantown, Md., 1976, Aspen Systems Corp.
6. Jonas, S., and Reimer, B.: Ambulatory care. In Jonas, S., editor: Health care delivery in the United States, New York, 1977, Springer Publishing Co., Inc.
7. Knowles, J.: The hospital. In Life and death and medicine, San Francisco, 1973, W. H. Freeman & Co. Publishers.
8. Mechanic, D.: Public expectations and health care, 1972, John Wiley & Sons, Inc.
9. Rogers, D. E., and Blendon, R. J.: The academic medical center: a stressed American institution, N. Engl. J. Med. **298:**940-950, 1978.
10. Rosengren, W. R.: Sociology of medicine, New York, 1980, Harper & Row, Publisher, Inc.
11. Torrens, P.: The American health care system, St. Louis, 1978, The C. V. Mosby Co.
12. Twaddle, A., and Hessler, A.: A sociology of health, St. Louis, 1977, The C. V. Mosby Co.
13. U.S. Department of Health, Education, and Welfare Public Health Service: Health United States: 1978, D.H.E.W. Publication no. PHS 78-1232, Washington, D.C., 1978, Office of Research, Statistics, and Technology.
14. U.S. Department of Health, Education, and Welfare Public Health Service: Health United States: 1979, D.H.E.W. Publication No. PHS 80-1232, Washington, D.C., 1979, Office of Research, Statistics, and Technology.
15. Williamson, J., Cunningham, F., and Ward, D.: Quality of health care in HMOs as compared to other setting, Unpublished paper prepared for the Office of Health Maintenance Organizations, Rockville, Md., 1979, Department of Health, Education, and Welfare.

Chapter 11

Physicians as professionals

In Chapters 9 and 10 we have looked at some components of medical education and at some of the organizational features of the hospital and ambulatory care settings in which physicians and other providers train and practice. In this chapter we turn to the *professional context* of medicine, a subject that has a direct bearing on the ways that physicians and other providers are trained, practice, and interact with one another and with patients.

The study of professions and of what it means to be "a professional" is a major area of sociologic study, and physicians probably have been the most extensively analyzed species of the genus *professional*. Our objective in this chapter is to indicate why it is important for medical care providers to understand, even superficially, the nature of professionals. Such knowledge will help them to better understand various aspects of their own work and that of their subordinates and superordinates in the medical care system. Awareness of the attributes of physicians as what is termed *dominant professionals*, for example, sheds light on various facets of doctor-patient, doctor-doctor, and doctor-nurse interactions. An appreciation of the characteristics of professionals helps explain why frictions almost inevitably occur between the professional staff and the administrative staff of institutions such as hospitals. As a final example, the sociology of professions offers insights into why the self-regulation of physicians, and indeed of all professionals, is problematic and of mounting concern as a matter of public policy.

The characteristics of professionals

Why is it so difficult to get into medical school? Why is medical training so long and arduous? Why do physicians, once they have finished training, find themselves at the top of the medical hierarchy, able, by and large, to set the terms of their work?

Sociologically, the answers to questions such as these have much to do with the characteristics of professionals. Sociologists differ, often sharply, as to which of their various perspectives on the professions best explains various features of modern American medicine. Nonetheless among sociologists who view professions as distinct from other occupations, there is fairly good agreement about the defining characteristics of a profession.*

Professions, *first*, are identified as *service-oriented occupations* that *apply systematic bodies of knowledge* (e.g., clinical or legal) *to problems that a society views as highly relevant to its central values* (e.g., health or justice). *Second*, as professions develop, they *establish formal institutions* such as medical schools to transmit their increasingly specialized knowledge to new generations of professionals. *Third, entry* into a profession *is highly selective;* applicants must meet specific formalized criteria that are set by the professionals themselves. That is, the members of a profession act as *gatekeepers* for entrance into the profession.

After initial acceptance as a candidate for a profession, *fourth*, there is a period of *long formal training.* As noted in Chapter 9, learning the substantive materials required to be a particular type of professional is not the only reason for the long period of formal training. A second important function of such training is *anticipatory socialization:* learning, usually informally and often latently, what is expected of you in your *social role*, for example, as a physician, nurse, lawyer, or researcher.

A *fifth* characteristic of professionals is establishing some sort of *formal recognition of expertise.* That is, once the period of professional training is over, one is certified or licensed to practice a profession. Here, too, those already in the profession occupy gatekeeping functions by determining the standards of competency that must be met before a person can be recognized as a physician or a specialist in a certain field of medicine.

Sixth, perhaps the most important characteristic of professionals is *autonomy.* Professionals want, and usually are granted by society, the right to determine many aspects of their own work and that of their field as a whole. The exercise of autonomy ranges from setting the hours that one will work to relying on peers to judge the quality of one's work and behavior as a professional. As occupational groups seek to attain professional status, autonomy usually is one of their most desired objectives. And once achieved, it is an aspect of their work that professionals, individually and collectively, will struggle fiercely to maintain. A fear of losing their autonomy, for example, has been one important reason that many members of the medical profession have vigorously opposed national health insurance, group practice arrangements, and other departures from their traditional solo practice, fee-for-service way of working as physicians.

Seventh, and closely related to norms of autonomy, professional groups traditionally draw up *codes of ethics.* These codes state general rules of proper behavior with one's peers and patients or clients and reflect the insistency on a profession's right to determine the standards of its members' work and conduct.

Eighth, to help perpetuate a profession over time its members establish *formal*

---

*References 2, 7, 12, 26, 33, and 35.

organizations such as the American Medical Association that usually become highly autonomous, self-governing institutions. As such, professional organizations acquire many of the characteristics of a bureaucracy, a change that often leads to friction between their governing bodies and the membership.

The characteristics just discussed underlie two additional corollary characteristics of professions. *First, they are occupations that carry with them high prestige. Second,* particularly because of the professional's autonomy and prestige, *other occupational groups often try to emulate the requirements for becoming a professional and/or the work characteristics of professionals.* The history of pharmacy, for example, shows how pharmacists have adopted some but not all of the characteristics of a profession, so that pharmacy today is viewed by sociologists as a "quasiprofession."[15,36]

As one thinks of the range of providers involved in medical care, our discussion should begin to suggest why *physicians* are viewed sociologically as *dominant professionals.*[17,18] By virtue of their training and certification as medical experts as well as their actual and symbolic roles in caring for the sick, physicians sit atop the medical hierarchy. They exercise a *high degree of autonomy* in their work, are answerable to no higher *professional authority,* and *exert strong control over the work of those below* them. Moreover, outside of the medical domain itself physicians are accorded an almost uniquely high social status as compared with other professional and occupational groups.

There are a number of other characteristics of professionals related to those described that can be problematic for the recipients of their expertise and for the larger society in which they work. These characteristics tend to generate public unease or criticism of the methods and objectives of professionals and "watchdogging" of their activities. First, in part because of the specialized knowledge and techniques they have mastered through their long training, professionals tend to define *doing good* for the recipients of their services as meaning the use of their most sophisticated skills and techniques. In medicine this inclination helps to account for the occurrence of "technologic overkill"—using the most sophisticated diagnostic or treatment methods at a provider's disposal when, for a particular patient, simpler approaches would suffice.

A second problematic characteristic of professionals, also related to the nature of their training, is that they tend to impose their *professional culture*—values, interests, and goals—on their recipient population, as contrasted with their specialized knowledge or skills.[7,24]

Third, reflecting the difficult gatekeeping requirements they have had to meet to be admitted to their profession and the fact that professions formally recognize expertise, professionals tend to place great value on *credentials.* That is, they are apt to evaluate other people by the formal degrees or licenses that they have obtained rather than in terms of their knowledge and abilities. Thus, for example, a norm in professional publications is to signal your status and expertise by stringing after your name as many "alphabet soup letters" as possible, for example, John Doe, DSc, MD, MPH, FRCP.

Fourth, professional organizations can operate as narrow *interest groups*. That is, when there is a conflict between the needs or interests of their clients or the public more generally and the needs and interests of the profession, the organization may act to protect the members of the "guild." Although this orientation is understandable in historical and sociologic terms, it is a characteristic of professions that is particularly apt to generate public distrust and efforts to reduce professional autonomy through legal and regulatory measures.

Finally, as we pointed out in Chapter 10, formal organizations such as hospitals also have their distinguishing characteristics as *bureaucracies*.[6] Because the characteristics of bureaucracies and of professions are basically incompatible in many respects, frictions and conflicts between the professional and administrative staffs of institutions such as hospitals occur frequently.[14] Professionals find it difficult to deal with what they perceive as the rigid structure and operation of the bureaucracy and its impersonality and seeming insensitivity to individual problems. Conversely, an institution's administrative staff is provoked by the "unwillingness" of its autonomy-oriented professionals to comply with the "rules of the system," for example, in terms of work hours, following standard organizational work procedures, or filling out forms. Differences in needs and objectives and in formal and informal work procedures are problematic for both camps, and the sources of conflict tend to be so poorly understood that attempts at conflict resolution often are not successful.

New professional roles

Although we are apt to speak of "a profession" such as medicine or nursing, professions are not monolithic, homogenous groups, nor are they static groups whose members share the same identities, values, and interests consistently over time. Rather, as analyzed by Bucher[9] with respect to a medical specialty, pathology, processes of specialization and changes in occupation lead to the formation of new groups or *segments* within a profession. These segments, as Bucher writes, "tend to take on the character of social movements. They develop distinctive identities, a sense of the past, and goals for the future; they organize activities and tactics which will secure an institutional position and implement their distinctive mission."

In part because of the need to master and deal with constantly growing bodies of knowledge and skills, medicine and nursing have become increasingly specialized professions. New segments have emerged frequently within various specialties, such as radiotherapy within radiology, and new specialty groups have formed, with their own distinctive organizations and certification procedures. In recent years, for example, nephrology and family practice, once segments within internal medicine, have become recognized specialties in their own right.

Additionally, the field of medical care has given rise to a variety of *new occupational groups*, such as dieticians, physical therapists, physicians' assistants, licensed practical nurses, and genetic associates, who work under the supervision of the professionals in their service area. Over time, for reasons noted earlier, many of these occupational groups begin to copy various characteristics of their professional counterparts. Thus they may form their own organizations, develop formal academic programs and certification procedures, and sometimes change the name of their occupation to one they think is more professional sounding. For example, dieticians now refer to themselves as clinical nutritionists, and genetic associates have changed their designation to genetic counselors.

Defining new roles: turf problems

The development of new segments and specialties within a profession and the effort of other occupational groups to more closely approximate the nature of a profession is seldom, if ever, a smooth process of social change. For example, those whose work roles are being modified or newly created and those in related roles with whom they interact usually must deal with various types of "turf problems." These include, first, problems of *role specificity*—defining the tasks and authority of the new professional or occupational group. Second, there are problems of *role conflict*—dealing with the real or perceived overlaps between the competencies and duties of new and existing roles and with the anxieties and hostilities that these occupational boundary problems create.

In terms of the relationships between physicians and nurses and between various segments of the nursing profession these problems of role specificity and role conflict are illustrated by the development of the *clinical nurse specialist*.[1,29] Like other new and expanded roles for nursing such as the nurse practitioner the graduate level clinical nurse specialist represents "a translation of the rather traditional domain of nursing into a repertory of intellectually based, autonomously performed, and interprofessionally planned nursing functions."[29] These specialists, for example, participate in the diagnostic process in terms of their patients' nursing needs and develop and carry out detailed, individualized nursing care plans.

From a sociologic perspective it was predictable that the emergence of the clinical nurse specialist role in the late 1960s caused conflicts within nursing and between nursing and medicine. Within nursing, for example, head nurses and supervisors saw the clinical specialist as a threat to their organizational authority until it became clear that the specialist's role did not include supervisory functions. Conversely, until the clinical specialists demonstrated that their primary skills and function lay in direct patient care, there were concerns that this type of academically trained graduate nurse would be "too good" for such work. Some physicians in turn saw (and still see) these highly trained and skilled nurses as impinging too closely on their expertise and on their traditional authority over nurses. In a 1975 survey of physician acceptance of various types of new health professionals clinical nurse specialists were described by some physicians as "uppity," "overeducated," and too "stirred up" by their multidisciplinary academic training.[28]

The role conflicts and specificity problems that have accompanied the emergence of the clinical nurse specialist also need to be understood in relation to the history of nursing and its relationships with medicine, for nursing, despite its long historical roots in early civilization, is still a developing profession in the process of carving out its own unique identity.[10] As a developing profession, it is dealing with many internal conflicts about the appropriate academic training and work of its members, with issues of governmental controls and with questions about how nurses should relate to physicians in delivering medical and health care.

As our brief example of the clinical nurse specialist suggests, sorting out the roles of and relationships between the many professional and occupational groups in medical care is a difficult task for providers. And it is an even more formidable challenge for patients. When one adds the job of learning the many types and features of medicine's institutional settings, it is clear that working in, being a patient in, or trying to rationally manage the medical care "system" are extremely complicated tasks. Moreover, as we have indicated, that system is not a static one either professionally or institutionally. It is a social system in which *change*, planned and unanticipated, *is a constant feature*, causing flux and tensions for all who participate in it. As Reeder and Mauksch[29] observe, "an inevitable concomitant of social change is disequilibrium among the various groups contributing to the organization and workings of the changing system. As knowledge increases and values shift, forces emerge which require drastic accommodations in the social structure."

Professional organizations

Another important component of the professional context of medical care is the role of formal professional organizations. The multiple functions performed by such organizations can be illustrated by looking briefly at the American Medical Association (AMA), which in 1980 numbered approximately 40% of U.S. physicians in its membership.

As illustrated by the history of the AMA, which was founded by a small group of 100 physicians in 1846, *professional organizations are created to serve many needs and objectives of their constituencies.*[11] These include providing a vehicle to transmit the "culture" of the profession; establishing criteria for admission to and exclusion from the profession and training and certification requirements; lobbying formally and informally for legislation favored by its membership; and, as suggested by the latter political function, providing structured ways of protecting the group against threats to its authority, autonomy, and other professional interests.

The first decades of the nineteenth century in America were a period of often vicious sectarian strife among practitioners of the healing arts, and holders of the doctor of medicine degree were only one of many groups claiming medical expertise and competing for public recognition.[32,34] The origins of the AMA and the promulgation of its first Code of Ethics in 1847 lay in the efforts of doctors of medicine to gain authority over their rivals and to establish the practice of medicine as their province alone. "To become preeminent," Chapman[13] observes, "the medical profession required a strong organization capable not only of overcoming rival professional groups but also of disciplining its own members when they violated the rules of the guild. The code of 1847 was designed with these requirements in mind, and for many years it served the profession's needs well."

Generally viewed today as a politically conservative organization the AMA in earlier decades was a leader in major health care and medical education reforms, speaking and acting authoritatively as the "voice of American medicine."[11] Currently, with the proliferation of specialty and subspecialty organizations, whose members often have sharply divided views and interests on issues such as health insurance, the AMA has become a less homogenous, united, and powerful organization.

Both politically and professionally, however, the AMA still exerts enormous influence over the nature of the medical profession and of medical care in the United States. Politically it remains a major influence nationally and locally through its affiliated state and county associations. One of its major political goals is to protect the autonomy of the profession. Thus, for example, it has fought vigorously against encroachment on fee-for-service practice in the form of national health insurance and against efforts by agencies like the Federal Trade Commission to regulate aspects of practice such as advertising by physicians.[27] It also continues to fight, as it has since 1847, to maintain its effective dominion over the practice of medicine in its both self- and public protector role as "traditional foes of cultists and quacks."[30] In this arena the AMA's long battle against chiropractic became a major issue in 1979 when it was sued for restraint of trade by chiropractors. One of the organization's responses to this suit and to related legal and regulatory actions was a softening of its long, uncompromising opposition to chiropractic. In a move that drew strong criticism from its membership and from other leading medical figures as well, the AMA voted in 1979 to no longer brand chiropractic as an "unscientific cult" or to hold that voluntary professional associations by physicians with chiropractors are "unethical."

Another spectrum of the AMA's role as a professional organization is represented by its major efforts in continuing medical education programs and the publication of a large number of professional journals. Much of the organization's influence over the profession also comes from its quasi-official functions. These include joint approval with the American Association of Medical Colleges (AAMC) of medical schools, which in turn sets the granting of medical licenses by state licensing boards, and also joint approval with the American Hospital Association (AHA) of hospitals for postgraduate physician training. Moreover, as Mechanic[25] notes, "since federal programs frequently use as criteria for reimbursement or federal support certification approval by such organizations as the AMA, the AAMC, and the AHA, the standards promulgated by these interest groups have effects beyond the functions performed."

As these brief notes on the AMA suggest, professional organizations serve many functions for the groups they are created to represent. Some of their roles, such as establishing standards of professional competency and performing educational functions, are explicit and formalized. Others, such as acting to protect their members' domain and interests, often are more latent and informal and are harder for those within and without the organization to identify clearly. One increasingly controversial aspect of professional organizations that we will touch on in the next section is how effectively they exercise social control mechanisms over professional performance and behavior.

Professional social controls

In part reflecting broader societal concerns about the roles and responsibilities of professionals in our society the nature and effectiveness of the social controls exercised over medicine and its practitioners are receiving increasing attention by the profession and by various lay groups, the media, legislatures, courts, and regulatory agencies.

Sociologically, the term *social control* has two distinct meanings. First, it refers to the measures communities or societies use to influence, regulate, or discipline individuals. Second, social control refers to the ability of individuals or groups, on their own initiative, to regulate themselves. In simple terms, the source of social controls may be *external* or *internal*. Controls also can be *formal* or *informal* in nature, for example, a malpractice trial verdict or the exercise of pressures by colleagues to change one's behavior.

As a start toward understanding how professional social controls operate, then, we can develop a simple four-way typology that locates types of controls by their external or internal source and formal or informal nature. As seen in Table 15, controls can be *external-formal, external-informal, internal-formal,* or *internal-informal;* in many cases, *controls also involve one or more combinations of these types.*

In this section we will focus on issues about the profession's system of *internal* controls over the *individual physician's* competency, performance, and behavior. What formal and informal means does the profession have in these areas, and are they exercised effectively? The subject of external controls in turn will be discussed in Chapter 12, primarily with reference to economic and regulatory factors affecting the profession.

Table 15. Types of social control in medicine*

Nature	Source	
	External	**Internal**
Formal	State licensing standards Regulatory agencies Legal statutes Malpractice rulings Boards of registration and discipline	Utilization review committees Tissue committees Grand rounds Mortality conferences Codes of ethics Hospital privileges
Informal	Mass media pressures Lay referral systems Exercise of informed consent by patients	Professional socialization Ward rounds Staff meetings Patient referrals Face-to-face criticism

*From Swazey, J., Klerman, G., and Neville, R.: Regulatory models for therapeutic innovations: surgery and drugs, unpublished paper, 1974.

As the fairly simple level of analysis in Table 15 suggests, sociologists are only beginning to develop an adequate understanding of social controls in medicine. There is a great deal of ideology and often angry rhetoric about the ability of physicians to regulate themselves or about the effects of externally imposed "bureaucratic" controls on medicine and its practitioners. The often heated dialogue and debate tend to obscure the fact that we do not know much about the range of controls involved in medicine, how those controls interact, and how well or poorly they work in various areas of physician performance and behavior.

Acquiring such knowledge is not only theoretically important for our understanding of the professions and their governance but has significant *social policy implications* as well. Those implications include such interrelated decisions as who should determine standards of physician competency and professional behavior, what constitutes the appropriate types and mix of controls to ensure as far as possible that those standards and norms are met, how should violators of standards and norms be detected, and how should violations be dealt with.

Further, to draw an analogy from medical therapeutics we need to identify the functional and dysfunctional effects of existing control "regimens" before seeking to alter them or introduce new controls. Potential new controls in turn should be treated like therapeutic innovations. That is, they should be subject to a careful assessment of their probable risks and benefits and evaluated for their "safety and efficacy" before they are established as "standard treatments."

Professional self-regulation

Like other professionals, as we have pointed out, physicians maintain that they have a right and are able to govern themselves. This claim is tied both to the autonomy of professionals and to the socially endorsed presumption that they will act in the best interests of their clients. In principle, then, a group of professionals should work together as what sociologist Barber[3,19] has called a self-regulating "company of equals." By this term Barber referred, first, to a social group whose members ideally are "roughly equal in authority," such as the members of a group practice, the attending staff of a hospital, or a group of interns or residents. In terms of professional norms, second, such a group should be "self-directing" and "self-disciplined." That is, the members of the group, because of their professional training and socialization, should have a *shared morality* that enables them to regulate the group's behavior. If the individual's own conscience "is not strong enough, the disapproval of others [in the group] will control him or lead to his exclusion from the brotherhood."[3]

In actual practice, however, few would dispute the assertion that self-regulation is problematic among physicians. In presenting examples of problem areas our purpose is not to point an accusing finger at physicians, for we recognize that *self-regulation is a difficult matter for all professional groups.* But because of the nature of their work the needs for an effective system of self-regulation among physicians are extremely high. We hope that this discussion will encourage readers to think about the following questions: What types of values about the exercise of professional responsibility are you learning in your training? How are you acquiring these values? How have you responded or would you respond to a social control issue within your "company of equals," for example, observing cheating on an examination or a colleague's patient workup that you thought was dangerously inept? How would you act if you observed negligence or incompetency in a senior physician from whom you need a recommendation for an internship or a fellowship or in a colleague with whom you practice? These are difficult questions but ones that each professional will have to deal with one or more times in training and practice.

No one is certain quantitatively how big a problem medicine has with providers whose competency or behavior does not meet professional standards nor, more generally, do we have a good sense of the comparative magnitude of social control problems in the various professions. Here we will briefly note four documented areas of social control problems in medicine that have been examined by physicians as well as by outside observers. The first such area is clinical research. In clinical research, for instance, one can cite failures to comply with federal and institutional requirements for prior review and approval of research protocols; failures to meet legal and ethical requirements for obtaining informed, voluntary consent of research subjects; and problems of deliberately falsifying data. Here, as in other areas, it is hard to estimate the frequency of these deviations from accepted standards, but that such deviations do occur is unarguable.[4,20,23]

Second, physicians may commit various types of legal violations that tend to be "overlooked" by their peers. These include, for example, writing illegal or unreported prescriptions for narcotic or psychopharmacologic agents in violation of the Controlled Substances Act or submitting fraudulent reimbursement claims to third-party payers such as Medicare and Medicaid. Third, physicians, like other individuals, may engage in various types of sexually or otherwise socially deviant behavior that is professionally problematic when it occurs in the context of interactions with patients.

Fourth, there is the problem of the "impaired physician," a subject that is now beginning to be openly recognized and dealt with by the profession. This term refers to the estimated 5% to 10% of practicing physicians whose competency is affected by psychiatric disturbances, alcoholism, or drug abuse.[21] A related social control problem is how to deal with those physicians who, whether by virtue of inadequate training or skill, physical or mental deficits, or substance abuse problems, are technically incompetent.[21]

The extent to which physicians become aware of these sorts of problems in colleagues and the ways they deal with them vary in part with the type of practice setting. Thus, for example, it usually is much easier for physicians to spot a colleague's technical incompetency if they are working together in a hospital setting, as compared to determining incompetency in a physician engaged in a solo practice. Comparably, physicians in a hospital setting have many more types of formal and informal social controls at their disposal, if they choose to exercise them, to deal with the incompetent or behaviorally "deviant" physician than do physicians practicing independently in a community.

When physicians do recognize problems in their colleagues, they have certain patterned responses that vary somewhat by practice setting. Most often these responses involve efforts to deal with the "violator" within the confines of the group, usually by informal means and, more rarely, by exerting formal pressures or sanctions. In hospitals, for example, one type of informal social control used by physicians to deal with an impaired or otherwise incompetent colleague is "grayzoning," that is, arranging coverage for the care of the incompetent physician's patients.[22] This practice has two objectives: first, to prevent harm to patients and, second, to protect the reputation of the physician and permit him or her to continue to practice. Other types of informal internal controls include efforts to modify behavior through face-to-face confrontations or the use of peer group pressure and slowing or halting patient referrals.[16]

If these types of informal control efforts fail, physicians may choose to exercise more formal types of internal controls. Invoking more formal controls is a decision that rests on many factors, including how serious the norm violations are judged to be in relation to the severity of the sanctions likely to be imposed. Formal controls range from discussions at morbidity and mortality conferences to such actions as complaints to a hospital's executive committee and removal of hospital privileges and complaints to and censure by local medical societies. Although loss of hospital privileges is considered as extremely severe sanction by those *within* the institution, it may in fact do little to control a particular physician's problem, since he or she seldom is prevented from obtaining privileges at other hospitals.

As this last point suggests, physicians, like other professionals, are faced with a difficult moral and often legal issue when they know that their self-regulatory efforts are not succeeding or are inadequate. How *do* they and how *should* they balance what they perceive as a conflict between duties to their colleagues and duties to patients and society? Even in terms of acting to trigger internal controls, much less "going public" with a problem, professionals also weigh the costs to themselves and their careers in terms of how colleagues may respond to someone they view as a "whistle blower."

From what we know about the exercise of social controls in medicine, physicians seldom turn to *external* sources to modify or sanction a colleague's professional behavior or deal with the colleague's technical incompetency. The boards in each state that are legislatively empowered to license and discipline physicians, for instance, rarely receive a physician-initiated complaint.[31] In 1975, for example, the Massachusetts Board of Registration in Medicine was given added powers by the state legislature to sanction physicians with measures ranging from reprimands to loss of licenses. Between 1975 and 1980, to our knowledge, only *one* physician has signed a complaint against another physician in the 1000 or more complaints received by the board.

Sociologically the reluctance of physicians to fully use the range of internal social controls at their disposal, and even greater reluctance to invoke external controls, is understandable. As the description of the "company of equals" suggests, for example, the education and socialization of physicians are geared toward self-direction, employing their own knowledge, skills, and internalized professional morality in the practice of medicine. In part reflecting the professional norm of autonomy, the emphasis is on what Bosk[8] terms *professional-self control*, or the individuals' control of themselves as professionals.

Other reasons that account for the frequent failure of internal social controls include the common tendency to overlook or normalize "deviant" behavior in those with whom we associate closely, a topic that was discussed in Chapter 4. Additionally, physicians, like other people, may choose not to respond to even flagrant cases of incompetency, negligence, or deviancy in a colleague on the rationale that "there but for the Grace of God, go I." "We are all fallible," this line of reasoning goes, "and if I protect my friend and colleague, perhaps I will be similarly guarded from exposure and sanctions if I should lapse in my performance or behavior."

Finally, when internal social controls fail to correct what professionals judge to be serious problems with a colleague, why are they so reluctant to use external controls? The answer to this question in part lies in the characteristics of professionals that we outlined earlier. Public exposure of the fact that some professionals are technically, behaviorally, or morally deficient, it is feared, will diminish the public's high esteem for and trust in the profession and, most worrisome of all, lead to an erosion of professional autonomy.

By seeking to keep knowledge of social control problems within the confines of the group and at the same time too often failing to deal adequately with those problems, however, professionals invite the very types of external controls and consequent loss of autonomy that they fear most. Those outside of medicine (and other professions as well) increasingly are becoming aware of the types of social control problems that we have noted and concerned about the ability of professionals to deal with them in ways that adequately protect the public.

In *Forgive and Remember*, a study of the development and exercise of social controls in a surgical residency training program, Bosk[8] draws an important distinction between *professional-self* control and professional *self-control*. By *professional-self* control Bosk refers to individuals' *internal* control of themselves as professionals, based on both personal values and the technical and moral standards acquired during professional training. Professional *self-control* in turn refers to the *shared exercise* of controls among physicians as necessary to maintain professional standards in the group. The term *professional self-control*, as Bosk[8] points out, "underscores the corporate responsibility of the profession to regulate its own internal affairs." And, as he suggests, our knowledge of how physicians manage this duty "suggests . . . that there is a hypertrophy of professional-self control and an atrophy of professional self-control."[8]

There are major theoretic differences among sociologists as to *why* self-regulation in medicine is so often inadequate. Indeed, as Bosk[8] observes, "social control is the criterion variable that distinguishes one sociological perspective on the professions from another." Although these theoretic differences are beyond the scope of this section, it is important to recognize that they are not only academic arguments. As we have indicated, how one interprets the reasons for self-regulation problems in medicine and other professions has major social policy implications. If, for example, one views the activities of a profession such as medicine as motivated primarily by a desire to protect a "monopoly" on its sphere of work,[5] it suggests (1) that physicians are only concerned with those internal social controls that will protect their self-interests and (2) that *external* controls are the only way to effectively regulate physicians in the public interest.

In our view it is overly simplistic to think that *any* profession's activities have a single motivating force behind them that accounts for the adequacy or inadequacy of its self-regulatory mechanisms. Thus it is equally unrealistic and harmful to the profession and the public to assert (1) that physicians have few, if any, internal social controls and little, if any, desire to do anything in the way of self-regulation beyond protecting their self-interests or (2) that if left alone physicians are perfectly capable of adequate self-regulation because they will always seek to protect the interests (health) of their patients and the public more generally.

What physicians and those concerned with their work need to do, we would argue, is to begin paying far closer attention to identifying and strengthening the often very subtle processes of social controls that do exist within the profession. Students and their teachers, for example, particularly during residency, can become more aware of the types of values that are transmitted in the process of clinical training and the ways that those values are expressed vis-á-vis social controls. A conscious awareness of socialization processes and professional values is a necessary first step in strengthening those social control mechanisms that are present but often fail to work to the satisfaction of either the medical profession or the public.

References

1. Baker, C., and Kramer, M.: To define or not to define: the role of the clinical specialist, Nurs. Forum **9:**41, 1970.
2. Barber, B.: Control and responsibility in the powerful professions, Political Sci. Q., p. 599, Winter 1978.
3. Barber, B.: Science and the social order, Glencoe, Ill., 1952, The Free Press.
4. Barber, B., Makarushka, J., and Sullivan, D.: Research on human subjects: problems of social control in medical experimentation, New York, 1975, Russell Sage Foundation.
5. Berlant, J.: Professionalism and monopoly, Berkeley, Calif., 1976, University of California Press.
6. Blau, P.: Dynamics of bureaucracy, Chicago, 1963, University of Chicago Press.
7. Bledstein, B.: The culture of professionalism, New York, 1976, W. W. Norton & Co., Inc.
8. Bosk, C.: Forgive and remember: managing medical failure, Chicago, 1979, University of Chicago Press.
9. Bucher, R.: Pathology: a study of social movements within a profession. In Freidson, E., and Lorber, J., editors: Medical men and their work, Chicago, 1972, Aldine-Atherton.
10. Bullough, V., and Bullough, B.: The care of the sick: the emergence of modern nursing, London, 1979, Crown Helm.
11. Burrow, J.: AMA: voice of American medicine, Baltimore, 1963, The Johns Hopkins University Press.
12. Carr-Saunder, A., and Wilson, P.: The professions, Oxford, 1933, Clarendon Press.
13. Chapman, C.: On the definition and teaching of the medical ethic, N. Engl. J. Med. **301:**631, 1979.
14. Coser, R.: Authority and decision-making in a hospital: a comparative analysis. In Freidson, E., and Lorber, J., editor: Medical men and
their work, Chicago, 1972, Aldine-Atherton.
15. Denzin, N.: Incomplete professionalization: the case of pharmacy. In Freidson, E., and Lorber, J., editors: Medical men and their work, Chicago, 1972, Aldine-Atherton.
16. Freidson, E.: Doctoring together: a study of professional social control, New York, 1975, Elsevier.
17. Freidson, E.: Professional dominance: the social structure of medical care, New York, 1970, Atherton Press.
18. Freidson, E.: The profession of medicine: a study in the sociology of applied knowledge, New York, 1970, Harper & Row, Publishers, Inc.
19. Freidson, E., and Rhea, B.: Processes of control in a company of equals. In Freidson, E., and Lorber, J., editors: Medical men and their work, Chicago, 1972, Aldine-Atherton.
20. Gray, B.: Human subjects in medical experimentation, New York, 1975, John Wiley & Sons, Inc.
21. Green, R., Carroll, G., and Buxton, W.: The care and management of the sick and incompetent physician, Springfield, Ill., 1978, Charles C Thomas, Publisher.
22. Holoweiko, M.: Grayzoning, Medical Economics, p. 187, Feb. 19, 1979.
23. Katz, J., Capron, A., and Serf-Glass, E.: Experimentation with human beings, New York, 1972, Russell Sage Foundation.
24. Levine, S., Scotch, N., and Vlasak, G.: Unraveling technology and culture in public health, Am. J. Public Health **59:**237, 1969.
25. Mechanic, D.: Physicians. In Freeman, H., Levine, S., and Reeder, L., editors: Handbook of medical sociology, ed. 3, Englewood Cliffs, N.J., 1979, Prentice-Hall, Inc.
26. Parsons, T.: Professions. In International encyclopedia of the social sciences, New York, 1968, Macmillan, Inc.

27. Peck, R.: Why the FTC has declared war on doctors, Medical Economics, p. 29, Aug. 6, 1979.

28. Record, J., and Greenlick, M.: New health professionals and the physician role: a hypothesis from the Kaiser experience, Public Health Rep. **90**:241, 1975.

29. Reeder, S., and Mauksch, H.: Nursing: continuing change. In Freeman, H., Levine, S., and Reeder, L., editors: Handbook of medical sociology, ed. 3, Englewood Cliffs, N.J., 1979, Prentice-Hall, Inc.

30. Relman, A.: Chiropractic: recognized but unproved, N. Engl. J. Med. **301**:659, 1979. (Editorial.)

31. Rosenberg, C.: Are those tougher doctor-policing laws really working? Medical Economics, p. 106, April 12, 1979.

32. Rothstein, W.: American physicians in the nineteenth century: from sects to science, Baltimore, 1972, The Johns Hopkins University Press.

33. Rueschemeyer, D.: Doctors and lawyers: a comment on the theory of the professions. In Freidson, E., and Lorber, J., editors: Medical men and their work, Chicago, 1972, Aldine-Atherton.

34. Stevens, R.: American medicine and the public interest, New Haven, Conn., 1971, Yale University Press.

35. Vollmer, H., and Mills, E., editors: Professionalization, Englewood Cliffs, N.J., 1966, Prentice-Hall, Inc.

36. Wardwell, W.: Limited and marginal practitioners. In Freeman, H., Levine, S., and Reeder, L., editors: Handbook of medical sociology, ed. 3, Englewood Cliffs, N.J., 1979, Prentice-Hall, Inc.

Chapter 12

Medicine and American society: toward a new social contract?

Throughout the past decade a refrain has been heard from many quarters that this is a "time of crisis" for medicine. A glance at some of the titles of books about medicine, for example, conveys a sense of deep concerns about the status of medicine in the United States and the objectives it should pursue in the years ahead: *Where Medicine Fails*,[41] *Doing Better and Feeling Worse*,[8] *Medical Nemesis*,[21] *The Medical Offenders*,[27] *The American Health Empire*,[9] *In Critical Condition: The Crisis in America's Health Care*.[23]

In this final chapter, in part by looking at what sorts of crises are being perceived in medicine, we will consider the role of medicine as a social institution in American society. It is obvious that medicine, considered as a body of knowledge and skills about the causes and treatment of disease and illness, is constantly changing and evolving. Although it may be less readily apparent, medicine also changes and evolves over time as an institution with certain roles or functions within a society and also has various functions in different societies.

The chapter will focus on the type of *social contract* that exists between the medical profession and the public, a contract that is seen most directly in doctor-patient relationships, and at some of the ways that the contract seems to be altering.*

It is important, particularly for those most directly involved in medical care, to have some grasp of medicine's role within the social system and of how that role may be changing. The nature of the social contract between the medical profession and the larger society of which it is a part is an important determinant of how all providers, not only physicians, are trained and work. And, more broadly, that contract says much about how our society views and deals with health and illness, both within and without the medical care system.

Providers, patients, and the public: stress points

The relationship between medicine and American society has been an often turbulent one.[40] When viewed historically it thus seems doubtful that the various

---

*Portions of this chapter are adapted from Swazey, J.: Health, professionals, and the public: toward a new social contract? Philadelphia, 1979, Society for Health and Human Values.

issues and concerns now being voiced about medicine in the United States have many unique elements or mark any sort of unprecedented "crisis." It is clear, however, that the institutional and professional roles, respectively, of medical practice and the physician currently are being challenged from many quarters. Some of these challenges derive directly from problems in medical care, whereas others reflect broader sociocultural events in contemporary American society.

In this part of the chapter we will look at some of the concerns about medicine that are being voiced from within as well as without the profession. The topics covered are divided into five areas: (1) the costs of medical care, (2) the views of medicine expressed by various groups of "critics," (3) concerns being raised by patients or those who profess to speak on their behalf, (4) the imposition of external controls on medicine, and (5) concerns being raised by physicians or those who profess to speak on their behalf. These topics illustrate the fact that there are many different perspectives on the strengths and weaknesses of American medicine, on what should be done to improve it, and on the likely effects of current changes and interventions.

The cost of medical care

Perhaps the single aspect of medical care that all commentators seem to agree constitutes a major problem, if not a crisis, is cost. Anyone who recently finished medical school thousands of dollars in debt or anyone who recently received a hospital bill need not be reminded of the economic realities that are pressing providers, the public, and the government to assess what we need, want, and can afford in the way of medical care. To both the medical profession and the public, according to 1979 surveys, cost is the major problem confronting medicine and health care in the United States.[2]

The reasons for the worries about cost are suggested by the following summary of national health care expenditures[10]:

> In 1977, the nation's health care spending exceeded $160 billion—four times the 1965 amount. Real per capita spending (i.e., net of general inflation) increased 94 percent from 1965 to 1977. *Public sector spending rose seven times over, from $9.5 billion to $64.4 billion.* Federal Medicare alone is doubling from 1976 to 1980, i.e., up from $18 to $36 billion. The Fiscal 1980 Budget projects $52 billion for 1982. Most of this government spending is open ended and not controllable. Health care spending is seriously straining the Federal budget.*

Although the basis for concern is clear, the reasons for the escalating costs of medical care are far more complex. The list of contributing causes is almost endless. It includes such factors as (1) inflation, (2) a lack of cost control incentives in

---

*From Enthoven, A.: Health care cost control through incentives and competition: consumer-choice health plan. In Miset, G., editor: Socioeconomic issues of health 1979, Chicago, 1979, American Medical Association. Reprinted with the permission of the American Medical Association.

the nonprofit care sector, (3) an increase in demand for and insurance coverage of medical care by the population in general and by previously underserved groups in particular, (4) the increased use of sophisticated, costly diagnostic and treatment technology, (5) the growth in numbers of nonphysician medical care personnel, (6) the increasing proportion of medical care that is provided in hospitals, which adds to costs in numerous ways, (7) the high level of government investment in research and development relating to every aspect of medical care, and (8) increasing malpractice claims and higher malpractice insurance rates.

Though the rising costs of medical care pose concerns in and of themselves, they are heightened by concurrent problems in all segments of the economy. Responses to the rising costs of medical care range from fervent statements of concern from patients, physicians, and government officials, including several Presidents of the United States, to a series of voluntary efforts and specific laws and regulations aimed at cost containment.

For our purposes in this chapter the details of efforts to curb or reduce the costs of medical care are less important than the fact of the efforts. "Cost containment" seems firmly ensconced as a major issue and slogan for the 1980s. However reluctantly, discussion about the explicit rationing of health care services is beginning to surface at the national policy-making level.[24,37]

A major value conflict will have to be dealt with in addressing the problem of costs and the possibility of rationing. For, as we discussed in Chapter 4, our society increasingly is endorsing and acting on the value that all its citizens have a *right* to medical or health care.[43] The notion of medical care as a right has been supported publicly by the Congress and the last five U.S. Presidents. Legislation such as Medicare and Medicaid has been passed and various national health insurance plans proposed to help ensure that such a right is not denied by lack of financial resources. Such developments indicate that American society through its political institutions is expected and intends to extend more care to more people. Efforts to act on the belief that medical care is a right in terms of providing services that are available, accessible, and affordable thus appear to be on a collision course with powerful and escalating concerns about the costs of such care. The goals of extending services and cutting costs are not completely mutually exclusive. But their joint pursuit inevitably will generate discord and necessitate some difficult decisions that will affect both providers and recipients of medical care.

Critics of medicine

Beyond cost there are many diverse opinions about what is right and wrong with American medicine and about what could or should be done to bolster its strengths and correct its defects. In this section we will briefly characterize the viewpoints of some of the critics of medicine, including physicians, by arraying them in groups along a quasi-political spectrum.

Conservative critics. The analysts of medical care who can be characterized as conservative critics reflect a laissez-faire political and economic tradition. In this tradition, as represented in economics by Friedman,[15] marketplace mechanisms are held to provide the soundest and freest way to distribute goods and services, including medical care. To conservative critics the medical care system in the United States, based on a fee-for-service principle, is fundamentally sound although not perfect.[38,39] The best way to improve medical care, from this viewpoint, is to place a greater reliance on strong market mechanisms. Correspondingly, government controls in areas such as the cost and availability of services should be decreased or abolished entirely.

One of the best known expositions of this conservative perspective is that by Sade (a physician).[38] Medical care, he argues,

> is neither a right or a privilege: it is a service that is provided by doctors and others to people who wish to purchase it . . . Problems such as high cost, few doctors, low quantity of available care in economically depressed areas may be real, but it is naive to believe that governmental solutions through coercive legislation can be anything but shortsighted and formulated on the basis of political expediency. The only long-range plan that can hope to provide for the day after tomorrow is a "nonsystem"—that is, a system that proscribes the imposition by force (legislation) of any one group's conception of the best forms of medical care.*

Liberal critics. To liberal critics a major problem with medical care in the United States is its organizational inefficiency. In contrast to conservatives like Sade, the liberal call is not for a "nonsystem." Rather, as expressed by one of the foremost liberal critics, Sen. Edward Kennedy,[23] it is to remedy "the inefficient and disorganized system of American health care." A better coordinated, better managed system, liberal critics argue, would correct many of the inequities in the availability and quality of medical care services in the United States. Here the demand is for more and more effective *planning*, for example, to provide coordinated services for special populations such as children and the elderly, offer regionalized services for particular problems such as cancer, or develop systems to monitor the quality and costs of services.

A second major thrust of liberal reformers of medicine over several decades has been the enactment of some form of national health insurance (NHI). From the liberal perspective health or medical care is viewed as a right, and the many NHI proposals introduced to Congress have been seen as a necessary means to ensure that people are not denied this right because of a lack of financial access.[23,42] According to 1979 opinion surveys the majority of the American public (67%) shares the liberal critics' belief that we need NHI. This is one area of conflict between the public and what is generally characterized as the conservatively oriented medical

---

*Reprinted by permission from The New England Journal of Medicine **285:**1288, 1971.

profession. For at the end of 1979 only 38% of physicians surveyed by the American Medical Association believed there was a need for NHI, a sharp decline from 53% in 1978.[2]

Radical critics. The most extreme critics of American medicine fall into two major camps. One group represents a Marxist tradition of political and economic criticism of the United States' democratic and capitalist principles, focused in this case on medicine. The other group can be characterized as "visionary" critics who, like many social utopian theorists, urge a return to a simpler "golden age."

A representative example of the Marxist-radical vein of criticism is *The Exploitation of Illness in Capitalist Society* by Waitzkin and Waterman.[45] To these analysts, as the title of their monograph suggests, the major problems with medical care in the United States reside in the system's capitalist, for-profit underpinnings. Physicians and medically related industries, they hold, have developed a monopolistic system that precludes "humane health care."

> Because the demand for health care is virtually limitless, individual professionals and medical-industrial corporations have discovered great sources of profit in illness. Like the exploitation of workers by capitalists in Marx's scheme, the enterprises of medical capitalism do not hesitate to exploit patients. Medical imperialism contributes to this process, since patients ultimately bear the burden of medical expansion in the form of rising health costs. Because the power distribution in American medicine favors the providers rather than the consumers of health care, exploitation of illness and suffering persists.*

Visionary critics. The *visionary critics* of medicine, exemplified by Illich, seem on the surface to share many of the Marxist critics' views. In his much-discussed book *Medical Nemesis*, for example, Illich[21] seems to echo many of the Marxist critics' charges about a "medical-industrial complex" that, as seen in the growth of medical technology, is bent on exploiting illness for monetary gain. Read more closely, however, Illich's views as to why "the medical establishment has become a threat to health" really are a highly conservative, traditional Christian-Catholic attack disguised as a Marxist argument.[14]

Illich sees modern medicine as turning the "world . . . into a hospital ward." He calls for a greater reliance on personal initiatives for our health, for a resumption of individual autonomy and responsibility to combat the social and clinical iatrogenicity for which medicine is responsible. Medicine's greatest threat, according to Illich, is that it has eroded "the healing power in sickness, patience in suffering, and fortitude in the face of death. . . ."[21] To Illich, as Fox[14] observes, "this state is not only morally dubious, but also spiritually dangerous. Because it entails the 'hubris' of what he deems arrogant and excessive medical intervention, it invites 'nemesis': the retribution of the gods."

---

*From Waitzkin, H., and Waterman, B.: The exploitation of illness in capitalist society, Indianapolis, © 1974, The Bobbs-Merrill Co., Inc.

Challenges to Aesculapian authority

The literature concerning criticisms of medicine, in sum, involves a spectrum of views about what is wrong with medicine as a social institution. In assessing the critics' charges, as well as the rebuttals by their opponents, we would emphasize the importance of being critical oneself. In particular it is necessary to distinguish those charges and countercharges that are based on accurate data about medical care from those that rest primarily on ideologic convictions.

Many of critics' charges are leveled against what they view as defects in our *system* (or nonsystem) of health care or medical care and the political and economic bases on which it rests. A second and related theme involves the medical profession's role. This strand of criticism includes charges about medical imperialism, medicalization, iatrogenicity, and excessive power over patients. These criticisms of the medical profession seem to have two major components. First, as discussed in Chapter 4, they involve a questioning of how the medical profession, and society more generally, are defining health and illness and medicine's role in relation to health and illness. Second, they involve a complex questioning, some old and some new, of what has been termed the physician's "Aesculapian authority." This authority, as we discussed in Chapter 5, involves a blend of sapiential, moral, and charismatic authority.

If the concept of Aesculapian authority is linked with the characteristics of physicians as professionals that we discussed in Chapter 11, one gains a sense of why physicians, as a class of professionals, have occupied a social role that involves special types of authority and a high degree of autonomy. That authority and autonomy, however, now is being challenged on a number of fronts. One front, as we have seen, is manned by the critics of medicine, for whom medicine often serves as a useful lightning rod on which to focus broader ideologic attacks. A second front, which we will touch on in the next section, involves a number of concerns about medicine voiced by patients and those who profess to speak for them.

Patient concerns

Much like "health care is a right," "patients' rights" has become a slogan and rallying point for a broad range of issues and concerns about medicine in the United States. These include a number of legal and ethical issues relating to the provider-patient relationship and to the delivery of care by hospitals and other institutions, a collection of interests that fall under the rubric of the "consumer movement," and perhaps most diffuse, a number of concerns relating to the "human dimensions" of illness and its care.

Patients rights. At various places in the text we have noted that major shifts in the nature of doctor-patient interactions have been prompted in recent years by legal and ethical affirmations of various patients' rights. Two such rights involve requirements for informed, voluntary consent to participation in clinical research and consent to treatment, both of which have had powerful effects on the profession's norms regarding candor or "truth telling." Another rights' claim, which we noted in Chapter 8, is the "right to die." Debate and action on this "right" has generated a series of court cases and a voluminous literature on the refusal of life-saving or life-prolonging treatment by competent patients and on how such decisions should be made on behalf of incompetent patients. A related and growingly "hot" area of patients' rights in relation to treatment decisions concerns the refusal of treatment by hospitalized psychiatric patients.[12,29]

Other active areas on the patients' rights front are growing demands for a right to review and possess a copy of one's medical records and growing concerns about the protection of rights, privacy, and confidentiality, particularly given the growth of computerized data banks.[46,47]

These sorts of patient rights' issues, while specific to medicine, also reflect broader concerns about rights in our society. Their origins, contents, and effects need to be assessed in the context of the values that have given rise to concerns, popular movements, and laws about civil rights, prisoners' rights, women's rights, privacy, and freedom of information. Current issues in medicine should not be looked at in isolation but in the context of medicine as one of many social institutions undergoing significant change.

Consumer activism. As we noted in Chapter 4, consumer activism in health care and medicine has many linkages with drives for patients' rights. Increased consumer activity ranges from an insistence on and assumption of greater personal responsibility for one's health and medical care[4] to more involvement in planning and overseeing medical care delivery at local, regional, and national levels.[17,44]

The range of interests and activities that can be catalogued under the banner of the consumer movement in health or medical care should be viewed in relation to the more general phenomenon of consumer activism in our society. This activism in turn is related to social currents such as a resurgence of political populism, a distrust of the power of experts, and a desire to gain more control over many aspects of our lives. In terms of a larger social context, however, we also need to recognize that the American people's interest and involvement in health and medicine *are* extraordinarily high. To some observers of the American scene, as we noted in Chapter 1, the attention, personal involvement, and resources that we devote to health, illness, and medicine indeed are excessive.

The patient as a person. Another somewhat more diffuse aspect of lay challenges to the physician's role and the orientation of medical care revolves around the wishes for a more patient-oriented medical care system. As expressed in the title of the influential book *The Patient As Person* by Ramsey,[36] many people feel that medicine, particularly in hospital settings, has so focused on the technologic management of disease processes that it has become overly depersonalized or dehumanized. The challenge here is not to the physician's technical expertise but rather to the nature of the acts of *caring for* patients in which that expertise is embedded. It is in simple terms a wish that physicians would discuss "Mr. Jones, the person in Room 603 who had a myocardial infarction," instead of discussing him as "the MI in 603."

On balance, the vast majority of the American public (88% in a late 1979 survey) is satisfied with the *quality* of medical care.[2] What does seem to disturb people, however, especially when they are cared for in an institutional setting, is a feeling of being treated as disease-object, with the attendant types of communication problems that were discussed in Chapter 5. What people want when they become ill, many people are saying, is *personal as well as technically competent care*. This may explain why, despite the growing trend toward group practice arrangements, only 33% of the public say they would approve of being treated by a group of physicians instead of a personal physician.[2]

Physicians and other providers, as many within medicine recognize, can strike a better balance between technically proficient and humanistic care.[34] The two are not mutually exclusive, as students have sometimes suggested when they ask: "What would you rather have, a warm and understanding doctor who doesn't know his medicine too well or an impersonal doctor who really knows his medicine?"

Moreover, as Potter[35] has argued, providers too need a patient-as-person orientation toward their work if they are to fully realize the rewards of being a medical professional.

> Patients who cannot be known in their individual selfhood and through awareness of the context and history of their lives, cannot be perceived as persons in the full sense. Thus, not being known as persons, they cannot give back to health professionals personal satisfactions of the deepest kind. One cannot be a friend to a sick kidney nor receive affection from a gall bladder . . . One can of course get money for dealing with such ailments . . . Or, one can strive for good repute within the profession and become famous for skill in treating such cases. Or one can exercise power within the hospital for which one's skills may seem indispensable. . . .
>
> It is the mark of the successful fool, however, to believe that such things insure a high quality of life. Without the opportunity to share interior lives of others, to bear the burdens and to delight in the joys of those we hold in mutual respect, such rewards turn out to be hollow even as the philosophers of every generation have said. So a physician who settles for depersonalized practice, entered into for the external rewards which may be purchased from the proceeds of that practice, is converting medicine from an honorable profession into another job, the rewards of which are extrinsic to its performance.*

Among all the professions, as Potter suggests, medical care providers because of their social role can experience both unique frustrations and rewards for their efforts. They render their services at times of great importance in people's lives, for example, at birth, infant development, childhood, adolescence, adulthood,

---

*From Potter, R.: Does medicine care about those who cure? The Guthrie Bulletin **46**:89, 1976.

pregnancy, child-rearing, and also when people are disabled and dying. People entrust their care to providers not only at times of great happiness but also at times of personal pain when they are most vulnerable. To the extent that providers cannot only *try* to be sensitive to their patients but can *actually* be sensitive and effective because they understand their patient's life situation and the social forces that influence their provider-patient encounters, the provider's work will be more fulfilling.

External controls over medicine

The fourth set of issues that we will touch on is the burgeoning of external controls over providers and the delivery of medical care.[5] As we pointed out in Chapter 11, social controls can be divided, at least for analytic purposes, into the *internal* or *self-controls* exercised by individuals or groups and the *external* controls exercised by various social agencies. We also noted that many types of social controls have both internal and external components. In medicine, for example, Boards of Registration and Professional Standards Review Organizations are legislatively mandated at state and federal levels, respectively, but operate essentially as peer controls by physicians.[18]

Internal and external controls, further, are not mutually exclusive. That is, it is not the case that medicine, or other professions, will be governed *either* by internal controls *or* by external controls. For as Barber[3] observes:

> Because the power of the professions is based on esoteric knowledge, acquired through extensive specialized and continuing study and training, its successful development and application require a considerable amount of self-control or autonomy for those who perform professional functions. . . . But self-regulation is always complemented by some external regulation. All specialized social tasks, and perhaps especially those that are most esoteric and most powerful, are subject to some external regulation and control.*

Barber's point is supported by the historical review by Chapman[6] of the physician's autonomy as the medical profession developed in England and the United States. Beginning in fourteenth century England he writes, "the story is one of intermittent and progressive limitation of autonomy and, somewhat later, modification of the right to create and maintain monopoly. But through it all, the special social [role] of the doctor is visible and, to an extent, determinant."

The five major steps in the development of external controls traced by Chapman are (1) malpractice law, (2) the requirement that the medical profession (in seventeenth century England) follow the laws of due process, (3) licensure requirements, (4) the enactment of restraint of trade laws, and (5) quality control laws and

---

*From Barber, B.: Regulation and the professions, Hastings Center Report **10**:34, 1980.

regulations designed to set standards for and monitor various aspects of physician performance.

From a historical perspective, the legal and regulatory controls over medicine are not unique developments in the relation between the medical profession and American society. The types of external controls represented by the role of the courts in areas such as malpractice litigation and defining patients' rights in treatment decisions, legislation affecting physician reimbursement, the creation of Professional Standards Review Organizations, and the antitrust activities of the Federal Trade Commission need to be assessed as part of a continuous process of defining how and by whom medical professionals and their work will be governed.[18]

Although internal and external professional controls are coexistent, however, their relative balance does vary over time. At present, as Barber[3] notes, "we are seeing expressions of complaint and distrust, and of the need for new regulatory standards and mechanisms for all the professions." Medicine, as we have suggested, is at the epicenter of these calls for increasing external controls. This is the case for reasons that are specific to medicine and because medicine is a lightening rod for more general concerns about the power of experts and about the values of equity and autonomy in our society.

Physician concerns

Critics of medicine, patients and those who speak on their behalf, and policy-makers include physicians among their numbers, for physicians too have diverse views on the strengths and weaknesses of American medicine. Many physicians, in short, are concerned about the sorts of problems we have noted already, such as the costs of medical care, inequities in access and quality, the need for stronger peer review mechanisms, and the quality of patient care. In this section we will look briefly at four additional sets of concerns voiced by some members of the medical profession: the need for a greater emphasis on disease prevention, patient care problems, changing practice arrangements, and an erosion of the physician's Aesculapian authority. This is by no means a comprehensive listing. But, together with the topics dealt with earlier in this chapter and others raised throughout the book, it suggests the range of issues and challenges perceived by physicians as they examine their relationships with patients and with American society more generally.

Disease prevention. One theme that has long prevailed in criticisms of medicine by physicians, as we pointed out in Chapters 2 and 4, is that the impact of medicine on health has not been as significant as it could be. Physicians such as John Knowles and Charles Epstein have argued that too many of medicine's resources have been directed toward technologically complex, expensive, and only marginally effective curative care. In their view far too little attention and effort have been directed to disease prevention and health promotion.

Among those who advocate a greater focus on disease prevention, some, like Knowles, hold that major responsibility for the promotion of health lies with the individual citizen, who can and should eschew unhealthful habits and behaviors.[25] Others, like Epstein, assert that our political and economic system must assume a new, more responsible role in protecting workers and society from industrial wastes and toxic and carcinogenic chemicals used in manufacturing and agriculture.[11] Both viewpoints, however, agree that to date the impact of curative medicine on the overall health of the nation has been inadequate, and both call for greater expenditures of governmental and professional efforts as disease prevention.

Patient care problems. For providers the essence of clinical medicine is caring for patients. At the same time physicians, nurses, and other medical professionals find certain aspects of patient care to be particularly problematic and stressful. Some of these problem areas are recurrent, endemic features of provider-patient interactions, which we have looked at in Parts I and II of this book in relation to topics such as careseeking decisions, doctor-patient communication, compliance, rehabilitation, and the dying patient.

In earlier chapters we also touched on two other more recent facets of patient care that are posing many difficulties for individual providers and for professions such as medicine and nursing more generally. The first is related to the major shift in morbidity and mortality patterns that has occurred in recent decades. Because the leading causes of illness and death now are the chronic diseases rather than infectious and other acute diseases, providers must be prepared to deal with an expanding population of elderly patients, who often suffer from several concurrent chronic illnesses. With few exceptions these illnesses are not yet amenable to prevention or cure. Thus both providers and patients must cope over time with disorders whose etiology often is not well understood and whose symptoms can at best be palliated.

This point in turn is related to a second contemporary facet of patient care that we have discussed. We are in an era in which the scope of what society views as medicine's responsibilities is an expanding one. Providers increasingly must contend with the fact that they are asked to deal with social problems for which they have had little or no training. Powerful social forces can impede or destroy their best treatment and prevention efforts with patients. Additionally, providers are asked to handle social or psychologic problems such as substance abuse, delinquency, gambling, and child abuse as if they were medical diseases with a definitive etiology, natural history, and cure.

These social problems, though they contain threats to health, are not well understood in terms of traditional medical competencies in the areas of etiology, diagnosis, prognosis, and treatment. With very few exceptions medicine has been unable to substantially alter, modify, or reduce such problems for society as a whole or even for particular individuals. The net effect on medical care providers has been to include yet another huge category of problems in its domain for which it can do little and for which it is being faulted for an inadequate performance.

Changing practice arrangements. Another changing facet of medicine to which physicians and other providers are finding they must adjust is their modes of practice. These changes include new professional roles for nursing, as we noted in Chapter 11, that are altering the traditional dyadic relationships between nurse-physician and physician-patient and the nurse-physician-patient triad. As pointed out in Chapter 10, we also are witnessing the growth of team care, group, multi-specialty, and other practice arrangements and of prepaid health care plans. These developments, as Parsons[32] predicted in 1964, suggest that modern medicine's characteristic solo practice, fee-for-service physician practice model may prove in the future to have been a nonviable stage in the evolution of medicine as a social institution.

Another major change that appears to be on the horizon, related to the economics of medical practice, is what one investment broker describes as "the beginning of real competition in medicine."[19] Two trends toward a more competitive medical marketplace are the growth of proprietary services and insurance plans that provide incentives to patients and physicians for seeking and delivering more efficient and lower cost care.

Proponents of these developments argue that institutionally based medical care, particularly in hospitals, has been predominantly a nonprofit enterprise and therefore not subject to the competitive market forces associated with the for-profit business sector. For this reason and because the consumers or purchasers of medical care do not, in reality, have "free choices" about the types or sources of care they receive, medicine in twentieth century America has had little incentive to operate efficiently and cost effectively.

Cost containment, as we have observed, has become a major policy issue in government and medical circles. Many economists and policy analysts, however, feel that the costs of medical care *cannot* be controlled by either government regulations or voluntary efforts under our present delivery and reimbursement systems.[31]

To its advocate the growth of *proprietary* or for-profit medicine is a delivery approach that can provide more efficient and cost-effective medical care. But as seen in the debate that has surrounded the growth of National Medical Care (NMC), a physician-owned company that operates a nationwide chain of lucrative dialysis centers, proprietary medicine is highly controversial.[26] The controversy has several components: feelings of moral unease about proprietary medical care, concerns about conflicts-of-interest for kidney specialists involved in for-profit dialysis centers, and worries about NMC, in part because of its substantial medical and political influences, monopolizing renal dialysis in the United States.

Advocates of NMC counter these criticisms by appealing to the merits of efficiency and free enterprise and suggest that, if need be, NMC should be regulated like a public utility such as AT&T.[26] More generally its proponents see proprietary medicine as an inevitable and positive economic development in medical care. In the judgment of one leading investment broker, for example[19]:

Because of the growing economies of scale associated with the increased capital and technological intensity of health care . . . the impact of increased competitive forces is predictable: the takeover by specialized or integrated health-care service companies . . . of much of the functions currently handled by independent physicians, dentists, and, to a lesser extent, hospitals. The reason is that only such companies will be able to survive in an increasingly competitive environment . . . The eventual result will be a huge, highly concentrated, mostly for-profit, U.S. health-service industry that in total will eventually dwarf the pharmaceutical industry.*

A second trend toward competition took shape in 1980 in the form of various bills filed in Congress that seek to "increase health care competition . . . [by modifying] employer and employee purchase of health insurance."[1] These bills reflect three related perspectives: (1) that privately initiated cost containment efforts in the form of changes in health insurance reimbursements can succeed, (2) that such changes can be effected by providing a competitive financing and delivery market, and (3) that establishing and supporting such a competitive market is "the only truly responsible position for the medical profession to take in its defense against increasing government encroachment."[20]

Efforts to stimulate changes in the financing and delivery of medical care in the direction of more private sector competition and less government controls basically rest on the conviction that "the key issue in cost control is how to motivate physicians to use hospital and other resources economically."[10] This is necessary, as explained by policy and management expert Enthoven,[10] because:

> The main cause of the unjustified and unnecessary increase in costs is the complex of perverse incentives inherent in today's dominant system of health care financing. Most doctors are paid on a fee-for-service basis which rewards them for providing more and more costly services, whether or not more is necessary or beneficial to the patient. Hospitals are reimbursed for their costs, so they are rewarded with more revenue for generating more costs. . . .
>
> Most consumers have health insurance which leaves them with, at most, a weak financial incentive to question the need for or value of services. . . . Furthermore, benefits for more than two-thirds of the workers in private industry health plans are paid for entirely by employers, so that many workers have little or no knowledge of or concern over how much their health insurance costs.
>
> Within this financing system, the question of how best to spend a limited amount of money for the health care of a population is never even posed. Providers of health care services (mainly doctors and hospitals) are not required to set priorities, look at alternatives and make hard choices. Such a system must produce inflation in prices and waste in the use of resources.†

If the trends toward more proprietary medicine and more competitively structured methods of financing and delivering medical care gain momentum, they could

---

*Reprinted by permission from The New England Journal of Medicine **302**:978, 1980.
†From Enthoven, A.: Health care cost control through incentives and competition: consumer-choice health plan. In Misek, G., editor: Socioeconomic issues of health 1979, Chicago, 1979, American Medical Association. Reprinted with the permission of the American Medical Association.

have significant effects on not only the costs of medical care. Modes of physician practice, government as well as private reimbursement policies, public and private cost containment efforts, and individual decisions about seeking and offering care might all be modified in the years to come.

Challenges to Aesculapian authority

There is, finally, a strong current of concern among physicians that the ways society is responding to many of the perceived problems with medicine is steadily eroding their authority and autonomy *as professionals*. Such erosions are seen to be occurring, for example, at the individual doctor-patient level in stronger legal requirements for consent, in calls for "second opinions" before accepting a physician's diagnosis or treatment plan, and in views that patients should participate in a more collegial manner with their physicians.

As individual providers and as members of a class of professionals, many physicians also see their expertise and autonomy being diminished by shifts from *individual to collective* and from *private to public* decision making. These shifts seem to be occurring in many areas of decision making in our society once left largely to the wisdom of experts. In medicine the move toward more collective decision making is illustrated in various areas of quality control, cost reimbursement, and resource allocation once primarily the province of the individual physician's judgment. A related pattern of more public decision making is illustrated by the growing role of the courts in treatment decisions and by the increasing requirements for lay participation in various groups concerned with the physician's practice and performance and with the organization and delivery of services.

As we pointed out in a preceding section, the most visible and powerful forms of collective and public decision making with respect to medical practice are laws and regulations. And, as we have suggested, it is the imposition of these formal external controls that many physicians see as the greatest threat to their professionalism. The fears here are mixed ones. They range from a loss of medicine's dominance of the health-illness care sector, to a diminution of the physician's "professional dominance" in relation to other providers, to a decline in the social status and income of physicians, to concerns about negative consequences for patients and their care.

To some physicians external controls threaten the survival of medicine as a profession. This perspective is expressed by Dr. Francis A. Davis, publisher of *Private Practice*, in an editorial entitled "The Death of Free Doctors." Commenting on proposed regulations for prescription drug labeling and advertising issued by the Food and Drug Administration in 1979, Davis[7] wrote: "The FDA continues to promote programs that interfere with the physician's ability to care for his patients. . . . [B]ecause these regulations will require the practice of 'cook book' medicine, we will no longer be able to conduct our practice as professionals. Who is going to suffer in the end? The patient."

To other physicians such as Chapman[6] the external regulations are not seen as a threat to the viability of the medical profession. Rather, they represent a challenge to its members to act as change agents, utilizing the great deal of autonomy they have been granted by society to develop and exercise effective peer controls.

> [T]here is surely no reason to believe that American society now wishes to destroy the medical profession by removing all traces of its autonomy. On the contrary, the special status, both social and economic, of the profession is under no massive and immediate threat. But the obvious message of the times is that the profession should retain the most fundamental aspect of its autonomy in order that it may apply it, in the public interest and in its own, to the setting of expert and ethically defensible standards, and to the creation of effective monitoring mechanisms.*

As these statements indicate, some providers feel beleaguered and infuriated by current challenges and the prospect of further changes in medicine and will resist efforts to deal with them. Others recognize changing needs and situations and seek to stimulate new ways of dealing with them. Although the work of all providers will be shaped by new events and conditions, only a fraction of providers will attempt to shape the future themselves.

We hope that this book has made clear that rendering effective medical care requires more than technical competence and mastery of new biomedical knowledge. It also does and will require an understanding of the *social forces* that influence the acquisition of illness, the delivery and use of medical services, the scope of provider responsibilities, provider-provider and provider-patient interactions, patient outcomes in treatment, and the many ethical issues confronting medicine. It also will require a willingness to become socially and politically engaged in efforts to better the public's health.

The traditional contract: the authority, rights, and role of physicians

The concerns, criticisms, and challenges with which medical professionals now are dealing do not in our view constitute a historically unique time of crisis for American medicine. But the types of issues we have looked at do suggest that we *are* in a transitional period in which the relationship or social contract between physicians and patients and medicine and society is being renegotiated. In this section we will look at some of the central elements in the contract that have governed medicine as a social institution in our society for the past century. Then, in the final section we will consider some of the elements that might be contained in a revised social contract, one that will be shaped in part by those now training as medical care providers.

---

*From Chapman, C.: Doctors and their autonomy: past events and future prospects, Science **200:** 851, May 26, 1978. Copyright 1978 by the American Association for the Advancement of Science.

Physician rights and the doctor-patient relationship

In earlier chapters we have looked at the physician's role in terms of the doctor-patient relationship and in terms of doctors as professionals primarily from a sociologic perspective. Another way to look at the traditional social contract between physicians and patients or society is to examine how the rights and duties of physicians have been defined.

In an essay analyzing claims about the rights of physicians Jonsen[22] points out that *theories of rights* "are offered to explain the fact that people make certain broad claims about how others should act or refrain from acting toward them. . . . [The] justification [for claiming a moral right] must be an appeal to some value that the claimant considers authoritative and presumes that others will recognize."

Jonsen goes on to observe that as one looks at the development of medicine as a profession in the United States, physicians have claimed two main *moral rights*. Both claims have been presented as moral rights because they "assert that the physician should exercise jurisdiction over a range of activities; others are obliged to acknowledge this and are not to interfere."[22]

The first claim is that only those who ascribe to certain tenets of medical thought and practice have a right to be called doctors and to practice as physicians. The second set of claims holds that physicians have a special *fiduciary relationship* with their patients.* There are three key aspects of this fiduciary relationship. First, it is *controlled* by the physician. Second, it is *based on trust* in the physician. Third, the physician should be trusted and should be in control because of his greater *expertise and autonomy* and because of his *benevolent intent* to use his skills in the best interests of his patients.

These two sets of claims to moral rights were embodied during the latter half of the nineteenth century in medical licensure and practice acts and in the Code of Ethics promulgated by the profession's major organization, the American Medical Association.

Medical licensure and practice acts have given legal substance to the moral entitlements claimed by physicians. The medical license is legally protected in the courts as a property right and as such, Jonsen[22] observes, "provides a paradigm for an entire philosophy of physician rights during the past century."

> Physicians can conceive their practice as if it were a property; they bring it into existence by their training and their labor; they offer its benefits to those who seek them. Those seekers enter implicitly into a fiduciary contract in which they entrust themselves to the physician's benevolence and his science. The physician, for his part,

---

*These proclaimed rights, Jonsen suggests, have been based partly on the social contract doctrine of John Locke (1632-1704). The essence of Locke's[28] social contract theory is his doctrine of *individual rights*, among which he held the right of property to be preeminent. Locke's social contract is a *fiduciary* one based on *trust* in which those who yield certain rights or liberties to their government do so with the belief that the government will act in their best interests. The government, that is, has both rights and correlative duties.

can fulfill the contract for conferral of the benefits only if he sets the conditions and oversees the compliance of the patient. The services that the physician renders are discrete and can be priced and purchased.*

As was discussed in Chapter 11, codes of medical ethics throughout history also have embodied moral claims about the rights and duties of physicians in relation to one another and to patients and society. In analyzing these codes various physicians, historians, and philosophers have pointed out two major ways that they reflect what are now seen by many as major problems in the relationship between the medical profession and society. First, they observe that the codes have been oriented more toward the profession than toward patients and often have dealt more with etiquette than with ethics. Second, they have observed that the codes reflect what May[30] calls the "conceit of philanthropy." That is, the codes assume "that the professional's commitment to his fellow man is a gratuitous, rather than a responsive or reciprocal, act flowing from his [being a physician]." The AMA's code of 1847 and less explicitly its code of 1957, for example, place their emphasis on *duties and obligations of patients and the public to physicians* based on what they have received from the physician. There is no corresponding statement of the physician's duties and obligations being based on those "gifts and services he has received from the community."[30] To May these codes thus reflect a profession that views its members as highly self-sufficient, wise, and generous people who have taken on themselves "the noble life of service." At least in their codes, that is, the medical profession sees itself as *giving* to the public and *being owed* in return. In place of this "conceit of philanthropy" May urges a notion of *"covenantal indebtedness"* that acknowledges the "reciprocity of giving and receiving" in professional relationships.[30] That is, the medical profession's view of its rights and duties, as embodied in its ethical codes, needs to be reshaped. It needs to reflect a social contract notion that recognizes a mutual indebtedness: the *giving* of training, autonomy, and trust *by society and patients to physicians as well as the giving of skills and services to society by physicians.*

Health, illness, and modern medicine

Another set of ideas that are important to understanding present and possible future relationships between medicine and society has to do with the nature of medicine as a social and cultural institution in relation to our views of the nature and meaning of health and illness. We have discussed this subject before in terms of what seems to be our expanding views of health and illness. In this section we will consider the topic from a slightly different perspective, placing our views of health, illness, and medicine in a comparative evolutionary framework.

---

*From Jonsen, A.: The rights of physicians: a philosophical essay, Washington, D.C., 1973, National Academy of Sciences—Institute of Medicine.

In modern Western society we tend to take the nature of medicine as applied science and the type of care that it entails for granted. It seems to be the self-evident and obvious way of treating disease and illness. But cross-culturally and historically, as Parsons[33] observed, "the comparative evidence is overwhelming that illness . . . has been interpreted in supernatural terms, and magical treatment has been considered to be the appropriate method of coping with it."

A supernatural view of illness and its care in turn creates a very different patterning in the relationships between health, healers, and the public than we are used to. These differences help us see that modern medicine has been and is an evolving institution. Viewing medicine in a comparative evolutionary framework, for example, Fox[13] points out that the health-illness-medicine complex in postprimitive or archaic societies "is tightly interlocked with the predominant institutions of an archaic society—kinship, religion, and magic—which are themselves closely interwebbed."

An archaic society's medical perspective on health and illness is a metaphysical one in which illness is "unnatural." Ideally, [illness] ought not occur, and empirically, it would not, without the intervention of transhuman forces, mediated by human agents who are either intentional or unintentional evildoers." Because of the way it views health and illness, "archaic medicine is focally concerned with explaining the '*why's*' as well as the 'how's' of illness; and it equates the diagnosed meaning of illness with its etiology and ultimate cure."[13]

Knowing how other cultures and other ages have viewed health-illness-medicine helps us understand the social and cultural context of *modern medicine*. In Parsons' view modern medicine's significance as a major social institution has two principal sources. The *first* involves *medicine's structure and function in the social system*. Medical practice is a social system mechanism for dealing with illness in the populace. It involves institutionalized professional roles and patient roles, which include certain obligations and expectations on the part of providers and patients. These roles serve in part to protect the functioning of the social system from the disruptive effects of illness in its members.

Parsons and his followers hold that the *second* source of medicine's societal significance lies in its *cultural and religious relationship to life and death*. "Both the experience of illness and the act of caring for the sick . . . are related to the ultimate conditions of man's existence that [are] the ultimate core of religion."[13]

In modern society, however, illness is both structurally and conceptually separated from kinship, magic, and religion. Illness now is seen as a natural rather than unnatural phenomenon. It is caused by impersonal physical or psychic factors rather than by transhuman forces. And, on the whole, ill persons are judged to be in a state for which they, their families or ancestors, or gods or spirits are not responsible.[13]

Given modern medicine's explanatory system those empowered by society to define, diagnose, certify, and treat illness are not kin or practitioners of magic or religion. They are instead scientifically trained medical professionals. And the primary task of the modern medical practitioner is to explain and deal with the *hows* of illness and not, as in archaic medicine, with the "whys."

Modern healers are expected to determine the causes of illness chiefly in terms of pathophysiologic processes and to develop and use biomedical means to prevent, cure, or at least palliate illness. This view of illness, as we discussed in Chapter 4, is modeled on a germ theory view of disease. A disease is a separate objective entity, distinct from the person who contracts it, and once rid of it a person will be "normal" or healthy. In this model, accordingly, the physician's *primary responsibility* is to deal with the disease-object, not with the diseased person and not with the cultural and religious context that involves the "whys" of illness.

Toward a new social contract?

Contemporary medicine, as we have indicated in this chapter and throughout the book, is facing major challenges and undergoing what seem to be important changes. These challenges and signs of change suggest that American medicine and the society of which it is a part are moving into a "postmodern" stage of their evolution. If so, what sort of social contract will define the relationships between health, illness, and medicine and between physicians, other providers, and patients?

In trying to see the shape of things to come we indeed are looking through a glass darkly. Forecasting the future is a notoriously risky art. But we believe that a sense of medicine's evolution as a social institution, coupled with a sense of events in present-day medicine and American society, gives us some reasonable guidelines for making some predictions.

As we view future or postmodern American medicine and society the fiduciary social contract relationship that we have known between physician and patient will not completely disappear but it will be a substantially altered one. It will not, like the dinosaur, become an extinct species because society will continue to vest in the physician the primary authority and responsibility for diagnosing, certifying, and treating illness. This role means that the physician will continue to have a high level of technical or sapiental expertise and will continue to be viewed as the "symbolic personification of medicine's capacity to help and heal."[13] And for these reasons we will continue to enter into a voluntary social contract type of relationship with physicians.

The nature of that relationship, however, as well as the relationship between physicians and other providers, should be more egalitarian, flexible, and responsive than it has been in recent times. In part, that is, the contract should incorporate some of the ideals of a *covenantal relationship*, in which a mutuality of giving and receiving between providers and patients, and the medical profession and society, is more fully recognized.

The attributes of a covenantal relationship would help to substantially and positively redefine the rights and obligations of physicians and patients. If we move toward such a redefinition, however, it will be important to establish and maintain as much symmetry as possible in the rights granted to and the responsibilities expected of both physicians and patients and of the medical profession and society more generally. That is, rights and responsibilities need to be seen as correlative.

If, for example, our society endorses the value that health or health care is a right, we also need to assume a reciprocal obligation to accept a greater individual and collective responsibility for our health. The assumption of this obligation, in turn, will contribute to a more informed and actively participatory role for the lay person-patient in health maintenance and illness care.

A recasting of the patient role into that of a more informed and involved participant will further reshape the fiduciary aspect of the doctor-patient contract. The once relatively blind nature of the public's and patient's trust in the physician is being, and increasingly will be, replaced by a trust that in some ways is more reasoned and realistic. It is a trust tempered by a better knowledge of the uncertainties and limitations of medicine and of the individual and collective roles of society's members in preventing or combating many forms of disease and disability. It also is a trust involving a more informed and consenting entrance into a patient role.

For these and other reasons the contract will reflect more openly what we think has been a long-standing and healthy, but largely latent, ambivalence in our attitudes toward medical professionals. It also, and more importantly, will broaden and deepen the rights and obligations of patients (or prospective patients).

But in granting more entitlements to patients we could be creating a new type of problematic asymmetry in the rights and responsibilities of physicians. For example, we view ethical and legal affirmations of patients' rights, particularly the right of informed, voluntary consent to treatment, as positive recent developments. But in establishing these patient's rights we need to guard against a too radical shift from a paternalistic, authoritarian physician model to what Gadow[16] calls a "consumer model," in which physicians (or nurses) become mere technicians executing patients' decision about their treatment and management.

Other types of asymmetries could be created by our expanding notions of what constitutes health and illness and by the broad types of sociomedical responsibilities that many feel should be assumed by providers, particularly in ambulatory care. These developments portend a social contract in which providers incur new or expanded responsibilities at the same time that their rights are being restricted or reduced in various ways. These responsibilities include dealing with the range of the "human condition" problems society is defining as within the rubric of health and province of medicine (a counterpoint to what in other respects is a more realistic appraisal of medicine's capabilities). They also involve asking medical professionals to help us with our renewed efforts to grapple with age-old religious and philosophic questions about the nature and meaning of life, illness, and death in a way that suggests a move toward a cosmologic orientation like that of archaic medicine.

Many in our society still would echo George Bernard Shaw's dictum that "all professions are conspiracies against the laity." Today, in turn, many professionals feel that Shaw's dictum should be reversed. What we speculatively see as the nature of a new social contract binding together health, medicine, providers, and the public is one, on balance, that we think will redress many aspects of the traditional contract that have been unhealthy for both professionals and the public. Our optimism, however, is tempered by a sense that the contract could again be too asymmetric, this time on the side of the patient and public. We need to be keenly aware of the reciprocity between rights and responsibilities or obligations and not err too far in the direction of increasing the public's medical care rights and at the same time reducing the rights of physicians while adding to what we feel are their professional obligations. It is not fashionable these days to voice a concern about the rights of physicians. But, as Jonsen[22] reminds us, "the question about physicians' rights is, in the last analysis, a question about how a strong and important profession can both preserve its essential functions and serve the insistent needs of society."

References

1. American Medical Association: Hearings on "pro-competition" bills to be held, Legislative Roundup **21**:3, 1980.
2. AMA insights, J.A.M.A. **243**:23, 1980.
3. Barber, B.: Regulation and the professions, Hastings Cent. Rep. **10**:34, 1980.
4. Belsky, M., and Gross, L.: How to choose and use your doctor: the smart patient's way to a longer, healthier life, New York, 1975, Arbor House Publishing Co., Inc.
5. Burger, E.: Protecting the nation's health: the problems of regulation, Lexington, Mass., 1976, Lexington Books.
6. Chapman, C.: Doctors and their autonomy: past events and future prospects, Science **200**:851, 1978.
7. Davis, F.: The death of free doctors, Private Practice **11**:7, 1979.
8. Doing better and feeling worse: health in the United States, Daedalus **106**:entire volume, 1977.
9. Ehrenreich, B., and Ehrenreich, J.: The American health empire, New York, 1970, Random House, Inc.
10. Enthoven, A.: Health care cost control through incentives and competition: consumer-choice health plan. In Misek, G., editor: Socioeconomic issues of health 1979, Chicago, 1979, American Medical Association.
11. Epstein, S.: The politics of cancer, San Francisco, 1978, Sierra Club Books.
12. Ford, M.: The psychiatrist's double bind: the right to refuse medication, Am. J. Psychiatry **137**:3, 1980.
13. Fox, R.: Medical evolution. In Loubsen, J., et al., editors: Explorations in general theory in social science, vol. 2, New York, 1976, The Free Press.
14. Fox, R.: The medicalization and demedicalization of American society, Daedalus **106**:9, 1977.
15. Friedman, M.: Capitalism and freedom, Chicago, 1962, University of Chicago Press.
16. Gadow, S.: Advocacy: an ethical model for assisting patients with treatment decisions. In Wong, C., and Swazey, J., editors: Dilemmas of dying, Boston, 1981, G. K. Hall & Co.
17. Gosfield, A.: Consumer accountability in PSROs, University of Toledo Law Review **6**: 764, 1975.
18. Grad, F., and Marti, N.: Physicians' licensure and discipline, Dobbs Ferry, N.Y., 1979, Oceana Publications, Inc.

19. Greenberg, D.: Money and health care, N. Engl. J. Med. **302:**978, 1980.
20. Havighurst, C.: Private cost containment—medical practice under competition. In Misek, G., editor: Socioeconomic issues in health 1979, Chicago, 1979, American Medical Association.
21. Illich, I.: Medical nemesis, London, 1975, Calder & Boyars Ltd.
22. Jonsen, A.: The rights of physicians: a philosophical essay, Washington, D.C., 1973, National Academy of Sciences—Institute of Medicine.
23. Kennedy, E.: In critical condition: the crisis in America's health care. New York, 1972, Simon & Schuster, Inc.
24. Klarman, H.: The financing of health care, Daedalus **106:**215, 1977.
25. Knowles, J.: The responsibility of the individual, Daedalus **106:**57, 1977.
26. Kolata, G.: NMC thrives selling dialysis, Science **208:**379, 1980.
27. Lewis, H., and Lewis, M.: The medical offenders, New York, 1970, Simon & Schuster, Inc.
28. Locke, J.: Second treatise on civil government, Chicago, 1955, Gateway Editions, Ltd.
29. Mathews, D.: The right to refuse psychiatric medication, Medicolegal News **8:**4, 1980.
30. May, W.: Code or covenant or philanthropy or contract? In Reiser, S., Dyck, A., and Curran, W., editors: Ethics in medicine, Cambridge, Mass., 1977, Massachusetts Institute of Technology Press.
31. Misek, G., editor: Socioeconomic issues of health 1979, Chicago, 1979, American Medical Association.
32. Parsons, T.: Social structure and personality, Glencoe, Ill., 1964, The Free Press.
33. Parsons, T.: The social system, Glencoe, Ill., 1951, The Free Press.
34. Pellegrino, E.: Humanism and the physician, Knoxville, Tenn., 1979, The University of Tennessee Press.
35. Potter, R.: Does medicine care about those who cure? The Guthrie Bulletin **46:**89, 1976.
36. Ramsey, P.: The patient as person, New Haven, Conn., 1970, Yale University Press.
37. Russell, L.: Technology in hospitals. Medical advances and their diffusion, Washington, D.C., 1980, The Brookings Institution.
38. Sade, R.: Medical care as a right: a refutation, N. Engl. J. Med. **285:**1288, 1971.
39. Singer, P.: Freedoms and utilities in the distribution of health care. In Veatch, R., and Branson, R., editors: Ethics and health policy, Cambridge, Mass., 1976, Ballinger Publishing Co.
40. Stevens, R.: American medicine and the public interest, New Haven, Conn., 1971, Yale University Press.
41. Strauss, A., editor: Where medicine fails, Transaction Book 4, 1970, Aldine Publishing Co.
42. Veatch, R.: What is a "just" health care delivery? In Veatch, R., and Branson, R., editors: Ethics and health policy, Cambridge, Mass., 1976, Ballinger Publishing Co.
43. Veatch, R., and Branson, R., editors: Ethics and health policy, Cambridge, Mass., 1976, Ballinger Publishing Co.
44. Vladeck, B.: Interest-group representation and the HSAs: health planning and political theory, Am. J. Public Health **67:**23, 1977.
45. Waitzkin, H., and Waterman, B.: The exploitation of illness in capitalist society, Indianapolis, 1974, The Bobbs-Merrill Co., Inc.
46. Westin, A.: Computers, health records, and citizen rights, Washington, D.C., 1976, U.S. Government Printing Office.
47. Westin, A.: Medical records: should patients have access? Hastings Cent. Rep. **7:**23, 1977.

Index

Patient(s)—cont'd
   physicians providing health education for, 41-43
   and providers and public, stress points between, 257-261
   and relationship with physician; *see* Doctor-patient relationship
   rights of, 262-263
   seeking medical care and; *see* Careseeking
   sick role of, 121-128
   views of, on physicians, 120-121
Patient care problems, physician concern with, 267
Physical disability; *see also* Disabled persons
   adjustment to; *see* Rehabilitation
   nature of, and rehabilitation, 163-164
Physician(s)
   active role of, 121-128
   Aesculapian authority of, 120
   assessing deviance and, 106-110
   authority of, 139-140
   authority, rights, and role of, 271-275
   becoming a, 211-229
   candor of, and dying patients, 191-196
   and careseeking; *see* Careseeking
   changing status of, 16-17
   classified by type of practice, 236
   concerns of, 266-270
     changing practice arrangements, 267-270
     disease prevention, 266-267
     patient care problems, 267
   disagreement among, on what requires medical attention, 73
   follow-up, and effect on compliance with medical regimen, 153
   impact of dying patient on, 204-206
   and informing patients of environmental hazards, 56-58
   and interactions with colleagues, 14
   locations of, 73-74
   maldistribution of, 225
   -patient interactions; *see* Doctor-patient interactions

Physician(s)—cont'd
   -patient relationship; *see* Doctor-patient relationship
   patients' views of, 120-121
   -population ratio, 73
   pressures of time and, 14-15
   professional interactions and status of, 13-17
   as professionals, 242-255
   rights of, and doctor-patient relationship, 272-273
   role of
     changes in, 13
     changes in public views of, 137-138
   as social control agent, 104-110
   specialization of, 74
   from student to, 220
   visits to, 118-120
     classified by age and income, 77
     and health consciousness of Americans, 20
     reasons for, 90-91
     statistics on, 119
     United States, 89, 90
   and working with hospital team, 15-16
Political organizations and disabled persons, 177
Pollution, legislation concerning, 52, 53
Poverty
   and not seeking medical care, 74-75
   and nutrition and illness, 27
   and relationship to careseeking, 75, 78-80
Practice arrangements
   changing, 267-270
   group, 235-237
   private, 235
Prescription drugs, consumption of, 20
Primary care, 100-104
   definitional issues of, 100-102
   providing, 102-104
Private practice, 235
Professional interactions of physicians, 13-17
Professional organizations, 247-249